A Relational Theory of W

MW00610854

Drawing on Chinese cultural and philosophical traditions, this book offers a ground-breaking reinterpretation of world politics from Yaqing Qin, one of China's leading scholars of International Relations. Qin has pioneered the study of constructivism in China and developed a cultural approach, arguing that culture defined in terms of background knowledge nurtures social theory and enables theoretical innovation. Building upon this argument, this book presents the concept of "relationality," shifting the focus from individual actors to the relations amongst actors. This ontology of relations examines the unfolding processes whereby relations create the identities of actors and provide motivations for their actions. Appealing to scholars of international relations theory, social theory and Chinese political thought, this exciting new concept will be of particular interest to those who are seeking to bridge Eastern and Western approaches for a truly global International Relations project.

Yaqing Qin is Professor of International Studies at China Foreign Affairs University, Executive Vice-President of China National Association for International Studies, and a Global Fellow at Peace Research Institute, Oslo. Previously, Qin was on the Resource Group for the High-Level Panel on Threats, Challenges, and Change, organized by the then UN Secretary-General Kofi Annan. He has served on numerous national and international editorial boards, including Global Governance, East-West Centre Policy Studies Series, and the *Chinese Journal of International Politics*. His academic interests include international relations theory and global governance, and he has written for numerous journals, including *International Studies Review*, *Chinese Journal of International Politics*, and *International Relations of the Asia-Pacific*.

A Relational Theory of World Politics

Yaqing Qin

CAMBRIDGE
UNIVERSITY PRESS

CAMBRIDGE
UNIVERSITY PRESS

University Printing House, Cambridge CB2 8BS, United Kingdom

One Liberty Plaza, 20th Floor, New York, NY 10006, USA

477 Williamstown Road, Port Melbourne, VIC 3207, Australia

314–321, 3rd Floor, Plot 3, Splendor Forum, Jasola District Centre, New Delhi – 110025, India

79 Anson Road, #06–04/06, Singapore 079906

Cambridge University Press is part of the University of Cambridge.

It furthers the University's mission by disseminating knowledge in the pursuit of education, learning, and research at the highest international levels of excellence.

www.cambridge.org
Information on this title: www.cambridge.org/9781107183148
DOI: 10.1017/9781316869505

Originally published in 2012 by Shanghai People's Publishing House as *Relations and Processes*, written in the Chinese language by Yaqing Qin (ISBN 9787208106482).

© Shanghai People's Publishing House 2012

First published in English by Cambridge University Press in 2018, rewriting and translation by Yaqing Qin.

© Shanghai People's Publishing House 2018

First published 2018

Printed in the United States of America by Sheridan Books, Inc.

A catalogue record for this publication is available from the British Library.

Library of Congress Cataloging-in-Publication Data
Names: Qin, Yaqing, 1953– author.
Title: A relational theory of world politics / Yaqing Qin.
Description: New York : Cambridge University Press, 2018.
Identifiers: LCCN 2017049406 | ISBN 9781107183148 (hardback) | ISBN 9781316634257 (paperback)
Subjects: LCSH: World politics. | International relations. | Constructivism (Philosophy) | Social sciences – Philosophy. | Multiculturalism.
Classification: LCC D288 .Q56 2018 | DDC 327.101–dc23
LC record available at https://lccn.loc.gov/2017049406

ISBN 978-1-107-18314-8 Hardback
ISBN 978-1-316-63425-7 Paperback

Contents

Figures

Tables

Preface

I

My father once took me to Mount Tai, the most famous mountain in Northeast China, when I was a teenager. As we were climbing, he told me to recite a short poem by a well-known Chinese scholar-poet, Su Shi (1037–1101). It is about Mount Lushan, another famous mountain in China. The poems go as follows:

> I see a range from one side and a peak from another,
> I have different views from above or below, from far or near,
> I fail to get the true face of Mount Lushan,
> Simply because inside the mountain I myself stand.

My father told me on the spot that you see a different image from a different angle even if you are observing the same thing. In addition, you can only see one image at one time without being able to see the whole picture simultaneously because you yourself are an observer from within.

It seems quite true of society and social scientists. Every social scientist is an observer from within society and can see only one side of it at one time. The whole picture perhaps exists, but no human can see it as it is. A different angle is significant, for it provides people with a different image they cannot see from other angles. A new image implies creation.

Cultures provide different angles for observation and different perspectives for understanding and interpretation. Culture is the shared background knowledge of a community of practice. It is true that there are commonalities across cultures, but there are also differences among them. These differences enable observers to have different angles from which they observe. As Su Shi's poem tells, an observer sees the mountain as a peak from one angle and as a range from another. It is not that the mountain changes; rather it is the angle of the observer that changes. It is exactly the reason why culture is a rich resource for theoretical invention and creation.

Society is similar. There are common features of a society anywhere, and power, authority, norms, and rules exist in every society. But how to understand and interpret such phenomena depends very much on the background knowledge of a cultural community, which has formed, accumulated, and developed over long history and practice. Gradually it has become part of their life, shaping their way of thinking, speaking, doing, and representing, just as people from different parts of the world have different mindsets and speak different languages. It is not a question of being true or false; it is a matter of perspectives.

I define culture in terms of shared background knowledge. However, I do not agree with the view that places background and representational knowledge in a dualistic structure. Theorists of the international practice approach argue that there is a representational bias in social theorizing, which overemphasizes the role of representational knowledge and overlooks the significance of practical knowledge. This dichotomization of representational and practical knowledge is misleading. Representational knowledge is produced by people embedded in background knowledge. Academicians who generate representational knowledge are members of a community of practice, sharing completely the background knowledge of this community. Representation is practice, and doing academic work is practice, too, reflecting important elements of the background in which the producer of representational knowledge is embedded. Since background knowledge is the unintentional and preintentional that make the international function, as Searle argues, representational knowledge grows out of the background knowledge and the two are complementary and mutually reinforcing. A knowledge producer can hardly create some representational knowledge irrelevant to or different from the background in which she grows and develops. Background enjoys ontological priority and provides nutriment for representational knowledge to be generated; at the same time, representational knowledge articulates and reinforces important elements of background knowledge. They are the two sides of the same phenomenon.

Civilization-based cultures provide perhaps the most significant angles for observation. The more distant the two cultural communities are from each other, the more different are the angles they provide. It is because the background knowledge that defines them has more different and distinct elements inside. Western culture is obviously different from Chinese culture, which is in turn very much unlike Islamic culture. If culture is defined in terms of background knowledge and if background knowledge provides different angles for observation of social facts, it is crucial to explore cultural resources for innovation in social theorizing. In the discipline of International Relations (IR), scholars in the West have done a great deal in this respect, finding and refining significant concepts and perspectives for their knowledge production and reproduction. Non-Western cultures, however, remains very much an underexplored land.

II

This book is organized around a key concept: relationality.

One of the most significant concepts of Western scholarship is, perhaps, "rationality." It is a key word of the representational knowledge of the West and comes from the background knowledge of Western communities, fully explored and continually refined by Western knowledge producers especially since the Enlightenment. It has contributed remarkably to progress in many areas. It constitutes a most important worldview which believes in the universal and ultimate rationality and reflects the understanding and interpretation of Westerners about the natural, the social, and the human.

What then can we get from the angle of the Chinese culture? I argue that "relationality" is perhaps to Chinese what rationality is to Westerners. As rationality, relationality is a key concept that has been embedded in the long practice of Confucian communities. It has been repeatedly emphasized by ancient Chinese thinkers such as Confucius, Mencius, and many others thereafter. It comes from Chinese practice and in turn has influenced Chinese practice for millennia. To some extent, Chinese society is called a "relational" society, meaning that the social is first of all a nexus of relations. Unfortunately, it remains an underexplored concept in modern times, especially since China met the West. As a result, it continues to be highly significant in practice, but fails to be refined as a significant element of the representational knowledge.

A careful conceptualization of relationality is therefore very much needed. To do it we should begin to ask some fundamental questions that are behind the concept itself. First, what is our world and what is our world composed of? It is a question of ontological significance. Although some IR scholars oppose discussion on ontological issues, it is highly important, for the answer to such questions sustains where one starts theorizing. Mainstream scholarship in the West largely sees the world as composed of discrete and independent entities acting and interacting, very much with the push of outside forces. An application of this logic to the social world leads naturally to a belief that individual actors are entities independent of one another and each is endowed with *a priori* properties and attributes. A clear identification of their properties and attributes will tell us what they are and how they behave. Rationality is indeed a great discovery, for it defines clearly and succinctly the characteristic attributes of human beings: They are egoistic individuals, always ready to maximize their self-interest at the lowest cost. Starting from rationality so many influential social theories have been developed, from economics through sociology to political science. Thus, I argue, this most significant concept of rationality is a spirit that has haunted the field of Western social theorizing and is rooted in the soul of Western knowledge producers. And I further argue that it is a concept drawn and refined from the practice of Western societies and a frame from which the world is seen and interpreted. It is an angle, a perspective, or a worldview that influences members of Western communities when they try to observe, understand, and conceptualize what is around them.

Relationality comes from a different angle. Chinese tend to see the world as one composed of complex relations, relations among the heaven, the earth, and the human, relations among humans, and relations among all things under the sun. In the social world it pays special attention to human relations in society. Its focus is not on the individual actor, but on relations among them. Its emphasis on human relations leads to some meaningful corollaries. In short, it holds that self-existence is simultaneous with coexistence; that self-identity is formed in and through social relations; and that self-interest is shared with other-interest and collective interest. Contrary to many who believe that traditional Chinese culture values collectivity at the cost of individuality, Confucianism values both. Because it places special emphasis on relations among actors, it holds that self-existence, self-identity, and self-interest are all related to other-existence, other-identity, and other-interest. In society, for example, self-existence is significant, but the self exists simultaneously with others. It is therefore wrong to argue that self-existence comes before or enjoys ontological priority over coexistence, and vice versa. It is also true of self-interest. While self-interest should be recognized as legitimate and significant, it is hard to define in isolation. Since the self exists simultaneously with others, their interests are related, shared, and realized through joint effort. It is mistaken to assume that self-interest is of primacy and it is equally mistaken to assume that collective interest comes before everything else. For Confucianism, a balance of the two is the key to a healthy society and governance, for they depend on each other for articulation, realization, and evolution.

The relational theory takes "relation" as its central piece and conceives the world in general and the international relations world in particular as composed of dynamic relations. Then how do we understand the multiple relations that connect actors in such a world? What is the nature of such relationships? How should such relations be managed? These questions are relevant in terms of both epistemology and methodology. The Chinese *zhongyong* dialectics provides a useful lens in this respect and it is also the methodology for my relational theory throughout. It assumes two poles, *yin* and *yang*, or the feminine and masculine forces in both nature and human affairs, and believes that all in the universe is made by the interaction of these two forces. Since the *yin-yang* relationship is representative of all other relationships, it is the "meta-relationship." The *zhongyong* dialectics studies the relationship between these two opposite forces. It first of all posits that the basic state of this meta-relationship is harmony. From such an assumption it is inferred that all relations are fundamentally harmonious and are able to be managed as such. This postulation about the basic state of the meta-relationship differs fundamentally from the Hegelian dialectics, which also assumes two opposite forces but at the same time interprets their relationship as fundamentally conflictual. Second, *yin* and *yang* are immanently inclusive of each other. Unlike the opposite terms in the Hegelian philosophy, which are interactive but not immanent, *yin* and *yang* are of each other and within each other. They are simply two inseparable parts of the same whole. In the final analysis, therefore, conflict between the two is ontologically baseless, while the basic state of harmony is well grounded. Third, *yin* and *yang* are complementary. The two inclusively interacting items complement each other in a dynamically interpenetrating process. *Yin* and *yang*, or any pair of seemingly contradictory polar terms, such as cold and hot, weak and strong, nothing and something, etc., are complementarily related to each other so that they together create life and lead to a balanced form of life. The balance is not static, for it is always maintained through the dynamic complementation of the two extremes. The strength of one pole implies simultaneously its weakness, which is necessarily made up for by the strength of the other pole, and vice versa. *Yin* and *yang*, fundamentally different from the Hegelian thesis and antithesis, constitute co-theses which are inclusive of and complementary to each and whose immanently dynamic interaction enables what I term "coevolutionary harmony." This dynamic interaction is at the same time a process of generating new life, which inherits from both co-theses but is irreducible to neither.

From these basic assumptions, we may get a logic of relationality. It means that human action is based on relations. The IR literature has discussed some important logics of human action. The logics of consequences and of appropriateness, for example, are the mainstream arguments, one dealing with the instrumental aspect of human action, and the other highlighting the normative dimension. Even though in recent years the study of international norms has become a conspicuous project in IR research, due mainly to the rise of social constructivism, people can hardly tell which, interests or norms, is more important as a mover of human action. The logic of practicality is said, in theory, to have ontological priority over other logics. It is so indeed. Practicality provides the ontological foundation for any other logics that are concerned with human action. But in the actual analysis by practicality scholars, it has been equaled with other logics, making the debate between the logic of practicality on the one hand and the logics of consequences and appropriateness on the other one that tries to figure out which logic is more significant as a base for action. The logic of relationality argues that a social actor weighs carefully the various relationships involved before she takes an action. Instrumental rationality works only when the relationship between actors has been defined. A business person's rational action toward her customers may not be rational and is even irrational when she does the same to her family. Norms are useful as an important mover of action in society, but norms are designed more to govern relationships rather than individuals. Each of the five cardinal relationships defined by Confucius has a corresponding norm to govern and manage such a relationship. Filial piety is the norm for the father-son relationship and sincerity for the relationship between friends. There is no norm that comes into being without a relational context. In this sense, the logic of relationality enjoys priority over the logic of consequences and appropriateness. Or rationality is defined in terms of relationality. At the same time it comes from long practice, and therefore the logic of practicality has ontological priority over the logic of relationality.

These assumptions constitute the major part of the relational theory. It sees the world as one composed of complex relations and the social world as one composed of human relations, giving "relation" an important ontological status and assuming humanity as the key to the understanding of the social. It employs the Chinese *zhongyong* dialectics as its major device of epistemology and methodology and with this dialectics argues that the basic state of the various and multiple relationships is harmony. It also proposes the logic of relationality, which holds that human action is based largely on relations. The simultaneity of self-existence and coexistence, of self-identity and co-identity, and of self-interest and co-interest indicates that relationality is a key concept in understanding human action in the social context. In short, from a different angle, we see a different world and a different social world; from such a world we develop a theory of relationality; and with such a theory we may reconceptualize some key ideas in international relations.

III

There are three parts in the book. Part I posits that culture provides one of the richest resources for social theory construction and knowledge production. Of course cultural influence is not linear and does not provide direct causality. Rather culture, defined in terms of shared background knowledge, shapes the mindset, the way of thinking and doing, and the worldview of knowledge producers who are also members of a certain cultural community. Since background knowledge tends to be inarticulate and unreflective, its influence is often subtle and imperceptible, but it is everywhere, bearing on everyone embedded in a cultural community, which is also the prototype of a community of practice.

Chapter 1 discusses the two approaches to social theory construction: monism and pluralism. The former holds that natural theory and social theory are not substantially different and therefore should follow the same logic of theorizing. It implies that reality is the same everywhere and its explanation should be the same accordingly. It thus denies a place for culture to play a role in theory development. Pluralism, on the other hand, argues that the social world is not identical with the natural world and that social theory also differs from natural theory in that the former is not only to explain, but also to understand, interpret, and even construct and create. Ideas, values, mindsets, and worldviews therefore matter a great deal. The monist approach is self-closed and would naturally lead to a poverty and decay of social theory, while the pluralist attitude provides an open system in which various nutriments, including culture, may prosper the growth of social theory in general.

Chapter 2 focuses on one concept: the metaphysical component of the theoretical hard core. Culture matters for social theory development mainly through its long and invisible influence on the mindset of students who generate social knowledge. It is most deeply reflected by the metaphysical component of the hard core of a social theory. The hard core defines a social theory, but it is not a monolithic whole. Rather it consists of two parts: the substantive and the metaphysical. While the former perceives, the latter conceives. Once the substantive component receives signals from the outside world, they are sent to the metaphysical component for understanding, interpreting, and constructing. The substantive component deals with the more material and visible out there and the metaphysical component digests them and provides meaningful feedback. It is exactly this metaphysical component that is nurtured and informed by the background knowledge that comes from the long practice of a cultural community.

Chapter 3 further explores how the metaphysical component may contribute to theoretical innovation. Knowledge producers who come from different cultural communities are likely to have different mindsets and therefore produce different metaphysical components of the hard core for a social theory. Observers may see the same thing, but their angles are different and their understanding and interpreting differ accordingly.

The different understandings and interpretations are valuably positive rather than negative, for each angle may provide a fresh and meaningful theoretical perspective. They greatly encourage innovation for social theorizing. Since the metaphysical component is quite decisive in theoretical innovation and since it is nourished in culture, defined in terms of shared background knowledge, efforts to explore cultural resources for social theory development should be encouraged for the prosperity of the social sciences.

Chapter 4 uses the Western mainstream IR theory, referring mainly to neorealism, neoliberal institutionalism, and social constructivism in the United States and also including the English School of IR theory, as typical cases to illustrate the importance of the metaphysical component of the theoretical hard core. Deeply implied in the metaphysical components of these theories is an element deeply embedded in the background knowledge of Christian culture and explicitly articulated by generations of knowledge producers in the West. It is individualistic rationality. It is a big idea indeed, and has produced enormous influence on theorizing especially since the Enlightenment. IR is no exception. All the three major paradigms in the United States share this key element in the metaphysical component of their theoretical hard cores. It is true that they have identified different master variables that influence the behavior of the individual actor. They are, respectively, distribution of capabilities, international institutions, and normative ideas. But all the big three theories depend on individualist rationality to work as social theories. It is instrumental rationality for neorealism and neoliberalism and normative rationality for constructivism. The English School used to be a distinct theory with its initial idea of "international society" to distinguish itself from mainstream American theories in the post-WWII years. But with the rise of Wendtian constructivism, the English School and American constructivism found a ready echo in each other and normative rationality was identified as a shared element in their metaphysical component. The convergence of American mainstream IR theories, and between the American mainstream and the English School, seems to be no accident. It is the shared metaphysical component in their theoretical hard cores that has led eventually to such a happy rendezvous.

Part II develops a relational theory of world politics. It explores the Confucian philosophical and cultural tradition so that a different angle can be found to see the world. Chapter 5 describes the world from a Confucian perspective of ontology: a world of relations and a universe of relatedness. Furthermore, the social world is seen as one of human relations. It is ontologically significant because a world of relations differs from a world of atoms. In such a world, relations become the pivot of society and accordingly should constitute a most important unit of analysis. Actors in such a world are relators, relating and being related all the time. As mentioned above, self-existence is simultaneous with coexistence, self-interest simultaneous with collective and other-interest, and self-identity is shaped in and through relations. In short, to relate is human. The social world is a relational world and humans are relational animals. It subverts the dominant assumption that the world is composed of discrete individuals who follow the logic of individualistic rationality.

A major epistemological scheme and methodological device is presented in Chapter 6. It is the Chinese *zhongyong* dialectics. The discussion of this dialectics is unfolded in a comparison with the tenets of formal logic and the principles of the Hegelian dialectics. It differs from formal logic mainly in its particular emphasis on a "both-and" rather than an "either-or" way of thinking and on its appreciation of the "middle" rather than its exclusion. Two opposite arguments, for example, are not taken as one being true and the other false. Rather there may well be something reasonable in each and both of them. It agrees with the Hegelian dialectics in that both understand things as consisting of polarities and their development through the interaction of such polarities. It differs from the Hegelian dialectics in that the *zhongyong* dialectics interprets the basic state of the relationship between the two polarities as harmonious while the Hegelian dialectics sees conflict as the nature of such relationship. This difference is fundamental. The two polar terms, seemingly opposite, are in fact two sides of the same phenomenon, immanently related and inclusively interdependent, relying on each other for life and for the production of new life. It does not deny the fact that conflict exists, but does deny it an ontological status. Conflict is a necessary deviation from harmony. There are no such dichotomous terms such as "thesis" and "antithesis"; there are only concepts like "co-theses." Thus the *zhongyong* dialectics always tries to find the appropriate middle where the common ground lies, while the Hegelian tradition tries to diagnose the key contradiction, which is key to crumpling the old and creating a new synthesis.

The proposed relational theory explains human action and Chapter 7 puts forward the logic of relationality. It argues that a social actor takes action in a relational context and therefore bases her action on relations. It is not an argument against the logics of both consequences and appropriateness, both of which take individualistic rationality as the sustaining assumption, instrumental rationality for the former and normative rationality for the latter. The logic of relationality holds that social actors are rational because they are relational in the first place. It is relational rationality. As the well-known example by Wendt shows, the

US nuclear policy toward Britain differs fundamentally from that toward North Korea. It is not an issue of double dealing; rather it is a consideration and action based upon different relationships. Every state does the same. It is also true of norms. Actors are able to apply norms to action only after they know well what relationship constitutes the context where norms are to be applied. Norms for a Hobbesian anarchy differ from those for a Kantian community because the nature of relationships among actors in a jungle is fundamentally unlike that in a community marked by friendship. What action to take and what norm to apply depend very much on the nature of relationships. Relations select.

Part III provides from a relational perspective a reconceptualization of power, cooperation, and governance respectively in Chapters 8, 9, and 10. Chapter 8 discusses power. As a key concept, it is commonly taken in IR as the ability to overcome resistance and realize one's interest, making others do what they otherwise would not do or wish to do what they otherwise would not wish. It is understood that power is influence based upon resources and that resources are possessed by the individual actor as her essential property. However, if it is assumed that self-existence is simultaneous with other-existence, and coexistence and self-interest simultaneously shared with other-interest, then power may well come from relations among actors and is more the ability to co-empower rather than to coerce. Just as *yin* and *yang*, they are always in an ongoing process of co-empowering, complementing each other and making up for each other's weaknesses. As such, power is sharable and exchangeable. It enables actors to overcome and destroy, but also enables them to empower and produce. The negative dimension of power has been more than fully explored, perhaps because international politics has been defined largely as the struggle for survival through overcoming the threat in anarchy, but the positive dimension has long been unduly neglected, thus making the power of power politics even more powerful.

Chapter 9 provides an alternative answer to the question "Why do actors cooperate?" Cooperation research has largely been carried out around the basic assumption that the individual actor is an egoist, trying to maximize her interest at the lowest cost. Whatever is the motivation for cooperation, it is the individualistic rationality that makes independent decisions. From the perspective of relational theory, I suggest that relatedness is a primary mover for cooperation and hypothesize that the more intimately related the actors are, the more likely they are to cooperate. Family members are the least egoistic in their dealing with one another and close allies in international relations are more ready to help each other. A single-move prisoner's dilemma (PD) game leads naturally to defection, while an iterated one is more likely to produce cooperation. No matter what other causal mechanisms work there, the shadow of the future or the expectation of continued relationship, for example, one factor is significant: The two players become related after their first encounter. It is the relatedness between them that makes a difference. Cooperation in a relational world is thus realized through three mechanisms: kin selection, the Confucian improvement or reciprocity, and Mencius optimality. Kin selection most explicitly shows how intimate relatedness promotes cooperation, reciprocity indicates that continued relationship makes cooperation more likely and easier, and Mencius optimality tells that a community of harmonious relations provides the best overall condition for its individual members to realize their self-interest. In a relational world, a serious obstacle to cooperation is kins-person's dilemma (KD), or relator's dilemma, which occurs when one cooperates with a related actor, and she has to defect from another equally related actor, even though she wants to cooperate with both. In world politics, therefore, to get related facilitates cooperation and, furthermore, how to manage relations constitutes a major problem for decision-makers.

Chapter 10 discusses global governance. The IR theoretical literature on governance is perhaps the narrowest in scope and the most destitute in content. With some discussion of hegemonic stability as the background, it has grown mainly out of the study of rules and regimes, which became a most attractive research area. It is not an exaggeration to say that the globalizing tide since the late 1980s and early 1990s has been accompanied by the dominance of neoliberal institutionalism, with almost all the emphasis placed on governance by rules embedded in international institutions. It is undeniable that rules and regimes are extremely important, but governance does not rely completely on one single model. In other fields, governance should and can be explored in a much broader sense. Scholars of business management, for example, have been studying relational governance for years, especially since the rise of Asian firms. The model of relational governance, within the framework of my relational theory, contains three important factors: trust, relations as the governed, and governance as a process of relational management. "Trust" is not in the instrumental sense as the business management literature has defined it in its dealing with relational governance. It is genuinely human and provides the foundation for a fiduciary community. A security community, for example, is first of all a fiduciary community where members genuinely believe that force is not a means to solve conflict. The governed in the relational governance model is relations among actors rather than actors *per se*, shifting the focus of governance from individuals to relations among them. Furthermore, global governance, and in fact any form of governance, is a process of relational management. It is a process of negotiating socio-political arrangements that manage complex and multiplex relationships in a community to produce order so that members behave in a reciprocal and cooperative fashion with mutual trust evolved over a shared understanding of social norms and human morality. Of course, relational governance is also one of the many models for governance and a synthetic model of rule-based and relation-based governance may prove more practical and effective.

IV

The relational theory of world politics proposed in this book tries to see and interpret the international relations world from a different angle, the angle of relationality. It is not out of thin air. Rather it comes from the long practice of Confucian communities and constitutes an indispensable part of their background knowledge. It has been extensively discussed and refined by generations of Confucian scholars and therefore is perhaps one of the most important concepts, if not the most important, in the representational knowledge that they have generated.

To relate and be related is human. Relations are significant in every society and the concept of relationality goes far beyond Confucian communities. Despite the fact that there are various understandings of relations, relationality as social practice is everywhere and generically human. It is, however, a very much underdeveloped and underexplored concept in the global academic world. To some extent, it has been overshadowed by the dominant concept of rationality, which has been a great idea in Western culture. Individualistic rationality has been so significant in modern times and is related to many of the human ideals and pursuits such as freedom, independence, and dignity. Together with it there have been great theories and institutions. But at the same time rationality becomes the ultimate word and the most powerful super force that has been moving farther away from humanness. The process of theorizing in IR, for example, is at the same time a process of dehumanization. Enormous efforts have been made to reduce to the minimum the complexity, reflectivity, and potentiality embedded in humanness so that general laws may be found to regulate and predict human behavior and to develop universally applicable theories. Gradually it has become an integral part of the shared background knowledge and the academic culture of Western societies.

But, what is the soul of IR as a discipline and what is the essence of world politics as practice? It is humanness. World politics, or politics of any kind, is human in the first place. Devoid of this spirit, there would be no world politics and no IR. To foreground relationality in social theorizing, therefore, is perhaps a small step toward bringing humanness back to the study of world politics.

Acknowledgments

I began to have an idea to develop a relational theory of world politics when I joined scholars from various countries in the project entitled "Why is there no non-Western IR theory," organized by Amitav Acharya and Barry Buzan in 2005. The inspiration I got from it is that it is far from sufficient simply to discuss why there is no non-Western theory. Rather it is more important to develop non-Western IR theory so that IR can become a genuine global discipline. As I was writing my paper for the project, "Why is there no Chinese international relations theory," this initial idea loomed larger. I started thinking about an IR theory from a Chinese perspective when the project was completed and the findings in the form of seven articles were published in the *Journal of International Relations of the Asia-Pacific* in 2007. My sincere thanks therefore should go to Acharya and Buzan as well as all the participants in the project, for the initial idea was inspired by the dialogue, discussion, and debate. In addition, Acharya and Buzan have discussed with me many times over the past ten years. Their valuable suggestions are highly appreciated.

I published in Chinese the book *Relations and Processes* in 2012 with Shanghai People's Publishing House (SPPH), which was my first effort to develop a systematic theory of IR by exploring Chinese cultural and philosophical thoughts. During the five years between 2007 and 2012 when I was writing the book, many of my friends and colleagues helped me with their time, advice, and even unconditional support. I would like to thank Peter Katzenstein in particular, a long-time friend who always encourages and inspires me intellectually and academically. I am also very much grateful to the following: Wang Yizhou, Chen Yue, Liu Debin, Zhu Liqun, Sun Jisheng, Wei Ling, Gao Shangtao, Tang Shiping, Guo Shuyong, Fang Changping, William Callahan, David Blaney, Arlene B. Tickner, Joshua Ramo, Benjamin Creutzfeldt, and many others. I owed a lot to my doctoral students, among whom my draft was often first discussed. They were young and energetic, having from time to time interesting ideas that refreshed me and their enthusiasm always encouraged me to keep on working. My sincere thanks also go to Fan Weiwen, who was the editor for my first book in Chinese years ago and has helped ever since, and Pan Danrong, editor for *Relations and Processes*. Thanks to the trust developed over decades, I have had several of my books published by SPPH, including my translations of Western IR classics.

In 2013, soon after my book was published in Chinese, I got an opportunity to join the fellow program of the Weatherhead Center for International Affairs at Harvard University. The six-month stay there provided me with a peaceful mind and an invigorating intellectual environment and enabled me to concentrate on my academic pursuit. It is by the Charles River that I began to consider publishing a monograph in English. I am grateful in particular to Alastair Iain Johnston, whose knowledge about Chinese culture inspired me greatly. My thanks also go to Karl Kaiser, who invited me to many of the talks and conferences he organized, and Kathleen Molony, who helped me to interview many distinguished scholars at Harvard in various fields from IR to anthropology. It is also at Harvard that I had intensive discussion with Zhao Tingyang, a Chinese philosopher who happened to teach there. His global thinking was most stimulating and, also as a well-known cartoonist in China, he has drawn the cartoon for the cover images for several of my Chinese books.

I appreciate indeed the suggestions by the anonymous readers invited by Cambridge University Press, the most valuable of which was that I should not simply translate into English my Chinese work *Relations and Processes*, but rewrite a book developing a substantial theory on relations. It was more challenging, but most interesting. I took it. During this process of rewriting, I have got various kinds of help and inspiration from the following people to whom I express my heartfelt thanks. They are: Wang Zhengyi, Yuan Zhengqing, Su Changhe, Gao Fei, He Yin, Chen Dingding, Wang Cungang, Wu Zhicheng, Sun Xuefeng, Shang Huipeng, Chih-yu Shih, Brantly Womack, Robert Ross, Astrid Nordin, Yong-Soo Eun, L.H.M. Ling, Patrick Jackson, Dan Nexon, Tim Dunne, and Collin Wight. In particular I would like to thank my colleague Dr. Ji Ling, who has helped me a great deal, finding materials, making figures, and proofreading parts of the manuscript. Without her help I could not have completed the manuscript in time.

My sincere thanks also go to Mr. John Haslam of Cambridge University Press who has offered his professional abilities for this project from the very beginning. Ms. Julie Hrischeva, Mr. Toby Ginsberg, and Ms. Margaret Humbert, editors of my book, have been very patient with me and helped me out many times when I was at a loss.

Over the years, several old friends of mine, especially Zhao Deliang, Zhang Songtao, and Wang Enmian, have always encouraged me to develop a social theory from a new perspective. Their rich knowledge in Chinese culture and philosophy, understanding of Western civilizations and intuition in the relationship between everyday practice and knowledge production have provided me with happy inspirations.

Support from my family has always been indispensable during the whole process. My heartfelt thanks go to all of them, Li and Su in particular. The book is written in memory of my father, Guangzu Qin, a medical doctor who taught me to work hard even in time of hopelessness and to stand as a virtuous person even in time of adversity and distress.

Part I

Culture and Social Theory

1   Social Theory and the Multicultural World

The universality of social theory has long been both a dream for realization and a topic for debate. Theory of the natural sciences is almost universally acknowledged as universally applicable, and, following this logic, the behavioral revolution in International Relations (IR) seems to have won an overwhelming triumph in the debate between the scientific school and the traditional approach, making universality the standard for evaluating a social theory. Mainstream theorists of IR, especially those in the United States, have persisted in the principles of the natural sciences, trying to develop theories that are universally valid, across time and space and beyond culture and geography.

At the same time, challenges to this mainstream belief have also been persistent. It is true that a well-established social theory should have broader applicability and gain more validity, even though no social theory is completely universal in the final analysis. However, it is absolutely necessary to discuss how a social theory originates in the first place. Social theory may well aim at universality and it is in a sense justifiable, but no theory starts from a temporo-spatial null, in a uniform homogeneity, and with an initial universal meaning. A social theory tends to originate in a particular geo-cultural setting, which shapes the practices of the cultural community and thus defines the efforts to develop theory, too. Social theory is therefore from the very beginning imprinted with the characteristic features of the cultural community of its origin, for it is this community that shapes the background knowledge of its members and thus provides the menu for the theorist to choose throughout the process of her theoretical construction. Furthermore, the theorist herself has lived in this community, being immersed in its culture, following its practice, and thinking spontaneously and effortlessly as a member of the community. In other words, social theory bears a cultural birthmark, which will be with it even when it becomes a well-established theory with a higher level of universality. This birthmark is indelible.

It is thus clear that I place particular emphasis on culture as a significant incubator and shaper of social theory. In fact, culture used to be taken as an important factor for social studies. "In the 1940s and 1950s, much attention was paid to culture as a crucial element in understanding societies, analyzing differences among them, and explaining their economic and political development."[1] In IR, "from the 1940s to the 1960s culture played a meaningful part in IR theory and research."[2] However, in IR, as well as in other disciplines of social studies, culture as an analytical element declined conspicuously in the United States later on due largely to the triumph of the behavioral revolution and the rise of the ambition for grand and scientific social theory. Even with the revived interest in culture as an explanatory variable since the 1980s, culture seems to be used mostly for analysis of actors' behavior and has never had a place in building and developing IR theory. I intend to explore the link between culture and social theory construction, arguing that to a significantly large extent, culture shapes social theory. It is not a far-reaching exaggeration to argue that the social sciences are in fact the cultural sciences, for "nature" is paired with "culture" rather than "society." It is undeniable that social theory is developed by people, who are cultural beings and have deeply embedded background knowledge of the cultural communities where they are brought up. In this sense, social theory is a product of culture. As to exploring how and why culture shapes theory, we need first to discuss social theory and analyze the two major approaches to social theory building and development.

Theory and Social Theory

Theory is a system of ideas. No matter whether it is in the natural or the social sciences, theoretical construction means to systemize ideas[3] and produce abstract knowledge.[4] Immanuel Kant has made a meaningful

---

[1] Harrison and Huntington 2000, xiii–xiv.   [2] Lapid 1997, 5.

[3] The definitions of "theory" in *the Oxford English Dictionary* include, *inter alia*, : (1) "A scheme or system of ideas and statements held as an explanation or account of a group of facts or phenomena; a hypothesis that has been confirmed or established by observation or experiment, and is pronounced or accepted as accounting for the known facts; a statement that is held to be the general laws, principles, or causes of something known or observed;" (2)"Systematic conception or statement of the principles of something; abstract knowledge or the formulation of it: often used as implying more or less unsupported hypotheses." The Compact Edition of the Oxford English Dictionary, 3284.

[4] The definitions of theory by *Webster's Dictionary of the English Language* include, *inter alia*,: (1) "the body of generalizations and principles developed in association with a field of activity ..."; (2) "the coherent set of hypothetical, conceptual, and pragmatic principles forming the general frame of reference for a field of inquiry ..."; (3) "abstract knowledge." Webster's Third New International Dictionary of the English Language, 2371.

definition of "system" by referring to architectonic. It is meaningful because it shows clearly why we should take theory as a system of ideas or systematic knowledge. He says,

By architectonic I understand the art of systems. Since systemic unity is that which first makes ordinary cognition into science, i.e. makes a system of a mere aggregation of it, architectonic is the doctrine of that which is scientific in our cognitions in general, and therefore necessarily belongs to the doctrine of method.

Under the government of reason, our cognitions cannot at all constitute a rhapsody, but must constitute a system, in which alone they can support and advance its essential ends. I understand by a system, however, the unity of manifold of cognitions under one idea. This is the rational concept of form of the whole, insofar as through this domain of the manifold as well as the position of the parts with respect to each other is determined *a priori*.

For its execution, the idea needs a schema, i.e., an essential manifoldness and order of the parts determined *a priori* from the principle of the end.[5]

I do not mean here to discuss Kant's ontological position, his argument on the rule of reason, and his means-end justification, but what is important in his understanding of theory is the difference he makes between an "aggregation of ideas" and a "system of ideas." His differentiation of "system" from "aggregation" indicates the essential quality of theory and his "one idea" refers to a system or a "schema" of thoughts. Thus, "a system of ideas" provides a general definition of theory. It is acknowledged by Amitav Acharya and Barry Buzan as they point out one of the important conditions for IR theory: "its contribution identifies it as a systematic attempt to abstract or generalize about the subject matter of IR."[6]

It seems true that there is little argument or disagreement about this general definition of theory, but controversies and debates flare up when social theory is drawn into the picture. One of the most conspicuous disagreements is whether social theory is the same as natural theory, behind which is the argument as to whether the social world is the same as the natural world. In the study of IR, for example, Kenneth Waltz distinguishes between "theory" and "thought," arguing that Raymond Aron and Hans J. Morgenthau provide mere realist thoughts and not realist theory because theirs do not "take the fateful step beyond developing concepts to the fashioning of a recognizable theory,"[7] which, among others, has distinctive dependent and independent variables to explain the causality.[8] Robert Keohane discusses "rationalistic" and "reflective" approaches to the study of international institutions, believing that the latter is "less specified as theories," need to develop testable

---

[5] Kant 1997, 691.   [6] Acharya and Buzan 2007, 292.   [7] Waltz 1995, 71.   [8] Ibid., 70.

hypotheses, and carry out "systematic empirical investigations."[9] Martha Finnemore believes that the English School of IR cannot be qualified as theory in a strict sense.[10] It is clear that all these scholars have a deeply internalized yardstick to judge what social theory is and their primary benchmark is no doubt the principles for theory construction in the natural sciences, underlined by a strong positivist worldview, one that has existed in the background knowledge of the IR community, especially in the United States, represented by mainstream theorists there and reinforced by IR students elsewhere in the world.

Acharya and Buzan, in a project for exploring non-Western IR theory,[11] gave two different definitions of social theory: "the harder positivist, rationalistic, materialist and quantitative understandings on one end of the theory spectrum, and the more reflective, social, constructivist, and postmodern on the other."[12] Their categorization of hard positivism and soft reflectivism, similar to the distinction of "scientific" and "hermeneutic" theories by Martin Hollis and Steve Smith,[13] has important implications: The former, dominating in the study of IR in the United States, recognizes only one form of social theory, i.e. theory that fits into the "hard positivist definition" and stresses "being scientific," which means the provision of neat explanations, including hypotheses with clear causality, rigorous empirical testing, and a deductive approach to observation. Causal mechanisms are considered the objective of theorizing and empirical testing is the method for "scientific" research. The latter, or the reflective definition, is much "softer," requiring putting forward meaningful questions, setting out systematic ideas, and developing a set of concepts and categories for the production of abstract and general knowledge.[14] Acharya and Buzan label correctly their own approach as the "pluralist view," for it recognizes various

---

[9] Keohane 1989a, 174.   [10] Finnemore 2001.

[11] Acharya and Buzan organized a project entitled "Why is there no non-Western IR theory: reflections on and from Asia?" The participants were mainly scholars from Asian countries. The title suggested that it was a challenge to the monist approach to IR theorizing. The organizers were puzzled by the situation: On the one hand the Western IR theory cannot readily answer questions that have arisen from a globalizing world and on the other hand there is no non-Western IR theory that is recognized by the academic IR community. The participants listed several causes that have led to such a situation, among which the one that all were agreed on was that IR remained massively dominated by Western thinking though it was now a global activity. However, "the case studies" in the project, as the two organizers said, "point to the existence of abundant intellectual and historical resources that could serve as the basis of developing a non-Western IRT that takes into account the positions, needs and cultures of countries in the region." Acharya and Buzan 2007, 427.

[12] Ibid., 291.   [13] Hollis and Smith 1990, quoted in Dougherty and Pfaltzgraff 2001, 22.

[14] Acharya and Buzan 2007.

forms of theory through identifying a "theory spectrum," including hard positivism, the soft reflectivism, and perhaps some others in between.[15]

Buzan uses "pluralism" and "monism" to tell the methodological position of the English School theory of IR from that of the American mainstream IR theory. He has argued that American mainstream IR theories, such as neorealism and neoliberalism, take a monist approach to social theorizing, for they believe that all theory, natural and social alike, should follow the single and same set of standards, while the English School adopts a pluralist approach, for example, taking history into serious consideration.[16] For the purpose of this study, I will explore in some more detail the two approaches of monism and pluralism and analyze their implications for the construction of IR theory, especially in non-Western cultural settings.

Monism

Monism holds that the natural sciences and the social sciences are both scientific by definition, and therefore the ontology, epistemology, and methodology should be the same.[17] Science aims at finding laws, laws in the natural world and laws in the social world, too. The most important or the essential law, by the influence of the Enlightenment, is causality. For every effect there must be a cause. In this sense, there is little difference between the natural and social sciences. International studies used to be more flexible, combining a multiplicity of factors such as history, law, and culture. However, IR in the post-WWII United States, especially since the behavioral revolution, has typically reflected the positivist and scientific tendency. Monism has become the signboard of the mainstream American IR theory and exerted strong influence in the rest of the world.

Monism seeks homogenization of social theory. In Robert Cox's words: "In the Enlightenment meaning universal meant true for all time and space – the perspective of a homogeneous reality."[18] Inspired by Cox,

---

[15] Ibid., 290–291.   [16] Buzan 2001.

[17] Patrick Jackson has discussed in detail dualism and monism. He defines dualism as an ontological stance whose "central presupposition is a kind of gulf or radial separation between the world and the knowledge about the world," and monism as its opposite that does not posit such "a radical gulf and does not begin by separating things and thoughts as dualism does." Monism assumes a fundamental continuity of knowledge with the world. Jackson 2008, 132, 133. I do not use here the term of monism as Jackson does. Rather I argue, with Acharya, that the opposite of monism is not dualism, but pluralism, for it covers more areas and concerns competing ontological positions even inside the social sciences.

[18] Cox 2002, 53, quoted in Acharya 2014, 3.

Acharya criticizes the dominant meaning of universality in today's IR discipline as follows:

The dominant meaning of universalism in IR today is what I would call a monistic universalism, in the sense of "applying to all." It corresponds closely to Enlightenment universalism, which may also be called "monistic universalism." ... And the Enlightenment has a dark side: the suppression of diversity and justification of European imperialism .... In IR theory and method, such universalism manifests as a way of much arbitrary standard setting, gatekeeping, and marginalization of alternative narratives, ideas, and methodologies.[19]

Since there is only one set of standards, there is necessarily only one form of theory. Furthermore there is only one form of social reality, too. Representative of this approach is no other than Kenneth Waltz, whose monumental work of *Theory of International Politics* in 1979 seems to have won the decisive battle for the scientific school over the traditional school in IR. For him, IR theory is a set of laws and must satisfy three conditions: It is a distinct system of the international; it indicates with clarity the causal directions; and it is parsimonious and rigorous.[20] He admires Newton's theory of universal gravitation, for it "provided a unified expla-nation of celestial and terrestrial phenomena. Its power lay in the number of previously disparate empirical generalizations and laws that could be subsumed in one explanatory system ...."[21] He stresses the universal oneness, the explanatory power, and the empirical testing, and his struc-tural realism is indeed an imitation in the international relations world of the Newtonian theory in the natural world: An international system with anarchy as its ordering principle, a systemic structure with the distribu-tion of capabilities as its most distinctive feature, and rational nation-states as the like units of the system, who abide by the principle of anarchy, weigh rationally the structural balance of power, and take action through a means-end calculation.[22] In this way Waltz does not only establish a distinctive system of international polity clear of all other features and develop a systemic and scientific theory of international politics, but more importantly, he sets the homogeneous standards for evaluating an IR theory. A theory is qualified as a theory if and only if it satisfies the conditions set forth by this homogeneity. The publication of *Theory of International Politics* not only marked the triumph of structural realism over other strands of IR theories, but also started an era of Waltzianization of IR theory, which is characterized by using one set of overwhelmingly positivist standards for evaluating all IR theories: It is qualified as a theory if the Waltzian standards are satisfied; otherwise it is dismissed as a non-theory. Thus the standard-setting and gatekeeping

---

[19] Acharya 2014, 3.   [20] Waltz 1995, 67–82; Waltz 1979.   [21] Waltz 1979, 6.   [22] Ibid.

role of the Waltzian phenomenon is much more influential than his substantive theory of structural realism. Later comers within the mainstream camp, despite the fact that they have strongly criticized the assumptions and hypotheses of structural realism, have followed closely Waltz's logic of theorizing, the positivist principles, and the scientific methodology. The emergence of neoliberal institutionalism and social constructivism, rather than fundamentally challenging Waltz, have in fact proved and reclaimed the victory of Waltzianization and of homogeneity in IR theoretical development. Its powerful influence or perhaps unconscious violence has continued to exist in a dominant way up to date.

Homogeneity means, by necessity, exclusion. The mainstream of the American IR studies, for example, offers little recognition of the reflective approach, and scholars of mainstream theories, especially the "big three" in the United States, simply refuse to give credit to it. Waltz believes that anything that does not follow the positivist tradition cannot be qualified as "theory": Non-positivist studies provide mere thoughts, for they are the "kind of work that can neither provide satisfactory explanations nor lead to the construction of theory. Such studies cannot explain the causal mechanisms with certainty and clarity."[23] Keohane, in his influential presidential address to the International Studies Association in 1988 entitled "International Relations: Two Approaches," contrasts the rationalistic approach with the reflective approach, arguing that the former is hard while the latter is soft, very much like the Acharya-Buzan categorization, and that the former is positivist while the latter is analytical; that the former is rigorous while the latter is complex; that the former aims at finding the causal mechanisms while the latter seeks coherent arguments. Keohane explicitly supports the former and believes that the rationalistic approach, despite the fact that it is not perfect, has made remarkable achievements, for it successfully explains actors' behavior. Scholars who use this approach are self-conscious about the methodology and their products are widely recognized.[24] As for the reflective approach, Keohane puts forward sharp criticism, saying:

Indeed, the greatest weakness of the reflective school lies not in deficiencies in their critical arguments but in the lack of a clear reflective research program that could be employed by students of world politics. Waltzian neorealism has such a research program; so does neoliberal institutionalism, ... Until the reflective scholars or others sympathetic to their arguments have delineated such a program, and shown in particular studies that it can illuminate important issues in world politics, they will remain on the margin of the field, largely invisible to the

---

[23] Waltz 1995, 68–69.   [24] Keohane 1989a, 160.

preponderance of empirical researchers, most of whom explicitly or implicitly accept one or another version of rationalistic premises.[25]

Keohane's criticism of the reflective approach in fact indicates his belief that such an approach cannot produce qualified social theory because it does not have theoretical hypotheses and pays little attention to rigorous empirical testing. His emphasis on a clear research program, on causality, and on the function of explanation shows that what in his mind constitutes theory is the positivist one or the so-called scientific one and other theories can be only on the margin of IR studies until they change and live up to the scientific standards or until they become the same with rationalistic theories like Waltz's and his own. Before they become the same as positivist and scientific theory they are no theory at all. Keohane, with his neoliberal institutionalism, has not reduced the significance of Waltzianization. Rather, he has helped the Waltzian way of theorizing to further establish itself as a universal standard. Gary King, Robert Keohane, and Sidney Verba again stress the importance of causal inference and further define the model process of scientific research by dividing a research design into four components: the research question, the theory, the data, and the use of the data, making the standards for being scientific more specific and operational.[26] As one of the most influential textbooks in IR methodology, *Designing Social Inquiry* tells IR students the right way to carry out scientific inference in qualitative research.

The scientific standards and positivist assumptions embedded in the mainstream IR theory of the United States have thus become the only yardstick to judge whether or not a self-claimed theory is a theory. Martha Finnemore expresses similar views about theory in her criticism of the English School. She again argues that the English School does not produce theory, that it lacks clarity in methodology, and that therefore its effort for theory building is not successful. American IR studies focus on causal relationship, make clear hypotheses on it, and try to find it in rigorous testing, while "much of the English School work does not fit well into the independent/dependent variable language that dominate the

---

[25] Ibid., 173. Keohane later realized the importance of ideas in international relations. The book coedited by Judith Goldstein and himself was entitled *Ideas and Foreign Policy: Beliefs, Institutions, and Political Change* (Goldstein and Keohane 1993). However, his rationalistic way of thinking did not change and the ideational factor was treated as a mere additional causal variable. As the editors said, ideas helped actors to clarify principles and conceptions of causal relationships, and to coordinate individual behavior, but they do not "challenge the premise that people behave in self-interested and broadly rational ways" Goldstein and Keohane 1993, 5.
[26] King, Keohane, and Verba 1994, 13.

American IR," making it "difficult for the American scholars to incorporate it into their research."[27] Even Wendtian social constructivism follows very much this tradition, supporting the positivist standards and explicitly hypothesizing the constitutive causality. It is exactly because of this characteristic that the constructivism developed by Alexander Wendt has become a mainstream theory of IR in the United States. It is the fact that most English School scholars lack the clarity about causal relations between operational variables that prevents it from completely entering the mainstream in the United States.[28] It would not qualify as a social theory by merely raising meaningful questions, setting out systematic ideas, and developing a set of concepts and categories for the production of abstract and general knowledge.

It should be abnormal or even absurd to take non-positivist theories as non-theories, but it is the case today because of the persistent dominance of the positivist mainstream in the theoretical discourse of IR despite voices against it.[29] Robert Crawford, from a different perspective, sharply points out such dominance. He has found that American IR theory has a conspicuous tendency and strong ability to change a heresy or a heretic theory into a paradigm. The English School is a telling example. It started as a unique theory that the American mainstream paid little attention to in the so-called inter-paradigm debates until it was "discovered" by the American mainstream, especially the key concepts of international society, international cooperation, and international regimes. Once discovered, it has become supplementary to the mainstream study of international regimes and institutions rather than a unique and original theoretical system of its own.[30] Even inside the United States, a similar story is seen. John Ruggie has argued that the rise of constructivism can be traced to such classic roots as Weber,[31] who believed that the social sciences are differentiated from the natural sciences because the former has the task of interpreting the meaning of social action. However, it is clear that the social constructivism developed in the United States soon merged into the mainstream and became a positivist research program and that the study of international norms, for example, is now a "scientific" discourse with the independent/dependent variable language, having been rigorously tested through either

---

[27] Finnemore 2001, 509 and 510–512.
[28] Ibid. I will discuss it later on, arguing that the situation is changing not only because of the effort made by the English School to join the American mainstream, but also because of the fact that they do share something essential that makes their integration easier.
[29] See Smith, Booth and Zalewski 1996; Tickner and Wæver 2009; Tickner and Blaney 2012; Tickner and Blaney 2013.
[30] Crawford 2001, 6–7.   [31] Ruggie 1999, 217–222.

quantitative inference or case studies.[32] In this way, exclusion is both the result of homogenization and a way to reinforce homogenization through either elimination of alternatives or assimilation of dissidents.

Monism is also cultural nihilism. It is perhaps the most profound and effective way for hegemonic dominance, for it negates completely historical heritages and cultural traditions, and denies their important role in the construction of social theory. Whereas there is plenty of criticism against the poverty of the monist approach to social theory, there is little questioning about the connection between culture and theory building. For international studies, a monist, from her view and standard of social theory, would argue that there should be no national borders, for IR theory, and any theory indeed, if it is scientific, is universally applicable, across time and space and beyond geography and boundary. The two criteria to evaluate whether it is a scientific theory or not are universality and replicability, which constitute the absolute and ultimate standard for theory evaluation.[33] Accordingly, there can be schools of theory, but there cannot be theory with national labels. Nobody, for example, can say Newton's theory is British and Einstein's theory is American or Jewish, for no matter where it originates it is true everywhere. It is also true in the social sciences. Any theory should have rational assumptions and falsifiable hypotheses, and must go through rigorous testing so as to reach scientific conclusions. Theories, such as the English School, do not fit into these standards, and thus cannot be defined as theory.[34] Concepts based upon local and practical knowledge are termed false concepts, and efforts to construct social theories with a local focus are criticized as either un-scientific or culturally nationalistic.

This is a clear and categorical inclusion/exclusion dichotomy. Consciously or unconsciously, monism draws a single line to distinguish theory and non-theory, to define a strict boundary to tell knowledge which is inside from non-knowledge which is outside. As David Blaney and Arlene Tickner have criticized: "IR ... fails to see alternatives because those who make it assume the West, its science and its development as the universal 'norm'."[35] If this disciplinary view dominates, then even if some advocate pluralism and encourage dialogue between the mainstream IR and the marginalized theories, such plurality can only be one "that evolves within a (narrow) space allowed for by the United States and Western European core, which exercises a strong disciplinary

---

[32] For example, *International Organization* published many articles on international norms, most of which follow the positivist and therefore scientific tenets. See *International Organization* 59 (Fall 2005) and 61 (Winter 2007).
[33] Kagan 2009, xi and 1.   [34] Finnemore 2001.   [35] Blaney and Tickner 2013, 7.

function in terms of the theories, concepts, and categories authorized to count as knowledge of world politics."[36]

Fundamentally, it is a matter of culture. Underlying the monist view of theory building, it is the monism that embraces the "self-culture" as the only rational culture, advanced and superior, and regards the "other cultures" as simply non-rational, backward, and inferior. They should catch up and become the same as the self-culture. Since I argue that culture plays a particularly important role in social theory building, this monist view of culture implicitly but fundamentally believes that only the Western culture works to make theory, and other cultures cannot produce key concepts, provide proper categorization, and therefore are not qualified as resources of social theory. It thus denies completely the multiple possibilities for the prosperity of social theory and plays the role of gate-keeping to prevent other cultures from producing systematic knowledge. The result, in fact, would be the demise of IR knowledge as well as the eventual fall of the mainstream IR theory dominant in the discipline today, for they simply would have nothing to dominate over and would therefore prepare themselves for the final demise.

Pluralism

The second view, pluralism, argues that the social world differs significantly from the natural world, for the latter focuses more on matter, while the former is lived by people with the students and the studied both as human beings. In social sciences, therefore, no study is value free and they cannot treat human beings, who are the studied, as iron, gold, or mechanical parts. The social sciences should try to find social laws, but equally important, they need to understand social meanings and interpret social phenomena. It should encourage multiple interpretations, just as artists and architects express the observed from their respective perspectives. Furthermore they create social facts, give meanings to make the social come alive, and construct laws through human agency in this process. The social sciences thus differ essentially from the natural sciences. It is the latter function of understanding and interpreting that natural theory does not have and therefore becomes the characteristic feature of social theory. And this feature is so significantly primary because it is human in nature.

Pluralism, by definition, does not seek and work for homogeneity. As the broader definition by Acharya and Buzan of IR theory goes, they include contributions that are substantially acknowledged in the IR

---

[36] Ibid., 4.

academic community as being theory, self-identified by its creators as theory, and recognized as a systematic attempt to abstract or generalize about the subject matter of international relations.[37] Pluralism does not privilege one type of theory over others and can help find theories of a local produce.[38] The most recent advocate of pluralism is the Global International Relations (GIR) agenda put forward by Acharya in his presidential address to the Annual Convention of the International Studies Association, in which he outlines the important dimensions of the GIR agenda, including pluralistic universalism; use of world history rather than just Greco-Roman, European, and US history as its foundations; incorporation of existing theories and methods; integration of regional and area studies; and eschewal of exceptionalism, and recognition of multiple forms of agency.[39]

Since respect of diversity is the essential idea, pluralism is an inclusive rather than exclusive approach to social theory construction. Acharya expresses it clearly in his explanation of the GIR project, whose mission is to "chart a course toward a truly inclusive discipline, recognizing its multiple and diverse foundations," because the discipline of IR "does not reflect the voices, experiences, knowledge claims, and contributions of the vast majority of the societies and states in the world, and often marginalizes those outside the core countries of the West."[40] It requires a new understanding of universalism or universality. In contrast to the monistic universalism, Acharya proposes a pluralistic universalism as the foundation of his GIR project. As the opposite to monistic universalism, it is, using Tickner's words, "to uncover stories about forgotten spaces that respect difference, show tolerance and compassion, and are skeptical about absolute truths."[41] For IR, it specifically encourages:

comparative studies of international systems that look past and beyond the Westphalian form, conceptualizing the nature and characteristics of a post-Western world order that might be termed as a multiplex world, expanding the study of regionalisms and regional orders beyond Eurocentric models, building synergy between disciplinary and area studies approaches, expanding our investigations into the two-way diffusion of ideas and norms, and investigating the multiple and diverse ways in which civilizations encounter each other, which includes peaceful interactions and mutual learning.[42]

Perhaps the most profound significance of pluralism, as well as the most relevant dimension to this study, is its recognition of cultural pluralism, its encouragement of civilizational dialogues, and its respect of cultures as firm groundings for theory construction. Max Weber has described such

---

[37] Acharya and Buzan 2007, 292.   [38] Ibid., 290.   [39] Acharya 2014, 3.   [40] Ibid., 1.
[41] Tickner 2011, quoted in Acharya 2014, 4.   [42] Acharya 2014, 1.

functions of the social sciences, believing that the social sciences can be an independent system, for it differs from the natural sciences in terms of the purpose of social studies. Human beings have a special faculty, that is, their ability to create and construct meaning for the social world, or in Weber's words, "to take a deliberate attitude towards the world and to *lend it significance*,"[43] while matter in the physical world does not have such a capacity. In the study of the social, the most significant purpose is to understand the social meaning of human agency. Meaning belongs to the ideational domain, and therefore the social world is very much concerned with ideas and meaningful actions, i.e. practices that these ideas are embedded in and create in turn. The natural world, on the contrary, is fundamentally about matter, which exists objectively and has a homogeneous ontological status, and the study of such a world aims to find objective laws about the properties of the material. As such, explanation is the most appropriate way. Objective laws exist, identical everywhere and all the time. (Even this view is questionable today.) Human beings, as explorers, can at the best find such laws and retell them as representational knowledge. The social sciences are not alike. Subjective existence and intersubjective reflection are normal phenomena in the social world, and even "social facts" are often conscious or unconscious social constructions, subject to change all the time. Thus, in the social world, there are at least two purposes of scholarly pursuit, both to find law-like patterns of action if they exist and to understand the meaning of social subjectivity and intersubjectivity. Understanding, both as an epistemological approach and as a methodological device, is indispensable in social studies.[44] In addition, understanding itself, by definition, includes interpretation, which unavoidably involves human agency through the activation of their practical knowledge, for social facts themselves are products of social practices.[45] By definition, interpreting is multidimensional, for it depends on the human beings who do the interpreting. According to Wang Yangming (1472–1528), a Chinese philosopher in the Ming Dynasty, interpreting occurs when the knowledge in one's heart/mind and the object being observed meet and combine.[46] Different people tend to have different interpretations of the meaning in a social setting and observers and the angles of observation matter a great deal. People from different cultural or even subcultural backgrounds may understand differently the meaning of a Van Gogh, a Matisse, or a Qi Baishi,[47] for the observers have different background

---

[43] Weber 1949, 81, quoted in Ruggie 1999, 219, emphasis in original.   [44] Qin 2004.
[45] Carr 1964; Alker 1996.   [46] Wang (Yangming) 2014.
[47] A late master of traditional Chinese painting.

knowledge and different collective experiences, which lead to different ways of interaction between the painting and the observer. The dialogue itself is a process of understanding and interpretation. For such a process, there is perhaps only one correct answer in the natural world, but there are many answers in the social world, none of which can be judged as absolutely correct or wrong. Pluralism is thus the characteristic feature of social studies, and human agency, activated by practical knowledge, is the crucial factor in the construction of social theory. Nothing social is as rigorous as linear causality and no law is so neat as Newton's law of universal gravitation or Einstein's theory of relativity.

A pluralist, therefore, believes that it is perhaps justifiable for the natural sciences to claim no national or geographical borders, but that social sciences can have national boundaries, which are not purely geographical, but mainly geo-cultural. When national borders fit fairly well with cultural ones, a national label is justifiable, for it is not the national borders that matter and what really matters is culture. A Chinese IR theory, for instance, is first of all related to the Chinese culture rather than the Chinese territory, to the ideational rather than to the physical. When the so-called "non-Western IR theory" is discussed, it is more cultural than geographical. Geography matters if and only if it fits with a cultural sphere.[48] We have just discussed the importance of understanding and interpreting as epistemological and methodological devices in the social sciences, which are exactly embedded geo-culturally. Understanding is cultural, for it is based upon the practice of a particular cultural community. It is human and social in the first place and no social science is over and beyond the human. Western brides wear white at the wedding, while white is the color for funerals in China. The social meaning of color differs because of the different practices of the two cultural communities. Time and space, cultures and collective memories, and ways of thinking and doing may well lead to different ways of understanding and therefore interpreting. In other words, different cultures nurture and are nurtured by different practices over time, and practical knowledge thus produced, accumulated, and fermented, in turn, leads to different understanding of the seemingly same "objective" fact, reproducing and representing different meanings in their ideational schema. Theory as a system of ideas follows this logic, inseparable from the culture, history, language, and ways of thinking and doing of a particular community of practice. It is exactly in this way that theory is initiated in a cultural setting and always bears its birthmark.[49] Karl Marx speaks of history, saying that history is made by people, but "they do not

---

[48] Nisbitt 2003.   [49] Zalewski 1996.

make it just as they please; they do not make it under circumstances chosen by themselves, but under circumstances directly found."[50] It is also true of social theory. It is made by people, but they do not make it just as they please. People make social theory under circumstances defined by the practical knowledge embedded in their cultural communities. No matter how a social theory is created and developed, it is related with the culture of its origin and it is created by cultural humans. When we use a national label that reflects a culture to indicate its cultural birthmark, it is not only justifiable, but also most reasonable.

Pluralism thus legitimizes the production of systematic knowledge in general and of IR theories in particular outside the boundary drawn by the Western mainstream and opens the door to social theory construction in non-Western contexts and cultures.

Social Theory Construction

Having discussed the two approaches to social theory construction, we need to come back to the general definition of theory, that is, "a system of ideas." The monist approach does not go against this definition, but limits it to a particular type of theory – the hard positivist one – and refuses to recognize other types as theory. The pluralist view also conforms to the general definition, but has a much broader and more open definition of social theory. The English School, dependency theory, feminist IR theory, and perhaps even more, are all theories if they constitute a system of ideas and a coherent scheme of knowledge. They may not have clear dependent and independent variables, may not focus on finding the causal relationships, and may not provide neat and rigorous explanations. However, they do use historical, social, and humanitarian phenomena for reflective analysis, and they do develop concepts and analytical frameworks for understanding and interpretation. In the social world, we need explanation, and we also need understanding and interpretation. In IR, different theories exist in terms of ontology, epistemology, and methodology, but if they constitute a system of ideas and are recognized as such by the academic community in general, they are theories. There is and cannot be a single set of standards for the ultimate judgment.

We insist on the general and broad definition of theory and social theory, not only because it is a widely accepted definition, but also because it cherishes an open mind for theoretical construction and stands as a fundamental opposition to discursive hegemony. It has several connotations. First, theory is about ideas, human ideas. No matter

---

[50] Ruggie 1999, 278.

what theory it is, it is constructed by humans through human practice. Since it is human, human agency is indispensable in theory construction and development. But human agency does not work completely as it pleases. It is conditioned, to paraphrase Marx's saying again, by circumstances directly found and immediately experienced. In IR, structural realism, neoliberal institutionalism, social constructivism, dependency theory, and the English School are all human products and have been produced in relevant circumstances. As such those who have produced them are enabled and constrained by the circumstances, too. It is culture that provides the most meaningful circumstances and therefore constitutes a most ready treasure house where new ideas and concepts can be discovered. On the one hand, therefore, we need to explore the cultural resources for theory development, believing that the multiplicity of cultures facilitates production of social theory; on the other hand, we also need to remember that a social theory will always bear this cultural birthmark and absolute and complete universality is impossible.

Second, theory must be a system of ideas. Thoughts can be systematic and can also be sporadic and disparate. Spontaneous inspiration produces great poetry, but cannot by itself create social theory. A system of ideas includes clear definitions, key concepts, and logical reasoning that makes the definitions and concepts meaningful and coherent. Mainstream American positivist IR theories reflect systemized ideas, and so do the English School, dependency theory, and feminist theory. They may have very different approaches to theorizing, but they all fit into the general definition of theory. There is no reason to exclude any one of them, just as none of them can claim that positivist theory is no theory simply because they are different in ways of organizing ideas. When the question "Why is there no non-Western International Relations theory" is raised, there is no doubt that the Western mainstream IR theory plays a crucial role in gatekeeping. However, we also need to reflect seriously on one more question: "Do non-Western IR scholars consciously develop concepts, carry out conceptualization, and systemize ideas for theorization by exploring the resources of their own cultures?"

Third, there are many paths to systemize ideas and thoughts. Pluralism is the key word here, because if we use only one set of yardsticks to judge, there would be no theoretical prosperity and intellectual progress, and knowledge production and reproduction would be retarded in a homogeneous fiefdom. As Burchill and Linklater have pointed out, theory is defined not as merely being "scientific," and cannot be limited to the one function of explaining. Positivist theory of

IR is only one of many.[51] The American positivist mainstream is a particular form of IR theory and cannot be taken as the theory and even more cannot be used as the standard to evaluate other theories. Theory should be in the plural form, or paraphrasing Peter Katzenstein's definition of civilizations, they should be "plural and pluralistic":[52] Across cultural communities it is pluralistic with many theories of different background knowledges competing with and complementing one another, and within a cultural community it is plural with many theories of different types competing with and complementing one another. This is the precondition for theoretical prosperity. It is perhaps understandable that theorists wish to make their respective theory the theory. However, no matter how influential it is, no theory can ever be the theory and the development of a theory is always going through a process of debating and competing with other theories. A theory, as well as any other form of knowledge, is dead at the moment when it becomes the theory.

The insistence on the broader and more general definition has another important dimension, which is related to the concept of "worldview." When Buzan used the terms of monism and pluralism, what he had in mind was perhaps more methodological and therefore used "methodological monism" and "methodological pluralism" to indicate that the difference lies largely with the methodology.[53] I argue that what they reflect is much more than a mere methodological dimension. Rather they represent different worldviews. Monism is sometimes termed "naturalistic monism" to indicate the belief that the natural and social sciences follow the same logic and therefore should follow the same way of theory construction.[54] It is true that the debate started in the discussion of the two types of sciences, and it is also true that the debate in IR seems to have started from the disagreement over methodology. But for my study here it is much more than a view that "the social sciences can be built on the same model as the natural sciences."[55] More relevance lies in what may be labelled as "cultural monism," which, perhaps an extension of naturalistic monism, believes that social theory produced in one cultural community is and should be perfectly universal and valid across cultural communities, for the multiple cultures that exist in the world differ only in one thing: whether it is an advanced culture or a backward culture. The "advanced" culture represents the correct and rational, while other cultures should follow this role-model and eventually become it.

Such a view is much more than merely methodological. It is indeed a worldview. As we discussed in the previous paragraphs, monists not

[51] Burchill 1996, 1.   [52] Katzenstein 2010a.   [53] Buzan 2001.   [54] Ruggie 1999, 219.
[55] Nicholson 1996, 130.

only believe that the natural sciences provide the standard for all sciences, but also hold and even take it for granted that social theory created in one societal and cultural setting is universal all over the world, no matter what culture it is applied to. The underlying assumption is that reality in different cultural settings should be essentially the same, for universal theory must rest on universal reality. Even if the reality in another culture or society seems different, it should eventually become the same or it should be made the same. If we should take the monist view, especially in the second sense, then there would be indeed no other form of social theory except the hard positivist one. Thus, cultural monism has created a self-closed system with homogeneity as its goal, exclusiveness as its distinct feature, and uniform application as its belief. By definition, such a system cannot achieve lasting prosperity despite momentary magnificence, for it represses the creativeness grounded on other cultural resources.

I tend to interpret pluralism as more cultural than methodological, too. Cultural pluralism rests on a belief in the plurality of social reality. As social reality is largely constructed through human practice and as many different kinds of human practice exist in the world, there cannot be only one social reality. In other words, there are many worlds with various realities, both the terms in the plural. Berger and Luckmann hold that reality is socially constructed. "What is 'real' to a Tibetan monk may not be 'real' to an American businessman."[56] Similarly, Searle argues that social reality is constructed and maintained by custom and habit, that is, by practice based upon background knowledge.[57] If this is the case, culture plays a most important role in the construction of social realities, for it is closely related to custom and habit, or to the practice of members of a particular cultural community. Monism is underpinned by the belief that there is only one reality throughout the world, across and beyond cultures and civilizations. It is exactly because of this belief that a particular set of standards for evaluating social theory is taken for the universally applicable standards. Recognition of plural realities as well as recognition of realities as social construction thus paves the way to the recognition of cultural pluralism.

A good example is Acharya's encouragement for grounding IR in world history rather than in just Greco-Roman, European, and US history.[58] The mainstream IR theory rests almost exclusively on the history of the Westphalian international system, especially its anarchic nature, without realizing that it is only one of the many international relations histories, or one of the many international relations realities that have existed in the

[56] Berger and Luckmann 1966, 3.   [57] Searle 1995.   [58] Acharya 2014, 3.

world. The dominant worldview, formed, embedded, and distilled from culture and through history, very much indicates what order is to be established. While recognizing that the Westphalian institution is made as a reality by rationalistic agents with strong individuality featured by sovereign identity, we need to see and understand that other histories may not be like it and may present different realities in relations among nations or peoples. In other words, there is no singular reality, but only plural realities. Balance of power, for example, was a Westphalian reality. But it was in fact what the agents made of it, just as Wendt's discussion of anarchy goes. The Tribute system was also a historical reality in East Asia for hundreds of years, where balance of power and anarchy were neither a reality nor a systemic feature at all, for the agents there made realities different from what has been found in the Westphalian international system. Following the advice by Berger and Luckmann on the sociology of knowledge,[59] we need to analyze how and why agents in different settings construct different realities, rather than to apply the reality of one geo-cultural space to the whole social universe. Similarly, concepts derived from the Westphalian reality are ones from a particular geo-cultural locale and may not apply to other geo-cultural settings, and, moreover, different concepts may well be derived from other cultural communities. It is also indicated by feminist IR, the reality of which differs very much from the reality of mainstream IR theory.

Pluralism not only recognizes the existence of multiple realities, but also embraces the multiple ways of perceiving the social world. Let's again use the example of the English School theory of IR. Scholars of the English School mainly turn to reflective thinking and logical reasoning, and rarely can we see in their analysis neat scientific hypotheses with the beauty and rigor of equations in physics, indicating the causal relationship between clearly defined independent and dependent variables. They seldom use mathematical modeling and quantitative statistical analysis.[60] Rather, they may well put forward an original idea or thought, design a set of key concepts, and then construct a systematically coherent framework through historical reflection and logical reasoning, discussing how the

---

[59] Berger and Luckmann 1966.
[60] According to Tim Dunne, the English School originated with "the fundamental questions of 'international society'" (1998, xi). He uses the term of "three preliminary articles" to describe the characteristic features of the English School, including a particular tradition of enquiry (an awareness of a body of literature, a set of central questions, and a common agenda), an interpretive approach, and a belief in the normative nature of international theory. These features are in contrast with those of American mainstream IR theories. Particularly, the second article, an interpretive approach, expresses a clear position against the scientific approach dominant in the United States. See Dunne 1998, 6–11.

international system works and what international society means. It appears indeed to some that the debate between the English School and the American mainstream is one about methodology. In fact the difference is more about how they see and understand the international relations world. While analysts in the United States were exploring the international system in every detail, English School scholars put forward and analyzed the key concept of "international society," thus making a theory primarily around the systemization of this idea. Later on, Buzan developed Bull's theory and focused on the evolution of international society to world society, taking into consideration the post-Cold War trend of globalization.[61] The system-society debate is in fact a debate between two worldviews extended to the field of IR. The former takes the international relations world as a system with discrete and like units, which resembles a billiard table with an external force driving the billiards to interact, while the latter understands the international world as a society, with rules, norms, and values binding its members together. It is well acknowledged that the greatest contribution of the English School is its big idea of "international society," the invention of which rests on a world perceived differently from what American IR scholars see. Without such a worldview there could have been no invention of the concept of "international society." For me, it is this different angle for observing the world, or different worldview, rather than mere methodological dissimilarity that has made the English School.

Even greater difference can be seen between the Chinese and the Western worldviews. Monists take the natural sciences and the construction of natural theory as their model. The underlying reason is that the world out there, or the natural world, is what they explore in the pursuit of knowledge. It is undeniable that modern sciences started in the West. It is also understandable because people in the West have spent much more time and energy exploring the natural world, trying to know it and to control it. "Matter" has thus become one of the biggest words that attracts generations of talents. In other words, the worldview of Western societies is very much around the word "matter" in the natural world, which is both something to know and something to exploit. Most of the material achievements by humans have been made through the efforts based upon this worldview. Moreover, the success of the West in sciences and technologies in terms of accumulated knowledge and material achievements have led to the belief that such a success is fungible and extendable to other fields, such as the social world. Even if the social world has conspicuous differences, it should be made into something

---

[61] Buzan 2004; Bull 1977; Vincent 1986.

similar to the natural world. Despite the protest and criticism from all the post-modernist strands, it is reasonable, although arguable, to say that this worldview focusing on the natural world and the material thereof continues to dominate.

The worldview of the Chinese is quite the opposite. It starts with the human rather than nature, focusing on the human heart/mind rather than on things and matter. It has never taken the natural world as a separate space and has never considered "matter" as what they should spend much time and energy studying. The Chinese tradition is to place more emphasis on humans rather than matter, for the decisive factor in the world, both natural and social, is human. While Westerners have tried to discover and create knowledge in the process of their exploration of nature, Chinese have paid much more attention to finding and exploiting knowledge in their own heart/mind. It is not to argue that traditionally Chinese did not pay any attention to nature, but they did understand nature in a way different from their Western counterparts. Confucianism, for example, has a profound belief that truth as well as knowledge is not out there for us to discover, but lies within us in our inner selves. As Feng Youlan (Fung Yu-lan) comments:

In another place, he [Mencius] said: "All things are already in us. Turn our attention to ourselves and find there this truth: there is no greater delight than that." ... Happiness and truth are in our mind. It is in our own mind, not in the external world, that we can seek for happiness and truth.[62]

Thus Chinese may turn inward to their inner selves for knowledge and truth rather than go to the external world. Similarly, they also feel that the cultivation of the human heart/mind is the most important and most difficult work. In particular, it is far more significant than the control of the natural world. While readers may well admire Hemingway's old man who singlehandedly struggles against the storm or sympathize with Melville's Ahab who fights against Moby-Dick, the biggest challenge, for the Chinese, rises always from one's own heart/mind and a profound person is one who daily examines himself and controls unhealthy desires.[63] Control of nature is not easy, but control of one's heart/mind is the most difficult. Education in the West may teach more about how to

---

[62] Feng 1991, 587. (Fun Yu-lan, is the spelling used for the *Selected Philosophical Writings of Fun Yu-lan* published in 1991, which includes most of his important works. The standard translation of his name is now Feng Youlan. In the following chapters, therefore, I will use Feng Youlan instead of Fung Yu-lan.)

[63] Confucius et al. 2014, 5. Later Confucian scholars have followed and interpreted this line of reasoning, stressing the importance of self-cultivation. Zhu Xi (1130–1200) advocated "eradicating human desires and maintain the heavenly principles," and Wang Yangming (1472–1528) argued that the most difficult thing in the world is not to eliminate bandits in the greenwood but to "eliminate the bandits in one's heart."

understand nature and find natural laws, while education in traditional China was first of all the most important means to cultivate one's heart/mind. Thus this Chinese worldview is more human-based, and more introspectively oriented. It is worth exploring what big idea or ideas can be found and what social theory can be developed in a culture that focuses more on the human. This is the effort I am making throughout this book.

Conclusion

Social theory is shaped by culture. Monism holds that natural theory and social theory are of little substantial difference, for both are used to explain reality. It implies that reality is the same everywhere and that the path to explain reality should be the same. No matter where a theory is initiated, it is and should be universal in the first place and therefore culture matters little for theoretical development. By definition, it denies the role of culture, i.e. ideas, values, attitudes, perspectives, worldviews, etc., in the building of social theory. Pluralism, on the contrary, argues that the natural sciences and the social sciences are of significant difference, for the latter is not only for explanation, but also for understanding and interpreting social reality, and moreover for constructing social reality, too. If understanding and interpretation are added to the process of social theory building, culture becomes significant, for such understanding and interpretation are based on practical knowledge that is developed through generations and embedded in a particular cultural community, or that is created by and creates a cultural community. Culture, therefore, matters. Different cultures may produce different social theories.

We place emphasis on pluralism in general and cultural pluralism in particular, for in an increasingly globalizing world with more cultural communities joining in international and global affairs, the multiplicity of cultural resources may provide a rich treasure trove for the prosperity of social theory construction and intellectual dialogue. If we want to make it come true, a pluralistic approach to social theory construction is necessary. And, furthermore, it has been recognized that there is basically no non-Western IR theory, and that there exists in IR a hierarchical structure which sees a division of labor between Western scholars who theorize and non-Western scholars who provide raw data.[64] To change this situation, non-Western scholars need to consciously explore their own cultural resources for social theory construction and for the enrichment of the existing edifice of IR knowledge. Such effort is a must.

---

[64] Wemheuer-Vogelaar et al. 2016; Maliniak et al. 2014.

2　Theoretical Hard Core

The previous chapter argues that culture shapes social theory. In this chapter I intend to answer a related and fundamental question: How does culture shape social theory? My presumption is that culture matters in social theory construction. In other words, culture leaves an indelible birthmark on a social theory through shaping the mind of the cultural beings who produce knowledge and develop social theory. It means that a social theory is initially constructed in a particular geo-cultural setting, which defines the practice of the cultural community and thus orients the efforts to develop theory, too. Different cultures may produce different social theories. I thus provide here a tentative answer: Culture informs and nurtures the metaphysical component of a theoretical hard core, out of which a social theory grows.

In this chapter I first argue that any social theory needs in the very beginning a theoretical hard core, or a nucleus, maturing from it gradually into a system of ideas through a process of nucleation. I further argue that the hard core is composed of two parts, the metaphysical and the substantive. The latter helps members of a cultural community observe and perceive empirical facts, while the former helps them understand and interpret such facts. Culture matters in theoretical construction exactly because culture is the sediment of long practices of members of a cultural community, making them tend to think and do in a culturally oriented way. It is their collective custom and habit, their common worldview and shared knowledge, thus becoming the lens through which they see, understand, and interpret. It is the angle from which one observes the world. Culture therefore provides the essential elements of the metaphysical component of the theoretical nucleus, without which no theory could even be started. In the following lines I will discuss these issues in detail.

The Theoretical Hard Core and Its Constitution

If theory is a system of ideas, then construction of theory is a process of organizing ideas and integrating thoughts into such a system. The American mainstream IR theory and the English School have gone through such a process of organization and integration, which structures ideas and thoughts in a logical and reasonable way so as to form an intellectual framework. So do feminist IR theory and dependency theory. If this understanding is correct, then a theory is a system with parts, of which the most important is the theoretical core. If we compare a theory to an intellectual system, the hard core is the nucleus from which a process of nucleation starts. It is like a life that starts from an embryo or a seed. The nucleus is thus the soul of the theory, for its forming, growing, radiating, and crystalizing constitute the whole process of theorizing. The smallest and core component is the beginning, deciding whether the system can stand, develop, mature, and evolve. Thus a theory, as a system of ideas, starts from a theoretical nucleus, a core that would give life to a sustainable theory.

Imre Lakatos' discussion of the hard core of a research program is highly inspiring in this respect. A set of theories form a research program, as he discusses in his book, *The Methodology of Scientific Research Programmes*, which by definition is a system of theories, somewhat similar to a meta-theory or paradigm. He holds that a research program should have two important components: the hard core and the protective belt, each having its own functions and both maintaining and sustaining the theory. The former decides the fate of the theory: If the hard core collapses, the theory is dead and abandoned. What is highly relevant here is his idea of the "hard core," which defines a research program and makes it different from other programs.[1] For the purpose of this study, I term it the "theoretical hard core," largely following Lakatos' definition of the hard core of a research program, and argue that it is applicable for a social theory, too. Theories, no matter whether they are about the natural or social worlds, have their hard cores and protective belts, with the former as the defining element of the theory and the latter as the flexible and expendable protection of the theoretical hard core from damage or destruction. Lakatos, even though strongly influenced by Karl Popper, argues against Popper's concept of the critical experiment, for he believes that a single and even critical experiment cannot falsify a theory if the hard core is not hopelessly damaged, or it is successfully protected by the belt. Unless the hard core collapses, a theory continues to stand.

---

[1] Lakatos 1978, 6.

Despite the fact that his discussion focuses more on the natural sciences, such as Newton's Laws of Motion and the Universal Principle of Gravitation, the concept of the theoretical "hard core" which defines and sustains a theory is enlightening.

The hard core is therefore the life of a theory. It makes one theory different from another and constitutes the identity of the theory: Once a hard core is being formed, a new theory is in the becoming. Although Lakatos does not discuss in particular the formation of a theory, he does point out that a research program starts from an initial model, growing gradually into a research program through testing and verifying. I term it a process of "nucleation," or a process of a hard core or a key idea of a theory being formed and growing, starting a related process of the formation of the theory itself. If this is the case, then we need to raise an essential question when we discuss a theory or a system of ideas: What is the hard core of a theory? In the natural sciences it is not that difficult. The idea of gravitation, for example, is the hard core, which then tells us that an apple would not fly into the sky unless some other forces over-power the gravity of the earth and that a spacecraft should overcome such gravity so as to fly into space. The causality is clear, indicating that the hard core is solid. In the social sciences, however, it is perhaps much more complicated, but the process of theorization is similar. Following some-what Wang Yangming's heart/mind theory and putting it in a most sim-plistic way, the hard core of a theory is an initial idea activated by an observation of some thing by a particular theorist.

The social sciences are human. The subjects and objects are both human beings and social beings, too, and therefore social studies cannot be value free and provide such simple, neat, and beautiful theories as Newton's and Einstein's, which indicate causality so directly and can be clearly expressed by mathematical formulas. The monist view has a fatal flaw, i.e. equating the social sciences to the natural sciences and copying the materialness, objectivity, and certainty of the latter directly or blindly into the former. At a certain level and during a certain historical period (such as the era of modernization), it seems that such efforts have made remarkable progress, but fundamentally it will fail, for it is non-human in the first place while the social world is primarily human. The history of the mainstream IR theory is a process of dehumanization, with increasing objectification and decreasing humanness. In IR, Waltz's structural real-ism is perhaps the closest in form to natural science theory, but its simplistic materialism and purposeful parsimony result in glaring flaws in explaining human behavior. It shows that social theory would fail if it should take humans as non-human and treat the objects of social studies as material and uniform. International systems, for example, are human constructions and may therefore vary across civilizations. Ever existing uncertainty in the social world creates opportunities for human creation. The performance of the Westphalian international system in Europe differs significantly from that of the Tribute international system in East Asia, though they share certain similarities. Theories based upon the performance and practice of the former then may not be the same as those based upon the latter and, similarly, concepts derived from the former may not even be thought of in the latter. To develop valid social theories, the human factor must go equally with and even weigh more than the material factor. (Even for the theory of gravitation, we perhaps also need to ask why Isaac Newton had such an idea while his Chinese contemporaries did not.) It is, therefore, necessary to differentiate the constitution of the hard core of social theory from that of natural theory and to break it up in order to study its constituent parts, paying special attention to the part which is more human and more cultural and which plays the role of understanding and interpretation, a defining feature of any social theory.

I argue that the hard core of social theory is composed of two parts, one substantive and the other metaphysical. The former is the component that plays the role of perception, taking signals from the real world and presenting them to the latter. It is more about observation, about substantive issues, and about the physical world. The metaphysical component plays the role of conception, processing signals through the ideational filter and representing them as a meaningful question. It is essentially about understanding, about worldviews, and about culture and philosophy. It embeds and brews meaning. In a certain sense, the former is more material because it deals with the "facts" out there, something like Searle's "intrinsic features of the world,"[2] and the latter is more ideational, attitudinal, and agent/observer-sensitive, for it treats the facts through a process of understanding and interpretation, with the observer's worldview as the most relevant background knowledge.

The two parts or components of the theoretical hard core, the substantive and the metaphysical, are complementary to and conditioned by each other.[3] They work simultaneously and interact in a way to have impacts on each other. For the purpose of analysis, however, we separate them in our discussion as two constituent components. As discussed above, the substantive component is related to the world out there, dealing with the objective facts based more on perception and receiving signals from the outside. For example, everyone can see poverty and

---

[2] Searle 1995, 9–13.
[3] As illustrated by the Chinese *ying-yang* diagram. See Brincat and Ling 2014, 4–5.

prosperity in life and war and peace in international relations. It is an objective fact, too, that Chinese soldiers went across the Yalu River into Korea in 1950 and the United States launched a war against Iraq in 2003. On the other hand, the metaphysical component is about the fundamental worldview, about conception, and about understanding and interpretation. It gives meaning to the facts and signals received through the substantive component. It does not only explain what causes poverty and war and what leads to prosperity and peace, but also interprets such facts. Thus it is very much an attitudinal judgment if we say that the Iraqi war was a major US effort to destroy a tyranny, or that it was a war by the wrong people, in the wrong place, and at the wrong time. Furthermore, the substantive component is more material, activated through direct contact with things out there at particular temporo-spatial points, and therefore is subject to empirical verification and falsification. The metaphysical component is not subject to such empirical testing. It is related to experience and reality, but not formed through the experience and reality here and now. The metaphysical component is a product of the long practice of a group, or people of a certain cultural community, representing their shared practical knowledge, manifesting their worldviews, and reflecting their ways of thinking and doing. It is not formed at any particular time and space. It is processual in nature, accumulated and formed during an open process of continued practice over a long history. Thus, it is the fruit of historical sediments and of the practical knowledge of a group of people.[4] Its importance lies in the fact that a real world fact, such as the poverty of the third world, is perceived and received through the substantive component of the theoretical hard core, goes through the metaphysical component to be processed as a puzzle, and comes out with a particular meaning given by this interpreting process. Thus the poverty of the third world can be seen either as a result of their domestic institutions and systems, or as an effect of the structure and functioning of the world capitalist system.

There is no doubt that the substantive component can make a difference. There are numerous facts out there, but the observer can only select some of them for her observation. At the turn of the century, there was a renewed debate in IR concerning the Hoffmann argument that IR is an American social science. In the 2001 book *International Relations – Still an American Social Science*, edited by Crawford and Jarvis, many authors recognize the dominance of the American IR in the

---

[4] As Hall and Ames have argued, a major difference of the Chinese modality of thinking from that of Westerners is that correlativity is a characteristic feature of the former while causality, the latter. Nisbett expresses something similar. See Hall and Ames 1995; Nisbett 2003.

discipline and at the same time they also largely agree that IR with a national identity exists.[5] For example, the United Kingdom, Canada, and Australia – scholars in these countries may raise different questions and take different approaches to international relations. The variations across countries are seen as a function of variations of the countries in question in terms of their international status, developmental levels, and other relevant factors. Canada may be interested more in the status and behavior of a medium-sized country while the United States tends to take itself as the leading player at the core of world politics and raises more questions about the entire international system and world order.[6] Continental European countries may also differ from the United Kingdom in their study of international relations.[7] It seems the debate reflected in this edited volume is more at the substantive level, which tells that the observer selects what to observe according to the material basis she, as well as her territory-based country, rests on. Scholars in the United States, for example, tend to study how a rising power may challenge the US hegemony and to argue that hegemony is good for stability. It is true, but even here the metaphysical component works in the background. Why, for example, does the observer select some facts and pay no attention to other facts?

One of the most important reasons why the theory of the natural sciences differs from that of the social sciences is that their hard cores are differently constituted, especially concerning the metaphysical component. The hard core of natural theories is more or less similar everywhere and the metaphysical component is, justifiably, neglected or taken for granted, because the same matter has the same properties, impartially defined and objectively conditioned. Iron is iron, no matter whether it is in Europe, Africa, or Asia. Even if there is a metaphysical part, it seems negligible. The social sciences, however, are human in the first place, and humans are in turn social and cultural beings. Theories of the social sciences therefore are unavoidably related to cultures and societies where humans are located and go through their everyday practices. It is such human conditions that provide social and cultural beings with their understanding and interpretation of the ego-alter interaction, the intersubjectivity, the interpersonal relationship, and the social world around them. These are ontological and epistemological, constituting shared knowledge and views about the world. It has fundamental impacts

---

[5] The exception is Tony Porter (Crawford and Jarvis 2001, 131–147), whose article, "Can There Be National Perspectives on Inter(national) Relations?," argues that nationality is an insignificant determinant of the study of IR. See Porter 2001.

[6] Nossal 2001, 167–186.

[7] Griffiths and O'Callaghan 2001, 187–201; Groom and Mandaville 2001, 151–165.

on the formation of the hard core of a theory, which is made and "fabricated" by thinking humans living in culture and society. Since the hard core is so important to theory formation, and since the cultural and social beings in the dual capacity of a social theorist and a member of a community are so important to the formation of the hard core, we need to discuss in more detail how the hard core of a social theory is related to human beings in social and cultural communities.

By a similar logic, the reason that a social theory may differ fundamentally from another is that their metaphysical components differ. Alexander Wendt, for example, has discussed two levels of questions: the first-order and second-order questions. He defines the second-order questions as those of social theory, concerning the fundamental assumptions of social inquiry, such as ontology and epistemology, and it is therefore in some sense comparable to my definition of the metaphysical component of the theoretical hard core here. The first-order questions concern issues in specific domains, for example, a social theory focusing on the family, or on the international system. He believes that one theory differs from another mainly in that the second-order theorizing is different and argues that his constructivism differs from Waltz's neorealism in that their ways of second-order, ontological theorizing are different. Waltz's is materialist and individualist while Wendt's is idealist and holist.[8] According to Wendt, the ontological and epistemological elements define a theory. Ole Wæver has provided another example. He argues that neorealism and neoliberal institutionalism reached a "neo-neo" synthesis during the 1980s because, using Kuhn's words, they were no longer incommensurable and their fundamental assumptions were converging – both sharing a rationalistic research program and a conception of science.[9] Wæver holds that neorealism and neoliberal institutionalism underwent a redefining in the 1980s toward an "anti-metaphysical, theoretical minimalism."[10] As a result they have become increasingly compatible.

It is correct if we take what Wæver means by using the term "anti-metaphysical" as a tenacious insistence by the mainstream on the material and scientific. However, I would argue that the neo-neo synthesis would be inevitable even though they seem to deal with different substantive issues in international relations, one with the international structure defined in terms of power distribution and the other, international institutions as the primary mover for cooperation beyond hegemony.[11] It is so because the metaphysical component of their

[8] Wendt 1999, 5–6.   [9] Wæver 1996, 162–163.   [10] Ibid., 162.
[11] Waltz 1979; Keohane 1984.

theoretical hard core is the same in the first place, best reflected by the monist worldview. Keohane himself agrees that neorealism and neoliberal institutionalism share a rationalistic research program. Being rationalistic is indeed the metaphysical component of their theoretical hard core, which brings the two theories together and defines them both as "rationalistic theories."[12] What I want to stress here is that the two mainstream theories share a worldview in a fundamental way, for they both see the world as composed of rationalistic individuals or actors, busy with seeking self-interest and constrained only by capabilities or contracts. It is this shared worldview that leads to the inevitable convergence of neorealism and neoliberal institutionalism.

The monist view takes theory as ahistorical and a-spatial, universally applicable anywhere and anytime. The General Principle of Gravitation is true no matter whether it is in the United States or Europe or Russia or China, so that spacecraft anywhere need to overcome that gravity of the earth. (In fact, it is now well known that this great principle is not universally applicable in terms of time and space. In this sense, the pluralist view is promising even in the natural sciences.) The pluralist view, on the contrary, takes seriously the roles of space and time, geography and history, and culture and practice when the formation and development of social theory are under discussion. If culture has important impacts on social theory formation, and if the metaphysical component of the theoretical hard core is the product of the long practice of a cultural community, then culture does matter, most conspicuously during the initial stage of theory construction. A social theorist is born, brought up, and living in a particular geo-cultural space and during a specific historical period. She has learned the language and lived the practical knowledge. The cultural community has provided her with a menu of thinking and doing, and she can hardly think and do something outside this menu, just as an international theorist who has lived in the tradition of the Westphalian international system can theorize neatly and rigorously about anarchy and balance of power, but cannot think and theorize about the ordering principle of the Chinese Tribute system or the Japanese Tokugawa system, where anarchy and balance of power seem to have had much less relevance.

In short, culture shapes the metaphysical component of the theoretical hard core and nurtures the nucleus of a social theory when it begins its life.

---

[12] Keohane 1989a, 171, 173.

Background, Practice, and Cultural Communities

Then a question is how this metaphysical component is shaped. My answer is that it is shaped and structured primarily by the background knowledge of a cultural community. To justify this answer, we need first to discuss three key concepts, background knowledge, communities of practice, and cultural communities, to see how they are related to one another and how they express the close relationship between culture and the metaphysical component of a theoretical hard core.

Background knowledge is a key term for the understanding of the metaphysical component. Many philosophers have discussed it and those of pragmatism and practice philosophy have placed a particular emphasis on it. John Searle's concept of "Background" is perhaps most typical and illustrative in this respect. He discusses in detail what Background means, as he says:

I have argued for what I call the thesis of the Background: Intentional states function only given a set of background capabilities that do not themselves consist in intentional phenomena. Thus, for example, beliefs, desires, and rules only determine conditions of satisfaction – truth conditions for beliefs, fulfillment conditions for desires, etc. – given a set of capacities that do not themselves consist in intentional phenomena. I have thus defined the concept of the Background as the set of nonintentional or preintentional capacities that enable intentional states of function.[13]

For Searle, Background is so important that it provides a context without which there would be no intentional states of function or no meaning for a word that seems to have no lexical ambiguity. In other words, Background constitutes the interpreting schemes. He has further described its functions, which, *inter alia*, are: enabling linguistic interpretation to take place, enabling perceptual interpretation to take place, structuring consciousness, and disposing an actor to certain sorts of behavior.[14] His discussion on the two important interpretive functions of Background is particularly enlightening. The first is the linguistic interpretation. "We don't interpret a sentence at the level of bare semantic content; interpretation rises to the level of our Background abilities." It is the background knowledge that draws the boundaries of our interpretation. With background knowledge, we "immediately and effortlessly interpret" the meaning of words in a sentence.[15] Then the function of perceptual interpretation tells us that with background we are able to see something as a certain sort of thing because we bring the background to bear on the raw perceptual stimulus, as Wittgenstein's duck-rabbit figure

---

[13] Searle 1995, 129.   [14] Ibid., 132–137.   [15] Ibid., 132.

may show.[16] By the same logic, we are able to provide some social event with a certain sort of meaning because we put it, often unconsciously, against our background repertoire, which enables us to interpret the event "immediately and effortlessly." A Chinese joke that makes every Chinese laugh may receive no ready response from a British audience, and vice versa, for they do not share the tacit knowledge that constitutes their frame of reference and do not understand the implications that derive from a particular culture.

Background knowledge lies behind the process of cognitive inclusion and exclusion, or the menu for choice of ideas. As Haugaard argues, we do not simply observe the world out there as objective reality.

we observe it by imposing our hypothesis upon it, which essentially constitutes categories of inclusion and exclusion. While Kant considers these categories as *a priori* and, somehow, transcendentally true, sociology and anthropology have taught us that these categories are multiple and variable. They constitute what Foucault terms a historical *a priori* . . ., which is a local tacit knowledge of thought particular to a period. I would argue that this is also what Kuhn . . . means by a paradigm. We interpret the world through categories of thought which constitute a [sic] historical (varied across time) and anthropological (across space) categories of meaning which entails local modes of inclusion and exclusion. Our knowledge of structuration practices is directly related to this knowledge. These broad categories of meaning, inclusion and exclusion, exist largely in our minds as *habitus* in Bourdieu's terminology . . ., or what Giddens . . . calls *practical consciousness* knowledge and Foucault terms an episteme . . ., system of thought or historical *a priori*.[17]

Whatever it may be termed, it is the tacit, practical, and background knowledge that enables people to take things for granted and to take some of the meanings for granted. In IR, it is perhaps the international practice approach scholars that have foregrounded the background. Wendt has discussed two types of knowledge, i.e., "explanatory knowledge" and "practical knowledge," the former being about why things happen and the latter about what to do. But he understands them as merely different attitudes toward time, for explanatory knowledge is backward-looking while practical knowledge is forward-looking. Despite this, he argues that practitioners need practical knowledge because they need to know what to do.[18] His misinterpretation is that they are merely understood as two kinds of knowledge, focusing on different temporal spaces respectively. The 2002 special issue of the *Millennium* discusses the practice turn and the pragmatic agenda of IR and the background is again brought up as associated with practice.[19] Scholars of the practice approach in IR have

---

[16] Ibid., 133.   [17] Haugaard 2012, 42.   [18] Wendt 2001.
[19] *Millennium* (2002) 31 (3).

provided a systematic discussion on background knowledge and pointed out the inseparable connection between background knowledge and communities of practice. Vincent Pouliot distinguishes between representational knowledge and practical knowledge, arguing that contemporary social theories have a strong "representational bias" and are therefore unable to account for nonrepresentational practices. It is rooted "in the evolution of Western thinking since the Enlightenment and the scientific revolution," and dismisses "local knowledge that makes sense in particular contexts" in favor of generalizable and abstract precepts.[20] Mainstream IR theories, as well as their respective logics such as the logic of consequences by rationalistic theory and the logic of appropriateness by constructivist theory, all reflect this representational bias. Following later Wittgenstein, Toulmin, Searle, and Bourdieu, Pouliot defines practical knowledge as tacit, inarticulate, contextual, local, experiential, and intuitional. It is in contrast to representational knowledge that is conscious, verbalizable, universal, intentional, rational, and abstract.[21] He stresses the important function of practical knowledge as the mover of action and points out that what people do in fact does not derive from representational knowledge, but from local, inarticulate, and practical knowledge. In *International Practices* edited by Emanuel Adler and Pouliout, they begin to use the term "background knowledge," to refer to the "stock of unspoken know-how, learnt in and through practice, and from which deliberate and intentional action becomes possible."[22] Such a definition goes well with Searle's concept of Background.

Background knowledge, understood as such, has significant implications for social theorizing, as well as for social action. That it comes from practice indicates the continuity of knowledge with the world, constituting a strong argument opposing the Cartesian dualism of thing-thought dichotomy, that it is nonintentional, inarticulate, and nonrepresentational means that it is experiential and even habitual,[23] and that it is knowledge growing out of everyday practices in particular communities provides legitimacy for the type of indigenously developed knowledge to stand as knowledge, reasonable and legitimate. These characteristic features of background knowledge at least inspire social theorizing in three respects. First, it is local. By definition, background knowledge comes from agents' experiences in a particular setting and crystalizes through practical engagement with all aspects of life. Unlike representational knowledge that comes from a transcendental, rational mind above practice and over time and space, it is knowledge evolving in a bottom-up way. Second, it is inarticulate and unconscious. When an agent begins to

---

[20] Pouliot 2008, 260.   [21] Ibid., 271.   [22] Adler and Pouliot 2011, 16.   [23] Hopf 2010.

acquire background knowledge, a learning process starts. But it is not like classroom learning; rather it is an unconscious process in which the agent learns in and through doing. Only getting it this way is the agent able to respond to a raw stimulus from the outside world "immediately and effortlessly." Third, it is plural and inclusive in terms of such fundamental questions as ontology and epistemology. In the editorial note of the special issue of the *Millennium* the editors say, "Instead of IR's fixation with absolute and exclusive ontological solutions, pragmatism encourages a multi-perspective style of inquiry that privileges practice and benefits from the complementarity, rather than opposition to, of different understandings of world politics."[24] Background knowledge is bound to be in the plural, for there are many communities of practice whose worldviews may not and cannot be the same. In this sense it is also inclusive, because its life lies in the exchange and dialogue among these communities rather than in its isolation. That one type of background knowledge is superior to another is a mere myth.

The return of background knowledge to the study of international relations is a recent phenomenon and aims to set the agenda for the international practice approach. One of the most important contributions it has made is that it relates background knowledge with communities of practice: A community of practice rests on background knowledge for its existence and socially meaningful patterns of action. As Adler says: "Practices are knowledge-constituted, meaningful patterns of socially organized activity embedded in communities, routines and organizations that structure experience."[25] Communities of practice are the social collectivity that develops, shares, stores, and maintains such knowledge, and in turn it is constituted and shaped by such knowledge. Epistemic communities, transnational advocacy networks, and critical communities, which IR scholars have studied before, are subsets of communities of practice.

For Adler and Pouliot, thus, background knowledge shapes a community of practice, which they defined as "a configuration of a domain of knowledge that constitutes like-mindedness, a community of people that 'creates the social fabric of learning,' and a shared practice that embodies 'the knowledge the community develops, shares, and maintains.'"[26] In an earlier study, Adler in discussing a community of practice, has emphasized such features as a community of people, shared practice, and "a repertoire of communal resources, such as routines, words, tools, ways of doing things, stories, symbols, and discourse,"[27]

[24] Editors of Millennium 2002 (31) 3: iii.   [25] Adler 2008, 198.
[26] Adler and Pouliot 2011, 17.   [27] Adler 2005, 15.

in which the members of such a community are "informally and contextually bound."[28] In the study of international relations, communities of practice are specifically defined as transnational, including communities of diplomats, of traders, of environmentalists, and of human rights activists. They are networks across national borders, as well as epistemic communities of like-minded people. Examples are given in such areas as diplomacy, deterrence, global climate change, humanitarianism (the Red Cross), and international law – very specific, issue-related areas where practitioners across national borders get together and work as a group with a distinct collective identity and a similar way of doing things.

It is clear that such communities of practice are important in today's international relations, for they rest not on the uniform representational knowledge that has dominated the social sciences for years and stresses background knowledge that both derives from and constitutes practice. The key concept is no doubt practice. As Adler and Pouliot define, "Practices are competent performances. More precisely, practices are socially meaningful patterns of action which, in being performed more or less competently, simultaneously embody, act out, and possibly reify background knowledge and discourse in and on the material world."[29] Such an approach to social studies in general and IR in particular is indeed innovative. It is a worldview, for it looks at the world not as a billiard table or an institutional entity, but as networks of communities in practical areas. "Think about the world neither as an assemblage of states nor as divided by borders and lines of national identification, but as transnational communities of practice, based on what people actually *do* rather than on where they happen to live."[30] Following such a worldview, analysts should change their perspectives about the world around them, rethink roles played by state and non-state actors, and take a fresh look at important aspects of international life, such as global and regional governance.

Even though areas such as security and environment are extremely important and practitioners from different nations may develop shared knowledge and become like-minded people over time and through practice, the definition of practice by Adler and Pouliot seems to limit a community of practice to merely transnational issue-related areas, as Adler has stated that background knowledge cements constellations of agents across borders.[31] Members of a community of practice, though from different nation-states, can have similar views and positions on

---

[28] Adler and Greve 2008, 196.   [29] Adler and Pouliot 2011, 6.
[30] Ibid., 24, emphasis in original.   [31] Adler 2005, quoted in Pouliot 2008, 259.

a particular issue area, whether it is human rights, environmental protection, climate change, or deterrence. However, if we go back to the concept of background knowledge, we may find communities of practice, bounded by shared, tacit, and even take-it-for-granted knowledge, may include much more than mere specific issues in international relations. Pouliot is quite correct in pointing out the most important dimensions of Bourdieu's definition of *habitus*, which has influenced him very much in developing the logic of practicality, as "a system of durable, transposable dispositions, which integrate past experiences and functions at every moment as a matrix of perception, appreciation, and action, making possible the accomplishment of infinitely differentiated tasks."[32] It is historical, relational, and dispositional. However, he has immediately exemplified it by using the term "diplomatic habitus," which is "a set of regular traits which dispose its bearers to act in a certain way,"[33] thus drawing a clear border line for the concept of communities of practice and limiting Bourdieu's definition to a more technical, specific, and issue-related level. It is justifiable, for any analysis needs to delineate its boundaries and it looks different but also fairly neat if the world is composed of communities of practice rather than nation-states. It is indeed a new worldview, but the fact is that the concept of communities of practice is broader than it is defined and applied by international practice approach scholars, and a redefinition may widen the horizon for academic exploration and provide yet another new view to look at the world.

It is relevant here to draw on Barry Buzan's discussion of the concepts of *"gemeinschaft"* and *"gesellschaft."* The former refers more to a civilizational community, more natural and with a strong sense of "we-ness," while the latter is more functional, an association, which may not have pre-existing cultural bonds, may be formed by regular and intense interaction, and may be qualified in a functional sense as a society.[34] Communities of practice, defined by Adler and Pouliot, seem to be more like what Buzan terms *"gesellschaft,"* whose members may not have prior identity and tight cultural bonds. They have gathered together to perform competently as members of a transnational grouping in various issue areas. Following Buzan's discussion, a *gemeinschaft* rests much more on traditions, cultures, civilizations, and therefore constitutes a much more coherent and steady community than the more functional *gesellschaft.* While the latter is more explicit and direct in terms of the behavior of its members, the former has a much deeper and more fundamental influence on the mindset of the people who have complete immersion in it.

---

[32] Pouliot 2008, 272.   [33] Quoted in Pouliot 2008, 272.   [34] Buzan 1993.

The prototype of communities of practice is a cultural community. It is more in the sense of *gemeinschaft* defined by cultures and traditions, by shared identities and worldviews. IR analysts often shy away from the involvement of culture in their studies, not only because it hardly fits into the neat rigor required by the positivist standards for "scientific theorizing," but also, perhaps, because of their fear of being accused of cultural relativism. Culture is no panacea, but no one can avoid the concept of culture in discussing "communities." If members of a social group are historically bounded and share inarticulate knowledge that makes their action meaningful and enables them to interpret action by others, then it is no other than a cultural community. Culture is naturally related thus to a community. As Richard A. Shweder says:

What do I mean by "culture"? I mean community-specific ideas about what is true, good, beautiful, and efficient. To be "cultural," those ideas about truth, goodness, beauty, and efficiency must be socially inherited and customary; and they must actually be constitutive of different ways of life.[35]

The diplomatic community of practice, an example often used by international practice approach scholars, is a group of diplomats from different countries who share the same diplomatic culture.[36] It is not "diplomacy" as a specific and functional area that makes the community. It is, rather the "diplomatic culture" that makes it. In fact Adler once said, "I also suggest that one should judge civilizations not for what they 'are' but for what they 'do.' That is, we should conceive of civilizations as dynamic, loosely integrated, pluralistic, and heterogenic *communities of practice* whose boundaries extend as far as their practices."[37] However it seems that he does not realize or does not want to point out that a cultural community is the prototypical form of communities of practice, historically formed and culturally tied together. When he is discussing the case of the Euro-Mediterranean Partnership, he says: "By culture, I mean neither what Huntington meant in 'The Clash of Civilizations' nor a romantic view of the Mediterranean cultural attributes – olives, wine, sunshine, and gorgeous beaches. Rather I have in mind the development of a relatively new type of preventive diplomatic practice that depends for its success on the political and social engineering of a Mediterranean 'we-feeling' or collective social identity."[38] It is clear that such a community of practice is first of all more issue related. By definition it is more functional

---

[35] Schweder 2000, 163.
[36] Pouliot 2016. In this book, Pouliot takes again his favorite example, the international diplomatic community, as one of practice and studies creatively how hierarchy is formed in this community through practice.
[37] Adler 2010, 68, emphasis in original.   [38] Ibid., 228–229.

than fundamental. For me, a community of practice may be one in a particular issue area, but its prototype and primary form is a cultural community, for background knowledge is most deeply embedded and habitually patterned behavior is most readily founded in a cultural community. Culturally nurtured background knowledge is thicker, steadier, and more natural than any technically formed background knowledge in a specific issue area.

Perhaps we can categorize communities of practice into three different types by a culturally relevant standard. The first is the macro-level community of practice, referring to civilizational communities of practice. In today's world, we talk about Western and non-Western cultures, and inside the non-Western sphere there are also many different cultures, such as the Chinese and Indian ones, as is the case within the Western cultural spheres. These civilizationally bound communities are macro-level cultural communities. Peter Katzenstein's study of civilizations in world politics, the ambitious three-volume work he has edited, seems to focus on the following civilizations: American, European, Chinese, Japanese, and Indian.[39] Samuel Huntington's study includes seven civilizations with potential tendency for conflict.[40] Feng et al. believe that there are five "cultural spheres" in the world, including the Chinese, the Christian, the Orthodox, the Moslem, and the Indian and the Chinese cultural sphere contains roughly China, Vietnam, Korea, and Japan.[41] The second is the intermediate-level of communities of practice, referring to such communities within a civilizational community of practice. It may also be called a subcultural community. Examples include communities based upon gender, socioeconomic classes, and religious and ethnic groupings. Such social groups exist within one civilizational community of practice, but have distinct experiences and ways of life of their own. Women feel about war differently from men and workers experience differently from capitalists. They practice in different ways and their worldviews may differ accordingly. The third is the micro-level category, referring to the issue-related community of practice. It is more functionally oriented. Such communities develop their issue-related culture through their everyday work as practitioners, and diplomats, human rights activists, and environmental protectionists belong to this category. The community of practice within the research agenda of international practice approach scholars goes mostly to the third type and functions mainly at the micro-level and with specific issues. All the three levels of communities are communities of practice because they all rest on

[39] Katzenstein 2010a; 2012a; 2012b.   [40] Huntington 1996.
[41] Feng, He and Zhou 2005, 495.

background knowledge. In other words, they are defined by culture, culture as the most conspicuous background, as ways of life, as shared knowledge for perception and disposition, and as schemes of understanding, interpreting, and giving meaning to social events.

Cultural communities are communities of practice and culture is therefore defined in terms of shared background knowledge. Culture refers to the way of life of a people who share a lot in terms of behaviors, values, beliefs, and perspectives without consciously knowing them. The worldviews, the attitudes, and the schemes for understanding and interpreting embodied in the metaphysical component of a theoretical hard core to fulfill its function as an ideational and intellectual construct are exactly the contents of background knowledge that have been formed over time and based upon the practice of a collectivity.[42] Culture thus defined means that a cultural community is a group of people bound by background knowledge and culture's significance lies in the fact that no community can be formed without culture. It is the most conspicuous yardstick to distinguish one group of people from another, the most reliable sources to create "we-ness," including the "we-feeling," "we-thinking," and "we-doing," and the most durable maker and marker of collective identity. Culture shapes the character, the personality, and the identity of a community. A community is called such because it has a shared cultural heritage and orientation. In other words, culture is the invisible bond that ties people into a community. Following David Hall and Roger Ames, who say in their discussion of the Confucian tradition, "'Confucianism' is a community, a society, and a living experience,"[43] we perhaps can also argue that Confucianism is a culture. It exactly reflects what background knowledge is and does.

I do not mean here to overstress the uniqueness of any particular culture. In fact, there is much in common across cultures. Chinese, for example, share a lot with Americans, as well as Americans with Japanese, even culturally. However, there are also distinctive ways of life especially among civilization-based cultures. Even for scholars of the international practice approach, communities of practice are treated as communities because they have already developed a culture by which its members have a similar mindset on the particular issues they deal with, whether it is human rights, deterrence, or environmental protection. Patrick Morgan's study of the practice of deterrence, for example, has showed in fact how a culture of deterrence is developed over years of practice and how it influences in this process the thinking and doing of the practitioners in this field.[44] This is perhaps why Adler uses the term "culture in action" to

[42] Qin 2013.   [43] Hall and Ames 1987, 24.   [44] Morgan 2011, 139–173.

describe a community of practice and stresses the significance of doing.[45] But culture is not only culture in action, it is also culture *for* action. In other words, culture defined in terms of background knowledge is in practice and on practice, reflecting what the community members do and disposing them for certain behavior and action. For the study of communities of practice, therefore, culture is a must.

Culture and the Metaphysical Component

The significance of culture, defined in terms of background knowledge, for social theorizing lies in the fact that culture cultivates and shapes the metaphysical component of the hard core, which is by definition the understanding and interpreting schema embedded in a social theory. Culture is both mental and material. The definition of the United Nations Educational, Scientific and Cultural Organization (UNESCO) is perhaps the most comprehensive, taking culture as the set of distinctive spiritual, material, intellectual and emotional features of society or a group. Culture encompasses, in addition to art and literature, lifestyles, ways of living together, value systems, traditions and beliefs. In the academic circles, definitions of culture tend to lean more toward the non-material and knowledge dimensions. Edward Tylor, for example, defines culture as "that complex whole which includes knowledge, belief, art, morals, custom, and any other capabilities and habits acquired by man as a member of society."[46] Wendt defines culture as common and collective knowledge, the former concerning actors' beliefs about each other's rationality, strategies, preferences, and beliefs, as well as about states of the external world, or "intersubjective understanding;"[47] and the latter concerning the knowledge structure held by groups which generate macro-level patterns in individual behavior over time.[48] Alastair Iain Johnston lists some of the definitions as the following: Glenn et al. define it as "the total knowledge existing within a society;" Wildavsky calls culture those codes enabling individuals to make much out of the little, like grand theories, paradigms, programs, from whose premises many consequences applicable to a wide variety of circumstances may be deduced; Keesing suggests that cultures are systems of cognition that relate people and communities to their ecology or environment in an evolutionary, symbolic relationship; Geertz holds that culture is a "system of inherited conceptions expressed in symbolic forms by means of which men communicate, perpetuate and develop their knowledge about attitude towards life;" and Schein and Barnes believe that

---

[45] Adler 2010, 68.   [46] Taylor 1871.   [47] Wendt 1999, 160.   [48] Ibid., 161.

culture is about unconscious and hidden standard operating procedures, scripts, and easy behavior ... routine, largely unexplained options followed by most people most of the time."[49] Then Johnston summarizes culture, more in the sense of political science, as shared decision rules, standard operating procedures, and decision routines, something that is learned, evolutionary, and dynamic. It is thus clear that scholarly definitions of culture are more knowledge-related and ideationally oriented.[50]

No matter how diversified the definition of culture is, therefore, the common core indicates that culture is shared knowledge about the way of life of a society and the way of thinking and doing of its members. It indicates worldviews and visions. As David Blaney and Naeem Inayatullah say:

"Culture" suggests human activity and creative capacities; the human capacity to construct, live and aesthetically express a form of life; human action to embrace and practise as well as critique and reform the "values and visions" of an inherited form of life. To use a different language, human beings live in the world according to a certain "vision" or "cultural representation." This "vision" sustains cultural life, constituting a way of life's specific identity in relation to the larger cosmos – its particular conception of what it means to be a human community in the world.[51]

Culture is thus by definition a most distinctive feature of human society, and ideas, worldviews, and attitudes are all factors that reflect a particular culture. It reflects at the macro-level common worldviews, collective attitudes, and communal behavioral codes, relating to how actors observe, experience, and engage with others and the outside world. In this sense, shared background knowledge is a most appropriate term as well as the most distinct feature of a culture, including not only a particular type of "preventive diplomatic practice," but also all aspects of life, such as the Mediterranean way of enjoying olives, wine, and sunshine. Using the concept of "Background" as Searle has defined, we can say that a cultural community is a group of people holding shared background knowledge and being like-minded in their way of thinking and doing at the macro-level. A most natural and representative form of communities of practice, therefore, is a cultural community.

The relevance of a cultural community as the prototype of communities of practice lies in the fact that the members of a cultural community in the first place share local and experiential knowledge, which comes before representational knowledge is formed, taught, and imposed, and continues as representational knowledge accumulates. Local and experiential knowledge is decentralized, bottom-up, and thus tends to be

---

[49] Quoted in Johnston 1995, 33. See also Shweder and LeVine 1984.
[50] Johnston 1995, 35.   [51] Blaney and Inayatullah 1998, 64.

heterogeneous. It relates agents and the world out there from the very beginning. This view goes against what Patrick Jackson has called "the Enlightenment dream," or "dualism," which views the social world as an "objective" existence and this objective world can be readily and radically separated from those who observe it. The separation of the world and knowledge of the world, of the facts and the observer of the facts, and of things and thoughts, constitutes the basic assumption of this Cartesian dichotomy. On the other hand it is what Wang Yangming terms "unity of knowledge and practice," which indicates a process of mutual inclusiveness and makes the two inseparable from each other, or it is also what Jackson names "monism,"[52] which "maintains a fundamental continuity of knowledge with the world and therefore does not give rise to an account of knowledge practices that aims at accurately reflecting the world's essential dispositional character."[53] It emphasizes the value orientations of the researcher and creative understanding and interpretation of the observer.

It is noteworthy that Jackson further interprets the Weberian "objectivity" and "scientific monism," as shedding light on social theorizing. In the first place Weber has denied the positivist sense of objectivity as he has argued:

There is no "objective" scientific analysis of cultural life – or, put perhaps somewhat more narrowly but certainly not essentially different from our purpose – of "a social phenomenon" independent of special and "one-sided" points of view, according to which, – explicitly or tacitly, consciously or unconsciously – they are selected, analyzed, and representationally organized as an object of research.[54]

Thus Weber has negated the view that we can accurately reflect the world out there and stressed that "We are *cultural beings*, endowed with the capacity and the will to take a deliberate attitude towards the world and lend it significance."[55] Weber has also pointed out that scientific research is more conditioned by researchers' "knowledge *interest* as it arises from the specific cultural significance that we attribute pertaining to the process in an individual case."[56] In all this discussion, the significance of culture to the value orientations of the researcher is explicitly expressed. As Jackson has commented, "the social sciences are productive of the world, beholden not to some existing set of objects or their

---

[52] Here the word "monism" used by Jackson is not the same as "monism" used in Chapter 1. "Monism" here is in contrast with "dualism," while in Chapter 1 "monism" is the opposite of "pluralism." The same word is used but expresses different meanings. I want to make this point clear to avoid confusion.

[53] Jackson 2008, 133.   [54] Weber 1999, quoted in Jackson 2008, 146.

[55] Weber 1949, 81, emphasis in original; quoted in Ruggie 1999, 216.

[56] Weber 1999, emphasis in original; quoted in Jackson 2008, 147.

essential dispositional properties but rather to the cultural values that orient the investigation from the beginning."[57] Clifford Geertz has once reiterated Weber's emphasis on significance and meaning, saying that: "Believing, with Weber, that man is an animal suspended in webs of significance he himself has spun. I take ... the analysis of [those webs] to be therefore not an experimental science in search of law but an interpretive one in search of meaning."[58] We may understand that Weber's "scientific monism," as Jackson has named it, makes three fundamental assumptions. First, the world and knowledge of the world cannot be separated; second, there is no absolute "objectivity" in social life, and the so-called "objectivity" is in fact socially and culturally constructed; third, knowledge about the social world is culturally oriented, for the meaning of social action is given by humans in a particular cultural setting.

Now we may come back to the formation of the metaphysical component of the theoretical hard core. As an ideational construct, it is essentially about understanding and interpreting, processing "facts" perceived by the substantive component. It is in this way that the metaphysical component is related to culture via background knowledge, for it is informed primarily from the background knowledge of a cultural community. There is not only a continuity of knowledge with the world out there, but also a continuity of a theorist with the culture she is embedded in, for she shares the background knowledge and constructs the metaphysical component of her theoretical hard core consciously or unconsciously with the internalized and inarticulate knowledge of the cultural community of which she is a member. She is first of all a cultural being and naturally takes a culturally oriented perspective, from which she lends significance to a social event or "fact." Rationality, I believe, composes the metaphysical component of the theoretical hard core for much of social theory in various fields, including IR, because it is an intellectual construct born and brought up in the Western culture and has constituted a key element of the background knowledge therein, developed, refined, and enriched by repeated intellectual efforts especially since the Enlightenment. It is basically impossible that such an idea would have been originally produced in the Chinese culture despite the fact that the Chinese civilization has an unbroken history of thousands of years, for it is of less significance within the structure of the background knowledge of the Chinese culture and therefore it seems to be off their menu for choice and for representation.

[57] Jackson 2008, 147.   [58] Geertz 1973, 5.

The metaphysical component is thus nurtured by background knowledge. The primary assumption here is that a theorist lives in a particular society and cultural community and there is an ideational as well as a practical continuity between her and the community of which she is a member. Fundamentally, a theorist carries out the practice and shares the background knowledge therein. Such knowledge provides the menu or context for her thinking and disposes her toward a certain mode of intellectual practice, which in turn helps her construct a social theory, starting from the formation of the theoretical hard core. Her imagination and intellectual activity can go as far as her practices and practical knowledge carry her, but she is hardly able to theorize about things outside the confines of the menu, unless she has experiences of two or more than two cultural communities.

Following Searle's logic, therefore, for a social theorist, the intentional state is to theorize on the social, and what matters are the nonintentional or preintentional capacities. These capacities enable her intentional state to function so that she may start to construct a social theory. Furthermore, these capacities come from her background knowledge that has been formed through years of living in a particular community of practice. The theorist, consciously or perhaps more often than not unconsciously, will turn to her background knowledge for inspiration and interpretation. She is not a transcendental super mind. If we believe that background knowledge informs the metaphysical part of the hard core of a social theory, and if we agree that background knowledge is in the plural form, that is, background knowledges, then it is reasonable to argue that the metaphysical component of the theoretical hard core may well vary across communities of practice, forming different views about the world around. For a long time in IR, however, the metaphysical component has not even been thought of and background knowledge has been largely neglected. The assumption that the mainstream IR theory is universally applicable has dominated the research programs through a deep level of internalization by theoretical practitioners both inside and outside the West.

There are several dimensions through which we can understand how background knowledge informs the metaphysical component. First, the metaphysical component shares the temporo-spatial dimension of the background knowledge. The theorist is able to theorize mainly within the temporo-spatial confines for the background knowledge of her cultural community. Past experience and history work actively here. As Bourdieu has pointed out, the *habitus* is a product of history and produces individual and collective practices in accordance with the schemes generated by history. "It ensures the active presence of past experiences, which, deposited in each organism in the form of schemes of perception, thought and action, tend to guarantee the 'correctness' of practices and their constancy over time, more reliably than all formal rules and explicit norms."[59] Western mainstream theorists of IR have had a ready reference, i.e. the Westphalian international system, which is in their history and has existed in the region where they have practiced, and from which their theoretical concepts have been put forward, including some key concepts of international studies – sovereignty, anarchy, and balance of power, as I have mentioned. But it is almost impossible for them to conceptualize about other international systems that have existed in history outside the West. Dependency theory was developed first by theorists of International Political Economy (IPE) in Latin America, whose experiences in their national economies disposed them to the argument that the global capitalist structure was the root cause of the underdevelopment of third world countries.[60] It is also true of feminist IR theory, a key argument of which is that women in war have experiences different from those of men.[61] An interesting fact is that many theorists of the feminist IR theory are female.[62] Most likely, it is not a mere coincidence.

Second, the metaphysical component contains the philosophical tradition of a cultural community. "Philosophical" here means fundamental questions of ontology and epistemology, reflected by more specific worldviews, perspectives, and ways of thinking and doing, which, as cultural sediments, constitute the background knowledge of a community and are shared by the metaphysical component of a social theory. It is particularly related to mental and intellectual activities, to the faculty of thinking about the self and the universe, about the material and spiritual, and so on. William James has related philosophy especially to thinking, saying that "Philosophy is the unusually stubborn attempt to think clearly."[63] A theorist shares the worldviews embodied in the background knowledge and the ways of thinking therein, which constitute her menu or context. For example, Hall and Ames have argued that there are two modes of thought, a transcendental one and an immanental one, the former being the Western tradition while the latter the Confucian tradition. The first mode believes that there are transcendental principles that exist eternally, immutably, and immaterially, providing an explanation for everything else in the universe. Aristotle's Unmoved Mover and Plato's Cosmos

---

[59] Bourdieu 1990, 347–348.
[60] See Frank 1967; Cardoso and Faletto 1979; Caporaso 1978.
[61] Goldstein 2001; Sylvester 1994.
[62] As Joshua S. Goldstein says: "Fortunately, other political scientists in those years – almost all of them women – were not so timid in developing feminist scholarship on war." Goldstein 2001, xiii.
[63] Quoted in Hall and Ames 1987, 29.

reflect this mode of thought. On the other hand, Confucianism believes that there are no such principles above humans and societies. A Confucian Cosmos, on the contrary, is a universe of correlativity, which stresses the interdependence and interconnection of all events, thus precluding any dualistic and transcendental language. The polar terms of *yin* and *yang*, for example, are complementarily related to each other, forming an organic whole and requiring each other for life and articulation. For a social theorist, such philosophical assumptions are always with her as background, which inform her worldviews, attitudes, and perspectives. It is hard for a social theorist with transcendental dualism as background to construct a social theory with the immanent worldview as her underlying presumption, and vice versa.[64] In other words, either transcendentalism or immanentalism is very likely to inform the metaphysical component of a theoretical hard core, rationality from the former and relationality from the latter, which may not be noticed or realized because they are deeply embedded in their respective traditional cultures and philosophies, or their background knowledge.

Third, the metaphysical component argument embraces pluralism in social theory construction. It is generally acknowledged that we are living today in a multicultural world. Background knowledge therefore varies across cultural communities. Katzenstein has pointed out that civilizations exist in the plural in the world and that civilizations are also pluralistic internally because there are many traditions and vigorous debates and disagreements.[65] If a cultural community is a prototype of communities of practice and if background knowledge is the key to defining such communities, then communities of practice exist in the plural, and so does background knowledge, elements of which may overlap and can also differ. In fact, an important yardstick to distinguish two different communities of practice is the difference in their background knowledge: different systems of durable, transposable dispositions in Bourdieu's words, and different nonintentional and preintentional capacities that enable intentional states of function, by Searle's definition. In today's world, for example, there are various cultural communities. At the macrolevel, there are civilization-based communities, such as the Western world, the Islamic world, and the Confucian world. It is reasonable to say that they have their respective sets of background knowledge, and it is perhaps also reasonable to say that the diversity of culture and background provides rich resources for innovative social theory. In IR, for example, the practice and performance in the Westphalian international system differs significantly from the practice and performance of the

---

[64] Ibid., 11–25.   [65] Katzenstein 2010a, 1.

Chinese Tribute international system. IR theories with a theoretical hard core cultivated by the Westphalian practices may not explain and interpret well phenomena in the Tribute system. Then at the intermediate and micro-levels there are numerous communities of practice, based upon their respective cultures, such as women's rights groups, environmental protectionists, and diplomats. The plural and pluralistic nature of such practices and experiences makes a pluralistic approach to social theory and social theorizing not only possible, but also inevitable.[66] Their respective background knowledge may nurture various theoretical hard cores. Even in IR, the background knowledge of a socioeconomic community of practice may lead to theories like dependency theory and that of a gender-based community of practice may result in a feminist theory of war. A theorist who is highly familiar with different international systems may provide a theory based on an in-depth comparison, questioning many key concepts, such as the "balance of power," which are familiar only in one international system but alien to other international systems.

Conclusion

Social theory depends on the metaphysical component of the theoretical hard core for its life and identity, which is the vital part informed by the background knowledge of a cultural community. Social theory therefore, bears its cultural birthmark because the theorist who constructs it lives the culture and is embedded in the background knowledge therein. No matter what reality is observed and perceived through the substantive component, it goes through this metaphysical component for understanding and interpretation. A theorist cannot theorize about something that is completely outside her background knowledge. If we fail to recognize the importance of culture as background knowledge in the development of social theory, then we would tend to take locally constructed theory as universally applicable.

The significance of the practice turn in the social sciences in general and in IR in particular lies in legitimizing creative social theorization. It realizes the importance of local and practical knowledge, which, though tacit, inarticulate, experiential, and even intuitional, sustains a community and defines the practice of the community. It tells, in terms of knowledge production, that social theory, as an explicit form of knowledge, starts from the local and the inarticulate. By definition, local knowledge is featured by its diversity and plurality. If we argue that the metaphysical component is informed by the practical knowledge of a certain cultural

[66] Qin 2011.

community, it must be in the plural because the world, as well as the international relations world, is composed of a multiple of cultures and cultural communities. This kind of understanding of theory construction goes with the pluralist approach discussed in the previous chapter, but with an emphasis on culture defined in terms of background knowledge.

In theory, the diversity of cultural communities in today's world should encourage original social theories to emerge and to grow. In reality, it is extremely difficult for a social theory to grow out of cultures other than the West. It is not surprising, as the non-Western world is a latecomer in terms of social theory development and as the monist approach is still dominantly influential in and beyond the West. In IR, for example, the theory that was initiated in the non-Western world and accepted by the Western academic community of IR is perhaps the dependency theory. It attracted attention around the 1970s in the United States, where chapters about dependence theory appeared in popular IR textbooks. But its influence was short-lived and the theory faded in the 1980s.[67] Somewhat a cousin of dependency theory, world system theory was not initiated in the non-Western world. In standard IR textbooks, there is literally no other IR theory that was born in non-Western cultural communities.

The potential for non-Western IR theory is great, especially as more non-Western nations have joined the grand trend of globalization. Civilizations and cultures of various kinds may prove rich nutriment for social theory construction. If we take the metaphysical component of the theoretical hard core as shaped by culture, then a serious exploration of cultural resources for theory may encourage more theoretical innovation. This is the topic for discussion in the next chapter.

---

[67] Blaney and Tickner 2013, 7–9.

3   Culture and Theoretical Innovation

Social theory contains a theoretical hard core, the metaphysical component of which defines the theory itself. In this sense, theoretical innovation is closely related to the metaphysical component. What is understood as immensurability is in the final analysis indicated by the immensurability of such components. Since the metaphysical component is informed and nurtured by culture, and since a social theory always bears its cultural birthmark during its life cycle, theoretical innovation tends to lie with the metaphysical component. We live in a multicultural world, which is composed of various cultural communities of practice, defined in terms of shared background knowledge. Such a world should provide rich resources for the prosperity of social theory development and innovation if the shackles of discursive domination were to be destroyed from the minds of people across the world and pluralism established to open more channels for meaningful dialogue to encourage theoretical innovation.

The Metaphysical Component, Incommensurability, and Theoretical Innovation

Now a question seems to be highly relevant: How does culture inspire and promote innovation of social theory? There are numerous works on social theory and theoretical innovation, and the concept of the theoretical "hard core" was also invented long ago and has been extensively discussed. However, few people have ever dissected it and related the metaphysical component to the construction of new theories. In the social sciences, inter- or intra-paradigm debates have been unfolded, but none of them have directly explored the composition of the theoretical hard core as an important source for incommensurability and therefore for theoretical innovation.

I argue that innovation of the metaphysical component enables innovation of social theory. A social theory is innovative because it has in its hard core a distinct metaphysical component which defines this theory and which is incommensurable with that of another social theory. Incommensurability used here refers, very much in the meaning given by Thomas Kuhn, to the fact that theories have different conceptual frameworks, belief systems, and interpretive mechanisms, based largely on different worldviews. As Kuhn has pointed out, theories are incommensurable because theorists of competing paradigms have different ideas, use different vocabularies and conceptual frameworks, and see the world in different ways due to their training and prior experience.[1] Michael Polanyi in his *Personal Knowledge* also argues that theorists from different backgrounds can have logical gaps between belief systems, thinking differently, speaking a different language, and living in a different world.[2] The factors mentioned by Kuhn and Polanyi are exactly those embedded in the metaphysical component of the theoretical hard core. These factors are effective in producing different theories. By this logic, theoretical incommensurability may well be caused by the difference in the metaphysical components that define social theories.

Thus, if we use incommensurability as a yardstick to evaluate whether a social theory is innovative, a highly potential resource for such innovation is culture defined in terms of background knowledge, which nurtures and shapes the metaphysical component of the theoretical hard core. As we discussed in the previous chapter, the two components of the hard core are related and complementary. Once an event occurs in the real world, the substantive component is the first to be activated and presents the event as a certain thing to be figured out. Then it goes through the metaphysical component as a puzzle to be processed, understood and interpreted, and given a meaning that leads to the decision for its solution. A social theory functions well if the two components work complementarily together. When we say that a theory is original and innovative, it may mean two things. First, the question that activates the substantive component of the hard core is new, not having been observed or systematically discussed previously. Many IR theories fall into this category. Power transition theory, for example, observed a phenomenon that had not been theorized about before and put forward an interesting question: What is to happen when the challenger is catching up in terms of capabilities with the hegemon in the international system? A new theory then was developed, providing an answer to the question by arguing that the probability of war between the two giants is the greatest and the system is most unstable during such a period.[3] It is no doubt an important theoretical innovation, changing a static international power structure

---

[1] Kuhn 1962.   [2] Polanyi 1998.   [3] Oganski and Kugler 1980.

into a dynamic power shift and still exerting much influence in today's study of international politics. However, it is an innovation at the substantive level, without innovative change of the ontological and epistemological assumptions of rationalistic IR theory in general. If we compare power transition theory with structural realism, they are akin to each other, akin especially in terms of their view of the international relations world, where material power dominates. Theories of this type belong to innovation within the range of "normal science" and have little to do with theoretical incommensurability.

Second, a new theory exists if the metaphysical component of its theoretical hard core differs from those of the established theories. In other words, it has a different worldview, a different interpretive mechanism, and a different perspective toward fundamental aspects of social life. Poverty in developing countries, for example, has been understood either as the result of bad domestic political and economic management or as the result of an unfair international economic structure and division of labor, leading to two incommensurable theories of political economy: the development theory and the dependency theory.[4] For the former, "Europe's past might be Asia's future" (and the future of Africa and Latin America, too) if Asia should follow suit,[5] and for the latter a revolutionary change of the structure of the international political-economic system is the solution, at least in theory. The fact out there is the same, but the understanding and interpretation of the problem through the metaphysical component differ. This is why the development theory and the dependency theory are incommensurable indeed: Their worlds are far apart. Another recent example is perhaps the international practice theory, which sees the world as composed of communities of practice rather than nation-states, thus fundamentally changing the global political landscape and distinguishing the theory from the mainstream.[6] It is of course possible for both the components to work creatively, but the second part, or the metaphysical component, is often more significant, for it is, because of its power in terms of understanding and interpretation, the soul and identity of a social theory. If there is indeed incommensurability between social theories, it is first of all because their metaphysical hard cores are not commensurable.

It is important to point out that theories dealing with different issues or problems at the substantive level may have a similar or identical metaphysical component at a deeper level. In this case, theories that appear different at first eventually converge and form

---

[4] See respectively Rostow 1966; Cardoso and Faletto 1979.
[5] Friedberg 1993/1994, quoted in Kang 2007, xi.   [6] Adler and Pouliot 2011.

a commensurable synthesis. The opposite is also true: Even if the real world problem is the same, theories with different metaphysical components will provide different understanding and interpretation of the problem and represent it with different meanings, as the development theory and the dependency theory have shown. In other words, incommensurability of the metaphysical components leads to incommensurability of social theories.

In IR, this is not uncommon. The eventual convergence of mainstream IR theories in the United States, it seems to me, is the result of the shared metaphysical component of their theoretical hard core: structural realism and neoliberal institutionalism first and rationalistic theory and Wendtian constructivism later. Since I will discuss this most interesting phenomenon later on, suffice it to say here that the more they move toward grand theories, the more apparent their shared metaphysical component becomes, and the more they tend to converge with one another. The three mainstream American IR theories discuss different aspects in the life of international relations: power, institutions, and culture, and there is no doubt that these are indeed important aspects of international politics. Their innovation lies in that each of them singles out and focuses on one aspect which the other theories have not paid much attention to. But some fundamental questions, such as how the international relations world is perceived and whether international relations is fundamentally human or non-human, are very much taken as a given, a definite and invariable given from the deeply embedded background knowledge they all rely on.

If we seek theoretical innovation by encouraging efforts of excavating and exploring the diverse cultural resources, especially those civilization-based cultures which are conspicuously different such as the Western, the Chinese, and the Indian, then we will indeed open new horizons for social theory in general and IR in particular, for hidden in these cultures are meaningful ideas that are yet to be systemized.

Culture as Resources for Theoretical Innovation

The incommensurability at the deeper level lies in that theories differ in their metaphysical components, their fundamental worldviews which are embedded most readily in culture defined in terms of background knowledge. Mansbach and Vasquez have correctly pointed out: "A paradigm contains within it a fundamental view of the world, and its assumptions act as lenses through which that world is perceived. 'Facts' rarely speak for themselves and make sense only when interpreted in the light of the basic assumptions of a paradigm."[7] The fundamental view of the world is most readily provided by culture and the embedded background knowledge. A late Chinese philosopher, Liang Shuming, also says that the fundamental difference between the Eastern and Western cultures lies in the difference in their ways of thinking, or their philosophies, which tend to dispose people of the former to understand and interpret the same issues differently from people of the latter.[8]

In this respect, an interesting discussion by William Callahan on specific IR theories sheds light on theoretical innovation. He compares the American IR theory, the English School, and IR theory with Chinese characteristics. In his article entitled "Nationalizing international theory: the emergence of the English School and IR theory with Chinese characteristics," he uses the concept of "big ideas" as a standard to differentiate IR theories, arguing that any IR theory with a national label must have a big idea, which is, for the American mainstream, "democratic peace," for the English School, "international society," and for the Chinese, "the *Datong*, or universal great harmony."[9]

Callahan's discussion of the big idea is related to a somewhat critical question: How to deal with intellectual and discursive domination in IR? What he wants to point out is that the English School and IR theory with Chinese characteristics both aim to resist and overthrow the American discursive hegemony in IR theory. Whether these theoretical efforts have such an ambition is arguable and theorists who work for such innovation are very much likely to wish to create some new theories to add to the intellectual treasure of IR theory, rather than to replace or displace competing theories such as the American mainstream. It is, however, important to notice that he has revealed an interesting fact: A big idea defines a big theory.[10] For him, the quality of the theoretical hard core is decisively ideational. This big idea is not only the soul of a theory shared by theorists, but also comes from the shared knowledge by members of a community including theorists and practitioners alike.[11] In other words, when a question is brought up and enters the knowledge system of an agent, it also enters a menu for interpretation and representation, relying more on the inarticulate background knowledge of the community of which the agent is a member. In 2003 the United States launched a war against Iraq, for the Americans firmly believed and repeatedly stated that Iraq had weapons of mass destruction, which could easily proliferate to terrorist groups. Colin Powell, then US Secretary of State, held hearings

---

[7] Mansbach and Vasquez 1981, 71, quoted in Wæver 1996, 159.
[8] Liang Shuming's view is discussed by Feng Youlan in his autobiography. Feng 2004, 164.
[9] Callahan 2002.   [10] Ibid., 6.   [11] Callahan 2004.

in all sincerity at the United Nations Security Council. Even though the investigation team did not find any such weapons in Iraq, the United States believed that the Iraqis had hidden or destroyed the weapons. Why did such things happen? It is the big idea of liberal rationalism that played a crucial role. The United States believed that the Saddam government was an anti-democratic, anti-peace regime and would do whatever it could. Thus, when the issue of Iraq came up, the solution by the United States was war, a solution based firmly on the big idea of liberal rationalism. It was, to a considerable extent, the background knowledge that provided Americans with a ready answer to the Iraqi issue and disposed them to military action against Iraq.

Unfortunately, Callahan has not gone further to explore why the American, English, and Chinese tend to have and can have different big ideas and why such big ideas are related to a country, a nation, or a particular geographical locale. If we should not stop where he stops, then we would go further to see why they have such big ideas, different and distinct. I argue that the big idea comes from the culture in which these scholars are immersed and it is in fact more related to the culture where a nation or a country is embedded rather than to a particular geographical location or nation-state *per se*.[12] A nation-state is largely a politically constructed entity, while a culture is a naturally growing process. The seemingly national label is thus a mere coincidence because of the overlap of the names of some nation-states and the cultures where they are embedded, such as American or Chinese or Indian. That a big idea comes from culture is of great importance for theoretical innovation. It does not come from the present, and neither does it simply represent what is present by rational reasoning. They are embedded in the cultural sediments and come from the practical knowledge of a certain community over long years. They are neither from purely rational reasoning nor from lofty ideal inspiration. They are the ideational product of a particular culture and constitute a perspective based on the world they perceive from their own angle. In terms of social theory, therefore, a big idea is related closely to the metaphysical component, which, as a perspective and worldview, works on the questions presented by the substantive component of the theoretical hard core. In other words, big ideas identified by Callahan in IR are the specification and reflection of a particular

---

[12] I agree with Shweder that one of the things culture is certainly not about is the so-called national character. The metaphysical component is nurtured and shaped by culture rather than a nation-state. It is labelled with the name of a nation-state simply because there is a high degree of overlap between the nation-state and the cultural community, usually a civilization-based cultural community, such as the Indian, Chinese, and Japanese. See Shweder 2000, 163.

worldview on phenomena in the international system or world politics. Theories differ in that their ideational parts, or the metaphysical components, differ. If this logic stands, it is reasonable to say that culture provides valuable, natural, and rich resources for construction of new social theories.[13]

Phenomena from the real social world are processed and represented by the agent through her ways of thinking. Different ways of thinking lead to different understanding, interpretation, and judgment. A rational solution in one processing system may not be rational in another, and a common practice in the former may not even exist in the menu of possible solutions in the latter. The processing mechanism is highly related to culture. In a social theory, it is functioned by the metaphysical component of the hard core. It is exactly this component that makes theory not just a mere instrument for certain conscious purposes as Robert Cox has stated,[14] but also as a reflection of a culture with firmly imprinted marks of history and practice of the cultural community. A social theory, no matter whether it is to understand or to change the social world, or to make normative judgment, or to provide solutions, reveals through the metaphysical component the worldview of a social grouping, the way of thinking of a cultural collectivity, and the practical knowledge of a human community. Thus, the metaphysical component defines a theory and makes it distinct from other theories.

This is why we say that social theory always has its cultural birthmark. It is in the first place produced in a particular cultural setting and the metaphysical component of the theoretical hard core is made in a particular community of discourse and practice. In this sense, culture makes social theory. A cultural community has shared practice, knowledge, and ways of thinking and doing. These are the sediments over long history and are embedded in the ways of thinking and doing of the cultural community. Different cultures are likely to shape different metaphysical components of the theoretical hard core and thus give birth to different social theories. The multi-civilizational and multicultural feature of the world tends to produce various social theories.[15] Such a pluralist view should encourage more theories to emerge.

By definition, the monist view opposes the idea that culture matters in theory building, for cultural sediments cannot have real impacts because theory is universal across time and space, civilizations and cultures.

---

[13] Ikenberry argues that every country has its own theoretical orientations, preoccupations, and debates. He characterizes American IR tradition as "liberalism in a realist world," arguing that the fact that liberalist America lives in the realist international system helps construct the lasting liberal-realist debate. Ikenberry 2009a.

[14] Cox 1986.   [15] Katzenstein 2010a and 2010b.

Robert Crawford has provided a vivid summary of the monist view, which he believes is the attitude that dominates the mainstream conception of IR:

The consensus to date is that IR is "international" only in subject matter and name, and pretty much a North Atlantic, disproportionately Anglo-American, preoccupation. This anomaly has generated occasional curiosity but generally failed to excite concern. National representation, it might be supposed, ought to play no role in assessing the health or viability of any scientific enterprise. At no point in the human struggle against disease, for example, do we feel compelled to ask whether our epidemiologists are from Bulgaria, Finland, or Tanzania. Why ought our equally pressing, and related, concerns with war, peace, dislocation, famine, wealth, poverty, genocide, environmental degradation, and so on, require the least bit of attention to nationality? Nationality, culture, location, and the myriad other constitutive elements of individual and group identities offer no prophylactic assurance against AIDS, no hedge against hyperinflation, and no shelter for radioactive fallout.[16]

What Crawford says reflects the fundamental assumption of monism. If we should take IR as physics or biology, it would not bear any cultural imprints and can only have one form, rigorously scientific and perfectly universal.[17] IR, however, is a social science directly related to human affairs, thus inseparable from human practice – their ways of thinking and doing. The process of theorizing in IR, therefore, is unavoidably mediated by normative values based on the practical knowledge of a cultural community where it is unfolding. The reason why "big questions" or "big ideas" for theories with national labels are different across nations lies in that the background knowledge of various cultural communities differs. When scholars of the mainstream American IR theory promote the hard positivist approach as universal, they seldom ask "whether the mainstream concept of IR is itself a reflection of values, attitudes, and predispositions forged in the cauldron of particular historical, cultural, and national experiences and circumstances . . ."[18] The result of such promotion, if successful (and indeed quite successful so far), could create a discursive and intellectual hegemony in theory building, taking the particular as the universal, deeming all the other particulars as alien heresies, especially those in

---

[16] Crawford 2001, 1.
[17] Even this is arguable, for medical science also has a cultural background to rely upon. The traditional Chinese medicine, for example, sees a patient and her disease differently from the Western medicine. See Ou 2005. Lou Yulie also argues that traditional Chinese medicine sees a human being as a whole system of which all parts are related. Such relations can be felt only when one is alive. Dissection as it is in the Western medicine will not do because when one is dead, such relations no longer exist. See Lou 2016, 124.
[18] Crawford 2001, 2.

other cultural communities, and homogenizing, marginalizing, or dismissing "alter" theories by the dominant standards. As a result it creates a domain of discursive domination where the phenomena observed are global, but theories for their explanation and interpretation are local ones claimed to be universal. It is a self-closed system, which could lead only to intellectual decay and thus prevent academic pursuit from moving forward to prosperity. Simply put, it kills innovation.

To prevent such a system from being an insurmountable obstacle, it is necessary to put the metaphysical component of the theoretical hard core within a cultural context, for the component itself is cultural in nature. Furthermore, to discuss culture, it is important to discuss the fundamental assumptions embedded in a culture defined in terms of shared background knowledge and bearing ontological and epistemological significance. A worldview, for example, is an overall understanding and interpretation of the world, natural and social. It is also a view of the world by members of a particular cultural community, both as common and collective knowledge, rather than by all the people under the sun. Worldviews are therefore related to culture in the first place. An agrarian culture, for example, usually sees human and nature as of one rather than one being the subject and the other object, for their fate seems to be tied together. It is universally acknowledged that our world is composed of multiple civilizations and cultures. Samuel Huntington's well-known theory of the "clash of civilizations" first of all recognizes the fact that there are many civilizations in the world. Only after making this basic assumption does he begin to discuss the properties of each civilization and the inevitable clash among them.[19] While scholars in any country who study civilizations cannot deny this fact, monists in IR seem to ignore it completely and therefore the concept of "worldviews" is seldom seen in their discussion. They take it for granted that there should be only one correct "worldview," and turn a blind eye to various worldviews and perspectives that exist in other cultural communities. Even less can they realize that inarticulate and tacit knowledge as background – worldviews and ways of thinking and doing, for example – are so important for the building of social theory.

A cultural community, in terms of language, history, and practice, has something in common with and something different from other cultural communities. A hunting cultural community may understand and interpret the world around it very differently from an agrarian community or a commercial community. It is thus not reasonable to say that there is only

---

[19] Huntington 1996.

one set of standards which has the sole authority to qualify or disqualify a theory and that there is therefore only one way to see the world, to build theory, and to produce knowledge. Criticizing realism, Ashley once said: "Neorealist theory is theory of, by, and for positivists. It secures instantaneous recognition, . . . because it merely projects onto the place of explicit theory certain metatheoretical commitments that have long been implicit in the habits of positivist method. It tells us what, hidden in our method, we have known all along."[20] What Ashley has emphasized is the perspective, the mindset, and the habitual way of thinking which are embedded in and reflected by positivism. It is for this reason, *inter alia*, Ashley has criticized realism for its poverty. In fact, American mainstream theories have a similar tendency because they have been so used to employing only one set of standards, based on their background knowledge, to theorize about phenomena in different cultures, against the colorfulness and richness of which the theories pale and show their poverty.

Ashley's criticism also points to the fact that the metaphysical matters. Positivism is not only a method, but also, perhaps more significantly, a worldview, deeply embedded in American culture and internalized to the extent that when the mainstream theories of realism, liberalism, and constructivism were being developed, those who were constructing them did not even realize it as a problem, let alone its weaknesses. If we should view the world as a causal totality, then whatever effort we make in theory building would focus on finding the causal mechanisms, and treat factors as independent and dependent variables so that causes and effects could be clearly identified. It is the appropriate approach because it is rational. By definition, furthermore, independent and dependent variables should not be correlated and a particularly emphasized dichotomy is thus firmly established in the worldview. Taking a different worldview, we could see the world as a relational complexity, and then make efforts to find how these relations work and are managed. The world is then not a collection of dichotomous sets, but a correlative whole and an immanent process, a perspective or a way of thinking different from the view that sees a lonely world of causality. The fact that I raise this issue here is not to judge which worldview is better because they are very likely to be complementary, but to point out that different ways of thinking are reflected in different cultures, for example, the Western culture and the Chinese culture, or the Western culture and the Indian culture. The assumption from it is that we may have different theories if we take such worldviews seriously and conceptualize them for the purpose of theory building and innovation.

[20] Ashley 1986, 280.

Recognition of the significance of culture for social theory building opens more channels for knowledge production and theoretical innovation. Different cultures nurture different worldviews, which in turn may shape the metaphysical component and give birth to different social theories. Kuhn argues in his discussion on the structure of scientific revolution that the excitement produced by the clash of two scientific cultures with a fundamental difference is much greater than that produced by two scientific cultures that are less different.[21] It is not only true of scientific cultures, but also true of civilizational cultures in general. Take the Chinese culture as an example, for it seems quite distant from Western culture. In a speech he made at a conference held by Columbia University in 1922, Feng Youlan, a well-known late Chinese philosopher, provides an answer to the question why there is no science in China from the perspective of traditional Chinese philosophy, saying that it is not because of the material conditions such as geography, climate, and economy, but because Chinese do not need science in their value system or their culture.[22] He argues that human beings seek goodness, which for Westerners lies mostly in nature, external to human beings, but for Chinese lies inside the human mind or the inner self of the human being.[23] It is a bold hypothesis. As Feng holds, Westerners, by their knowledge and way of thinking, believe that to know and control the material world is the most important work, while the Chinese, by their knowledge and way of thinking, to know and to control one's own heart/ mind or inner self is the most important thing. He uses two concepts to summarize the Enlightenment tradition and the usefulness of science – certainty and power, "Descartes said that it is for certainty; Bacon said that it is for power," certainty about the outside world and power over this world out there. He continues:

The Chinese philosophies … had no need for scientific certainty, because it was themselves that they wished to know; so in the same way they had no need for the power of science, because it was themselves that they wished to conquer. To them the content of wisdom is not intellectual knowledge and its function is not to increase external goods.[24]

Westerners tend to think about the outside world. "They first try to know it, and after getting acquainted with it, they try to conquer it. So they are bound to have science both for certainty and for power."[25] His argument itself is perhaps arguable, but what is inspiring in his discussion about the two cultures is that Chinese and Westerners differ in terms of their perception of the world and their conception of the

---

[21] Kuhn 1962.   [22] Feng 1991, 572.   [23] Ibid.   [24] Ibid., 594.   [25] Ibid., 595.

human and nature. The Chinese way of thinking and doing is more about their heart, their mind, and their inner self.[26] Feng says that modern Europe is trying to know, conquer, and control nature, while the Chinese have been trying to know themselves and sought a peaceful mind.[27] For such a people who place more emphasis on knowing and controlling the inner self, they may produce many rules for cultivating the self, but principles of science and objective laws about nature would not even be thought about, and therefore are not listed in their menu for choice. Certainty, one of the most important principles of rationalism, cannot even enter into the mind of a Chinese, and thus loses its significance in the traditional Chinese culture. Feng argues: "I cannot refrain from saying that the West is extension, the East is intension, and that the West emphasizes what we have, the East emphasizes what we are."[28] The Chinese culture in the final analysis focuses on the inner self and therefore introspection or the control, cultivation, and purification of one's own "heart/mind" has become a principle and precondition for good social order and harmonious social relations. What Feng has discussed is why Chinese are backward in the development of science and technology, but at a deeper level he implies that ways of thinking and doing are philosophically and metaphysically implanted in culture and that members of different cultural communities may have different views about the world, ego and alter, and the material and the social.

My argument that different cultures may produce different social theories by cultivating the metaphysical components of the theoretical hard core is not meant to replace one type of theory with another and to displace one type of discursive and intellectual hegemony with another. Western culture has made great achievements and given birth to great thoughts. Rationality, which is a most important concept developed in Western culture, has inspired and informed so many great theories. What I intend to do is simply to refer to a fact that cultures provide rich resources for social theorizing and can help lead to the prosperity of the discipline of IR. If we should follow only one set of standards and all researchers, or at least most of them, are testing to prove either how correct or how wrong a theory is, then "activit[y] commensurate with international relations theorizing may be noted, but is defined in terms of its consumption, replication, and imitation of what counts as theoretical activity elsewhere."[29] Even worse, it is defined not only by American mainstream IR scholars, but also by those who are carrying out such

---

[26] In the Chinese language, there is no dichotomous distinction between the mind and the heart. A single word, *xin*, is used for both. It both feels and thinks.
[27] Feng 1991, 592.   [28] Ibid., 595.   [29] Crawford 2001, 2.

activities elsewhere, consciously and unconsciously, through their belief in monism or their blind following of the monistic principles. The result is that their intellectual soil would be sterile, leaving so much treasure of thoughts wasted. On the other hand, if we should encourage theories growing out of different cultural backgrounds and see how they compete, debate, and perhaps complement one another, we would have a better intellectual inhabitancy. Let me again quote Feng, who says after pointing out that difference between the Western and the Chinese:

> The question as to how to reconcile these two [the Chinese and the Western] so that humanity can be happy both in body and in mind is at present difficult to answer. Anyway the Chinese conception of life may be mistaken. If mankind shall afterwards become wiser and wiser, and think they need peace and happiness in their mind, they may turn their attention to, and gain something from, the Chinese wisdom. If they shall not think so, the mind energy of the Chinese people of four thousand years will yet not have been spent in vain. The failure itself may warn our children to stop searching for something in the barren land of human mind. This is one of China's contributions to mankind.[30]

Social Theory: From Particularity to Bounded Universality

If we argue that social theory, especially its metaphysical component, is shaped by culture, the question of universality is unavoidable. Should we aim to create universal social theory or locally applicable theory? It seems to be an easy question, for a theorist, no matter whether she wants to develop meta-theory or medium-range theory, she expects it to be widely or even universally applicable. Some theorists have gone so far as to wish that their theory would not only be universally applicable, but also stand as *the* theory in their respective disciplines.

To this question, monism is likely to provide an affirmative answer. In Chapter 1, we discussed in some detail the monist and pluralist views for theory building. If we should take the monist view, all theories, no matter whether they are of the natural or social world, would be the same, universally applicable and geo-culturally insensitive. There is then only one set of standards, one form of theory, and one orientation for intellectual and scholarly pursuit. If a theorist does not aim to create universally applicable and universally verifiable theory, her work would be hopeless in the first place. The pluralist view, on the contrary, holds that the social world differs essentially from the natural world and therefore social theory is by definition and necessity different from natural theory. Such

---

[30] Feng 1991, 595.

difference exists in a society among different social groups, such as men and women, the elite and the grassroots, and the bourgeoisie and the proletariat. The difference also exists across civilization-based cultural communities, whose background knowledge cannot be identical. Otherwise, it would not be necessary to ask the question: "Why is there no non-Western International Relations theory?" In this line of reasoning, social theories bear the birthmarks of their respective cultures.

While the monist view denies completely this cultural birthmark by its belief in the perfect universality of any theory, the pluralist view tends to recognize the cultural origin of social theory. Theorizing with concepts from different histories, cultures, and backgrounds is welcome because it enriches IR knowledge as a whole. However, the argument that social theory originates from a particular geo-cultural setting may well lead to suspicion that such theory is able to gain universality at all. Furthermore, it may even cause worries about cultural parochialism and exceptionalism. Peter Katzenstein has emphatically pointed out that no culture or civilization should think itself as exceptional, neither the American nor the Chinese.[31] In proposing the Global IR project, Amitav Acharya expresses a similar point of view. While admitting that national and regional schools of IR can broaden and enrich IR, he is strongly opposed to cultural exceptionalism, which he defines as "the tendency to present the characteristics of one's own group (society, state, or civilization) as homogeneous, unique, and superior to those of others."[32] He then focuses on the importance of going beyond particularity, saying:

My test for national or regional "schools" of IR is that they must offer concepts and approaches that explain IR not only in that particular country or region, but also beyond. In other words, they must be applicable, at least to some degree, to the world at large. For example, the English School and the Copenhagen School, despite their biases and limitations, has offered concepts such as "international society," or "securitization," respectively, which have genuinely broader application beyond the UK or Europe and are used by scholars in other parts of the world ... To be credible, a Chinese School of IR must offer concepts and explanations that have relevance beyond China or East Asia, rather than simply capture China's behavior or the East Asian international system.[33]

Such worries are quite understandable and justifiable. An overemphasis on local characteristics may well go to the other extreme: Social theory is and can only be locally applicable. Furthermore cultural parochialism and exceptionalism deny the commonalities of humanity and may lead to disastrous results in both academic pursuit and human life as well. While great caution should be exercised against such extreme

[31] Katzenstein 2010b.   [32] Acharya 2014, 5.   [33] Acharya 2014, 5, fn.10.

narrow-mindedness and excessive parochialism, it is also necessary to realize that neither thorough universalism nor complete particularism is conducive to social theory building.

I argue that perfect universality is impossible. The noble dream for seeking such universality has already been smashed even in the natural sciences with the falsification of the Newtonian theories in different temporo-spatial fields and the rising of the theory of relativity and quantum physics. In fact, what Popper's principle of falsification through critical experiments tells us quite explicitly is that the aspiration for perfect universality is infeasible and unachievable.[34] For Popper, if a theory fails to be falsifiable, it is not scientific. Perfect universality has ever been an impossible mission especially for social theory, which is born in a particular cultural setting and whose bias is even greater than theories of the natural sciences. Since the background knowledge that defines one cultural community may differ from that of other cultural communities, perspectives and attitudes based on such knowledge, which shape social theory, are not likely to be the same. It is therefore easier to see the social theory born in one culture to be falsified in another.

To indicate the indelible cultural birthmark of social theory, I have made three interrelated arguments. First, social theory is defined by the metaphysical component of the theoretical hard core and incommensurable metaphysical components lead to theoretical incommensurability. Second, the metaphysical component is nurtured by culture defined in terms of background knowledge and reflected by worldviews, attitudes, and ways of thinking and doing. Third, culture provides rich resources for theoretical innovation because different cultures are more likely to produce different metaphysical components. It is reasonable to say, paraphrasing Kuhn's judgment, that the greater difference one culture has with another, the greater chance there is for theoretical innovation, innovation more fundamental and more revolutionary. In this sense, all social theories are local in the first place, born of the background knowledge of a cultural community. A social theory originates in a particular cultural setting and has its birthmark during its whole life cycle. No social theory can expect to wash off its cultural birthmark completely and no social theory can reach the ideal state of perfect universality. Starting culturally is not only a possible but also an innovative way for the development of social theory.

It is noteworthy that Acharya's passage cited above stresses "concepts" and "approaches," such as "international society" of the English School and "securitization/desecuritization" of the Copenhagen School.[35] While

---

[34] Popper 1959.
[35] For the concept of "securitization," see Buzan, Wæver, and de Wilde 1998.

the success of the English School or the Copenhagen School may well depend on its broader application than in Europe, it should be realized first of all that the key concepts that form the theoretical hard core are produced in the particular locale and with a particular *habitus*. Before becoming more mature schools of thoughts, they each started with a key concept without which they could not have become influential theories. Moreover, the two strands, i.e. the English School and the Copenhagen School, are still within the Western civilizational and cultural domain. If concepts and approaches should develop in a distant cultural and civilizational realm and if theorizing this way should succeed, then the locally stimulated innovation would be more conspicuous and meaningful.

Thus, while I agree with Acharya on his notion of a qualified social theory, that is, a theory applicable beyond its origin, I need to point out further here that a social theory is first of all to have local application. The metaphysical component is the product of the shared and practical knowledge of a particular cultural community and therefore in the first place depends on culture, exists because of culture, and lives with culture. It is a worldview and a way of thinking, carrying with it the meaning and value of the "we-ness," presented also for the "other" to know and interpret. Furthermore, the substantive component is more likely to receive signals that touch on the local nerves. As Kim Richard Nossal has noted, a conspicuous feature of the IR discipline is "America at the center," and hegemonic stability theory is "the 'theory' that has been invented by American scholars to 'account' for American leadership ... "[36] His survey of widely used IR textbooks leads to his conclusion that IR "remains a deeply 'American' enterprise, having changed little since Hoffmann was writing in the late 1970s," because these textbooks "portray the world to their readers from a uniquely *American* point of view: they are reviewed by Americans; the sources they cite are American; the examples are American; the theory is American; the experience is American; the focus is American; ... "[37] Nossal's criticism is sharp, but in fact he reveals a fact: It is natural that a social theory functions first of all to spontaneously respond to the local, reflecting local concerns and providing explanation and meaning for local facts. That is why it has what Acharya calls "biases and limitations." Since no theory is developed by the almighty and absolutely rational mind, biases and limitations are only natural, for the menu for the theorist to choose from is always limited by time and space, and by the practical knowledge of the culture she lives in. American mainstream

---

[36] Nossal 2001, 172–173.   [37] Ibid., 183.

IR theories, the English School, the Copenhagen School, dependency theory, feminist IR theory, etc., all have such biases and limitations, for none of them did not come from a particular cultural setting in the very beginning. To some extent, the biases and limitations are what necessarily go with the forming process of a theoretical hard core, especially its metaphysical component. It is the different biases and limitations that may well lead to theoretical innovation.

Robert Cox's discussion on social theory again sheds light here.[38] He has put forward three interrelated arguments. First, theory starts with a certain perspective; second, the perspective is related to a problematic; and third, the problematic comes from specific problems and issues in particular time and space.[39] Along this line, we can infer that a social theory cannot stand without a particular temporo-spatial site to start and sustain, and the perspective that a social theory starts with can be a view of a certain socioeconomic class and thus the theory can be a standpoint theory "*for* someone and *for* some purpose."[40] Although Cox still focuses on modern Western societies and socioeconomic classes and argues that their perspectives are the most important for theory building in such societies, he, as a leading thinker of the critical theory, enlightens us at a deeper level on the question of how theory is constructed. Since the initial perspective and the problematic come from some socioeconomic classes, they come from some cultural or subcultural communities which, as we have discussed, may have different initial perspectives and problematics once an issue arises in the real world. The English School, for example, seems to have started its debate with the American mainstream over methodological differences, but in fact, it is their initial perspective and the problematic that differed from their American counterparts and shaped the debate, with the American mainstream stressing the international system and the English School focusing on international society. It is not the methodological difference that has made the English School. It is the initial perspective of international society that has enabled the English School to develop a theory of its own. In addition, methodology, such as positivism or reflectivism, is in fact a worldview, too. This initial perspective, as I understand it, is close in meaning to the metaphysical component. As a theory is maturing, it may go beyond this initial perspective, but without it no theory can even get started. Realism and liberalism as theories of IR explicitly show their initial perspective, which goes back to the rationalistic worldview born out of the Enlightenment, and dependency theory has a clear initial perspective from practice in less developed peripheral economies which constitute

---

[38] Cox 1986, 207–208.   [39] Ibid.   [40] Cox 1986, 207, emphasis in original.

a sharp contrast to the development theory of comparative politics in the United States. Each initial perspective is related to a problematic, which Cox has explained as the initial dialogue between the maker of a social theory and the real world she tries to understand and interpret. It is a problem sensed by a human agency. It is conditioned by history and activated by present phenomena.[41] A social theory starts with this problematic and is constructed in the beginning by it.[42]

A social theory thus should first of all provide meaning and explanation for the particularity of which it is born. Without being able to do this, it cannot even come into being. For example, balance of power is a key concept of realism, classical realism and neorealism alike. This concept grew out of the European history and experience, rested firmly on the Westphalian international system, and has become an important element of the background knowledge there.[43] Using Cox's reasoning, the conceptualization of "balance of power" should have started with an initial perspective of the theorists who invented it, and become a problematic when its makers were carrying out a dialogue with the European international relations world around them, where specific issues were arising. Specifically and perhaps simplistically, the issue was individual sovereign states fighting against one another, the problematic was how to maintain systemic order in such a struggle for power, and the initial perspective was the rationalistic calculation that a balance, as that in the world of physics, would result in a most stable state. Thus the balance of power theory was first of all a response to the particular European international relations with sovereign states competing with and against one another. The solution it offered was to establish and keep a balance so that the probability of war could be reduced and order among nations better maintained.

Now it seems that the concept of balance of power has gone beyond its birthplace of Europe and has a very broad application. As Waltz has said: "If there is any distinctively political theory of international politics, balance-of-power theory is it," and it is a "theory that is generally accepted."[44] During the Cold War years, the US–USSR relationship was explained as a bipolar balance and the US–USSR–China relationship was seen as a triangular matrix to maintain an overall balance in the international system. But as people have explored in a much broader way histories of international relations and as the Westphalian international system has no longer been considered as the only international

---

[41] Cox's words are as follows: A problematic is a "historically conditioned awareness of problems and issues." Cox 1986, 207.
[42] Cox 1986.   [43] Gulick 1967.   [44] Waltz 1979, 117.

system that ever existed, the balance of power theory seems also to be questioned. When Edward Vose Guick discusses balance of power, he outlines four assumptions upon which balance of power rests: a state system, a clearly defined territory, relative homogeneity such as Europe, and rationality.[45] He, more as a historian than as a political scientist, thus draws a boundary for the application of the concept.

One type of criticism is that this theory does not explain order and disorder outside the Westphalian system. A comparative study by Victoria Tin-bor Hui has shown that balance of power can only account for one type of the sovereignty-based, individually oriented international system and cannot explain other types of international systems such as the Chinese international system. It compares China's Spring and Autumn and Warring States periods (656–221 BC) and Europe in the early modern period (AD 1495–1815) and finds that these two periods under discussion resembled each other with largely independent states fighting against each other. The outcomes, however, were totally different, the former becoming a unified empire under one ruler while the latter the international system of sovereign states balancing one another. "If the balance of power prevailed in international politics and the constitutional state triumphed in state-society relations, then why did the opposite outcomes occur in China? Is it because China was destined to have authoritarian rule under a unified empire as taught in standard Chinese history books? Alternatively, is it possible that the European trajectory was far more contingent than is presumed by the European perspective?"[46] In fact, she raises the question in the very beginning of her book: "Why is it that political scientists and Europeanists take for granted checks and balances in European politics, while Chinese and sinologists fail to take for granted a coercive universal empire in China?"[47] It may also be put as: "Why is it that political scientists and Europeanists do not take for granted a coercive universal empire in European politics, while Chinese and sinologists refuse to take for granted checks and balances in China?" It is not a play of words. It reflects the different perspectives and worldviews of theorists as cultural beings who are geo-culturally confined.

The balance of power theory's limitation or lack of perfect universality is also reflected in another study by David Kang, who has found that balance of power theory did not apply in East Asia's Tribute international system. According to balance of power theory, state actors together would prevent a rising power from becoming the dominator of the system and use all means possible, including a resort to force, to stop the rising power from growing overwhelmingly predominant. The underlying assumption

---

[45] Gukick 1967, 3–29.   [46] Hui 2005, 1.   [47] Ibid.

is definitely that balance brings about systemic stability and prevents major-power war. But in East Asia, from 1300 to 1900 AD, countries in the region did not balance China; rather they accommodated it. It seems to have contradicted "much conventional international relations theory."[48] Moreover, this lack of balance of power did not lead to disorder and war, for East Asia was characterized by its "comparative peacefulness" with many fewer wars than Europe during the same period of time.[49] His explanation is that "this accommodation of China is due to a specific constellation of interests and beliefs – a particular mix of identities and the absence of fear."[50] His answer is perhaps arguable and even highly controversial, but the observation he has made that the balance of power concept fails to explain the 600-year East Asian reality is inspiring. As he has pointed out, balance of power processes occurred in many other international systems, but "in the East Asia international system such processes barely registered in historical evidence. If balance of power theory is misleading in the other cases, in this case it is profoundly and fundamentally wrong."[51]

Balance of power theory, even though it was not applicable to the East Asian international system where such balance was not found and therefore no theory of balance of power was ever developed, continues to be a theory of importance. It is thus argued that even if a social theory does not go much beyond its origin, it is still of value and cannot be simply dismissed as not qualified as a theory. I do not mean to deny that a social theory should go beyond its origin and gain broader application; I simply want to clarify one important aspect: Any social theory is born locally and starts from understanding, explaining, and interpreting the local. As Cox has argued: "The more sophisticated a theory is, the more it reflects upon and transcends its own perspective; but the initial perspective is always contained within a theory and is relevant to its explication."[52] If I should understand Cox's initial perspective as similar to my metaphysical component, I would like to rephrase Cox's words and argue that a social theory is culturally bound at its origin and is always traceable to a culturally conditioned awareness of certain problems and issues. At the same time, it also tries to transcend the particularity of its cultural origin in order to gain more universality with general propositions or laws.[53] But, it is not the necessary condition for the recognition of a social theory.

I believe, with Acharya, that social theory can realize some degree of transcendence and gain more validity than as first constructed. Stopping

[48] Kang 2007, 4.   [49] Ibid., 36–41.   [50] Ibid.   [51] Ibid., 23–24.   [52] Cox 1986, 207.
[53] Ibid.

with cultural parochialism is to retard social theorizing and even bring it to a premature end. What I argue, therefore, is, paraphrasing Herbert Simon, "bounded universality." By bounded universality, I mean a social theory initiated in a geo-cultural setting can gain higher levels of application beyond the locality of its origin, even though it can never reach the state of perfect universality. At the same time, we need also to recognize the commonality of humankind, and thus a social theory needs to go beyond its birth place and gain more universal application to realize its own evolution. Both Acharya and Cox would agree, for they recognize the permanent bias and limitations of a social theory. For such transcendence, there are two approaches. One, and perhaps the most efficient, is power driven. In other words, if a social theory, especially the metaphysical component of its theoretical hard core, is promoted by a prevailing civilizational-cultural community, perhaps in the reduced form of a powerful nation-state, it may spread quickly and the underlying assumptions are accepted, consciously or unconsciously, and willingly or unwillingly. It is reminiscent of Foucault's discussion of knowledge, discourse, and power.[54] But what I want to argue here is that once a big idea is promoted by a powerful community like a so-called advance civilizational community or a strong nation-state, then social theories containing and reflecting the idea or the concept may go with the flag. It may not be a purposeful process, as Cox believes, but it is historically true, for a big power carries its practice all over the world and its ideas go with it around the world. Development of IR theories has witnessed such a process and the Acharya-Buzan project has shown that the American mainstream IR theory has maintained a dominant position in many other parts of the world.[55] It is a fact, but it is not the appropriate approach for social theory to gain universality, for it is imposing, with a strong sense of violence and even tyranny.

The second approach is through ideational exchange or cultural dialogue. An idea, a significant concept, or a theoretical hard core, born of a particular cultural community, is not easily understood by members of another cultural community, especially when the two communities are far apart physically and mentally. A study by Bleiker, discussing the cultural dimension of IR theory, compares the assumptions of neorealism and the philosophical views of Confucianism and finds that there are fundamental differences concerning ontological positions, understanding of reason, and perceptions of conflict and war. Thus Bleiker has commented on neorealism, "an ethnocentric theory may be able to account for one (systemic) source of conflict within a predominantly ethnocentric

---

[54] See Foucault 1972; 1991. [55] Acharya and Buzan 2007.

international system. Even in this narrow area, structural realism can only continue to be relevant as long as the international system is anarchical and culturally dominated by Western (realist) values."[56] Differences in terms of ontology and epistemology, and in worldviews, constitute a formidable obstacle indeed to successful cultural and civilizational dialogue, but it is not impossible to overcome such obstacles. Kofi Annan's promotion of inter-civilizational dialogue through the United Nations Alliance of Civilizations (UNAOC) provided a good and encouraging effort in this respect, but the realization of "many cultures, one humanity" still has a long way to go.

Therefore, I propose that the ability to provide understanding, interpretation, and explanation of local events and actions is the primary and minimum qualification of a social theory, while attainment of a broader application and a certain degree of universality, or bounded universality, is an aspiration and goal. At the same time, it should be understood that perfect universality is impossible. A theory is first of all produced in a particular culture, its meaning is understood and interpreted by other cultures, and then it aims to acquire "cross-cultural" or "inter-cultural" meanings. Gradually it may gain a higher level of universality and be applicable in more cultural communities. This requires a high level of communicative action, which not only enables cross-cultural understanding, but also has important impact on the renewal of cultural and background knowledge.[57] In the very beginning, no theory starts from a universal null, and in the end, no theory can remove completely its cultural birthmark. For this reason, I suggest that we need to go deep into a particular culture defined in terms of background knowledge and explore its fundamental assumptions about universe, life, and ways of thinking and doing. Then we need to crystalize them into a key concept or idea that constitutes the metaphysical component of the theoretical hard core, from which a systematic and coherent theory is to be unfolding and growing.

Conclusion

The metaphysical component of the theoretical hard core, nourished by the culture where the theorist lives, is a key factor in theoretical innovation. Since cultural resources are rich and diverse, development of new social theories is ever promising and, moreover, should be prosperous as more cultural communities are joining the increasingly globalized world.

[56] Bleiker 1998, 109.   [57] Habermas 1984.

Recent years have already seen much effort to develop IR theories by non-Western scholars and the Global International Relations (GIR) project encourages such effort.

However, the dominance of Western IR theory continues to be conspicuous. The findings from the 2014 Teaching, Research, and International Policy (TRIP) Project's worldwide faculty survey, which covers thirty-two countries, including more than ten non-Western academic IR communities, have shown clearly that IR is still a Western/American dominated discipline.[58] A most interesting point is that within this hierarchical structure of IR academic communities over the world, there is a division of labor wherein scholars in the West are responsible for theory production while the non-West supplies raw data for theory testing.[59] It may imply that the more non-Western scholars do in IR with this division of labor, the more they reinforce the domination of Western IR theory and the less they are able to develop theories by exploring their own cultural resources. There are many factors at work that makes this division of labor possible. In the 2007 Acharya-Buzan project, "Why is there no non-Western IR theory?" scholars from non-Western nations identified some of the most important factors: the Western/American disciplinary domination itself; non-Western IR communities as latecomers in theory construction; lack of institutional support, etc. Looking back, I feel that the project missed one important factor, that is, how to explore cultural resources for conceptualization and theorization. The present division of labor within the IR hierarchy will change if and only if non-Western IR scholars are culturally conscious to take nutrition from their own cultures defined in terms of background knowledge. If IR is to overcome Western dominance, it must offer concepts and theories that are derived from societies and cultures other than the West. A conspicuous problem is perhaps that non-Western scholars tend to use and test Western IR theories and seldom turn back to their own culture for inspiration, even though they feel that the Western domination should not be the normal state of art for the discipline.[60]

The discussion of the metaphysical component of the theoretical hard core points to a possible orientation – to explore deeply and carefully the cultural resources so that an initial idea, which will turn to become the metaphysical component of the theoretical hard core, may come in shape and develop gradually into a more mature theory through the process of nucleation. It is not to replace the existing IR theories, but to develop a theoretical concept from a non-Western culture that has been off the

[58] Maliniak et al. 2014.   [59] Wemheruer-Vogelaar et al. 2016, 18–19.
[60] Maliniak et al. 2014.

menu of Western IR theorists. The result is theoretical innovation as well as enrichment of the existing IR knowledge. In fact, the development of Western IR theories provides a telling example as to how social theory is constructed. The repeated exploration of the cultural resources, the continual refinement of concepts and conceptual frameworks, and the persistent effort to theorize and re-theorize – this long and tortuous process indicates, for example, how "rationality" has finally become a key element of the metaphysical component for many Western social theories. We will continue this discussion critically in the next chapter.

4 Individualistic Rationality and Mainstream IR Theory

The mainstream IR theory, which has been the dominant academic discourse and research agenda, is represented by three theories in the United States, namely, Waltz's structural realism (1979), Keohane's neoliberal institutionalism (1984), and Wendt's structural constructivism (1999). The debates and dialogues have been mainly carried out among these theories and numerous empirical works done to test the validity of the big three.[1] Over time, these theories have drawn the blueprints for the theoretical orientations and analytical frameworks. It is true that these mainstream theories are highly abstract and provide explanations for important phenomena in the international relations world in quite a parsimonious and rigorous scientific way: Structural realism tries to explain international power structure and its impacts on unit behavior; neoliberal institutionalism focuses on international institutions and their influence on unit behavior; and structural constructivism centers on international ideational structure and, via identity formation, its effects on unit behavior. Thus they have become what Kuhn has termed paradigms, meta-theories in the discipline, enjoying and reinforcing the scientific revolutions they started with, and integrating and assimilating occasionally other theories into their agenda.

What I argue in this chapter is that the mainstream IR theory has a common and commensurable metaphysical component in its theoretical hard core – ontological individualism. In other words, through their theoretical lenses, the social world is composed of individual actors, natural or corporate, and structures, material or ideational.

---

[1] According to "The Project of Teaching, Research, and International Practice (TRIP)," "the vast majority of scholars worldwide continue to view international relations scholarship as dominated by paradigmatic analysis." The TRIP surveys "confirm that currently constructivism, liberalism, and realism are the most established and most visible contenders for paradigmatic dominance." In addition: "In the 2006 survey, ... nearly 90 percent of scholarship considered to be paradigmatic by respondents consisted of work identified with the realist, liberal, or constructivist tradition." The TRIP 2014 survey shows that after ten years the situation has changed little. See Sil and Katzenstein 2010, 24, 25, 26, and 225; Wemheuer-Vogelaar et al. 2016.

Individualism is based upon what I term "entitism," a worldview that sees the world as one composed of entities, or independent and discrete substantive beings and objects. Related to this ontological individualism is the key assumption of rationality, both as a position of epistemology and as a device of methodology. In any structural theory, with such a worldview or metaphysical component, rationality, strong or weak, substantive or instrumental, is a necessary and convenient condition. In fact the dominant debates in IR, usually engaging one another among the big three, are called inter-paradigm debates, and their efforts have been made mainly to find problems with one another at the substantive level. What they have neglected is the fact that they share this special dimension of ontological individualism and its corollary assumption of rationality. The debates that have been carried out therefore try mainly to juxtapose different dimensions within this worldview to produce the effect that they differ essentially as social theories, materialism versus idealism, or traditionalism versus positivism, but what they do not see is that the way they look at the world is fundamentally similar, given their culturally oriented menu and background knowledge: a world of structures and units. As a result, mainstream IR theories tend to reach a synthesis at the metaphysical level after some initial debates at the substantive level.

In this section, I will discuss a tendency of theoretical synthesization by examining the prominent theories of neorealism, neoliberalism, and constructivism, the big three in the United States. I will also discuss the case of the English School to see how it has engaged with American IR theories. To a great extent, the construction of mainstream IR theories is quite a success, which is largely a result of the consistent and persistent effort to explore the rich resources of Western culture. Rationality, for example, is the key concept for many Western social as well as IR theories, especially those mainstream and prominent ones. It is exactly a concept that is culturally embedded and has crystalized through the tenacious exploration by generations of thinkers and scholars. Following Ole Wæver, I argue that the first major convergence is the neo-neo synthesis, which he believes is caused mainly by the shared rationalistic approach. I agree partially, but I would like to point out that this rationalistic approach is underpinned by ontological individualism. I also argue that Wendtian constructivism tends to synthesize itself with the mainstream because of its essentialist assumption about the agent and its emphasis on systemic structure. Then I will discuss the potential of a transatlantic rapprochement of the American mainstream and the English School, especially when the latter aspires to become a grand theory of IR.

A Neorealist-Neoliberalist Synthesis

Kenneth Waltz takes an innovative way of reasoning for his structuralism. He was the first IR scholar who systemized rigorously a structural theory of IR, and he has defined his structural realism explicitly and consciously as systemic theory, which he believes differs fundamentally from reductionist theory due to the fact that it focuses on the impacts of systemic factors on unit behavior. He has cut off unsympathetically all elements that do not belong at the systemic level, making his theory highly parsimonious. Although he does not deny that reductionist theory is theory, he does argue that such theory is not a theory of international politics because it tries to explain reality by tracing factors at the unit level rather than at the systemic level. Waltz says: "Theories of international politics that concentrate causes at the individual or national level are reductionist; theories that conceive of causes operating at the international level as well are systemic."[2] The publication of *Theory of International Politics* (1979) is both a deviation away from and continuity of Waltz's early work of *Man, the State, and War* (1959), which identifies three images, or levels of analysis, for the study of international relations, indicating that causal factors could be conceived of at the levels of the international system, the nation-state, and the individual, for any of them could cause international war.[3] *Theory of International Politics*, however, marks what I term "the system turn" for the discipline, shaping the later theoretical orientation and enabling a boom of "systemic theorizing" in IR.[4] The causes for unit behavior rest only at the systemic level and theories with causal variables at other levels are not qualified as theories of international politics. "Any approach to international politics that is properly called systemic must at least try to infer some expectations about the outcomes of state behavior and interactions from a knowledge of systems-level elements."[5] Otherwise, it is not "international" at all.

Waltz then sees a system in general as composed of a structure and interacting units, and an international system in particular as composed of the systemic political structure, and nation-states as the units in the system.[6] He further identifies the most representative characteristics of the international system: anarchy as the defining feature which differentiates an international system from a domestic system; nation-states as the units of the anarchic international system; and the distribution of capabilities as the structure of the international system. The last one, the structure of the international system, is what he believes the most important system-level element.[7] Because anarchy is the defining feature

[2] Waltz 1979, 18.   [3] Waltz 1959.   [4] Waltz 1979, 71.   [5] Ibid., 50.   [6] Ibid., 79.
[7] Ibid., 88–99.

of the international system and self-help the principle of the units in the system, then capabilities across the units, especially those of the most powerful units, are the most significant element of the international system. A highly parsimonious theory of international politics, somewhat like that in microeconomics and even physics, has thus been constructed, with anarchy as the overall condition for international politics to occur, the distribution of capabilities as the master independent variable, and state behavior the dependent variable. "The structure of a system changes with changes in the distribution of capabilities across the system's units. And changes in structure change expectations about how the units of the system will behave and about the outcomes their interactions will produce."[8]

Waltz's theory is self-coherent and consistent, and its three-part definition of the international system, i.e. anarchy, nation-states as the system's units, and the systemic structure in terms of distribution of capabilities, sustains the theoretical framework. Many critics have pointed to his focus on system-level elements at the expense of causal factors at other levels and neoclassic realism in fact has staged a return to domestic factors and taken exactly what Waltz calls a reductionist approach. However, it seems to me that the hard core of neorealism is not its system focus. For a social study, focusing on a certain level of analysis, whether it is the system or the individual, is more or less a methodological matter. As David Singer has argued, levels of analysis provide a convenient instrument for researchers to determine where they can identify their independent variable so that they may establish more conveniently their cause-effect hypotheses for testing.[9] What level a theory focuses on is more a question of choice and even realism itself has various versions using different levels of analysis or mixed levels of analysis. Hans J. Morgenthau, E. H. Carr, Henry Kissinger, and many other realists have aptly used mixed levels of analysis for their discussion of international relations,[10] even though their theories might well be classified as "realist thoughts but not realist theories."[11] Waltz's focus on the level of the international system and his identification of the systemic structure as the independent variable are theoretical innovations at the substantive level, which are to be followed enthusiastically by later theorists, but these factors do not represent the metaphysical component of his theoretical hard core. Furthermore, his definition of the structure is, distinct as it is, also at the substantive level, for it is

---

[8] Ibid., 97.   [9] Singer 1961.   [10] Morgenthau 1961; Carr 1964; Kissinger 1973.
[11] Waltz argues that realist scholars such as Raymond Aron and Hans Morgenthau have theoretical elements in their works, but theirs are not theory. As he says: "Morgenthau . . . described his purpose as being 'to present a theory of international politics.' Elements of a theory are presented, but never a theory." Waltz 1995, 71.

almost completely material and therefore more an observation of the tangible configuration of power than an ideational and fundamental assumption representing a perspective or attitude. But, Waltz is definitely a scientific mind. The logical form of his theory is a clear structure-unit framework in which the structure influences the unit, but what is the idea that makes up this form in the first place?

Hence is our question: What constitutes the metaphysical component of structural realism? It is ontological individualism and rationalism, which can be simply termed "individualistic rationality." If we look at the three parts of Waltz's definition of international structure, there is one of them that is obviously embedded in the long tradition of Western culture and embodied in the "Enlightenment dream." It is the assumption of the "like units," i.e. individual nation-states in the international system. For this crucial part of his definition, Waltz borrows almost completely from microeconomics and assumes that the unit of the international system is a rational actor. He argues:

Unrealistically, economists assume that the economic world is the whole world. Unrealistically, economists think of the acting units, the famous "economic man," as a single-minded profit maximizer. They single out one aspect of man and leave aside the wondrous variety of human life. As any moderately sensible economist knows, "economic man" does not exist. Anyone who asks businessmen how they make their decisions will find that the assumption that men are economic maximizers grossly distorts their characters. The assumption that men behave as economic men, which is known to be false as a descriptive statement, turns out to be useful in the construction of theory.[12]

Thus, Waltz's fundamental assumption is individualistic rationality, ontologically individual and epistemologically rational, which means that independent actors make decisions and take actions according to their rational calculation, especially about costs and benefits. This is exactly what makes nation-states "like units," just as firms in the market. The distribution of capabilities works only when there are such rational actors as the units in the system: They are able to consider their self-interests, taking into account the distribution of power in the system. The political structure of the international system works exactly as the market does: Its invisible hand functions only when there are economic persons as the interacting units therein. Waltz's rationality is very much the individual instrumental rationality, highly objective and cost-efficient, and free from such factors as emotions, feelings, and culturally specific norms. The "economic man" is called such exactly because he tries to maximize his interests so as to realize his goals at the lowest possible costs.

[12] Waltz 1979, 89

For me, this individualistic rationality underlies the neatly structured neorealism and, as a firm belief, an initial perspective, and a fundamental assumption, it constitutes the metaphysical component of neorealism's theoretical hard core. In other words, neorealism would have not even come into being as a grand theory without individualism as its ontological position and rationalism as the pivot of its working mechanism. Both are culturally embedded concepts.

Waltz's far-reaching influence, therefore, lies less in his innovation at the substantial level than in the way of theorizing through a structure and the units therein. For the causal mechanism of such a structural theory to work, ontological individualism and epistemological rationalism are absolutely necessary. It seems that any theory aiming at a systemic grand paradigm cannot help but follow this ontological and epistemological foundation laid so firmly by Waltz: An individual ego exists independently and seeks to maximize her interest rationally in an enabling and constraining structure. It is not a brand-new invention, for microeconomics has been established this way long before. But for IR, this Waltzianization of theoretical development seems to be highly influential. The neo-neo synthesis tells exactly this story: Neoliberal institutionalism and neorealism have materialized a high degree of convergence even though they seem to have been very different at first glance. In fact, neoliberalism started as a theoretical challenger to neorealism, and the two were considered paradigmatic theories of IR incommensurable with each other, around which a major debate unfolded among proponents of both theories and joined by scholars from various schools.[13] Ironically, the two were to converge eventually when the dust was settled.

If we merely look at the substantive level, neorealism and neoliberalism are indeed very different. The former focuses mainly on material power with a particular emphasis on the distribution of material capabilities in the international system, while the latter chooses international institutions as their most significant independent variable for the explanation of state behavior. The former has little confidence in cooperation, stressing that relative gains are what a rational actor values most, while the latter believes that cooperation is possible and absolute gains are more important than relative gains in international political economy.[14] The former takes international institutions as a mere function of power which have serious limitations and cannot have the final say,[15] while the latter holds that international institutions are needed by actors in the system and therefore it is explained by a demand rather than a supply theory, which

[13] See Baldwin 1993, Katzenstein, Keohane, and Krasner 1999; Kegley 1995.
[14] See articles in Baldwin 1993.   [15] Krasner 1991.

suggests the continued existence and functioning of international institutions even without hegemonic power to sustain them. Furthermore such institutions can encourage actors to cooperate and thus reduce the effect of violent power and anarchy.[16] These issues are substantive, covering important matters and concerns in international affairs. Because the two theories are different on such issues, they are considered "incommensurable" and therefore constitute two major rival paradigms in IR. In justifying this incommensurability, Jack Donnelly has said:

> Realists and liberal institutionalists do both assume that states pursue their self-interest; that is, that they are instrumentally rational. But they have very different *substantive* conceptions of rational self-interest. Mearsheimer views states as "short-term power maximizers." Liberals, however, see "rational" states as those that pursue long-term utility. They thus derive an account of international institutions that *is* incompatible with the no effects thesis.[17]

It is true that the substantive issues the two theories deal with are different. Even at the ontological level, neorealism and neoliberalism are not exactly alike. At least, the latter has been less material than the former, for international institutions are a superstructure rather than a mere material infrastructure. Goldstein and Keohane have even taken ideas as an important independent variable in their discussion of foreign policy.[18] However, if we consider the way of theorizing, the two theories seem to be quite similar. Neoliberal institutionalism is also a systemic theory, trying to find causal factors at the system level. When Keohane and Nye developed the complex interdependence model in 1977, they listed three characteristics of complex interdependence in world politics: multiple channels that connect societies, which draw non-state actors into the picture of international relations; absence of hierarchy among issues, which denies the utmost importance of the traditional security issues in international affairs; and reduced relevance of the military force as a means to realize national interests.[19] It is clear that these characteristics had little to do with levels of analysis, for they did not have a clear sense of developing a theory at the systemic level at that time. However, the restructuring of the power and interdependence model to a paradigmatic theory of neoliberal institutionalism later on seems to have made Keohane first seek systemic elements as explanatory factors for unit behavior and then drop the first important characteristic feature of the complex interdependence model by returning to the state-centrist position and taking states as "like units" as Waltz had done. Thus, neoliberal institutionalism accepts the several

---

[16] Keohane 1984.   [17] Donnelly 2000, 133–134, emphasis in original.
[18] Goldstein and Keohane 1993.   [19] Keohane and Nye 2001.

fundamental assumptions of neorealism about international politics: the anarchic and decentralized nature of the international system, the centrality and rationality of the state actor, and the causal mechanisms that link the former and the latter.[20] Like neorealism, it tries to begin with identifying a most significant causal factor, or the independent variable, at the system level and then takes it as the vital factor of the causal mechanism that links the system and the units therein. The success of neoliberalism lies in the fact it finds "international institutions," which reduces the degree of anarchy and facilitates international cooperation through providing more transparent information, lowering transactional costs, and exercising institutional awards and punishments. It is also neat and parsimonious and makes an important theoretical innovation by changing Waltz's formula of "structural selection" into one of "institutional selection." In this way, neoliberal institutionalism "should be regarded as a distinct school of thought,"[21] for it believes that international institutions in world politics are as fundamental as the distribution of capabilities in terms of explaining state behavior.

In fact, Keohane has stated clearly that he chose to develop a systemic theory that draws on microeconomics as Waltz had done, and made the central assumption that firms act as rational egoists. He has further explained that: "Rationality means that they have consistent, ordered preferences, and that they calculate cost and benefits of alternative courses of action in order to maximize their utility in view of those preferences."[22] When he discussed structural realism, he pointed out the three major assumptions of the theory: state-centrism, rationality, and power. The rationality assumption posits that "world politics can be analyzed as if states were unitary rational actors, carefully calculating costs of alternative courses of action and seeking to maximize their expected utility."[23] When Keohane moved on to further his analysis of Waltz's neorealism, he made the following comments:

The link between system structure and actor behavior is forged by the rationality assumption ... Taking rationality as a constant permits one to attribute variations in state behavior to variations in characteristics of the international system ... Thus the rationality assumption ... is essential to the theoretical claims of Structural Realism.[24]

As Keohane believes that the rationality assumption is a great contribution of neorealism to the study of international politics and IR theorizing, his neoliberal institutionalism makes the same assumption, arguing that international institutions influence state behavior through providing

---

[20] Keohane 1989b, 7–8.   [21] Keohane 1989b, 8.   [22] Keohane 1984, 27.
[23] Keohane 1989b, 40.   [24] Ibid., 41.

incentives to actors and they exist "because they could have reasonably been expected to increase the welfare of their creators."[25] In this respect, Keohane does hit the mark with a single comment: The rationality assumption is indeed the key link that enables a structural meta-theory to work and to enable systemic factors to have impact on the individual actor. For a systemic theory to stand, it is necessary to assume that units in the system are alike; and what makes them alike is that each of the units has a common and most important quality: They are rational. For nation-states, they have many similarities such as territory, population, government, and so on. But the essential sameness is that they are all rational egoists, seeking self-interest at the lowest possible costs.

Critics tend to see the neo-neo synthesis as the result of the failure of meta-theories to have paradigmatic incommensurability and to provide inspiring ideas and thoughts. In the mid-1980s, as a result, "we were no longer in the inter-paradigm debate,"[26] and the mid-1980s was exactly when Keohane's *After Hegemony* was published. It has been found that "the rationalist corner has reached the point where realists and liberalists agree more than 90 per cent, only discuss details and these details are tested with much mathematics . . ." What Ole Wæver has concluded is:

During the 1980s, realism became neo-realism and liberalism neoliberal institutionalism. Both underwent a self-limiting redefinition towards an anti-metaphysical, theoretical minimalism, and they became thereby increasingly compatible. A dominant neo-neo synthesis became the research programme of the 1980s. (. . .) No longer were realism and liberalism "incommensurable" – on the contrary they shared a "rationalistic" research programme, a conception of science, a shared willingness to operate on the premise of anarchy (Waltz) and investigate the evolution of cooperation and whether institutions matter (Keohane).[27]

Wæver's argument seems to indicate that the two theories, realism and liberalism, had been incommensurable before they became neorealism and neoliberalism because they had irreconcilable fundamental assumptions. Only after the redefinition which they took and which changed them did they become a synthesis without distinct and competing assumptions. However, it seems to me that they did share similar fundamental assumptions or worldviews in the first place and before they redefined themselves with the "neo" label. The difference between them lies in their respective tangible independent variables at the substantive level – power distribution for neorealism and international institutions for neoliberal institutionalism, while the similarity lies in almost everything else – an anarchic international system, states as the units, and

---

[25] Keohane 1984, 80.   [26] Wæver 1996, 161.   [27] Ibid., 163.

instrumental rationality as the principal assumption. More significantly, they share the fundamental ontological and epistemological
attitude in their theoretical hard core, which constitutes exactly what
the metaphysical component is about and the most significant similarity – individualism and rationalism – is represented by realism as
"*realpolitik* rationalism," and by neoliberals as "institutional rationalism," both of which presuppose ontological individualism. It is, therefore, the deeply embedded perspective of individualistic rationality,
sustained by the background knowledge of the Western civilization-
based culture, that has eventually brought them together and materialized the neo-neo synthesis. Consciously, they both have tried to seek
a different tangible, master independent variable and they have suc-
ceeded, thus seeming to be paradigmatically incommensurable; unconsciously, they both go to their culture for their key concepts, for an
initial idea, and they have converged because of and toward it. Both
their success and their convergence indicate how social theory is made
in a particular context and provide inspiration for theorists to see how
cultural resources can be sought, explored, and refined.

A Rationalistic-Constructivist Reconciliation

It seemed, at least to some, that the neo-neo synthesis provided in the
1980s an excellent opportunity for a middle-ground paradigm to emerge.
What happened was that rationalists and reflectivists moved toward each
other, i.e. "the increasing marginalisation of extreme rationalists (rational
choice) and of extreme anti-IR approaches (deconstructivists), and the
emergence of a middle ground where neo-institutionalists from the
rationalist side meet constructivists arriving from the reflectivist side."[28]

The rise of social constructivism in the United States owes much to
Alexander Wendt,[29] whose theory has successfully merged itself into
the American mainstream mainly because it provides a "via media"
between positivist epistemology and post-positivist ontology,[30] and
because it is explicit about the theoretical claims and offers clearer
research methods for investigating those claims.[31] It is most interesting
to trace the trajectory of this transformative process, which, in retro-
spect, looks so similar to that of the neo-neo synthesis: emerging as

---

[28] Ibid., 168.

[29] Zehfuss has identified three kinds of constructivism, represented by Wendt, Kratochwil,
and Onuf, which are closer to the mainstream IR than the more radical postmodern
constructivism. Here I discuss only the Wendtian strand, for it is the most influential in
IR. See Zehfuss 2002.

[30] Smith 2000, 151–152.   [31] Finnemore 2001, 511–512.

a theoretical challenge to the mainstream and eventually merging into it as another mainstream IR theory.

Wendtian constructivism has several underpinning assumptions of which the first, and perhaps the most important, as claimed by its proponents, is its idealist ontology. Wendt believes that his theory differs from neorealism because it has different fundamental ontological positions, concerning "the nature of human agency and its relationship to social structure, the role of ideas and material forces in social life, the proper form of social explanations, and so on."[32] It seems that he does not agree with Keohane, who holds that academic debates in IR should not be conducted at the purely theoretical level and who strongly opposes debates over epistemological and ontological issues in the abstract.[33] For Wendt, quite correctly, ontological issues are particularly important because they provide the lens to see the world. In other words, ontology is fundamentally about worldviews. For a new theory incommensurable to the existing ones to emerge, different second-order questions are a must. Constructivism differs from the dominant IR theories exactly in that it assumes an idealist ontology, following the age-old divide between materialism and idealism in Western philosophy. Wendt has criticized neorealism and neoliberal institutionalism, holding that they take the identity and interests of the agent as a given and the anarchy of the international system as a constant. What he wants to do is to trace back from where these theories begin and question the underlying assumptions of neorealism and neoliberal institutionalism. It is about the second-order question. He has placed repeated emphasis on the different ontology of his theory, as he argues:

Neorealists see the structure of the international system as a distribution of material capabilities because they approach their subject with a material lens; neoliberals see it as capabilities plus institutions because they have added to the material base an institutional superstructure; and constructivists see it as a distribution of ideas because they have an idealist ontology.[34]

The most innovative effort by Wendt is perhaps his well-cited argument that "Anarchy is what states make of it." It negates the fundamental assumption shared by neorealism and neoliberalism that international anarchy is a given and a constant. It is from this given that the self-help nature of the international system and therefore power politics are logically derived. For Wendt, neither the self-help nature

---

[32] Wendt 1999, 5.
[33] Keohane 1989e, 162. However, ontological and metaphysical presumptions cannot be avoided, as Keohane's own theory has shown.
[34] Wendt 1999, 5.

nor power politics can be logically and causally derived from anarchy. Rather it is the intersubjective activities of agents that create them. In other words, it is the interaction of the agents rather than the nature of the international system that constructs the meaning of anarchy.[35] Anarchy is thus first of all an ideational structure, constructed by agents and imbued with social meaning. Although Wendt placed emphasis on the mutual construction of the structure and the agent, especially in his earlier work, "The agent-structure problem in international relations theory," where he applied the structuration theory to provide the solution to the problem and argued for a reconceptualization of agents and structures as "mutually constituted or co-determined entities,"[36] it seems that the argument he forcefully made in the article, "Anarchy is what states make of it," leans somewhat more toward the agency, stressing agency, or more precisely agential intersubjectivity, as the creator of the structure. This constitutes a sharp contrast with the exclusive emphasis by neorealism and neoliberalism on the international structure.

The second characteristic feature of Wendtian constructivism is its epistemological similarity with neorealism and neoliberalism. Scientific realism provides the epistemological foundation for social constructivism and its essential assumptions, very much in line with transcendentalism, include "that the world exists independent of human beings, that mature scientific theories typically refer to this world, and that they do so even when the objects of science are unobservable."[37] Since the subject and the object are distinct and since the world and the knowledge about the world are separable and independent of each other, there is little problem for constructivism to use science to approach the reality, observable or unobservable, out there. Accordingly, Wendt has argued that there should not be a gulf between causation and constitution as some believe. He says: "Part of the gulf that separates positivists and post-positivists in social science stems, I believe, from a mistaken view of these two types of theorizing. Positivists think natural scientists do not do constitutive theory and so privilege causal theory; post-positivists think social scientists should not do causal theory and so privilege constitutive theory. But in fact all scientists do both kinds of theory; causal and constitutive theories simply ask different questions."[38] They are not contradictory, but closely related to each other, and may be inclusive of each other. When he discusses the different epistemological positions of scientific realism and empiricism, he has particularly pointed out the "unobservable causal mechanisms", i.e. those mechanisms "which make observable regularities

[35] Wendt 1992.   [36] Wendt 1987, 350.   [37] Wendt 1999, 47.   [38] Ibid., 77–78.

possible *work*."[39] This middle ground has led to some criticism that identifies Wendt with causal theorists; as Smith has said: "I read Wendt as seeing constitutive theory as a form of causal explanation."[40]

Constructivism started as a challenge to rationalistic mainstream IR theories especially through its idealist ontology and the debate has been quite heated between the two sides, which is called again an inter-paradigmatic debate after the one between neorealism and neoliberalism. However, a synthesis between rationalistic and constructivist theories seems to be well on the way when scientific/positive epistemology is repeatedly stressed. Wendtian constructivism has sought to enter the mainstream by identifying itself as a via media through its scientific positivism, and mainstream IR theorists have welcomed Wendt's demonstration that constructivism could be formulated in scientific terms and worked to make the seeming incompatibility compatible.[41] Clearly, they see that Wendtian constructivism has an underlying rationalistic assumption. Keohane has in fact made some interesting comments on Wendt's *Social Theory of International Politics*, saying:

> Perhaps surprisingly, he [Wendt] then accepts many of their [neorealists and neoliberalists] assumptions and arguments: that states exist prior to the system; that material interests and power (as well as institutions) are important causal factors; that meaningful science requires propositions that are potentially falsifiable with evidence. These admissions bring him substantially closer than his previous writing to what he calls "mainstream" IR, ...[42]

These important assumptions have made Keohane believe that "Wendt would just be a rationalist who had read Foucault."[43] Though Keohane holds that *Social Theory of International Politics* is somewhat away from the earlier Wendt and that Wendtian constructivism, as represented in the book, has a larger goal, the assumptions Keohane has mentioned have shown that structural constructivism does have obvious rationalistic connotations, which then enable it to be compatible with mainstream rationalistic theories in the United States. It is a success for Wendtian constructivism; it is also a success of Waltzianization; and it is perhaps even more a success for the worldview and philosophy behind the American mainstream IR theory.

By a similar logic, realists also see the compatibility of constructivism and realism, classical realism in particular. It is not merely about epistemology, but also, more fundamentally about ontology. Sterling-Folker holds that constructivism shares with realism an evolutionary ontology. For example, "Wendt's definition of the corporate identity contains an

---

[39] Wendt 1987, 354, emphasis in original.   [40] Smith 2000, 157.
[41] Keohane 2000, 126.   [42] Ibid., 125.   [43] Ibid.

implicit biological link because it 'refers to the intrinsic, self-organizing qualities that constitute actor individuality. For human beings, this means the body and experience of consciousness,'"[44] thus providing an ontological space for constructivism and realism to engage each other in a dialogue. Barkin suggests that elements of realism and constructivism should be combined to produce a new perspective for IR theory, which he calls "realist constructivism," for they have, despite their obvious differences, similar views in terms of the importance of power, the material understanding of human nature, the scientific approach, and the positivist orientation.[45] In other words, classic realism and constructivism share a lot in terms of ontology and epistemology and therefore their dialogue and fusion are conducive for theoretical development. *International Studies Review* organized a forum on a realist-constructivist dialogue, most of the contributors to which shared Barkin's basic contention that realism and constructivism are not as implacably opposed as has been imagined.[46]

A related question has been raised by the reflectivist/post-positivist theorists, although reflecting a critical rather than welcoming attitude, which basically denies the claim that the ontology in Wendtian constructivism agrees with that of post-positivism. Roxanne Lynn Doty believes that Wendt is no idealist, for he assumes that human nature is a material force and it is truly "puzzling as to how sociation, self-esteem, and transcendence can be considered material ..."[47] Furthermore, as Hayward Alker has pointed out, Wendt's insistence on the Cartesian dichotomy of idea and matter is the most serious problem for his theory. It is therefore not only Wendt's belief in science and his positivist methodology that have enabled his theory to merge with and converge into the mainstream, but, perhaps more essentially, because his ontological and epistemological dualism fits well into the Cartesian understanding of rationalism. In other words, it is his worldview. From the perspective of immanency which, as a most distinct feature of the Chinese philosophy and culture, holds that the body and the mind are always one and so are the material and ideational, this dichotomous worldview is perhaps the most serious problem with Wendt, for his constructivism first of all assumes that there is a transcendental omnipotence that separates the body and the mind, the material and the ideational, and the world and the knowledge about it. Fundamentally it is an issue of ontological as well as epistemological significance. When we look at the American mainstream IR theory, this dichotomy permeates.

---

[44] Sterling-Folker 2002, 90.   [45] Barkin 2003.
[46] "Forum," *International Studies Review* (2004) 6: 337–352.   [47] Doty 2000, 138.

The comments reviewed above have in fact shown a tendency for Wendtian constructivism and rationalistic mainstream theories to form another synthesis. While mainstream theorists see this opportunity mainly because of the epistemological compatibility, post-positivists question more the self-claimed idealistic ontology. Thus the positivist epistemology and the half-hearted idealism or even materialism in disguise are often said to be the main reason why Wendtian constructivism has successfully entered the American mainstream. It is even clearer with the publication of *Social Theory of International Politics* and some critics have noticed changes in Wendt's academic position, indicating that his later thinking is somewhat different from the important arguments in his earlier works, such as those in the "The agent-structure problem in international relations theory" and "Anarchy is what states make of it." In those earlier articles, the mutual construction is emphasized, as exemplified by his use of the structuration theory, a theory that tries to overcome dualism between the structure and agency and "to prevent the analytical separation of generative structures from the self-understandings and practices of human agents to prevent structural reification."[48] In his 1992 article, "Anarchy is what states make of it," intersubjectivity is very much emphasized, too. Anarchy is not a given, not a reality in the international system, but socially constructed configurations that are not "objective" like mountains or forests, and at the same time not "subjective" like dreams or flights of speculative fancy. They are, as most social scientists concede at the theoretical level, "intersubjective constructions."[49] In his 1999 book, he reiterates some of the important assumptions and arguments, but the theoretical gravity seems to have moved in favor of an overall meta-structure, which for constructivism is the distribution of ideas in the international system. A strong impression left by this work is that his emphasis on ontology leads to only one innovation, i.e. the change of Waltz's material distribution of capabilities into a non-material distribution of ideas. For this reason, Wendt's constructivism is no doubt a system-level theory. If we take into consideration what he has argued for the noncontradiction between the causal and the constitutive mechanisms, it is also an implicit causal theory linking the systemic factors and the unit behavior: The systemic structure of meaning constitutes the identities and consequently the interests of the agent,[50] which in turn cause the agent to behave in a certain and scientifically predictable way. Although Wendt has criticized rationalism, which he believes, correctly, constituted the hard core of neorealism and

---

[48] Wendt 1987, 355.   [49] Coulter 1982, 42–43, quoted in Wendt 1992, 406.
[50] Weldes 1996.

neoliberalism, the later agenda of the now mainstream constructivist research seems to have verified the tendency for a rationalistic-constructivist synthesis.

If we go some steps further, it seems to me that the success of Wendtian constructivism lies more deeply in the fact that there is an implicit but fundamental perspective: Individual actors are rational. From his earlier works, such as the highly influential "The agent-structure problem in international relations theory," Wendt assumes the structure and the agent as two separate entities in the first place, which go naturally back to the Western cultural and intellectual tradition of ontological individualism and, as such, have paved the way for his later structural theory of constructivism – assuming a self-organizing/independent individual agent at the unit level and a constitutive/causal structure at the international system level. This approach to the structure-agent problem is already very much a rationalistic approach, for it follows the structure-agent dichotomy and assumes the separation of the two in the first place. As Jackson and Nexon have pointed out:

Structurationism attempts to overcome the dichotomy between structure and agency, yet by developing terms like "co-constitution" and "co-determination," structuration theorists tend to reinforce the essential separateness of agents and structures. Two elements which are mutually constitutive are still two distinct elements.[51]

Separating the structure and the agent thus seems to be the first requirement for social theorizing at the systemic level. Then observing how the structure influences the terms of the agent is the approach to the construction of grand IR theory. To accomplish this process, a theorist, explicitly or implicitly, but necessarily, assumes the ontological significance of the individual as the unit *a priori* and her rationality as the necessary condition that makes the theoretical causal or constitutive mechanisms work. It is a deeply embedded way of thinking, which has permeated Wendtian constructivism and which became even more conspicuous when he intended to construct a grand systemic theory comparable to that of Waltz. It requires indeed a higher degree of reification of both the structure and the agent through the reification of international cultures.

As for reification, it is defined as the apprehension of human phenomena as if they were things, that is, in non-human or possibly supra-human terms. Wendt has cited appropriately the Berger-Luckmann definition, which is:

---

[51] Jackson and Nexon 1999, 295.

the apprehension of the products of human activity as if they were something else than human products – such as facts of nature, results of cosmic laws, or manifestations of divine will. Reification implies that man is capable of forgetting his own authorship of the human world, and further, that the dialectic between man, the producer, and his products is lost to consciousness. The reified world is, by definition, a dehumanized world. It is experienced by man as a strange facticity, an *opus alienum* over which he has no control rather than as the *opus proprium* of his own productive activity.[52]

In Wendtian constructivism, there are actually two levels of reification. At the systemic level, his discussion of the three cultures of anarchy, i.e. the Hobbesian, the Lockean, and the Kantian cultures, in fact, reifies the three cultures to an extent that is reminiscent of the rationalistic understanding of anarchy as an objective reality in the international relations universe. They are created by agents, but once created, have independent force over agents. Then it goes on to tell the reader that these are the structures of the international system which constitute states as units of the system. Meanwhile, at the unit level, the agent is also reified as more an object constituted and caused by the structure. The one-to-one correspondence of the three cultures to three kinds of agent's identity, the Hobbesian to enemies, the Lockean to rivals, and the Kantian to friends, makes the reification even more salient. As such, a divide between two entities – the structure and the agent – is completed. Again we have this familiar systemic theory of IR with the causal or causally constitutive direction from the system level to the unit level, no matter whether the system-level factors are explicitly or implicitly causal. It is true that Wendt's constitutive effect of the systemic factors has more to do with the construction of the identities and interests of state actors, but it is an extended causal chain that does not stop at the assumption of the *a priori* identities and interests, but goes way back to the formation of such identities and interests. It tries to answer the "what-question" *for* the "why-question." In the final analysis, a carefully organized and top-down theory fits well into what Waltz has defined as "the theory of international politics." It is therefore correctly termed "structural constructivism," which successfully changes the neorealist logic of "structural selection" and the neoliberal logic of "institutional selection" into a logic of "cultural selection." But this culture is not the culture defined in terms of background knowledge over a long history of practice of a community, but the cultures represented by a rationalistic mind in their reified forms of the Hobbesian, the Lockean, and the Kantian, a culture cut off from history, from practice, and from agency.

---

[52] Berger and Luckmann 1966, 89. See also Wendt 1999, 76.

An illustrative example is provided by the study of international norms as the most mature research agenda following the "constructivist turn"[53] in IR theory to date. Numerous articles and books have been published. It is readily understandable, for constructivism focuses on identity and interest formation and rests itself comfortably at the system level. The international norm, a distinct non-material factor at the system level, is a perfect phenomenon for setting up a constructivist agenda and carrying out scientific investigation. Since constructivism does not accept the invariability of identity of the state, what constitutes such identity is naturally a research question and a starting point as well for the constructivist approach.[54] Studies on and around international norms have so conspicuously appeared in mainstream IR journals, covering the whole life cycle of norms and including their formation, growth, spreading, and demise.[55] The focus, however, is how international norms shape the identity and interest of the state and therefore the behavior of the state, for "[n]orms ... constitute[] states/agents, providing them with understandings of their interest."[56] Norms have thus become a key independent and explanatory variable at the systemic level. With many prominent constructivist scholars as contributors, Peter Katzenstein edited an influential volume in 1996, using the traditional issue of national security but focusing on the role of norms and identities.[57] Finnemore published her work the same year, arguing that international norms embedded and promoted by international organizations shape and reshape state identities and interests through norm teaching. In a norm context, state actors follow the logic of appropriateness rather than the logic of consequences.[58] Finnemore's study is very much of a structural theory, identifying international norms, an element at the system level, as the independent variable, and interests of the state or other international actor, an element at the unit level, as the dependent variable. The most important argument of social constructivism, i.e. the mutual construction of structure and agency has almost completely disappeared, and the one-way causal/constitutive direction has ushered the constructivist study of norms well into the mainstream analytical framework for grand IR theory construction.

The journal of *International Organization* has helped since the mid-1990s set the agenda on the study of international norms, obviously

---

[53] Checkel 1998.   [54] Klotz and Lynch 2007.
[55] The journal of *International Organization* (59, Fall 2005), for example, carried a group of articles, focusing on the socializing role of international institutions. The five empirical articles provided a detailed study of the European Union as a socializer and norm spreader in various respects.
[56] Checkel 1998, 326.   [57] Katzenstein 1996.   [58] Finnemore 1996.

encouraged by the constructivist turn and committed to promoting the research effort on norms.[59] In the presentation of an overall design in norm spreading in Europe, Jeffrey Checkel raises the question of how international norms are spread and defines international institutions as the promoter and individual states as norm takers through socialization, thus determining the independent variable (norms embodied in international institutions), the intervening variable (socialization), and the dependent variable (norm acceptance).[60] The European Union itself is often named a "normative power." Many more articles, mainly case studies, have been published, unfolding a panoramic analysis of international norms. Most of them have at least the fundamental assumption of the constructive treatment of international norms: They work to shape and reshape the identities and interests of state agents.[61] However, despite their explicitly claimed opposition to rationalism, such studies have at least implicit rationalistic assumptions and connotations. It goes in fact back to the 1989 work by Friedrich Kratochwil, which examines "the role of norms in international life." Kratochwil has made three assumptions: First, rules and norms are guidance devices "which are designated to simplify choices and impart 'rationality' to situations by delineating the factors that a decision-maker has to take into account;"[62] second, norms, in addition to the role as guidance devices, are "the means which allow people to pursue goals, share meanings, communicate with each other, criticize assertions, and justify actions;" and third, rules and norms influence choices through a reasoning process, which is beyond the instrumental rationality and more about value-oriented practical reasoning.[63] Whatever norms are, they work first of all because norm-following individuals are "self-propelling, self-subsistent entities, pursuing internalized norms given in advance and fixed for the duration of the action sequence under investigation."[64] It is therefore clear that the study of international norms under the label of social constructivism assumes both individuality and rationality, explicitly or implicitly.

---

[59] See Klotz 1995.   [60] Checkel 2005, 801–826.
[61] There are exceptions, which include studies that find that norms at levels lower than the system play an important role. For example, Legro argued that the focus on the international system level neglected norms at the regional, national, and subnational levels. Acharya compared the spreading of two international norms at the regional level – cooperative security and humanitarian intervention, and finds that the former was accepted by the ASEAN nations while the latter was not, mainly because the former fitted well into the normative structure of the region while the latter did not. See Legro 1997; Acharya 2004.
[62] Kratochwil 1989, 10.   [63] Ibid., 11–12.   [64] Embirbayer 1997, 284.

Constructivists of various strands argue that the key difference between constructivism on the one hand and neorealism and neoliberalism on the other lies in their different ontologies. Norms, as shared and institutionalized ideas, are said to constitute identities and interests, rather than merely regulate behavior.[65] However, from most of the studies on international norms, we can see that an easier way to understand it is that norms as a structural element *causally* constitute the unit identities and interests, and therefore, *constitutively* cause state behaviors. As we see in *Social Theory of International Politics* as well as in *Theory of International Politics* and *After Hegemony*, a structural theory requires at least two variables, one at the system level and the other at the unit level respectively. It also needs a causal or disguised causal link between them. The agent, through its own "rationality," loses its agency and becomes the passive receiver who changes in accordance with the change of the systemic element, which is an exogenous factor placed on them through either teaching or learning, willingly or unwillingly, and which makes them behave as an economic person does in a market. It is the systemic force that socializes her to be such a person and behave as such. To successfully complete this process of theorizing toward a meta-theory, there must be an underlying assumption. It is individualistic rationality, instrumental or substantive. If this is not so clear in Wendt's structural constructivism, it is most conspicuous throughout the agenda of the study of international norms. The first of the mechanisms in Checkel's norm socialization design is "strategic calculation,"[66] meaning that following norms brings benefits. Although Checkel does not take it as socialization if it works alone, it definitely plays a role in norm acceptance and works as the first step in the process of norm socialization. Finnemore's discussion on UNESCO also tells us that developing countries are rewarded materially from their obedience to norms represented and promoted by international organizations.[67] Thus an element of rationality is always involved in the constructivist agenda of norm studies as a necessary link between the structure and the agent, indicating that materially self-organized individual actors, natural and corporate, are socialized by international norms to make rational decisions. It is the rationality based on norms, or "normative rationality." As in the previous neo-neo synthesis, we have a different independent variable at the system level, norms this time, and units with normative rationality to complete a paradigm of IR.

[65] Ruggie 1999.   [66] Checkel 2005.   [67] Finnemore 1996.

A Transatlantic Rapprochement

The success of Wendtian constructivism and the focus on the study of international norms seem to have introduced yet another similar tendency: the possible convergence of the English School with the American mainstream IR theory. The English School has developed around a key concept, that is, "international society," quite a unique perspective which has turned out to be the most important theoretical contribution of the English School IR theory and distinguished it from American mainstream theories.[68] However, the debate between the two started in the 1960s more as one over methodology, usually referred to as the second debate or the debate between the traditionalists represented by Hedley Bull and the behaviorists represented by some American IR scholars such as David Singer and Morton Kaplan.

Bull's attack on American positivists was quite merciless. However, the focus of his criticism of the American IR was not about the substances, but its methodological approach.[69] In his well-known article, "International theory: the cases for a classical approach," he argued strongly for the traditionalist approach and listed seven dimensions which the scientific approach failed. His emphasis was no doubt on the methodological position taken by American behaviorists like Kaplan and Deutsch. He did not believe such an approach could contribute to IR and was not entitled to replace the classical approach which he advocated and which he believed was one that followed the traditions of philosophy, history, and law.[70] He argued, "the scientific approach is likely to contribute very little to the theory of international relations, and in so far as it is intended to encroach upon and ultimately displace the classical approach, it is positively harmful."[71] He further advised that IR scholars should turn a deaf ear to the scientific methodology that was rising in the United States.[72] The debate was heated in fact by the counter-attack from the scientific camp, as Kaplan said: "Those traditionalists who have done a significant amount of historical research – and they are the exceptions – confine themselves largely to problems of diplomatic history that are unrelated to their generalizations about international politics."[73]

---

[68] Buzan 2001, 471. Many of the influential books by English School scholars have discussed and refined this central concept of "international society," enabling it to be a distinct theoretical concept with strong historical connotations. In fact many of the books contain this concept in the book titles. See Bull and Watson 1984; Watson 1992; Stern 1995; Roberson 1998. For a more recent discussion of the English School, see Linklater and Suganami 2006.

[69] Bull 1969, 38.   [70] Dunne 1998, 118–119.   [71] Bull 1969, 26.

[72] Dunne 1998, 122.   [73] Kaplan 1969, 56.

This line of comments on the nature of the debate between English School scholars and American behaviorists has been largely followed later on. Tim Dunne has argued that the first opponent among English School scholars to the unity of science is in fact E.H. Carr, who "recognised that in the process of analysing facts, social scientists transformed them. His recognition of no value-free enquiry in the social sciences received universal assent in the British Committee."[74] Andrew Hurrell has followed Bull closely and dwelled on the significance of "[k]eeping history, law and political philosophy firmly within the English School." He has argued that Bull took a method for his investigation of international relations that combined analytical and historical approaches.[75] Barry Buzan has also summarized, in a very much refined way, the characteristic features of the English School as methodological pluralism, historicism, and constructivism. He has particularly reminded the reader of the importance of methodological pluralism as a defining feature of the English School. After discussing the tripartite of the international system, international society, and world society, and the different methodological approaches related respectively to each, i.e. positivism to international system, hermeneutics and interpretivism to international society, and critical theory to world society, as presented by Richard Little, he emphasizes: "It is this explicitly pluralist (or multiple rather than competing paradigms) methodological approach that underpins the distinctiveness of the English School as an approach to the study of IR."[76] On the other hand, American social scientists have continued to criticize sharply the English School for its methodological pluralism. For mainstream American IR theorists, the methodological unity of science is an unnegotiable tenet, which seeks uniformities and laws beyond time and space.[77] The English School is unlikely to become a grand theory as Buzan has wished, for "[I]t would seem that grand theory requires a degree of cohesion and discipline that is antithetical to the methodological pluralism which has characterized English School work and which Buzan views as one of its strongest virtues."[78]

Whatever differences exist between the English School and the American mainstream, the methodological one has been admitted and even stressed or overstressed by many. However, methodological differences may not be a necessary condition for the incommensurability of two theories. The argument of positivism to international system, hermeneutics and interpretivism to international society, and critical approach to world society cannot stand because these different methodologies may

---

[74] Dunne 1998, 119.   [75] Hurrell 2001, 489.   [76] Buzan 2001, 476.
[77] Neufeld 1995, 34–35.   [78] Finnemore 2001, 509.

well be used for any study of social life. Wendt embraces scientific realism and tries to say that it can go well with the ideational ontology. American mainstream IR scholars, for example, have used extensively their scientific method to study international norms within the theoretical frame of social constructivism. Furthermore, as Tim Dunne has pointed out, the methodological differences may not be the only element in the debate.[79] In the interpretation by Buzan of methodological pluralism, it is pluralistic because it can embrace and include positivism. The more significant difference between the English School and the American mainstream in fact lies in the intellectual substance of the former, which is typically represented by the concept, or the big idea, of "international society." For me it is this intellectual substance that constitutes the metaphysical component of a theoretical hard core and that underlies and sustains the distinct characteristic of the English School.

In this sense, Buzan has quite correctly pointed out, "the main thrust of the English School so far has been to establish the Grotian/Rationalist element by developing the concept of international society."[80] It is this idea of international society that has enabled the English School to distinguish itself, especially from the American mainstream, which until the 1990s had focused more on the international system and been busy with establishing systemic grand theories like neorealism and neoliberalism. For this concept of international society, Bull's classic definition is:

A *society of states* (or international society) exists when a group of states, conscious of certain common interests and common values, form a society in the sense that they conceive themselves to be bound by a common set of rules in their relations with one another, and share in the working of common institutions.[81]

Such a definition involves a strong privilege for rules, values, institutions, and norms over merely material forces, which is also the key difference between an international society and an international system. As Bull has said, an international society presupposes an international system: The former has the distinct features of any society, such as values, rules, and institutions that tie members together, while the latter can be a mere billiard table type or an amalgamation of states which "may be in contact with each other and interact in such a way as to be necessary factors in each other's calculations without their being conscious of common interests or values, conceiving themselves to be bound by a common set of rules, or cooperating in the working of common institutions."[82] Although it is actually impossible to take the international system and international

[79] Dunne 1998, 124.   [80] Buzan 2001, 476.   [81] Bull 1977, 13, emphasis in original.
[82] Ibid.

society as two discrete entities because they are inseparable in reality, the strong normative inclination of Bull's discussion of international society, as well as his understanding of the nature of social theory, constitutes a sharp contrast with that of Kenneth Waltz, whose structural realism denies almost any place of values and norms in IR theorizing.

In this respect, later English School scholars are similar, showing a strong normative tendency in their work and taking it as one of the most important features of the School.[83] When Buzan and his colleagues made great efforts to expand the concept of international society to a world society through serious historical studies, the unit of analysis changed accordingly. "In the ontological sense, world society starts from individuals and is in clear contrast to the state-based ontology of international society."[84] But the distinctive normative preference has continued and been even more conspicuously emphasized, whether it is an international society of states or a world society of individuals. For example, Buzan and Little in their monumental work entitled *International Systems in World History* distinguish between two systems, the mechanical and the socially constructed. The former is basically material, while the latter is composed of sentient units. They say:

When units are sentient, how they perceive each other is a major determinant of how they interact. If the units share a common identity (a religion or a language), or even just a common set of rules or norms (about how to determine relative status, and how to conduct diplomacy), then these intersubjective understandings not only condition their behavior, but also define the boundary of a social system.[85]

However a tendency appeared when Wendtian constructivism success-fully joined the American mainstream IR theory, and together with it the constructivist study of international norms has been firmly and vigor-ously established as a major research agenda for the American main-stream. Then there comes a tendency of rapprochement between the English School and the American mainstream via the "via media" of Wendtian constructivism. Some believe that such a rapprochement is due to the fact that the English School and the American mainstream IR both have been moving toward the middle ground. Wæver has, for example, made the following comments:

The English School is a respectable and historical approach which includes quasi-philosophical and historical reflection, and especially it interrogates deep institutions in the system. Thus, it can relatively easily be linked to more or less post-modernist notions, an emphasis on the cultural colouring of international

---

[83] Vincent 1986.   [84] Buzan 2001, 477.   [85] Buzan and Little 2000, 104.

systems and especially the general "radical" interest in thinking the basic categories of the international system instead of taking them as mechanical givens. At the same time, the classics of the English School, especially Bull's *Anarchical Society* is a comprehensive, seemingly straightforward discussion of the actual system with relatively clear, operational concepts. Thus, the American mainstream can find a moderate way to extend its institutionalism in a not too dangerous way by using Bull (and reading him almost as a regime theorist or neoliberal institutionalist). The new wave of English School enthusiasm thus ties in with the attempted *rapprochement* between reflectivists and rationalists, with the deradicalisation of reflectivism and the rephilosophisation of the rationalists.[86]

Wæver has perhaps thought more along the methodological line and thus used the rationalistic-reflectivist categorization, as Keohane did, in discussing the American mainstream theory and the English School. To some extent, it is true. More importantly, however, it is related to the concept of international society, which is an intellectual construct rather than a methodological choice. The English School invented this important concept differently from that of their American counterparts, which made the world of international relations look different: Whether the world should be taken as a billiard table system with discrete units or as a society with units connected by norms and institutions does make a difference for the study of world politics. The American mainstream has accepted the English School neither because both are moving toward the middle ground, nor because both are beginning to embrace a methodological eclecticism marked by the deradicalization of reflectivism and the rephilosophization of rationalism. In fact, positivists in the American mainstream have up to date continued not to recognize the English School as a scientific theory. A more important reason for such a rapprochement is perhaps that IR communities across the Atlantic are beginning to share a similar agenda, which has enabled the two approaches to come together.

This agenda is the study of international norms. It used to be the distinctive feature of the English School, differentiating it from the American mainstream IR theory. It is no longer so. Since Wendtian constructivism successfully entered the rank of American mainstream IR theory and became one of the big three, the agenda of the international norm study has been established as one of the most important and conspicuous areas for scholarly pursuit. Wendt's *Social Theory of International Politics* in 1999 placed great emphasis on the social and his middle ground in terms of ontology and epistemology enabled his theory to be one of the three main paradigms in the American IR literature and at

---

[86] Wæver 1996, 169–170, emphasis in original.

the same time sacrificed as an opportunity cost the fundamental assumptions in his earlier works, such as "The agent-structure problem in international relations theory" and "Anarchy is what states make of it."[87] As discussed above, culture is reified into the Hobbesian, Lockean, and Kantian international cultures, which as an overall independent variable determines the order of the system, the identities of the units, and therefore their interest and behavior. More specifically, a clearly pivotal concept is no doubt the international norm, which reflects the essence of the international cultures interpreted by Wendt. Later developments of social constructivism in the American academic circles have witnessed very much a focus on international norms. Numerous research papers have then been published to enrich the agenda of international norm studies. The international norm, like its predecessors of power distribution and international institutions, has become a new academic attraction because it makes the reified international culture have a more specified and operational concept, tangible and testable. It is not only a problem of, as Smith has questioned, whether or not the study of the social can be "scientific," but also a problem of materializing the non-material, as Doty has argued. Through such efforts, the concept of "international society" has become a more universally accepted and promoted idea of international studies across the Atlantic. At least it has gone beyond Europe and joined the American mainstream in the new IR research agenda.

English School scholars have fairly successfully realized this commonality. Buzan argues that there has already been the linkage and interplay between American constructivism and the English School concepts of international and world society, and that there has been some linkage between the English School and those engaged in International Political Economy (IPE), regime theory, and globalization. Of course, he believes that the English School should "make more substantial inroads into the US IR community than has been the case thus far," especially in terms of the centrality of norms, rules, and institutions to both approaches.[88] American constructivists have at the same time recognized the influence of the English School in their theorizing, especially the effort to add to IR theory important social elements, which have almost no place in the rationalistic theories of neorealism and neoliberalism. Wendt acknowledged the contribution of the English School when he said that the English School treats the international system as a society governed by shared norms and is therefore the forerunner of contemporary constructivist IR theory.[89]

---

[87] Wendt 1999.   [88] Buzan 2001, 484.   [89] Wendt 1999, 31.

The rise of social constructivism in the United States and the establishment of the research agenda on international norms have created the opportunity for the transatlantic rapprochement. Studies on norms seem to be moving toward another ambition for a grand theory. Again, we have a familiar structure of international norms which, through individualistic rationality, shape and reshape the identities, interests, and therefore behavior of the units. This "normative rationalism" stresses that international norms select through the rationality of the agent. As I have argued, such a grand theory requires ontological individualism which assumes that the independent individual agent is rational. Rationality can be instrumental, institutional, normative, or in any other form. No matter what form it takes, it is the root of the metaphysical component of the theoretical hard core that informs much of the mainstream IR theory. The transatlantic rapprochement is realized mainly because they share, to a large extent, a metaphysical component in their theoretical hard core: ontological individualism and epistemological rationalism. It is not a mere methodological concept. It is a deeply embedded worldview. No matter whether it is *realpolitik* rationalism, liberal rationalism, or normative rationalism, they have a common denominator, which is exactly the historical and cultural sediment of the West. It is important not only to see the ramifications of this denominator, but also to be clear about the denominator itself. The methodological differences continue to exist, but the metaphysical component of the theoretical hard core seems to show increasing similarity. Hence, the transatlantic rapprochement.

Conclusion

What then has enabled the process of paradigmatic synthesization to materialize? Why is there the interesting phenomenon that IR theories, once aiming at a grand theory, go gradually together even though they started as if they were irreconcilable challenges to the existing dominant theory? From the above discussion of the three rapprochements, I tend to conclude that it is because these grand theories share a common metaphysical component in their theoretical hard cores, which is ontological individualism together with epistemological rationalism. It is an essential element of the sediment from the "Enlightenment dream" and the vital part of background knowledge that defines Western culture particularly since the Enlightenment.

Constructing a grand theory in IR has followed this rationale deeply embedded in the cultural condition and forcefully reinforced by Waltzian neorealism. It is the so-called systemic theorizing. It has an irreconcilable and deeply rooted worldview: The world is composed of structures and units. The structures can be material and ideational, and the agents can be natural and corporate, but the two entities, the structure and the unit, are indispensable. This kind of theory has at least several requirements. It must assume ontological individualism, meaning that the individual is an independent entity and exists in a structure that is over her and can be separate from her ontologically. At the same time, it must assume epistemological rationalism. For any structural forces to work on the individual agent, the latter should have three essential attributes: First, the agent is an independent entity, able to stand by and for itself; second, it must be able to reason, no matter how passive and even hopeless once she is within the structural frame; and third, all units should be alike and what makes them alike is rationality. Their reasoning can be instrumentally rational, which defines the rationalistic IR approach, and it can also be value-oriented, or normatively rational, which defines the constructive approach and much of the English School literature. Theories that refuse this fundamental worldview are almost impossible to converge with the mainstream, as more radical post-modernist theories have shown.

People may argue that many theories which are inside the mainstream category do not insist on this worldview and try to look at the irrational or non-rational dimensions of international relations. Graham Allison has, for example, discussed three models of decision-making, two of which, the organizational and the governmental models, are considered at least non-rational.[90] In fact, Allison's decision-makers are all rational, and instrumentally rational, actors. He used the concept of "economic man" for his rational actor model, which requires clear goals and objectives, good judgment about alternative policy proposals, logical consideration of possible consequences, and ability to make rational choices to maximize the decision-maker's interests.[91] Using the same logic, decision-makers in all three of Allison's models are rational whether they are organizational officers or governmental bureaucrats: They are rational at different levels. The governmental bureaucrats, for example, are rational from the perspectives of their respective agencies and they rationally equal their goals and objectives to the national ones. Furthermore, if Allison's study is more at the micro-level and rationality is more a quality of individual decision-makers, then a systemic theory like neorealism requires individual rationality as a pivot to enable the theory to work and find regularities so as to qualify it as a grand theory.

I am not arguing that ontological individualism and epistemological rationality are wrong. They have grown out of the background knowledge

---

[90] Allison 1977.   [91] Ibid., 29–30.

of the cultural practices of Western societies and become highly representational knowledge especially since the dawn of modernization of the West. As a core concept, it has helped to establish abstract theories of the ideal type in many fields of academic pursuit. A worldview that combines ontological individualism and epistemological rationalism thus has made great contributions to intellectual inquiry and academic progress. Because of the leading role of the West in the process of modernization, and because this worldview grasps some essential dimensions of human activity, it has gone far beyond the geographical boundary and gained global influence. It came from the background knowledge, became the foreground and representational knowledge, and then completed its glorious retreat to the background which many have believed and applied even without being conscious of it.

The mainstream IR theory is thus not only something we should criticize, but also something we should learn from. It relies heavily on concepts, such as individualistic rationality, deeply embedded in the culture where it is born and grows, and uses such concepts to be the nucleus to shape its theoretical hard core. It is easy to see how the concept of rationality, a key concept for much of mainstream IR theory as well as for many social theories in the West, has been excavated, explored, and exploited. During the long process of its development, it has been repeatedly refined to help form theories in various fields, from economics to sociology to IR. Individuality, another key concept in the Western culture, has not only contributed remarkably to theory construction, but also to business management, social development, and political progress. It has also contributed to human liberty. The independent and self-conscious individual, armed with rationality, has become the symbol of modernization. It is indeed the "modern man," or an ideal type in the West.

Hence my question: If we should purposefully take an alternative worldview to look at the international relations universe, and if we should acquire such an alternative by consulting a different menu from some different cultural background knowledge to form the metaphysical component of our theoretical hard core, then how should the world look and what kind of theory could we construct? This is the question to which I will try to find some answers in the following chapters.

Part II

Relation and Relationality

5   A World of Relations

If rationality nurtures the metaphysical component of Western mainstream IR theories, then relationality may well be its counterpart in Confucian communities, both having sociocultural origins and both having values of application beyond their respective geo-cultural boundaries. Relationality is a characteristic element of the background knowledge that has been formed and evolved in practice and over history in the Confucian cultural sphere, which sees the world as one of relations and the social world as one of human relations. I use this concept to constitute the metaphysical component of the hard core for a relational theory of world politics because it represents a worldview, a way of thinking and doing, and a perspective that differs from those mainstream IR theories which take individualistic rationality as their theoretical nucleus.[1] In this chapter I will outline a relational theory of world politics centered on the concept of relationality by defining the key concept of "relation," discussing actors as relators and delineating some underlying assumptions sustaining the relational theory. I first of all raise very much an ontological question: What is the world? Put it in a different way, how is the world perceived? I believe that culture nurtures worldviews, which in turn help understand and interpret the world in general, the social world included. Then I will discuss three key concepts: relations, relators, and relational webs.

Relations and Human Relations

A World of Relations

The relational theory rests on the fundamental assumption: The world is a universe of relatedness. It is true of both the natural and the social worlds. In the natural world, everything is related to everything else; in the

[1] Qin 2009a.

social world, everyone to everyone else; and across the natural and social worlds humans and things are also related. Together they constitute a whole cosmos. It looks different from the world perceived and conceived by mainstream Western IR theories, for at the metaphysical level such a Confucian world is visualized as composed of continuous events and ongoing relations rather than substantial objects and discrete entities. If we use a chessboard as an example, the Chinese see more the lines that link the pieces rather than the pieces themselves. This relatedness decides that relations are real and important. In other words, without relations nothing would happen and the world would be a non-world.

The fluid and moving relations provide the dynamics of this cosmos and therefore there is no need for exterior forces to empower it. Since all are related to all, there is nothing that is not related. In fact there is no such a thing as a transcendental being, principle, or force that is above this interrelated whole and decides for actors entangled in the relational context therein. Hall and Ames define strict transcendence in the following way, "*A* is transcendent with respect to *B* if the existence, meaning, or import of *B* cannot be fully accounted for without resource to *A*, but the reverse is not true." They argue further that the Anglo-European philosophical tradition requires the presumption of this strict definition of transcendence and therefore they have an all-mighty and all-rational God.[2] For the Chinese, however, the concept of transcendence is alien and, accordingly, there is no such thing as an absolute rational mind that transcends the relational complexity. The Chinese do not have an absolute God that is omnipresent, omnipotent, and omniscient; rather the Chinese worship their ancestors because they are intimately related even though the ancestors are no longer in this world. The intimate relationship guarantees that the ancestors in the other world will bring to their offspring in this world auspicious luck and good fortune. Their worship rests on thinking from relations rather than on relying on supernatural forces. This is the Confucian cosmos, which Hall and Ames describe as an immanent cosmos – everything is in everything else and all are related to one another as well as to the context, and correlativity is the most significant word in this world.[3] Ontological substantialism provides a deeply embedded worldview that has biased the Western mainstream IR theory toward an international relations universe composed of discrete objects and self-subsistent actors. From a relational perspective, however, the world represents itself always as a complexly relational whole in which actors live and co-live, act and interact.

---

[2] Hall and Ames 1998, 190.   [3] Hall and Ames 1987, 12–17.

For a relational theory of world politics, it is necessary to define the key concept of "relation" explicitly and clearly so that it can constitute the metaphysical component of its theoretical hard core. The term of "relation" is in fact as old as the existence of human beings and discussion of relations can also be dated back to ages ago. Moreover, relational thinking has been seen in many social writers in both the West and the East. Mustafa Emirbayer, for example, discusses the two approaches of social studies: substantialism and relationalism, believing that Heraclitus, Marx, Simmel, and Foucault reveal a clear relational tendency, more often than not mixed up with substantialism, while John Dewey and Norbert Elias are the two scholars on whom Emirbayer himself as an advocate for a relational sociology has drawn heavily.[4] Business practitioners have long understood the importance of relations and usually established a special unit in their firms called "public relations." And in many countries governments have followed suit.

A highly systematic and in-depth study on relational approaches in sociology in recent years is perhaps Mustafa Emirbayer's "Manifesto for a Relational Sociology," which outlines a relational/transactional perspective for the study of social phenomena. He argues that in sociology the most important issue is not "material versus ideal," "structure versus agency," and "individual versus society," but substantialism versus relationalism.[5] His relational perspective is established as a criticism of and an alternative to substantialism, which holds that "it is the substances of various kinds (things, beings, essences) that constitute the fundamental units of all inquiry. Systematic analysis is to begin with these self-subsistent entities, which come 'preformed,' and only then to consider the dynamic flows in which they are subsequently involved themselves."[6] For substantialists, relation "is not independent of the concept of the real being; it can only add supplementary and external modifications to the latter, such as do not affect its real 'nature'."[7] Emirbayer's relational perspective constitutes a sharp contrast to substantialism by reversing its basic assumptions and "depict[ing] social reality instead in dynamic, continuous, and processual terms."[8] For his purpose, Emirbayer, very much inspired by John Dewey, and perhaps North Whitehead, defines and characterizes relations implicitly and explicitly in the following way. First, relations are connections between terms or units, linking persons, places, meanings, and events.[9] Second, relations are multiple overlapping and intersecting socio-spatial networks, for society itself is a relational

---

[4] Emirbayer 1997.   [5] Ibid., 282.   [6] Ibid., 283–284.   [7] Ibid., 284.   [8] Ibid., 281.
[9] Ibid., 294.

setting. Third, relations are transactional processes,[10] which are ever unfolding and ongoing rather than static ties among inert substances. The terms or units "involved in a transaction derive their meaning, significance, and identity from the (changing) functional roles they play within that transaction."[11] In short, to be relational is to be transactional. Relations as connections, networks, and processes play the most important role in society and therefore should be the key to social analysis.

In the IR literature, it is Patrick Jackson and Daniel Nexon who have done the pioneering work in proposing a theory of "processual relationalism" (the p/r approach as they term it), drawing on Emirbayer's monumental work on relational sociology. Like Emirbayer, they do not explicitly define relations, perhaps taking it for granted that it is a concept too familiar to be clarified. From their discussion, however, it is clear that the concept of "relation" is largely similar to what Emirbayer implies in his 1997 article but with more emphasis on what they call "reification." They also structure a dualistic contrast between substantialism and relationalism in the beginning and define their processual relationalism as follows:

Relationalism, on the other hand, treats configurations of ties – recurrent sociocultural interaction – between social aggregates of various sorts and their component parts as the building blocks of social analysis (Tilly 1996: 2). These configurations of ties give rise to what we normally refer to as entities. Because ties are not static "things," but ongoing processes, a more accurate term for this kind of analysis is processual relationalism (hereafter, simply "p/r").[12]

It is fairly clear here that relations are ties between social aggregates and their component parts. They are no longer something like the milieu or background against which entities interact; rather they are dynamic, creative, and transformative. Furthermore Jackson and Nexon have introduced four key concepts for their p/r approach: processes, configurations, projects, and yoking. Processes are defined as "a causally or functionally linked set of occurrences or events which produce a 'change in the complexion of reality'."[13] They in turn define processes in world politics as they say, "many processes in world politics can be conceptualized as 'ties' between entities. Examples might include circulating currency, extracting revenue, prosecuting war and bargaining." Thus relations are ties between entities, even though, unlike the substantialist assumption that entities come before processes, they argue that "entities do not exist absent processes and relations and (most) processes and relations do not exist without entities."[14] The concept of configuration is defined as

---

[10] As for a philosophical discussion on process, see Whitehead 2010; Lowe 1966.
[11] Ibid., 287.   [12] Jackson and Nexon 1999, 292.   [13] Ibid., 302   [14] Ibid., 304.

"a particular pattern of ties and/or processes."[15] The configuration of sets of processes and its special form is "projects," referring in particular to reified configurations with agency,[16] which is perhaps the most meaningful component of the p/r approach. Thus, relations are implicitly defined and interpreted as ties related to the concept of processes. Sometimes they are used interchangeably, for configuration is defined as a particular pattern of processes and also as social relations.[17]

The p/r approach in fact places emphasis on a particular type of relationship, the relationship between reified processes (configurations) and entities, arguing that entities are formed and/or transformed by such processes. There is, hence, the argument of "relations before states." The valuable insight is that entity formation becomes a research question and the state, for example, in international relations is definitely not a given fact but an entity that should be problematized. It is thus necessary first to question how the state is formed. Based upon the first three concepts of processes, configurations, and projects, Jackson and Nexon use the concept of "yoking" to discuss how entities are formed, for "the existence and persistence of such entities must be accounted for in a theoretically informed fashion."[18] They further use "yoking" to mean the connection of two or more proto-boundaries (sites of differences) to form an entity and rationalization of such an entity mainly through discourse so that it becomes formalized with properties and attributes. It is exactly by this reasoning that processes produce entities, as historical processes have produced the state in international relations.

The theory of relational sociology by Emirbayer and the logic of the p/r approach by Jackson and Nexon are both highly inspiring. Their emphasis on the ontological significance of dynamic and ongoing social processes, their way of linking processes with entities, and their reconceptualization of such key concepts in social life as power, equality, and the structure-agency problematic, cast new light on the study of world politics in general and on my relational theory in particular. However, there are some problems inherent in their discussion.

First, neither of them has explicitly and clearly defined the key concept of "relation." They use the term throughout their discussion sometimes interchangeably with processes and sometimes not. They used "ties" and "connections," seemingly to refer to and even be interchangeable with "relations." But such terms are still so elusive that it is not easy to grasp the connotations of the concept of "relation" as it is. The concept of "relation" is therefore too general to be workable. We still need to ask the fundamental question: What is relation?

[15] Ibid., 304.   [16] Ibid., 292.   [17] Ibid., 306.   [18] Ibid., 307.

What does relation mean in social life? And what is its role in international relations? Second, it is essentially entities that are related. In other words, relations refer to ties between entities although such entities are created by processes. Once created by processes the entity becomes at least for the moment an independent being or thing, which is the product of the joint effort of processes through the mysterious yoking. Substantialists believe in the pre-existent and self-subsistent entity, while Emirbayer and Jackson/Nexon believe in the process-produced entity. Their entities are still entities that can stand alone with their properties and attributes. They are related, but not immanent to each other, while those in the Confucian cosmos are first of all immanent. Being externally related differs fundamentally from being immanently related. Third, especially with Jackson and Nexon, relations refer more to something between the aggregates and the units, or between the "yoked processes" and the entities. Such a relationship is actually one between the creator and the created. The revolutionary contribution is that the dynamic and transformative aggregates defined in terms of reified processes give rise to an entity, such as the nation-state in world politics. However, there is something familiar if one thinks about structuralism: Processes replace structures and perform a similar function in entity formation, including identities, properties, and attributes of the entities. In this one-way traffic, we are not clear about the agency of the units in such processes: They seem to be passively created at a particular historical moment *by chance* when some processes happen to have some powerful yoking effects. From a structural or quasi-structural perspective, relations or processes are before actors, but from an agential perspective, relations cannot come before actors.

In addition, and perhaps most relevantly here, the concept of relation is basically non-human. For Emirbayer, "relation" is a general term: It tends to be highly general and may involve human and non-human factors. Fundamentally, however, it does not take human relations as the key. It is similar for Jackson and Nexon, in whose study the human element is further reduced. The yoking effect that finally produces the entity is basically a temporo-spatial chance with few human elements involved. In other words, nothing would happen if the necessary processes were not related perhaps by chance. Relations among humans and human actors, including corporate human actors such as nation-states in world politics, are very much left out of the picture. It is magnificent to see dynamic processes yoked by a magic touch that relates them for creative production of the entity, but at such a great historic moment there is little room for human agency. The Confucian cosmos is also one of relatedness among things, people, and people and things, but humans are always a key factor, most creative and full of agency.

A Social World of Human Relations

For the relational theory, relations are first of all human relations. Since they are human relations, they involve indispensable human agency. Even though the concept of "relation" can be seen in a highly general way, referring to connections among places, events, occurrences, processes, people, and whatever is in the universe, in the social world, it is, for my relational theory, fundamentally about ties among humans. In other words, the social world is a world of human relations: It is not relations in general; it is human in the first place. With this important point in mind, let us see how human relatedness is discussed in the relevant literature.

Confucianism, as the mainstream of Chinese culture, gives priority to human relations.[19] Most sociologists and psychologists who study Chinese society or people, consciously or unconsciously, also focus their analysis on human relations. Fei Xiaotong, a late Chinese sociologist who once studied in the UK, compares the Western and Chinese societies through a field study of human relations in a typical southern Chinese village, arguing that the Chinese view a social world as ripples in a lake, interconnected with each other and forming concentric circles.[20] It is not composed of discrete organizations, but of overlapping relational circles of people linked together through differentially categorized social relationships. He calls it the "differential mode of association (*chaxu geju*)."[21] Everyone is the center of her social "ripples" and numerous social actors have made an enormous relational complexity, overlapping, mutually penetrating, and constituting the social totality. This Chinese view of the world is, as Fei argues, in sharp contrast to the view of Westerners that the social world is one consisting of individuals, standing on their own and independent of one another.[22] Richard Nisbett compares the Greeks and the Chinese. After pointing out that the Greek social life was independent and they thought of themselves as individuals with distinctive properties who constitute the primary units in society, he says the following about the Chinese:

Chinese social life was interdependent and it was not liberty but harmony that was the watchword – the harmony of humans and nature for the Taoists and the harmony of humans with other humans for the Confucians ... The world is

---

[19] Xu Zhuoyun 2006, 210.   [20] Fei 2012, 46.   [21] Ibid., 38.
[22] Fei 2012, 43. See also Gold, Guthrie, and Wank 2002, 10.

complicated, events are interrelated, and objects (and people) were connected "not as pieces of pie, but as ropes in a net." The Chinese philosopher would see a family with interrelated members where the Greek saw a collection of persons with attributes that were independent of any connections with others. Complexity and interrelation meant for the Chinese that an attempt to understand the object without appreciation of its context was doomed.[23]

It is a relational world, defined by the fundamental relatedness of human beings. It is neither a Hobbesian world of all fighting against all, nor a Lockean world of all competing with all, nor a Kantian world of all befriending all, but a Confucian world of all being related to, interdependent on, and inclusive of all. The key difference lies in the fact that the view of the world as composed of independent individual units constitutes the background of Western mainstream IR theorists while the conception of the world as one of interdependent and immanent actors locked in complex relations with one another and with the context shapes the Chinese mind. For the former, the unit must be an entity, an atom, and a self with subjectivity, however they are made; for the latter, nevertheless, the unit is a "selfless self,"[24] because it would be non-existent as a social being without the interdependence on and interrelatedness with others as well as with the context. In the Confucian social world, therefore, all social beings are situated and positioned in such a relational complexity, which defines them as such and which orients them toward certain actions with social meaning. A vivid picture of such a world is perhaps represented by the map of the human body in the traditional Chinese medicine indicating the main and collateral channels: a complex but fluid web of co-relatedness with nodes and connecting lines. Accordingly, health means a balanced, cooperative, and harmonious relationship among all the interrelated parts as well as the parts with the body as a holistic and organic system.

This conceptualization of the social world as one of relatedness, with humans as key relators, naturally refers first of all to blood ties and then to social relatedness, the notion that all social beings are related among one another. Persons are never seen as isolated beings with distinct properties and attributes. Rather they exist in the first place as social beings, connected in some meaningful way. One is the daughter of her parents, the wife of her husband, the mother of her daughter, and a friend of her friends. Similarly, Country A is a friend of Country B, a rival of Country C, and a foe of Country D. No matter what is the nature of the relationships, no one can escape the relations between herself and the specific others. These relations matter a great deal and constitute the background

[23] Nisbett 2003, 19.   [24] Hall and Ames 1998, 23.

against which an actor thinks and does. Furthermore, such conceptualization of the world tends to shift the focus from the individual actor in
isolation to the relational context where she is situated, which can be
termed "actor-context immanency." It is therefore context-oriented, paying great attention to the relationship between the actor and her social
context. If our attention focuses mainly on individual objects or entities in
isolation and our aim is to find with certainty the linear relationship
between such objects or entities, then we tend to neglect their surroundings or we even need to assume the surroundings as constants or as mere
milieus. However, if we conceive the world as composed of relations,
we cannot miss the important relationships between the actor and her
context. In more general terms it means relationships between humans
and nature, and in the social world it is about relationships among
humans and relationships between the actor and the context which is
composed of her total relational circles. In other words, an actor is always
related to the context, or the totality of her relations. People exist in the
complex relational context, without which, none of them are existent at
all; and without their existence, there is no social world at all.

For the purpose of this study, therefore, I first define relations as human
relations, that is, as relations among human beings and as relations
between a human being and her social context defined in terms of her
total relationships. It is not a mere reduction of the general term of
"relation" to social settings. While it goes with the argument that relatedness characterizes both the natural and the social world, it places particular emphasis on the humanness of relations. International society is first
of all a human society, bearing all of its defining features. Humanness is
hence a most distinct feature of my relational theory. In other words,
humans are what they are because of relations and would no longer be
what they are if they were not relational. At the same time the social
world is what it is because of human relatedness and would no longer be
what it is if it was devoid of such relatedness. Humans are the most vital
and most meaningful. It is a Confucian statement, explicitly expressed by
Mencius. This constitutes the key argument of my relational approach
that differs from Jackson-Nexon processual relationalism, which may or
may not be human. Relation for them is a general and impersonal force
whose presence brings about the configurations of processes as the creator of the individual entities. Relation for me is not only the reified
configurations of processes that play the crucial role in entity/state formation. They are also, perhaps more importantly, what define the meaning of life for humans throughout their existence as such. International
relations in the final analysis are human relations and an international
actor would not exist if there were no significant others and if there were

no relations between them. As Ho, a psychologist, points out, although the importance of relations has been recognized in social psychology everywhere and therefore the concept is not unique to Asia, they tend to be interpersonal in Asian societies.

Interpersonal relations are of crucial importance [for Asians] not only historically in the formation of the human character but also contemporaneously in defining what it means to be human throughout the individual's lifetime. The life of the individual is incomplete! It derives its meaning only from the coexistence of other individuals. Without others, the very notion of individual identity loses meaning. In this sense, Asian conceptions of social existence are relation centered.[25]

Second, relational human actors are immanent to each other as well as to the relational context. It means that these social beings are more inclusively becoming during the process of their interaction. They are not two separate entities that happen to come into interaction, as much of the network theory assumes. Moreover, they are parts of a whole that tend to share an immanent intersubjectivity, which the network literature largely does not assume. It is vividly reflected by the Chinese cosmological diagram, which expresses what is meant by the concept of "self-in-other" and "other-in-self," each living inside the other and each depending on the other for life. In a cultural community, for example, people in the process of their intersubjective practices tend to share a lot of "properties and attributes" that have become the significant meaning of their life and make them what they are. Confucianism stresses the importance of the relational environment because how and to whom one is related may decide what kind of person one becomes, for the moment one is related to significant and specific others, one is part of them and immanent to them. In other words, properties and attributes are forged through the self's relations with significant others and with the relational totality she is embedded in. Mencius' mother is said to have moved three times simply to find a better environment inhabited by moral people for her son. Norbert Elias may also place emphasis on the importance of one's relational circles in forming and reforming the individual when he discusses the behavior of the people in medieval times within the courts and the unplanned processes that developed and spread such behavior.[26] Humans are relational animals. At the moment one is related to others, the relator and the related are inclusively intersubjective and immanently becoming. Immanent inclusivity is a key assumption of my relational theory and this point will be further deliberated on when I discuss the *zhongyong* dialectics.

[25] Ho 1991, 82–83.   [26] Elias 1939/2012.

Third, mutual constitution and enabling between the relational context and actors in such a context is a primary assumption of the relational theory. As my relational theory is human in the first place, one's relational context means the totality of relations one has at a temporal-spatial moment. It is a relational web in which one is embedded. There is no one-way traffic between the actor and her relational context. A most valuable contribution by Jackson and Nexon is their argument that processes create actors, who are not pre-existing with anterior essential properties as substantialism assumes. Processes are defined as relations and therefore "relations before states" in world politics. I agree with them in that relation, or the relational context as I term it, shapes actors, including their identities and behaviors. However, actors are constitutive of relational processes at the same time. In other words, it is not that relations come before actors, but that relations and actors are processual simultaneities. Grand theories tend to pay more attention to macro-level factors, structures or processes. It is always a problem rather than a necessary negligence. Except for blood relations, which, as such, do not exist in international relations, all social relations are simultaneous with social actors. They are immanent in each other and cannot be artificially separate. Actors are always actors in relations and relations are always relations with actors. No one can exist without the other. Giddens has tried to use structuration to solve the problem of dualism between structures and agents and Wendt seems to have been inspired by Giddens in his earlier works to solve the same problem in international relations, but has turned out to be a structuralist during the course of building a grand theory of international politics, thus having to assume the separateness of the structure and the agent and to draw a one-way direction causal/constitutive arrow. It seems that this one-way traffic eventually leads to a blind end. The relational complexity is dynamic and constitutive and at the same time it is constituted by actors within. When relators relate themselves, they are simultaneously weaving their relational webs. When we argue that processes constitute actors, we should not forget that actors are also active and help create simultaneously the processes in which they are embedded.

Such a definition has three implications. The first is that relations are confined to connections and ties among humans, who can be natural persons and corporate persons as well. In world politics, states are still the most conspicuous actors. It is not to deny that other corporate persons like inter-governmental organizations, non-governmental organizations, technical communities of practice, and transnational networks, have been getting much more significant in their roles and functions on the stage of world politics. It is not to exclude individuals who sometimes may play a crucial role. Summit diplomacy has an important function of connecting national leaders and allowing them to establish a kind of personal relationship. However, for the purpose of this study, it focuses on state actors and treats them as humans. Second, human relations by definition have a strong embedded human element. They can be rational, non-rational, and irrational. Their rationality, however, is not that of a super mind which can carry out pure reasoning as formal logic shows. They are rational as humans and in the sense of relationality, or we may call it relational rationality. It is not even the bounded rationality as Herbert Simon has defined because human rationality is always related to human relations rather than to perfect/imperfect information.[27] Sometimes they can even be quite emotional, as all humans are. Khrushchev's notorious banging on the UN table with his shoe in 1960 may have shown an emotional response to the worsening relations between the Soviet Union and the West. Human relations are of different types and vary in degrees of intimacy and importance. Blood ties are the most intimate and are little subject to change. They are therefore the super-stable relationship. However, except for blood ties, most relations are social relations, relations that constitute society and that humans live with in their social life. Third, social relations are subject to change. Two nations, for example, may start as close friends but end up as deadly enemies. China and the Soviet Union were allies in the 1950s and 1960s, became foes in the 1970s and 1980s, and improved their relations in the 1990s. Now the two seem to be very close to each other in their strategic relationship. Since relations are subject to change, management of relations is of utmost importance in politics as well as in society.

Relations as a Unit of Analysis

The worldview that sees the universe as one of relations has methodological implications. If relation is the key concept, then for social studies, the primary unit of analysis should be relations rather than actors *per se*. An actor, at the moment of her social existence, is simultaneously relational. It is not a detached, material, and physical being as the mainstream IR theory assumes about the nation-state and the actor's socially meaningful action can only occur in this relational web. Thus, as Ambrose King understands and cites Liang Shuming, a leading Confucian scholar active in the 1940s in China:

---

[27] Simon 1955 and 1985.

Chinese society is neither *ko-jen pen-wei* (individual-based), nor *she-hui pen-wei* (society-based), but *kuan-hsi* based (relation-based). In a relation-based social system, the emphasis is placed on the relation between particular individuals: "The focus is not fixed on any particular individual, but on the particular nature of relations between individuals who interact with each other. The focus is on relationship." In other words, in the Confucian system, man is socially situated in a relational context – man is a "relational being."[28]

Liang's argument has in fact pointed out the two levels of analysis often used in social analysis: the systemic and the individual. In IR, Kenneth Waltz identifies three levels or, as he has called them, three images – the individual, the state, and the international system, and locates causes of international war at these three levels.[29] A pioneering work exclusively discussing this question is David Singer's influential article,[30] "The level-of-analysis problem in international relations," which identifies two significant levels: the state at the micro-level and the international system at the macro-level. While the international system is the most comprehensive level, enabling researchers to observe at the macro-level, the state is the specific level, helping researchers to study strategies and policies at the micro-level. Since then more studies have been done to make an even clearer division of levels of analysis. James Rosenau has identified five levels, i.e. the individual, role, government, society, and international system.[31] In these studies, the focus is exclusively on the tangible entities in international relations, and, as Liang has said, either on the individual basis or on the holistic basis. None of them includes "relations" as a level of analysis.

Building on these studies, Bruce Russett, Harry Starr, and David Kinsella have put forward a six-level framework, from the micro to the macro: individual decision-makers, roles of decision-makers, governmental structure, characteristics of the society, international relations, and the world system.[32] A great contribution of the Russett-Starr-Kinsella framework of the levels of analysis is the addition of "relations" as a level of analysis, indicated by "international relations" above domestic societies and below the international system. However, this concept of "relations" is a substantialist understanding of the term. According to the authors: "The actions of states toward each other are affected by the relationship between them, which, in turn, is determined by the characteristics of the two states."[33] They further explain by using the example of democratic peace, saying, that "democracies are only more peaceful in their relations with other democracies and that their relations with authoritarian regimes

---

[28] King 1985, 63; Liang 1949/2012, 76–91.   [29] Waltz 1959.   [30] Singer 1961.
[31] Rosenau 1982, 11–17.   [32] Russett, Starr, and Kinsella 2006, 10–19.   [33] Ibid., 18.

can be quite aggressive."[34] Thus, their purpose of adding "relations" to their analytical framework is to find "what can be learned from the interactions between states that cannot be explained by the characteristics of each individually (their society, governments, or leaders)." Their "relations" therefore is meaningful only in a substantialist way because the relations are reflected by the characteristics of each state in the dyadic situation, for example, peace between two democracies. It means pseudo-relations or relations at the superficial level, for it is still rooted in the characteristics of the two pre-existent states with essential properties and defining characteristics. It is not relations in its genuine social meaning, and, moreover, it is not relations that imply inclusivity and immanency.

If the pivot of society is relations and if the focus is on relations rather than on individual units, knowledge about society should first of all include understanding of social relations. Furthermore, if we believe that there exists an international society or even a world society,[35] then states or non-state actors in it, from a relational perspective, are actors in relations, relational beings as Liang terms it or, simply, relators. Therefore, analysis of world politics should start from a study of relations rather than taking nation-states as independent entities interacting in a rational way and in an atomistic universe. Social studies thus should take relations among actors rather than actors *per se* as the primary unit of analysis, as actors are constantly to relate and at the same time to be related.[36] Mainstream IR theories have to date focused mainly on the individual actor, whether it is an individual decision-maker or a corporate person like a nation-state or an international organization. Network theories and studies have done more, focusing on the role of networking of social actors and drawing attention to transnational networks in international relations, but their problem is still to locate individual actors in the first place. Their nodes in the network are first independent agents and their network is one that links these discrete agents with their interaction. Keck and Sikkink, for example, have studied the transnational networks of advocacy, but their first effort is to find who starts such networking.[37]

---

[34] Ibid.   [35] See Bull 1977; Buzan 2004.

[36] A most interesting study by Robert Axelrod et al. of carcinogenesis shifts the focus from the existing cancer theory to a new understanding based on evolutionary cooperation theory. The existing cancer theory interprets cancer from an individualistic view, holding that "individual clones of cancer cells evolve independently from one another, acquiring all of the genetic traits or hallmarks necessary to form a malignant tumor" (Axelrod et al. 2006, 13474). Axelrod et al. challenge this interpretation, believing that interactive relationships among malignant cells and between malignant and non-malignant cells help explain why cancer grows and develops. For example, "two nearby cells could protect each other from a set of host defenses that neither could survive alone" (ibid.). They in fact have changed the unit of analysis from the individual cell to relations among cells.

[37] Keck and Sikkink 1998.

Finnemore and Sikkink have analyzed the life cycles of international norms by first identifying the norm "entrepreneurs."[38] The stereotypical way of finding an "independent" agent with distinct properties and attributes is always there with them. Furthermore, the grand theories, i.e. the three American mainstream IR paradigms, all take the state as their primary units, pre-existing and self-subsistent. Wendt's weak materialism reflects his hesitation in this respect, but for building a grand theory, he has to sacrifice the crucial assumption of mutual constitution and resorts to the self-organizing nation-state as his primary unit. In their repertoire, there is no such term of "relator" and neither is there a choice that "relations among actors" or "relations between actors and their context" can be a meaningful unit of analysis to start from. Because of this bias of mainstream IR theories, a major problem of IR as a discipline is that it does not have a well-developed theory of relations and does not seriously theorize on relations, even though it is called International "Relations" and accepted as such through common practice.

A social actor's identity is shaped by her relations with specific others and by her relational matrices. From the worldview that sees everything as related to everything else, it is derived that in the social world actors are related to one another and to the relational totality or the context where they are entangled. They are and can only be, therefore, actors in relations. Their existence is simultaneously relational and their subjectivity is borne out only through relations with others. In this sense they are relational beings indeed. As such, their identities and roles are defined by relations rather than by their own essential properties, which they, as relational beings, do not and cannot possess *a priori*.

Relators: Actors in Relations

Since all are related to all in an interrelated world, social actors are and can only be "actors in relations." In this sense, social actors are "relators" – they relate and are related, and they are relational creatures. This is naturally derived from the fundamental assumption or the worldview that relatedness characterizes the cosmos and human relations define the social world. No matter whether they are natural individuals or corporate agents, they are in the first place entangled in a relational complexity and cannot exist as discrete entities.

It is a question first concerning ontology. Mainstream IR theories, represented by realism, liberalism, and constructivism, tend to prioritize the ontology of existence, holding that the existence of the individual

---

[38] Finnemore and Sikkink 1998.

entity, or self-existence, is the foundation on which social studies should start their exploration. From such an ontology, it is natural to get the corollary that self-interest of the individual, who is assumed to be rational in the first place, is the driving force for action. A logical chain is thus formed: The primacy of the ontology of existence decides the independence of the individual actor with basic needs and self-interests, defining qualities and properties, which in turn orient her toward certain egoistic action. Furthermore, this ontology explains an actor's identity and hence interest. Realism and liberalism explicitly define identity as pregiven: The actor has her identity with properties and attributes and enters an interaction in a social setting with such *a priori* identity as an independent individual. Mainstream constructivism also acknowledges the primary and fundamental nature of the pregiven identity, although it recognizes that the secondary properties and attributes can change through intersubjectivity. Once the identity is determined, interest follows naturally, such as those developing countries described by Finnemore, which, having been taught by international organizations, began to define their identity as modern states and understand their interest accordingly.[39]

The proposed relational theory of world politics challenges these theoretical interpretations of existence, identity, and interest. For the proposed relational theory, the key word is relatedness, thus denying the primary ontological status of self-existence. Rather, it emphasizes the simultaneity of existence and coexistence, or of self-existence and other-existence. Also, the relational theory acknowledges the importance of identity in social life, but denies the belief that social actors have anterior identity. Rather, it argues that the identity of social actors is constituted through relations, meaningful only in a relational context. In addition, the relational theory agrees largely that interest motivates action, but denies the primacy of the exclusiveness of self-interest; it recognizes the importance of collective interest, but denies the privilege of collective interest over self-interest. I propose three primary positions here as the sustaining backups. They are coexistence, relational identity, and shared interest. My main arguments include: Self-existence is simultaneously coexistence; the identity of an actor is formed and reformed through relations with other actors in society; and self-interest always shares with other-interest as well as with collective interest. Simply put, it is about coexistence, co-identity, and co-interest. I will discuss them in turn in the following sections.

---

[39] Finnemore 1996.

Coexistence

The relational theory places particular emphasis on coexistence, or existence of the self in relation to others rather than existence in isolation. It believes that politics is an art of managing relations among actors who coexist in a particular temporo-space. Thus, a most important assumption is that of coexistence. It posits that existence always means relational existence and therefore self-existence is simultaneously coexistence with others. Coexistence means in fact the simultaneity of self-existence and other-existence. It posits that in a relational world, discrete, self-sufficient, and independent individuals do not exist. Rather, any individual or self is a continuous process between herself and others who she is related to. The self and the other are mutually conditioned for each other's existence and articulation for each other's life. In other words, humans are more relational becomings than self-organizing beings in social settings and their existence is necessarily relational existence. This important assumption implies both that the well related are fitter to survive and that the harmoniously related prosper.

It is of ontological significance and goes against two existing ontological positions: One is that self-existence has an ontological primacy over coexistence, and the other, coexistence comes before self-existence. Rather, my coexistence assumption places emphasis on the simultaneity of self-existence and coexistence, meaning that the existence of the self is at the same time a coexistence of this self with others in a social setting. Self-existence cannot stand by itself and does not come before or after coexistence.

Existence of individual entities is perhaps the primary assumption for much of modernist, scientific exploration. It holds that being is the beginning of life and thus the measure of everything. Since the world, natural and social alike, is composed of independent and discrete entities, the existence of such entities is of primary significance and the exploration of the properties, attributes, qualities, and other essential elements of these entities constitutes the main inquiry of humans to produce knowledge. It is also the core assumption for mainstream IR theories. Realism and liberalism both assume the privileged status of the individual entity, the sovereign, independent nation-state. Mainstream constructivism accepts this assumption. As Wendt says "States are people too."[40] Following what he calls the realist assumption, he argues that the state is a real corporate actor. It is not, as nominalists believe, a function of the individuals whose actions alone are actions that count. However, despite

---

[40] Wendt 1999, 215.

the disagreement of realists and nominalists on the status of the state, the underpinning assumption is that a real being or an actor, individual or corporate, is the unit who enjoys the primacy in terms of existence and whose existence is where social life starts and therefore should be the most significant aspect for social studies. The existence of the state, for example, is the foundation for realist IR theory, and the survival theme has dominated realist literature. Existence of the individual entity, or what is philosophically the "being," has long been the starting point for intellectual pursuit and knowledge production. This is an ontology of being, or an ontology of self-existence. It argues that existence of the individual entity comes before everything else, thus constituting the beginning of all inquiry for knowledge production.

A closely related argument is that the individual of ontological significance has her own independent self-interest. Furthermore, the self-interest of such an actor is the decisive factor that motivates her to action. Interest is what an independent actor naturally has, *a priori* defined, and can be ranked in terms of importance for the individual actor. Survival, for example, always enjoys priority, without which no other interest is meaningful. Based on an ontology of being, A. H. Maslow has put forward his famous hierarchy of needs, including physiological needs, security, love and belonging, esteem, and self-actualization, each representing a higher level along this hierarchical ladder. In international relations, national interest is not only considered the prime mover for state action, but is justified by Hans Morgenthau as the highest morality of the state whose existence comes before everything else.[41] For institutionalists, self-interest of the nation-state is the foundation, conflict of national interests among states is the problem, and international institutions are the solution.[42] Although for some classical realists, such as Morgenthau, power is both a means and an end, realists largely agree that power is the most reliable means to achieve the ends of the state, the most important of which is none other than survival in an anarchical international system through self-help. Mainstream social constructivists seem to question this assumption by arguing that interest comes from identity, which is in turn shaped through intersubjectivity.[43] However, they recognize the existence of self-organizing beings in the first place and interact afterwards, as indicated by the first encounter of Ego and Alter, which tells the story of two peoples, having pregiven primary identity and interest and then starting to interact with each other.[44] In international relations, only in the Lockean culture in which survival is no longer the concern of the state thanks to the sovereignty principle, does the state begin to seek interests

[41] Morgenthau 1961.   [42] Keohane 1984.   [43] Wendt 1999.   [44] Ibid., 187–189.

other than survival. Thus interest, either of an individual or a corporate person like the state, is defined *a priori* in isolation and the maximization of the self-interest refers to the best realization of this self-defined interest. A state, for example, can unilaterally define its interest, ranking from the most important to the least. Its primary requirement is the existence of an individual and isolated being with a status of ontological significance. It is exactly what the ontology of self-existence says and much of the Western IR theory literature holds.

The overwhelming importance of the ontology of existence has been questioned. Some argue for the primacy of the ontology of coexistence over that of existence, meaning that coexistence of the self with others comes before self-existence. Zhao Tingyang, a Chinese philosopher, puts forward his theory on what he calls the "ontology of coexistence" in contrast to the ontology of existence.[45] From a philosophical perspective, he argues that there are two worlds which are different in essential respects. The first is a "world of things" and the second a "world of facts." While the former is for science and logical reasoning, the latter is for humans and human ways of existence. Furthermore, since the world of facts is first and foremost concerned with human practice, the ontology in this world is more about "to do" than "to be," and the latter is the ontological concern of the world of things. In this world of facts, *"facio ergo sum"* replaces *"cogito ergo sum."* Zhao argues further that this "doing" defines the world of facts as necessarily one in which humans are involved.[46] Human agents do and, moreover, necessarily do together to create facts. Doing together means first of all the creation of intersubjective relations and the engagement in interactions. It is thus a characteristic feature of coexistence.

Zhao holds that this ontology of coexistence comes before the ontology of existence, because in the world of facts, the existence of the individual and self-organizing "I" is meaningless and therefore null. He explains:

The fundamental principle of the ontology of coexistence is that coexistence comes before existence. It means that there must be first of all a state of coexistence, only in which existence gains meaning. The presence of coexistence constitutes the only possibility for the significant state of existence.[47]

Zhao's world of things, to some extent, resembles the natural world, where the existence of any particular thing or matter is of primary importance, and his world of facts is like the social world, where humans are the primary actors that matter, as he defines "fact" as conscious action by humans and existence of facts always means doing together.

---

[45] Zhao 2009 and 2016.   [46] Zhao 2009, 24.   [47] Ibid., 26.

The existence of, say, iron or gold, is real and these matters have independent and different properties and qualities. Their existence is not defined by coexistence with other matters unless it is interfered with by some external forces. When we describe a thing as something, we at the same time isolate it from other things so that we can gain some certainty about its properties and group it with things of similar properties through categorization. It is reasonable because a thing or matter exists as it is. Furthermore, as a thing or matter, it does not face any question of choice and it has no ability to do. By a kind of mistaken extension, people tend to use such a worldview about the things to describe individual humans, confusing the two worlds as one and the same. It is highly misleading, because humans have the ability to think, to do, to choose, and therefore to create. Nobody is able to know for certain what her future will be simply because her possibilities are limitless thanks to her ability to think, to do, and to create, together with others. All the thinking, doing, and creating by the self are necessarily related to other human beings, for whatever one does in society has an impact on others. Without being related to others, what one does is not only meaningless, but also impossible. Doing inevitably involves others or doing requires first of all coexistence.

Zhao's contribution is to emphatically raise the question of coexistence as one of ontological significance, which goes against the ontology of being or self-existence, stressing the primacy of the status of the isolated individual. The processual relationalism proposed by Jackson and Nexon has a somewhat similar argument when they make the argument of "relations before states."[48] They use the distinction by Emirbayer between substantialism and relationalism, pointing out that the former takes "things" or "entities" as the ontological primitives of analysis because entities exist before interaction, while the latter "treats configuration of ties – recurrence sociocultural interaction – between social aggregates of various sorts and their component parts as the building blocks of social analysis."[49] Relations give rise to entities, such as nation-states. They further maintain that entities cannot be taken as static existence with *a priori* properties and refer to the fact that many IR theories have already begun to treat the state and other units not as mere pregiven entities. How the state is made and how the entity-properties of the state are produced has attracted scholarly attention. Thus they have cited as the epigraph for their article Martin Buber, "In the beginning is relation."[50] Relations come before the state because they give rise to the state, whose so-called constitutive properties and

---

[48] Jackson and Nexon 1999.   [49] Ibid., 291–292.   [50] Ibid., 291.

attributes are not pregiven either, but rather are made by such configurations of ties through yoking.

In this sense, actions and interactions between entities that do not change the essential properties are still within the framework of substantialism. Without studying how relations make the entity it is impossible to understand how the entity of the state has been historically made what it is now. The argument that relations come before states sounds like Zhao's theory, but in fact the two theories differ in their purposes. For Jackson and Nexon, the emphasis is on the production or creation of an entity by the configurations of ties. They focus on the process of entity formation without theorizing about relations between two or more agents. Zhao's, on the other hand, is more a Confucian understanding of human relations and his focus is on relations between two and more agents, whose existence is what I may term a "relational existence," or coexistence.

Although I agree with Jackson and Nexon on their main argument that social and historical processes produce entities, I do not agree with them, as I have briefly mentioned before, on a particular point of view: relations before states. It is reasonable to say that a particular form of an entity or an agent, such as the state, is produced by certain configurations of ties and therefore it comes after relations. In general terms, however, processes and agents are and can only be simultaneities. They simultaneously produce and constitute each other. If we put processes before agents, then who creates the processes that produce the agents? We may say that time and space conjoined then and there, and the entity was thus created. But who made the time and space conjoin then and there? I therefore maintain that relations and agents, in general terms, are mutually and simultaneously created and constructed. Prioritizing each over the other leads to a dualistic treatment as structuralism always does. My use of the concept of "relation" is thus more congruent with Zhao's, as clarified in the previous sections. It refers to human relations, relations between two or among more human agents.

I do not, however, agree with Zhao on the argument that coexistence comes before existence in the social world. If we follow such an order of ranking, we tend to believe that "existence is conditioned on coexistence,"[51] or even coexistence is the prerequisite for self-existence.[52] It goes to the dualistic structure of existence and coexistence again by separating the two and prioritizes one over the other. It does not agree with my underlying position that any dualistic structure tends to be biased and to mislead as well. It is often said that the Chinese culture is a culture of water and in fact an analogy is frequently used to describe the self and the collectivity:

---

[51] Zhao 2016, 8.   [52] Zhao 2010, 46.

The collectivity is the ocean and the self a drop of it. The existence of a drop of water is at the same time its coexistence simultaneously with many other drops from the ocean. If coexistence goes before and constitutes the pre-requisites of existence, and if the two are structured in a dualistic way, then the logic will be easily applied in terms of interest. Collective or group interest is prioritized over self-interest, subjugation or even elimination of which is justifiable in the name of the collectivity. It is not only misleading, but also tends to justify dictatorship or collective violence which suppresses legitimate self-interest in the name of the "state" or of any other collectivity.

The norm of "comfort level" is a telling example of the simultaneity of self-existence and coexistence. It is an Association of the Southeast Asian Nations (ASEAN) norm and has been practiced for years. It means that a decision is not to be made even if all participants but one agree to make such a decision. During the deliberation on a certain document to be completed as a collective decision, for instance, if one participant says that she does not feel comfortable with the document or part of the document, it will be further deliberated on and revised until a complete consensus is reached. If no agreement is reached, then the document will be shelved until a compromise is made in the future. During the decision-making process, there is no voting and no majority rule. If it is assumed that coexistence takes priority over self-existence, a majority rule is justifiable in the name of the collectivity at the sacrifice of the individual. However, if any single participant's attitude is taken into full consideration, individual self-interest is very much valued and in fact equaled to the majority interest. It is in the interest of the collectivity because the cooperative process is maintained without being broken; it is also in the interest of the individual for her position is fully respected. Extended to the ontology of existence, it means exactly that self-existence is simultaneous with coex-istence. They are mutually dependent and constitute conditions for both the individual and the collective life. Confucius never denies self-interest, always stressing the inclusiveness of self-interest and other-interest; and Confucius never denies the existence of the self, always stressing the mutuality of self-existence and other-existence. The Confucian motto, "wishing to be established himself, seek also to establish others," exactly expresses the importance attached to both the self and the other(s), and to both self-interest and other-interest. It is not that coexistence is priori-tized over self-existence. It is that they are simultaneously mutual and correlatively interdependent. Inclusive harmony of both creates an ideal condition for social life.

What I want to stress, therefore, is that in the social world self-existence and coexistence are simultaneities, mutually defined and conditioned. Existence always "exists" with coexistence: The self and the other define each other; their coexistence defines their respective existence and vice versa. In other words, self-existence gains meaning from coexistence and, on the other hand, coexistence cannot have significance without self-existence. They imply each other and participate in each other, rather than separate as two distinct forms of existence, one coming before the other and being more significant than the other. They are immanently inclusive, mutually constitutive and having no temporal sequences like causes and effects. In fact existence of any individual self in the social world is always simultaneous coexistence of this particular individual with others. Only by realizing that they are simultaneities can we understand why coexistence does not exclude or subjugate self-existence. Coexistence is always an inclusive system. The global system, for example, is by definition an inclusive system where various peoples and nations live together, and the interest of the globe is inclusive of the interest of each and all who live on this globe.

Discussing selfhood and identity, David Ho, a psychologist who studies socio-psychology in East Asia, also argues that in Confucian societies the characteristic feature for social behavior is "relationship dominance," in contrast to the Western individualistic pattern.[53] "Relationship dominance ascribes primacy of reciprocity, interdependence, and interrelatedness among individuals, not to individuals themselves." In such societies, the self is a relational self, one intensely aware of the social presence of other human beings, and her identity is relational identity, meaning that her identity is defined by her social relationships.[54] This is again what I call a "relational existence," or coexistence of the self with others. It is simultaneously and conjointly with the existence of the self.

Let me use the family analogy again. At the moment when a life is being formed as an embryo, it coexists with the mother. We cannot separate the two. At the moment when a baby is born, she coexists with other members of the family. Moreover it is impossible to say which comes first, her existence as an individual or her coexistence with her family members, for they occur at the same time. Some may argue that she is born by her mother or into this the relational nest of the family, but the nest bears little meaning to her before her existence. As Professor Tu Wei-Ming says: "A Confucian self devoid of human relatedness has little meaningful content of its own. Since the self in Confucian literature is often understood in terms of dyadic relationships, a Confucian man's self-awareness of being a son, a brother, a husband, or a father dominates his awareness of himself as a self-reliant and independent person."[55] If one's identity is defined in terms of one's personal relationships with others, one's

---

[53] Ho 1995, 116.   [54] Ibid., 116–117.   [55] Tu 1985, 114.

existence always goes together with one's coexistence with others to whom one is related.

In international relations, a state always coexists with other states and actors. It happens at the moment when it is a state. We may argue that a state, before it is recognized by others, exists as a *de facto* state. However, its identity is not accomplished, its meaning not fully realized, and it is still a non-state, or it is a state without appropriate and adequate social significance. That is perhaps why the Palestinians have always struggled for a universally recognized statehood. Even if we recognize it as a state *accompli*, its existence is also a *de facto* coexistence with other states. To be or not to be is the question, but it is always a question in a relational context. In this sense existence and coexistence both express the meaning of relational existence. Another example is provided by a study of grand strategies of major powers. Shih and Huang have found that the United States and China have different conceptual sources for designing grand international strategies. The former relies largely on the subjective "I," with a strong cognitive construction of the identity as a rule-maker, trying to convert other/others to the self's value-oriented expectations, and the latter assumes more the role identity of a rule-taker, attempting to adapt rather than to alter so as to maintain a stable relationship.[56] It is clear that the former is more atomistic and messianic while the latter is more relational and contextual. From a relational perspective, self-existence is of primary importance in the former while coexistence of the self with others characterizes the latter. It is in fact what Confucianism thinks about the fundamental question of the self-other relationship. For Confucianism, no self can ever exist "as an isolated individual, but as an active participant in the living community – the family, the province, the state, and the world."[57] The selfhood always "entails participation of the other" and "the reason for this desirable and necessary symbiosis of selfhood and otherness is the Confucian concept of the self as a dynamic process of spiritual development."[58]

Relational Identities

The proposed relational theory of world politics assumes that identities and roles of social actors are shaped by social relations. In other words, actors' identities are formed in the process of relating and being related. No absolute and independent identity of the self exists: It is constructed and reconstructed in relations with others and with the relational totality as a whole. For a Chinese: "There is no me in isolation, to be considered

[56] Shih and Huang 2015.   [57] Tu 1985, 114.   [58] Ibid., 113.

abstractly: I am the totality of roles I live in relation to specific others ...
Taken collectively, they weave, for each of us, a unique pattern of personal identity, ..."[59] Ho makes the following comments when he discusses
the selfhood and identity in Confucian societies:

> In Confucian cultures, the self is ... the *relational self*, one which is intensely
> aware of the social presence of other human beings. The appearance of others in
> the phenomenal world is integral to the emergence of the selfhood; that is, self
> and others are conjointly differentiated from the phenomenal world to form the
> self-in-relation-with-others. This, in short, is the phenomenological representa-
> tion of selfhood in Confucianism.[60]

Such relational nature of selfhood has been discussed by other scholars.
Lebra explains that, "in Japan, the term for the self is a *bun* compound
noun, *jibun*; the concept of *bun* (which means portion, share, part, of
fraction) implies an image of society as an organic whole, individuals
being parts of that organism."[61] It is impossible to argue which, the
parts or the whole, comes first and can determine the other. They come
together and define each other. Tu also holds that Confucian selfhood
entails the participation of the other. In short, the self is the self of the
other and vice versa.[62] This is what I call "co-identity."

A vivid analogy is *weiqi* or *go*, the board game that is said to have
originated in China and is very popular in Confucian societies such as
China, Japan, and Korea. The whole board, once it has pieces on it, looks
like the Confucian cosmos, for every piece is related to other pieces and
together they constitute the *weiqi* universe. For any single piece, there are
no anterior identities, pre-fixed properties, and constitutive attributes at
all. All pieces look alike. It is unlike the Western chess, for which every
piece has a predetermined identity, a king, a bishop, or a pawn, each of
which has clearly defined roles and functions to play according to pre-set
rules and regulations. But once a piece is placed on the *weiqi* board, it
gains meaning and performs functions through its relations to other
pieces. It is a game, but it reflects a way of thinking and an understanding
of the universe. As Hu Shi comments:

> There are natural and artificial relationships among humans. The former includes
> relationships between father and son or between brothers while the latter relation-
> ships between husband and wife or between friends. ... The Confucian philoso-
> phy of life holds that no person can exist independently and every human behavior
> is behavior of a certain human relationship, following the norm governing such
> relationship.[63]

[59] Nisbett 2003, 5.   [60] Ho 1995, 117, emphasis in original.
[61] Lebra 1976, 67, quoted in Ho 1995, 117.   [62] Tu 1985, 113–130.
[63] Hu 1919/1991, 83.

For an individual, it is her relationships with members of her family, organization, and social group that shape her identities. Multiple identities are normal because she is embedded in overlapping relational circles of various types and with different natures. Whether her action is rational or appropriate depends on the nature of her relationships to others. A rational action to one's father may not be rational to her classmate and even less to a stranger. The United States nuclear policy toward Britain differs fundamentally from that toward North Korea, as Wendt's classical example shows, because the special relationship defines the identity of the United States as an ally of the former and an enemy of the latter. Identities denote relationships among actors. They do not indicate individual properties and attributes. There is no such self-organized social being with pre-fixed properties and defining attributes. Humans are social beings and their identities are shaped first of all by social relations and their identities change as such relations change.

Alexander Wendt criticizes the individualistic approach to identity formation, which assumes that "[i]ndividuals must be constitutionally independent."[64] He argues that the individualistic approach follows the internalistic tradition of Descartes and believes the individual's self-determination of her thought leads to her action. "'[T]hought is logically prior to society,' and society is reducible to an aggregate of interlocking but independently existing 'idiolects.'"[65] He also discusses the holistic approach, which, in contrast to the individual approach, holds that thought is intrinsically dependent upon society. According to this approach, thought is externally shaped and the meaning of objects and events lies in "a relationship to the external world."[66] Wendt on the one hand recognizes the constitutive claim of the holistic approach and agrees with the view that people think through culture. On the other hand, he also endorses the idea of the individualistic approach that the self-organizing individual has her own motives independent of external influence. He tries to synthesize the two approaches, and then puts forward perhaps his own "via media" theory on identity formation. For this purpose he distinguishes between individuality *per se*, which refers to the properties of an agent's constitution that are self-organizing and independent of social context, and the social terms of individuality which refer to "those properties of an agent's constitution that are intrinsically dependent on culture, on the general Other."[67] Thus an agent's identity is both constituted externally through the understanding of the general Other and internally through her independent thoughts and motives. He uses George Mead's "I" and "me," the former denoting the agent's sense of

---

[64] Wendt 1999, 169.   [65] Ibid., 173.   [66] Ibid., 174.   [67] Ibid., 181–182.

herself as a distinct locus of thought, choice, and activity, while the latter, the meaning an agent attributes to herself when she is taking the perspective of Others.

Such a compromise, though seemingly making up for the weaknesses of both the individualistic and the holistic approaches to identity formation, has its own problems. The fact that the individuality *per se* and its social terms are divided as such tends to remind the reader of the dichotomy of the soul and the body, a Cartesian dualistic view in disguise. For the Chinese such dichotomy never exists. They do not distinguish between the internal and the external forces that work to form the actor's identity. For them, the two are always immanently correlated and in fact they are united in one-ness, in an ever-going process. As Jacques Gernet comments:

Not only was the substantial opposition between the soul and the body something quite unknown to the Chinese, all souls being, in their view, destined to be dissipated sooner or later, but so was distinction, originally separable from it, between the sensible and the rational. The Chinese had never believed in the existence of a sovereign and independent faculty of reason. The concept of a soul endowed with reason and capable of acting freely for good or for evil, which is so fundamental to Christianity, was alien to them.[68]

Emirbayer has systematically criticized the self-action and interaction schools of substantialism, which resemble in a certain sense Wendt's internalism and externalism.[69] Although the former takes the self as the locus of action while the latter shifts such focus onto the interaction among the entities, the entities themselves remain their essential properties which are unchanged throughout the whole process of interaction. As for the via media by Wendt, the identity issue seems to be more complex, for Wendt himself argues for the idea that interaction does change the identity of an agent. On this issue, Jackson and Nexon comment:

The answer is that the *entities* themselves – in both these examples, states – do not change in their constitutive properties; they remain states with the requisite attributes which define them as states. Rather, what changes are some of their variable attributes – how much power they have, the scope of their corporate identities, etc.[70]

For a relational theory, such a via media cannot stand, for the actor is relational in the first place without the presupposed properties and constitutive attributes, just as a piece of the *weiqi* game, which is identity-less

[68] Gernet 1985, 147, quoted in Hall and Ames 1998, 29.
[69] Emirbayer 1997; Jackson and Nexon 1999, 293.
[70] Jackson and Nexon 1999, 293, emphasis in original.

before being placed on the board. In fact, it is impossible to make a clear distinction between the individuality *per se* and the social terms of individuality, for they are immanently related, or they are one. The sense of the self and the sense by the other of the self are intrinsically related. As Hall and Ames point out:

> In the Confucian model where the self is contextual, it is a shared consciousness of one's roles and relationships. One's "inner" and "outer" . . . selves are inseparable. Here one is self-conscious, not in the sense of being able to isolate and objectify one's essential self, but in the sense of being aware of oneself as a[] locus of observation by others. The locus of self-consciousness is not the "I" detached from the "me," but in the consciousness of the "me."[71]

The concept of immanent inclusivity of "I" and "me" is reflected in the Chinese language, too. There is no independent subjective "I" and objective "me," for in the Chinese language there is no distinction between the nominative and the objective cases at all: The same Chinese character is used for both "I" and "me," for "he" and "him." Whether it is the nominative or the objective depends on its relations with other characters in a sentence. If we agree that the language structure reflects a certain people's way of thinking and doing, the practical use of the Chinese language in fact denotes the immanent relatedness. We may too take sovereignty as an example. Sovereignty is a Western concept, which, as Wendt argues, means both the intrinsic, self-organizing property of the individuality of the state and the recognition by others as such.[72] It also means a demarcation between "we" and "they." In the Chinese tradition, however, there is no such boundary, for whoever comes to the Chinese community and culture is Chinese.[73] Moreover, there are no such things as the invariable essential properties and constitutive attributes of an actor. As Nisbett comments, there are many different words for "I" in Japanese and in Chinese, reflecting the relationships between self and other: There is an "I" in relation to my colleague, "I" in relation to my spouse, etc. It is difficult for Eastern people to think of properties that apply exclusively to an isolated "I." Rather, it is "much easier for them to think of properties that apply to themselves in certain settings and in relation to particular people."[74]

That identities are formed in and through relations does not mean a binary of the self and the other, which is also a kind of relationship. There is a tendency in IR to argue that the self's identity can only be formed with a negative and hostile other, an outsider who poses existential danger and threat. Felix Berenskoetter discusses this tendency in

---

[71] Hall and Ames 1998, 26.   [72] Ibid.   [73] Qian 1994, 41.   [74] Nisbett 2003, 158.

detail and finds that the survival theme of realism as well as in other IR theories lies deeply in the Kant-Hegel conceptualization of the self-other binary.[75] Such a dichotomy at least has three implications. First it necessitates the specific other as a negative stereotype enabling the self to form its own identity. In other words, those who greatly facilitate or even decide the success of the self's identity formation are the enemies of the self. Second, the negative stereotypical other mainly represents itself in its difference from the self. As Berenskoetter points out, there is a belief that "identity 'requires difference' which is then turned into (negative) otherness."[76] Then the particular identity of the self is assured as good, coherent, and complete, and the other is depicted as evil, irrational, or mad. It implies strongly a messianic worldview that tends to assimilate and homogenize so that the self would acquire absolute security. Third, it is further accented by the assumption that the international system is anarchic and therefore self-help is the best strategy. In this anarchy, the Kant-Hegel conceptualization of the self-other relationship as a dichotomously conflictual one has flourished. "Leaving aside the view among some classical realists that states seek power as an end in itself, from Arnold Wolfers via Martin Wight to Kenneth Waltz and Alexander Wendt, across the theoretical spectrum scholars readily accept the assumption that 'survival' is a prerequisite to achieving any goal that states may have."[77]

To address this bias, Berenskoetter attempts correctly to insert "friendship" into the reading of international relations. In fact, both Berenskoetter and those scholars whom he has criticized have implied in their reading of international relations something from a somewhat relational perspective: While Berenskoetter argues for the case of friendship and holds that as an intimate relationship it should not be missed in international thoughts, those whom he criticizes look more at the negative relationship between the self and the other, arguing that self-identity is established necessarily through establishing a negative other. It is a question concerning a dialectical epistemology and will be discussed in later chapters. Suffice it to argue here that identity is formed through relations, positive or negative alike. Having said that, I would also like to point out that a relational approach pays attention to both positive and negative relations, but a key concern is how to change a negative relationship into a positive one. For a relator, the more friends she has, the more powerful she is; and the more intimate friends she has, the more secure she feels. In this sense, the relational theory sees not only the importance of friendship as a key concept in international relations, as Berenskoetter

---

[75] Berenskoetter 2007.   [76] Ibid., 658.   [77] Ibid., 652.

argues, but also takes making, maintaining, and expanding friendly and intimate relations as a wise policy and a practical strategy.

Identities are only meaningful when they are in a relational context. It is also true of roles. The Western chess game pre-defines the role of each piece and sets rules for the game by regulating each of the pieces according to its predetermined role. It is the same with the English language, which has a well-organized form of grammar and each word belongs to a pre-fixed part of speech with corresponding roles and functions stipulated by the formal grammar. None of the pieces in the Chinese *weiqi* game have roles at all before they are put onto the board or the relational web and they gain their roles only after they are related to other pieces at the moment they are being placed on the board. It is the same with the Chinese language. Chinese characters, for example, have no pre-fixed parts of speech and gain such roles only after they are put in a linguistic context and begin to be linked to other pieces. The same character can be a noun, a verb, an adjective, or an adverb, and can function as subjects, predicates, or objects, all depending on the ways it is related to other characters in a sentence. Furthermore it changes parts of speech as the context changes. In fact, the Chinese language has a history of thousands of years without a system of written grammar at all: How characters are related to one another decides what they mean and what function they perform. It was not until 1898 that the first systematic Chinese grammar book was written by a scholar who had studied in the West and used the Latin grammar to set the framework for the Chinese language.[78]

Shared Interest

If we agree that self-existence is simultaneously coexistence and the identity of the self is formed in relation to others, then self-interest, as derived from the assumption of self-existence, is only impossible to independently define in a social context. It is here necessary to challenge the conventional assumption of the social sciences in general and mainstream IR theories in particular, that is, the primary assumption of self-interest. The assumption from the perspective of the relational theory is that interest is always shared in coexistence and that it is therefore realized only through reciprocity. It recognizes the legitimacy of self-interest, but argues that self-interest and other-interest are shared in social life and can

---

[78] Ma 1898. It is the first systematic book on Chinese grammar whose author, Ma Jianzhong, studied in Europe and completed this book by mainly drawing on the grammatical structures of Western languages.

be defined only in relational terms. It can thus be well captured by the term "co-interest."

Based on the ontology of self-existence, it is easy to get the corollary that the independent self has independent self-interest, which comes from her essential needs and defining attributes and properties. As we have discussed, Maslow's hierarchy of human needs indicates why self-interest is so important: The more basic the needs are, the more exclusive they are. Survival, for example, is defined as the most basic need and therefore the core interest of the self, and conflict between the self and the other concerning survival is very often taken as a zero-sum game. Realism has always taken survival of the state as the most fundamental issue in international affairs where no central authority or government can protect you and self-help is the way of life. Even today, when the possibility of a state being completely wiped out is very low, territorial disputes, which are often seen as an issue related to the physical survival of nation-states, continue to be a highly thorny problem and often lead to worsening of relations and even to armed conflict between the parties concerned.

In addition, mainstream IR theories tend to take "common interests" as a category that exists in contrast to a different and opposite category of "no common interests." Keohane, for example, argues that the most important condition for institutional cooperation between actors is the existence of common interests. If there are no common interests, no cooperation whatever will take place.[79] The relational theory argues, on the contrary, that such a division between existence and non-existence of common interests is a false assumption, for interests are always shared once actors are socially related and therefore common interests always exist in a relational world. It is not a question whether or not common interests exist, but a question whether or not such interests are found or to be found. Unconscious negligence or deliberate suppression of common interests may well lead to a zero-sum game, while unconscious enlargement of or deliberate emphasis on common interests can lead to a positive-sum game. Common interest always exists as a potential. Even between deadly enemies there are common interests, as illustrated by the examples of the deliberate withholding of fire between soldiers of enemy states during the trench warfare in WWI[80] and the US–USSR negotiations on strategic arms during the Cold War years.

Furthermore, self-interest is taken as the driving force for action. A rational actor, being driven by her interest and calculating the costs and benefits, makes decisions for the realization of such interest. In IR theories, national interest has thus become a key word in a system

[79] Keohane 1984.   [80] Axelrod 1984, 73–87.

composed of egoistic nation-states. Realists argue explicitly for the most direct form of power, in terms of which national interest is defined,[81] and which is exercised for gaining national interest.[82] Institutionalists recognize the fact that interest is hard to gain by only one side of the parties concerned and therefore propose establishing international institutions to encourage both or all actors to gain interest.[83] To some extent, they realize that in a social situation it is impossible to unilaterally realize self-interest and therefore cooperation through institutions is the way to escape the single-round prisoner's dilemma (PD). But the base for action by institutionalism continues to be interest defined by the self and what it wants to do is to invent mechanisms that promote cooperation among egoist international actors who are rational self-interest pursuers at the same time.

On the other hand, as we have just discussed, some scholars argue that coexistence conditions self-existence, implying that collective interest is more important than self-interest. Starting from such an assumption, it is not difficult to say that for the realization of the former the latter can be sacrificed. If we are not careful enough, it is easy to be misled. Despite its real intentions, this line of thinking structures coexistence and existence, collective interest and self-interest in a dualistic way. It goes fundamentally against the Chinese *zhongyong* dialectics that denies dualism in the first place. The Chinese seldom see human interaction as an exclusively zero-sum game and believe that any game played by human beings implies shared interests which are to be found, but often neglected. Following the argument that coexistence comes before self-existence, we could be easily misled to the belief that individuals live for rather than with and through the collectivity and turn a blind eye to the saying and doing in which the collective or group interest is used as a sanctimonious and hypocritical excuse for sacrificing and nullifying self-interest.

The simultaneity of existence and coexistence provides a different picture. Existence is always a shared and relational existence. By the same logic, self-interest and collective interest are also shared. Because the existence of the self always means a coexistence of the self with the other or others, the interest of the self is shared with others by definition. There is no absolute and exclusive self-interest to start with. From a purely egoistic perspective, it is easier to define self-interest, as Maslow has done. But such definitions are not reliable because nobody lives in isolation. Consider Maslow's hierarchy of human needs. Survival, security, love and belonging, esteem, and self-actualization – which of them exists in a world with only one individual living in vacuum and

---

[81] Morgenthau 1961, 5.   [82] Waltz 1979.   [83] Axelrod and Keohane 1985, 85–115.

which of them does not need others to become true? The simultaneity of existence and coexistence means that self-interest is simultaneously shared with other-interest, but cannot be replaced by the latter, and vice versa. They are two in one, rather than one over the other as two discrete and independent categories. This understanding of interest differs from either the "individual-before-relation" argument or the "relation-before-individual" proposition. Its focus is on the simultaneity of self-existence and coexistence, of self-interest and shared interest, recognizing the mutuality and complementarity of both rather than putting them in a dualistic conceptual framework.

Again, it is worth reiterating here that I do not assume the primacy of coexistence over existence, for if it were true, an easy corollary would be that shared interest is over self-interest. The monopoly of interest by the collectivity is extremely dangerous and any self-interest would be ignored and even categorically denied. Just as self-interest is always shared with other-interest, it is also shared with collective interest. Neither can subdue the other. Mencius argues for a middle course when discussing self-interest and collective interest as follows:

The principle of the philosopher Yang was – "Each one for himself." Though he might have benefited the whole kingdom by plucking out a single hair, he would not have done it. The philosopher Mo loves all equally. If by rubbing smooth his whole body from the crown to the heel, he could have benefited the kingdom, he would do it. Tsze-mo holds a medium between these. By holding that medium, he is nearer the right . . . [84]

The existence of the self simultaneously involves and implies the participation of others. Thus the ontology of coexistence decides that egoistic rationality based upon the ontology of isolated self-existence is likely to be irrational once it is put in a coexistent context, as the single-move PD game shows. Interest is shared because it is defined first of all in a relational context. Furthermore, unlike institutionalism which is based on the ontology of existence, coexistence or relational existence presumes emphatically the shared nature of interest and at the same time stresses the joint effort of the self and other as a most reliable way to the realization of interest. A newly born baby, for example, needs to survive. Nobody denies that it is the most fundamental interest of the baby-ego, but this interest can be realized only through her parents or others who offer help. Since this interest is shared from the moment the baby is born or even conceived, the help of the parents is natural and out of their own will. A nation-state needs to survive and the threat to its survival is defined in

---

[84] Mencius 2014, 340–341.

terms of other nation-states. The well-known security dilemma describes in fact a situation where the survival of a state tends to be perceived as endangered by the increasing military forces of another related state.[85] In this sense, security is relationally defined. In the imagined world where only one self exists, security would never constitute a problem, just as the imagined situation where should God have created only one Adam, he would live happily (or unhappily) forever in the Garden of Eden. Both happiness and sadness come when there are relations among humans. However, no one can escape the reality that her existence is at the same time coexistence with others and her interest is necessarily co-interest with others.

During the Cold War years, for example, the survival of the Soviet Union was always defined in terms of threat from the United States, and vice versa. The United States and the Soviet Union had to live together, no matter whether they liked it or not. Realism usually takes survival as the most fundamental self-interest of an actor, but the survival of any actor involves the survival of others and therefore survival itself is a shared interest of the self and the other. The interest in survival of the United States was shared with the interest in survival of the Soviet Union. While the nuclear utilization strategy (NUTS) was primarily based on a unilaterally defined self-interest, the mutual assured destruction strategy (MAD) rested more on self-interest defined in terms of other-interest. If MAD implies the philosophy of "live and let live," NUTS rests more on the survival of the self without much consideration of that of the other. MAD was thus first of all a mutually guaranteed survival strategy because both sides eventually realized that their own survival depended on the survival of the other.[86] Strategic nuclear weapons are said to facilitate the cooperation of the two superpowers exactly because their lethal character and suicide effect made the shared nature of their survival interest most conspicuous. Their sense of self-interest comes from their relational existence. In recent years, common security has become a more popular concept in international relations,[87] showing that shared survival as a concept has been more widely accepted.

We may use another extreme example – territorial disputes. That interest is shared means that any solution to conflict is and must be a compromise on both sides; or both should benefit and at the same time pay a cost. It is a common argument that territorial disputes are zero-sum games. Most countries take territorial issues as the most important national interest. One side gains while the other side loses. If it were true in a wild jungle, in a "live and let live" world where negotiation rather than

[85] Hertz 1950.   [86] Keeny and Panofsky 1981.   [87] Acharya 2004.

force is the generally agreed approach, the most reliable solution would be that both sides make compromises. It is not a true or false choice, but one in which both win and both lose. Any win-win solution is at the same time a lose-lose solution, for winning something means simultaneously losing something else. Otherwise no lasting solution can be made. In a relational situation, a practical and realizable definition of self-interest is thus always based upon an inclusive consideration of the interest of related others.

Coexistence is even more a reality in the international relations world, which, as we have discussed, very much resembles a traditional agricultural village where you need to live with others, willingly or unwillingly. It is a matter of necessity rather than a matter of choice. The key element of coexistence is relations among actors. Think carefully about the cases discussed by game theorists and any of them involves relations at least between two players. Game theory, in fact, implies a strong sense of shared fate/interest of the players, for it has realized that an interest exclusively of and for the self is never achievable in a social situation, even though game theory is based on the ontology of existence and explicitly embraces the rationalistic model in terms of self-interest and interest maximization. Individual rationality seems to be a most reasonable principle because it justifies the argument that the ego works to gain her best interest. It has been so internalized that national leaders, following Machiavelli and Morgenthau, often justify their action in terms of national interest, as if it were the highest morality they always cherish. The problem with it is that the interest is exclusively defined and such interest in fact can hardly exist in a social world. The problem with the designers of games then is that they do not realize the shared nature of interest in society in the first place even though they recognize the fact that interest can be achieved through joint efforts. In other words, they start with exclusively self-interest and end up with a relational context. Any interest that appears as if it were purely of oneself necessarily involves the interest of others. You buy rice instead of wheat flour to satisfy your need for survival, and at the same time your action for self-interest involves the interest of both the farmers who grow rice and those who grow wheat. Self-interest exists, but it exists simultaneously with other-interest and collective interest as well.

Relational Webs as the Social Context

For the relational theory, I define the social context in terms of the totality of relations, which constitute complex and ramifying relational webs. Since "relation" first of all refers to the self's personal relations with others so that we start from the self, assuming that the self is related to others at the moment it begins to exist. For the purpose of analysis, we take a single self as the starting point although in reality there is no such a case that the single self ever exists. Each self has her relational circles which indicate the various types of relationships and their different natures. Traditionally, for example, the Chinese made a rough division between kinship and non-kinship, indicating how intimate relationships are. One's family usually represents the closest and some other relationships may also be important. The relational totality is a key factor because it is the social context which designates the sphere of activities of the actor. Furthermore, it is believed that if these relationships are well managed and run harmoniously, there naturally follow good governance and healthy social order.

Let me again use Fei's ripple analogy, which is most illustrative in describing the relational circles of the self. When discussing social relationships in Chinese society, he makes a comparison between the Chinese and the Western. He starts by mentioning that the Chinese word *jia* (family) is quite ambiguous about who are included and then he says:

In my opinion, the ambiguity indicates the difference between our social structure and that of the West. Our pattern is not like distinct bundles of straws. Rather, it is like the circles that appear on the surface of a lake when a rock is thrown into it. Everyone stands at the center of the circles represented by his or her own social influence. Everyone's circles are interrelated. One touches different circles at different times and places.[88]

The ripples look like concentric circles with the self at the center and radiating from it are the concentric circles that represent the total social relations of the self. The bigger the circles are, the larger the actor's sphere of activities is and the farther her influence can reach; and the farther away the circles are from the self at the center, the less intimately they are related and the less significant the relationship becomes. We may imagine that the self's relational totality is roughly composed of three-layer concentric circles as Figure 5.1 shows.

It depicts a picture of three-layered concentric circles of relationships and the dots on them indicate others that are related to the self. The primary circle includes kinship, the secondary friendship/partnership, and the tertiary a strangers' world. The most significant circles are the first two, but the tertiary circle, or the strangers' world, is a potential space to be explored. Within each circle, there are numerous sub-circles (not marked here), which also show the nature of the relationships between the self and the others, for example, close friends and average friends, deadly enemies or average enemies.

---

[88] Fei 2012, 42.

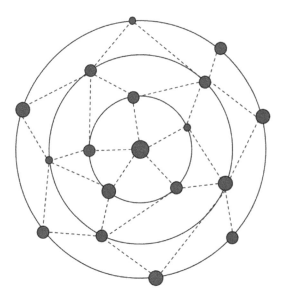

Figure 5.1: Three-layered relational circles

In international society, the most relevant is the secondary circle, but by definition relationships are transferable across the sub-circles: A close friend may become an average friend and a partner can be at the same time a competitor.

The self and the other are related by these continual and connecting ripples. However, each of the others, for itself, is also a self of its own and has its relational circles exactly like the self's. In society, there are numerous such "selves," and their relational circles are overlapping, cross-ramifying, interrelating, and interpenetrating, just as many spiders' webs overlap with one another. The self's relational circles and the relational circles of those specific others who are related to the self together constitute the relational totality of the self, which we may call the self's relational context. It is this relational context that makes up the self's social cosmos wherein she lives, acts, and interacts. We may imagine a simple triadic situation where three actors are involved: A, B, and C. Each has her relational circles and their circles are overlapping and interpenetrating, as Figure 5.2 indicates. The totality of the relations represented by the overlapping circles is the relational totality of each and all of the three. The relational theory holds that this relational totality or relational context is the pivot for understanding how humans act and where they gain the meaning for their social action as well as their life.

Figure 5.2: Three overlapping relational circles, representing A, B, and C

This relational complexity represents the space for the self to act and the field for her activities, just as a spider cannot move out of the web it has woven (but the weaving is a continuous process and the web can be ever enlarged, depending on the capabilities and efforts of the spider). The interests, objectives, and goals of the self are all realized or can be completely destroyed through its maneuvers on the web. The social web is thus engaging and entangling. This is what I term "relational enmeshment," an environment where an actor lives and cannot escape.

Let me again use the village analogy.[89] A traditional Chinese agricultural village offers a good illustration of the so-called relational enmeshment. It is a small place where everyone knows everyone else and all are related in one way or another. It was an agricultural community, with people gathering together in a settlement and tilling their farmland nearby. The villagers were born there and had little choice as to whom

---

[89] Qian Mu argues that an important difference in the mindsets of the Chinese and the Westerners lies in the fact that the traditional Chinese society was agricultural while the Western one was commercial. For the former, the family and the village constituted the pivots for society, while for the latter individualism dominated. Ge Zhaoguang also argues that a natural village was the primary unit of life in rural China. See Qian 2005, 34–35; Ge 2001, 8.

they were related. In many of the traditional Chinese villages, most of the villagers had the same family name, indicating that they were somewhat related, close or distant.[90] Since they lived together as villagers and since there was little mobility as their agricultural way of life determined, they usually stayed in the same village for life. All villagers were either relatives or neighbors, seeing one another every day. Such practices over millennia mean that they had to have and stay with lasting relationships among the villagers who knew one another well. The way of life might be different for a hunting civilization, for hunters had a much higher rate of mobility and more constantly changed habitats where they had different people and environments to relate themselves with. Today Chinese society, with a very fast pace of being modernized, has changed a lot with a much higher rate of mobility, but the culture and practice as well as the way of thinking formulated over years have lingered.

If we look at international society, it is perhaps more like the traditional agricultural village in this respect than a modern Western city, with the nation-states as the villagers. In international life, relations are usually something that state actors have little freedom to choose and relations tend to last for a long time. In other words, international actors in a relational enmeshment tend to find their relations with others immovable and durable. It is especially true of today's international society in the process of globalization, which is indeed depicted as a global village. Very much again like the villagers in a traditional agricultural community, any country in today's small international society knows every other country at least fairly well and has to stay with such relationships almost permanently. If Wendt is correct in describing international society as one with the Lockean culture as the dominant ideational structure,[91] then elimination of other nation-states is no longer the practice in it, or at least no longer the main practice. All the existing 200-odd nation-states can live long and have to be related with one another. Neighbors cannot move or be moved away and two states may terminate their diplomatic ties, but cannot terminate their actual relationships even as dead enemies. Moreover, no matter how far away two states are geographically located, they are related one way or another. The days are gone forever that two states far away from each other could be strangers and did not have to relate with each other. Barry Buzan, in discussing today's international society, has suggested that since an all-round world society is not feasible

---

[90] A typical example is Qufu, Shandong Province, where Confucius was born. Most of the people there have the same family name (*Kong*) with Confucius. It means that all the people with the family name of *Kong* are relatives and can be buried in the Confucian Graveyard after death.

[91] Wendt 1999, 279–297.

at present because of the real diversity in norms and practices in different regions, it would be better to form regional international societies whose members have similar values and identities.[92] In fact it is impossible. No matter how far the regions are geographically apart, inter-regional relations are real and there cannot be regional international societies standing as independent entities and treating each other as strangers. It is unimaginable that East Asia would move and function on its own without dealing with Europe, Africa, or America. It is also true of Europe. In the global village, nation-states are no strangers to one another. They have no choice but to be related among themselves, and do so virtually permanently, too.

Relations in international society therefore tend to be characterized by immovability and durability.[93] Actors are relational and nation-states have little choice but to relate and to be related. They are born into the relational complex and they cannot move away from it. For them, relations that constitute the social world begin to have meaning at the moment when they come into it. It is perhaps true that historical processes, through yoking, created nation-states, but for any particular nation-state, the relational world becomes meaningful only when it is being born into and enmeshed in it. Therefore, the simultaneity of relations and relators, especially of human relations and relators, is a distinct character of the relational theory, and the relational enmeshment, that is, the entanglement of the relator in relational webs, no matter whether or not she likes it, constitutes the relator's living habitat and the social context for her activities.

However, I need to clearly point out that the relational enmeshment argument does not mean to delete human agency, just as it does not exaggerate such agency. When Jackson and Nexon put forward the processual/relational approach and argue that relations come before states, agency seems to have an insignificant role to play. What they stress is that processes create actors, and therefore their argument may lead people to the understanding or misunderstanding that social processes are logically prior to the entities doing the interaction.[94] Although they do not define "relation" in explicit terms, it seems that for them relations are social interactions or transactional processes with little agential dynamics. A more thorough syndrome of "agential hopelessness" is explicitly

---

[92] Buzan has proposed this model, that is, "layered international society." While it is not possible to build a cohesive global international society, it is easier to establish a regional one because nations in a region have more shared values, cultures, and institutions. Thus we may have a European international society and an East Asian international society. See Buzan 2010.

[93] Zhai 2011, 48–49.   [94] Jackson and Nexon 1999, 301.

expressed by Hopf's logic of habit, which denies agency completely, because habit rather than agency does much of the work.[95] An agent largely follows robotically and monotonously its habit. Network theories are at the other extreme. For them, actors tend to come before rather than after relations and play a very dynamic role in establishing and developing relations, for they study the phenomena that actors actively and purposefully choose whom to relate with through social interaction so that the network may grow and function and norms may spread and work.[96]

The relational theory stands somewhere in between: While it realizes the immovability and durability of human relations, which constrain social actors, it also gives ample room for active agency. International actors, on the one hand, have little choice in deciding their relational totality: They have to relate or to be related with other international actors, whether they like it or not. On the other hand, what they are able to do and where their agency is given full play is the management of the relationships and of the relational totality they are enmeshed in. I argue that no states, nor any social actor, can escape the relational enmeshment, but it does not mean that they are prey caught hopelessly by such a social context. Rather, the relational web it is in has an enabling function, which, appropriately exploited, can facilitate the state actor's success, just as it constrains the actor's action at the same time. Furthermore, as to whether or not to have relationships with others a state actor has little choice, but as to how to manage the relationships and enlarge the relational circles it has huge room to maneuver. The United States cannot choose to move Cuba away from its doorstep, but can manage its relationship with Cuba and change its nature. China could take the United States as a deadly enemy in the 1950s, and fought against it in Korea, and also it could take it as a quasi-ally against the Soviet Union in the 1970s. In other words, the relationally enmeshed actor is able to manage the relationships and the relational context for gaining self-interest and for maintaining social order.

Such a description of the social world rests on an important assumption of the relational perspective. It is the understanding that the boundaries between relational circles are never clear, for there are no absolute dividing lines between the ripples or circles of relationships. Fei distinguishes between the ripple-like relational patterns of Chinese society and the rice-bundle pattern of Western society, arguing that the latter is a "group society," each discrete group standing independently and having a clear

---

[95] Hopf 2010.
[96] See Hafner-Burton, Kahler, and Montgomery 2009. See also Ward, Stovel, and Sacks 2011; Cook and Whitemeyer 1992; Wellman, Chen, and Dong 2002.

boundary that demarcates itself from other groups.[97] When we use such dualistic terms as in- and out- groups, self- and other-groups, boundaries, etc., we need to understand that these concepts and descriptions almost always imply a clear and definite line between the entities, and that the Chinese language has rarely seen society as such and is in fact quite barren in dualistic rhetoric. Fei in particular compares the term of "family" used in Chinese and Western societies to indicate this difference:

Families in the West are organizations with distinct boundaries. If a Western friend writes to you saying that he will "bring his family" to visit you, he knows very well who will be coming with him. In China, however, the sentence is very ambiguous. In England and America, a family will include the man, his wife, and his children who have not yet grown up. If he is bringing only his wife, he does not use the word *family*. In China, we often see the sentence "The whole family will come" (*hedi guanglin*), but few people can tell what family members should be included in the word *di* (family). In Chinese, the word *jia* (family) is used in many ways. *Jialide* (the one at home) can mean one's wife. *Jiamen* (Kinsmen) may be directed at a big group of uncles and nephews. *Zijiaren* (my own people) may include anyone whom you want to drag into your own circle, and you use it to indicate your intimacy with them. The scope of *zijiaren* can be expanded or contracted according to the specific time and place. It can be used in a very general way, even to mean that everyone under the sun is a *jia* (family).[98]

It is this ambiguity that creates opportunities. Ambiguity implies uncertainty, which in turn contains opportunity for creation. The future is uncertain so that human agency can play a significant role to create something new. If the future should be completely certain and determined, human agency would have no role to play at all. To manage one's relational circles may well mean to make one's relational context more favorable by getting others more intimate. Intimacy is indeed a key word in the relational theory. The family members are the most intimate. And, as Fei points out, the kind of relationship among family members is extendable to others who are not of one's family. Fei argues that kinship is a most intimate relationship, and it can be "extended to embrace countless numbers of people ..." The Chinese concept of "relation" differs from the Western one in the fact that for the Chinese relationships are seen as a gradual process from intimacy to distance. This gradual process necessitates the ambiguity and therefore the potentiality for relational management. The most significant character of social relations is how intimately or closely one is related to a specific other. For Westerners it is often whether this specific other is a member of the in-group or out-group. It is clear. For the Chinese, on the other hand, the line between

---

[97] Fei 2012, 41.   [98] Fei 2012, 41–42, emphasis in original.

these groups is blurred and changeable, and therefore manageable. Relations usually become less and less intimate as the ripples get less and less discernible: It is a gradually diminishing process without clear boundaries. When Chinese define their international partners, for example, they tend to use such different terms as all-weather strategic partners, comprehensive strategic partners, and strategic partners, indicating the decreasing intimacy of their relationships. In addition, since there are no clear demarcating boundaries, identities are subject to change more easily than in the in-group/out-group division: A comprehensive strategic partner may be degraded to the status of an average strategic partner, or vice versa. Han Yu (768–824 AD), a leading Chinese philosopher and writer in the Tang Dynasty, once said to the effect that once you come into China, you are Chinese; and if you go away into the barbarian, you will be barbarian.[99]

If intimate relationships can be extended boundlessly, just as the concept of "family" may be used to include all under heaven, then the opportunity of the self to manage her relational circles, at least in theory, is limitless. It is true that her relational totality defines the sphere of activities of the self. However, since the connectivity of the self's relational circles with others can extend theoretically the totality of her relations to infinity, the self's opportunities follow the extension. Actor A may make use of Actor B's relational circles if A is connected with B, and may also make use of Actor C's relational circles if B is connected with C, etc. In international society, as we have discussed, the relational totality is not infinite if we take nation-states as the primary relators, but the potential of a state to manage its relations and relationships is unlimited.

Conclusion

The Confucian worldview differs from that of Western societies in that it sees the world as one of relations rather than atomistic and discrete entities. It is especially true of the social world, where human relations are the most significant factor in their daily life and practice. Such a worldview tends to pay more attention to relations among members of a community rather than individual actors *per se*; to interdependence rather than independence; and to dynamic processes rather than static structures.

Once human relations are put in the primary place in social activities, coexistence becomes a most significant concept, for any relationship

[99] Quoted in Liu 2015, 59.

involves the existence of the self and its coexistence with the other. The self-other relationship is thus not only something indicating two interacting entities, but also a crucial factor that brings the two into an immanent coexistence. This assumption goes against the ontology of existence, which constitutes the mainstream understanding in the West of the universe and often leads to a dualistic interpretation of the social world. As Emirbayer comments: "Large segments of the sociological community continue implicitly or explicitly to prefer the former point of view [substantialism]. Rational-actor and norm based models, diverse holisms and structuralisms, and statistical 'variable' analyses – all of them only subsequently – hold sway throughout much of the discipline."[100] It is true of the way of thinking and practicing; it is also true of the mainstream social sciences including perhaps particularly IR. The relational theory, on the contrary, holds that ontologically neither existence nor coexistence has primacy over the other and both are simultaneously significant, for they live on and gain meaning from each other. Privileging each over the other will lead to a dualistic structure that goes against the relational understanding of the social world.

Based upon the assumption of coexistence, I argue in this chapter that the identity of a social actor is shaped and reshaped by her relations with others and her relationship with the social context. It is not something that the actor has as a pregiven. The simultaneity of existence and coexistence means that the identity of the self is related to that of significant others, for the self-other coexistence is the social condition on which one's identity is formed. Similarly, interest in a social setting is always shared. It is hard to define in absolute terms the self-interest without considering the conditions that shape it. Even survival, the most basic human need and the fundamental "self"-interest, is related to that of others, including one's deadly enemy, as illustrated by the US–USSR relations during the Cold War years.

Relations are everywhere, West and East alike. However, it has been largely absent from the dominant narrative in the West, which is reflected conspicuously in the intellectual and academic traditions. In the Confucian cultural communities, on the other hand, relational thinking has largely dominated in practice. As rationality is the most characteristic concept of Western societies, relationality provides the foundation of the Chinese social world. Relations in the Universe, especially between humans and nature, are the primary consideration for Daoism, while social relations, that is, relations among humans, constitute the pivot of Confucianism. Mencius has even said that people differ from other

---

[100] Emirbayer 1997, 281.

lower animals in that the former take relations among them as the most significant and understand the moral principles that govern such relations.[101] Social relations are seen as the starting point of politics, economics, and culture. Confucius identifies five cardinal relationships as the foundation of a society, and their appropriate maintenance by appropriate norms and codes is the necessary condition for good govern-ance and harmonious social order. Norms, governance, social order, and morality are therefore all for relational management. Even education aims to teach people to know the importance of using appropriate moral principles to govern and manage relations among them in society.[102] In the Chinese tradition, which rests to a larger extent on agricultural practice, relations permeate society, and management of complex rela-tionships for a sufficiently orderly society constitutes the soul as well as the art of politics. The logic of action is more relationally oriented and the realization of self-interest also tends to be sought in terms of relational management and joint optimization.

[101] Mencius argues that men do not differ much from other lower animals, but man, especially the superior (virtuous) men, "clearly understood the multitude of things and closely observed the relations of humanity" (Mencius 2014, 201).

[102] Mencius says: "When the five kinds of grains were brought to maturity, the people all obtained a substance. But men possess a moral nature; if they are well fed, warmly clad, and comfortably lodged, without being taught at the same time, they become almost like beasts. This was a subject of anxious solicitude to the sage of Shun, and he appointed Hsieh to be the Minister of Instruction, to teach the relations of humanity: how, between father and son, there should be affection; between sovereign and minister, righteous-ness; between husband and wife, attention to their separate functions; between old and young, a proper order; and between friends, fidelity" (Mencius 2014, 127–128).

6   Meta-relationship and the *Zhongyong* Dialectics

The previous chapter discussed the underlying assumptions of a relational theory with the key argument that the social world is composed of human relations. Generally speaking, the proposed relational theory centers on relations and assumes the ontological significance of relations in human society. Closely linked with it are the epistemological and methodological dimensions which sustain the relational theory of world politics. After "relation" is taken as the central piece of the theory then, questions follow: If we conceive the world in general and the international relations world in particular as composed of dynamic relations, how then do we understand the multiple relations that connect actors in such a world? What is the nature of such relationships? Without answering these questions, all complex and fluid relations and all overlapping relational circles would appear a complete mess.

To provide an answer, we need to discuss two concepts at the epistemological and methodological levels: the meta-relationship and the *zhongyong* dialectics.[1] The former is the prototype and the simplest form representing all relationships and the latter the way to understand and interpret the nature of this meta-relationship. In this chapter, therefore, I shall put forward the following three interrelated assumptions. First, the meta-relationship, as understood by traditional Chinese philosophy, is the relationship between *yin* (the feminine principle/force) and *yang* (the masculine principle/force) and all other relationships can be seen as derivatives of the *yin-yang* relationship; second, the approach to understanding the nature of the meta-relationship is the *zhongyong* dialectics, a long cherished Confucian worldview that may lay the epistemological foundation for understanding dialectically the meta-relationship;[2] and

---

[1] Qin 2010; 2014.

[2] The Chinese *zhongyong* dialectics contains mainly Daoist and Confucian ideas about the universe. I use the term *zhongyong*, a Confucian term, and call it a Confucian worldview because of two reasons. The first is that Daoism is more about relations between humans and nature while Confucianism is more secular and largely about human relations; the second is that Confucianism takes "*zhong* (centrality)" more emphatically as the most important element, stressing harmony as a dynamic state of appropriately centering.

third, the polarities contained in the meta-relationship, *yin* and *yang*, are in a continuous process of harmonization and keep moving toward central harmony, which, as the natural and ultimate state of the cosmos, characterizes the relationship between the polarities.

Since we posit that dialectics is a "metasystematic form of cognitive organization"[3] and constitutes the primary way of understanding the world in general and relations in particular, it is necessary to discuss it in detail. It is highly relevant because it tends to focus on the understanding of relations, starting from relationships between two objects or polarities. Furthermore, since the etymology of "dialectics" is about differences, disagreements, contradictions, and change, it is thus relevant to international relations especially in terms of conflict and cooperation.

There are two important traditions in terms of dialectical thinking. One is the Western Hegelian tradition (reflecting more the etymology of dialectics) and the other is the Chinese Confucian tradition, or the *zhongyong* dialectics as I term it (containing both Daoist and Confucian conception). Both Chinese and Westerners use the same word "dialectics *(bianzhengfa* in Chinese)," and the two traditions do share some important commonalities. They are by definition about relations between objects; they see things in polarities;[4] they discuss in particular change and transformation; and they may both have their respective meta-relationships, for example, being/nothingness in the former and *yin/yang* in the latter. However, the meaning of "dialectics" used in the two languages is not identical and in fact they differ significantly in important aspects.[5] It is better illustrated if we compare the Western and the Chinese ways of reasoning and thinking as well as the Hegelian and the Chinese dialectics, for there are indeed cultural differences in what is generally called dialectics and such differences have significant impacts on how people perceive and conceive relations among international actors. This chapter, therefore, first discusses the Western logical way of thinking and the Hegelian dialectics, then deliberates on the Chinese or *zhongyong* dialectics, and finally sees how the *zhongyong* dialectics shed light on the nature of relations and on the key question of cooperation and conflict in international relations.

Hegelian Dialectics and Conflict between Polarities

It is often understood that formal logic and dialectics are two different approaches and have different functions for understanding the world. To some extent, to be logical is perhaps undialectical, for formal logic

---

[3] Ho 2000, 1064.   [4] Schwarz 1964.   [5] Tian 2005.

and dialectical logic rest on opposite principles: the former on the principle of noncontradiction whereas the latter on the principle of contradiction.[6] Perhaps, in a general sense, it seems to be true. However, since they are two important organizers for thinking and interpreting rooted in Western societies, they are nurtured by the same cultural traditions and practices. In fact, formal logic and its principles agree with the Hegelian dialectics in many important respects despite their difference.[7] In this section, therefore, it is necessary to discuss the formal logic first.

Formal Logic and the Taxonomic Thought Pattern

Formal logic is perhaps one of the greatest inventions and it allows inference through pure formal structures without referring to any actual things or objects or experiences. Although traditional Chinese philosophers touched upon something like logic, the systematic logical inference through formal and absolute rules is undoubtedly an Aristotelian tradition. Its contribution to intellectual progression is remarkable. I do not intend to discuss in detail this way of reasoning, and only want to outline some important aspects that are relevant to the discussion of dialectics, especially to the Hegelian dialectics. Particularly relevant here are the principles of Aristotelian logic. The discussion of these principles by Peng and Nisbett and the application of such principles in their psychological study shed light on the influence of culture on thinking, reasoning, and behavior.[8]

The Aristotelian logic rests on three principles: the law of identity, the law of noncontradiction, and the law of the excluded middle. The law of identity holds that everything is identical with itself, or $A = A$. The second law stipulates that nothing can be both true and false. A and non-A, contradictory to each other, cannot be both true: If A is true, non-A must be false. Contradictory statements, for example, cannot both be true. The third law posits that any statement is either true or false, meaning that there is no middle ground for compromise. It is an either-or logic, either A or B, there can never be both A and B. Peng and Nisbett use the example of "student" to illustrate the three theorems: A student is a student (identity); a student is not a nonstudent (noncontradictory); and a person must either be a student or a nonstudent and she cannot be both (the excluded middle).[9] These principles are crucial to formal logic and the rigor of these principles guarantees that logic works as the

---

[6] Heine and Teschke 1996.   [7] Hegel 1991; Avineri 1972.   [8] Peng and Nisbett 1999.
[9] Ibid., 744.

appropriate way of reasoning and inference, although in practice the Greeks also valued the "middle way."

Formal logic, as a great device of thought organization, has contributed greatly to the progress of scientific studies. It is primarily a Western invention. During the thousand years' course of its development, it has helped humans to create and generate remarkable achievements. Some have argued that one reason for the Chinese to lag behind in science and technology in modern times is that they did not have formal logic and thus failed to develop the kind of logical reasoning and abstract thinking science needs. Formal logic is indeed a powerful discourse that helps and constitutes human mindsets. The relevant question here, however, is: What is implied in formal logic and its principal theorems Peng and Nisbett discuss? In other words, what are the necessary assumptions for logical reasoning to work?

For me, the first is what I call the taxonomy-oriented thought pattern.[10] Formal logic is a rigorously systematic way of reasoning and a powerful tool for abstract thinking. In other words, it requires a taxonomic system for qualitative categorization of objects in the first place. It is nurtured by and further nurtures this taxonomical way of thinking. Any logical inference is category-sensitive and requires everything to be put into well-defined and neatly demarcated categories. In all the three laws of formal logic, there are A and B, or non-A and non-B, all of which represent categories of people and things. A student represents one category and a nonstudent a different category. The periodical table of elements is a good example for it groups the elements of similar properties together, assuming that these things have defining and pregiven properties. The inert elements (He, Ne, Ar, Kr, Xe, and Rn) are neighbors to each other in the table because they are all gases whose essential property is inactivity. Nisbett's description of a psychological experiment showed this way of thinking clearly. In the experiment, three objects – a cow, a chicken, and some grass – were drawn on the board and Chinese and American children were asked to place two of them together. The American children were category-sensitive and placed the cow and chicken together because they both belonged to the "animal" category, while the Chinese put the cow and grass together because cows ate grass. Nisbett then commented, "the American children preferred to group objects because they belonged to the 'taxonomic' category, that is, the same classification term could be applied to both ..."[11]

Following this taxonomic pattern of thought, we then easily see that formal logic is an object-oriented approach. Objects, both in physical and

[10] Qin 2010.   [11] Nisbett 2003, 140–141.

social forms, are seen as discrete and independent of each other in the world and categorized according to the similarity or dissimilarity of their essential properties and attributes. The category of students excludes whoever is a nonstudent and the category of animals refuses to take in whatever is a non-animal. Thus an object is a real entity of a certain category, which is independent of other objects and of the context in which it lives. What is most important within this thought pattern is to put an object into a distinct category and then to determine the essential properties and defining attributes of the object, which distinguish it from other objects. Think about two objects, A and non-A. The theorems of formal logic would tell us that A cannot be non-A, and vice versa. Each is discrete, independent, and able to stand by and of itself, as either A with the essential A properties or non-A with the essential properties that A does not possess.

This object-oriented thought pattern naturally led to some consideration about two key concepts in both the natural and social worlds – change and certainty. Since each object is independently defined by its essential properties and attributes, then it may change in appearances and variable attributes, but its nature is non-changeable and its essential properties are non-transformable. Iron is iron and cannot be gold, and a cat is a cat and cannot be an eagle, any time and any place. For any common sense it is a fact. Underlying this, however, is the assumption of essential non-changeability, which, in turn, lays the foundation for certainty. The taxonomy-oriented thought process makes categorization the most important means of understanding objects in both the natural and social worlds. As an object behaves according to rules and laws because of their essential properties, and objects of some category according to some rules and laws, categorization helps to discern the rules and laws applicable to the relevant categories. Once the rules and laws are found, how the object behaves becomes clear and certain. The Newtonian object keeps its present position and status unless an external force works upon it. This principle has similar application in the social world. An actor has its own properties, free, impermeable, and independent of contexts and circumstances. A corporate, for example, is a business and one of its essential properties is seeking profits. No matter what happens, this essential feature will not change. If all actors are thus defined, there must be laws to enable or restrain their behavior and there must be contracts to bind them together within society. In international relations, for instance, balance of power, as an institution, is able to restrain the major nation-states in the international system, whose essential and non-changeable desire is to seek, maintain, and increase power, or "struggle for power."[12]

[12] Morgenthau 1961.

Rules and norms, once institutionalized, can also harness actors' independent behavior, govern instrumental instinct, and facilitate collective action.[13] Thus their actions are predictable and actors are certain about one another and about the order of their living habitat. The fundamental non-changeability leads to the belief in certainty, both encouraging tremendous human efforts and tenacious search to find the laws and rules to govern objects which are categorized according to their essential, invariable properties and attributes.

In addition, formal logic, especially the law of noncontradiction and together with the law of the excluded middle, leads naturally to an "either-or" mindset. Where the former refuses to equal A with non-A and the latter precludes a middle ground where something between A and non-A may have a co-living space, the either-or logic rules. Thus, Schrödinger's cat is ridiculous because it must be either alive or dead and a superposition of being both alive and dead is illogical and therefore fallacious and absurd. In the social world it leads in fact to a dichotomous structure with a clear boundary between the two objects. In some sense, polarities such as inner and outer, self and other, dynamic and static, strong and weak, big and small, black and white, and so on, all go with this logic. A nation-state, for example, is either essentially good or bad, and cannot be both good and bad. When someone says, "You are either with us or against us," it is also a typical reflection of this mindset. Although such an arbitrary rule organizes one's thought neatly, it achieves this at tremendous costs. As the communications theorist Robert Logman has commented, "The Greeks became slaves to the linear, either-or orientation of their logic."[14]

The Hegelian Dialectics and Synthesization Via Conflict

The Hegelian dialectics is a powerful and most influential tool to organize thoughts. It is a worldview that tells how people should see the world and reason about it.[15] Moreover, it is an approach and a schema for the discussion and understanding of social relations. In many studies of the social sciences and humanities, we can see its influence. It is perhaps the most conspicuous and sophisticated approach to deal with

[13] Keohane 1984 and 1989; Kratochwil 1989; Krasner 1983.
[14] Quoted in Nisbett 2003, 11.
[15] For the relational theory, the *zhongyong* dialectics is not a mere method; it is also a way of seeing and understanding the world. Brincat (2009) takes the Hegelian dialectics as almost completely methodological. I think that argument is too absolute. In many respects, both the Hegelian and *zhongyong* dialectics have both epistemological and methodological significance. And they are worldviews.

relations and relationships, for it structures things into polarities and explains their relationship. In this sense it may serve as a major approach to the understanding of relations in general and human relations in particular. Furthermore, and perhaps more significantly, the Hegelian dialectics is a typical device to provide an understanding of the self-other relationship in the thesis-antithesis framework, which, together with the third term in the Hegelian dialectics, the synthesis, is highly relevant to identity formation, especially in the international relations world.

We have discussed formal logic because, I argue, it is related to the Hegelian dialectics in important respects. Some may say, as mentioned above, that application of the principles of formal logic, like the non-contradiction theorem, is undialectical,[16] but a careful scrutiny of the primary assumptions of formal logic will reveal the fact that the Hegelian dialectics follows, consciously or unconsciously, rather than violates these assumptions, especially the taxonomic way of thinking, which provides a foundation for structuring the Hegelian dialectics. The thesis and antithesis are objects that belong to different categories and have different essential properties. They are fundamentally opposite to each other, just as the proletarian and the bourgeois classes in capitalist society, which belong to two completely different economic classes. Furthermore, the Hegelian polar terms are independent, discrete, and distinct. They are related, but they are also distinct. As Ling points out, the Hegelian dialectics may assume the mutuality of social relations: The Master and the Slave need to recognize each other as such so that a slave society exists. "But Hegel never really saw the Slave *inside* the Master and the Master *inside* the Slave."[17] They are two separate categories. Similarly and in more general terms, he never saw being inside nothingness and vice versa. "Being and nothingness are mutually related and remain absolutely distinct."[18] His polar terms are

---

[16] Brincat and Ling 2014, 6–7. Brincat cites Jameson who has argued that "the urge to decide between 'binary oppositions' is something motivated by the 'law of non-contradiction' and therefore *un*dialectical." It seems to be true that formal logic's law of non-contradiction leaves no room for contradiction while dialectics rests primarily on contradiction. In the light of this argument, something can be either logical or dialectical. It seems to me, and perhaps to many people outside Western cultural background knowledge, that it is another example of a dualistic "either-or" structure, a trap which it is easy for one to fall in. Formal logic and the Hegelian dialectics converge on one thing: the elimination of contradiction. Formal logic denies the existence of contradiction so as to eliminate any potential contradiction for the maintenance of the logical orthodoxy. The recognition of and emphasis on contradiction by the Hegelian dialectics are, in the final analysis, to eliminate or cancel out such contradiction. Understanding the Hegelian dialectics this way, we can argue that Cheng's analysis is not a misinterpretation while Jameson's is indeed dualistic and problematic.

[17] Brincat and Ling 2014, 3.   [18] Ibid., 13.

of qualitatively distinct categories and the mutuality between them is interaction between two related but distinct objects. Getting opposite objectives from different categories and structuring them as the polarities – this provides the cornerstone of reasoning by the Hegelian dialectics. As such, the Hegelian dialectics follows rather than violates the three important theorems of formal logic we have just discussed. We will explain this point in more detail in the following lines. Finally, Hegelian dialectics rests on contradiction, but its aim is to eliminate contradiction so that the principle of noncontradiction is satisfied. Even though the dialectical process is endlessly full of contradictions which drive progressive development, to overcome the tension and realize the potential through wiping out crucial contradictions for a new synthesis is always a major concern. As Heine and Teschke argue, formal logic and dialectic logic "do not face each other as absolute opposites (in orthodox thought as antinomies), but are capable of solution (transcendence)."[19]

Chung-ying Cheng, typically reflecting the way the Chinese understand Hegel, provides a succinct summary of the propositions of the Hegelian dialectics in the following way:[20]

1. The world is (subjectively) given as oneness (thesis).
2. The world realizes itself in terms of opposition and conflict between the given and its negation (antithesis).
3. The world develops and realizes a higher level of existence by sublating and synthesizing conflicting elements into a more integrated configuration (synthesis).
4. The world will move on according to this sequence in an indefinite progression which will ultimately approximate an ideal perfection.

It is important to notice that the Hegelian dialectics assumes an ever advancing progression of the world and it argues that such progression is realized in the form of the synthesis (or whatever it may be termed) through the interactive relations between the two objects as the given and the negation expressed by the terms of "thesis" and "antithesis." If we structure, for example, nature and humankind as such polarities, the Hegelian dialectics tells us that through continual interaction between nature and humankind progression will be realized. It is similar to reason that through continual interaction between the working class and the capitalist class social and historic progress will be realized in the form of

---

[19] Heine and Teschke 1996, 412.
[20] Cheng 2006, 36. Brincat criticizes Cheng, arguing that he misread and misinterpreted Hegel (Brincat and Ling 2014). He (Brincat 2009) also criticizes the post-modernist view that the Hegelian dialectics seeks homogeneity and dominance through eliminating difference. His question therefore is: Why do post-modernists and Chinese philosophers read Hegel this way?

a new society without any evil of the old one. The most relevant question here for my study, however, is how this progression is realized. In other words, if we take the relationship between the Hegelian polarities as having general significance, what is the nature of such relationship through which the progression is realized?

Perhaps the simplest answer is "conflict." In other words, the Hegelian dialectics is a conflictual dialectics because progression in both human affairs and the objective realities of the world is achieved through conflict between the polarities. The terms of "thesis" and "antithesis," or "given" and "negation," themselves imply antagonism and hostility. This conflict is taken as real and objective. It is normal and therefore unavoidable. Furthermore it should be welcome because it moves history forward toward perfection. The given and its negation struggle to achieve a new form of reality and of society. The Hegelian dialectics provides explanation for change, the process of which is "a process of disharmony. Consequently, disharmony, though objective, is not considered an evil or a destruction of value, but rather a necessity and even a tool for evolution and progression."[21] In this sense the Hegelian dialectics is highly radical, revolutionary, and even destructive, and consequently, its evolutionary progression is progression through *Aufhebung* and its construction of a new synthesis is a construction through destruction. A typical example in social studies is perhaps identity construction via the binary structure of the self and the other. Richard Ned Lebow argues that Kant and Hegel believe in the necessity to create a negative and antagonist "other" simultaneously for the construction of the identity of the "self."[22] Kant draws a clear line between the "us" society and the "other" society and believes that the price of order at home is conflict among societies. For him, the "us" society is maintained at the expense of "others."[23] For Hegel, conflict between the "us" state and the "them" state helps both to be more coherent and more aware of the identity of each. The Hegelian tradition thus sees the self and the other as independent categories structured in a dichotomous way, using "thesis" and "antithesis" to signify them and following the Kant-Hegel construct of the conflictual self-other binary in which the other is the negative and antagonist stereotype.[24]

This essential conflictual nature of the relationship between the interactive polarities seems to be rooted in the deeper structure of mutual exclusiveness in the Hegelian dialectics. The Hegelian dialectics assumes the simultaneity of the thesis and antithesis, each depending on the other for existence. But the two terms are independent, belonging to different

---

[21] Cheng 2006, 37.   [22] Lebow 2008.   [23] Lebow 2008, 475.
[24] Lebow 2008; Brincat and Ling 2014.

categories and having their respective essential properties. This exclusiveness in fact follows the first principle of formal logic of identity: They are two entities, forces, or principles interacting with each other, but they are not and cannot become each other. A equals A only, and it cannot be B. Rudyard Kipling, an English writer who lived long in India, once said, "East is East, and West is West, and never the twain shall meet," reflecting a deeply embedded dualistic way of thinking and mutually exclusive understanding of various civilizations and cultures. The exclusiveness also refers to the fact that the Hegelian dialectics follows rather than violates the third principle of formal logic, i.e. the principle of excluded middle. The polarities are neither mutually transformable nor reciprocally accommodative. It is hard to argue that the proletariat could become the bourgeoisie and vice versa. There must be some new form as the synthesis to reflect the elimination of tension between the two classes. There is no middle ground, which pushes the relationship further into an uncompromising struggle. If we deny the possibility for mutual transformability and accommodation of two different objects, forces, and principles, conflict is the only way to solve the contradiction between them for a noncontradictional nirvana.

To sum up, the Hegelian dialectics is first a conflictual dialectic, seeing the world as one consisting of categories independent of one another, each of which has its own essential properties that do not change and that define it and distinguish it from other categories. Thesis and antithesis stand opposite each other in a binary structure, such as slaves and slave-owners in a slave society and the proletariat and the bourgeoisie in a capitalist world. The nature of the relationship between thesis and antithesis is contradictory, conflictual, and confrontational. A new and higher level of synthesis is reached, if and only if the inherent and non-reconciliatory contradiction between them is resolved through revolutionary changes. In relational terms, it means that the relationship between the two objects is conflictual in nature, and this relational conflict is resolved if and only if one object or both objects disappear.

IR Framed in the Hegelian Dialectics

The discourse of social conflict by the dialectical approach has gone through the works of scholars who advocate and practice it in IR. Contradiction and conflict are seen as normal in social life. Hayward Alker and Thomas Biersteker have placed the dialectical approach on a par with the behavioral-scientific approach and the traditional approach, pointing out that dialectical theorists usually understand the world as a place of conflict between the existing order and its possible alternatives and they "have valued emancipation, favored structural revolutionary change, and have fundamentally challenged the legitimacy of the existing world order."[25] Change through conflict-driven crises has been a dominant theme in all types of dialectics in social sciences.

Furthermore, conflict is not only a normal phenomenon in life, but also a positive and active factor that pushes forward the development of history and humankind. At the micro-level, conflict is the necessary condition for identity construction. Richard Ned Lebow goes to the fundamental question of identity creation. He delineates the binary embedded in the Kant/Hegel philosophy and discusses the essential conflict assumption in international relations, that is, conflict as a necessary condition for identity creation. He says: "In philosophy, political science and politics, identity construction has routinely been assumed to require the creation of 'others'." Furthermore, the "others" are created as negative and antagonistic to the self. In Carl Schmitt's words, political identity "can be best formed in the course of violent struggles against the adversaries."[26] Hegel's dialectics structures this self-other binary, antagonistic in nature, and has been applied to state formation, holding that conflict is not only a natural constant in political and social life, but also a helpful factor for a state to build its identity. As Lebow comments: "Hegel rhapsodizes about the life of states as active and creative agents who play a critical role in the unfolding development of the spirit and mankind. Conflict among states, . . ., helps each to become aware of itself by encouraging self-knowledge among citizens."[27] Thus the positive self and the negative and adversarial other are locked in natural conflict, through which they succeed in making themselves what they are as the self and the other.

At the macro-level, conflict is the factor that pushes forward human history, for it is the prime mover for structural change and the catalyst for social transformation. Cox's critical theory is perhaps a pioneering work in IR that uses the dialectical approach to interpret change of international relations at the macro-level. His structure-counterstructure argument provides a telling example as to how the critical theory seeks to apply the dialectical method to explain and predict hegemony in world politics. As he argues: "Dialectic is introduced, first by deriving the definition of a particular structure . . ., and second, by looking for the emergence of rival structures expressing alternative possibilities of development."[28] A world structure is brought about and gains dominance by the fitting of the three important factors, that is, material capabilities, ideas, and

---

[25] Alker and Biersteker 1984, 125.   [26] Lebow 2008, 474.   [27] Ibid., 475.
[28] Cox 1986, 220.

institutions. Once a dominant structure is established, thus, the dialectical approach tries to explore the contradictions generated by the working of those factors and looks for a possible counterstructure. Dialectic is thus "the potential for alternative forms of development arising from the confrontation of opposed social forces in any concrete historical situation."[29] Structural change therefore is a function of confrontational social forces. By this logic, dialectics is both the epistemology and the methodology of conflict. It is such because it sees conflict as not only a normal phenomenon in human life but also the driving force for historical progress and social transformation. History itself is a process of change and evolution which are constantly pushed by conflict upon conflict. He compares neorealism and historical materialism. After correctly pointing out that both direct attentions to conflict, he continues to discuss their differences:

Neorealism sees conflict as inherent in the human condition, a constant factor flowing directly from the power-seeking essence of human nature and taking the political form of a continual reshuffling of power among the players in a zero-sum game, which is always played according to its own innate rules. Historical materialism sees in conflict the process of a continual remaking of human nature and the creation of new patterns of social relations which change the rules of the game and out of which – if historical materialism remains true to its own logic and method – new forms of conflict may be expected ultimately to arise. In other words, neorealism sees conflict as a recurrent consequence of a continuing structure, whereas historical materialism sees conflict as a possible cause of structural change.[30]

It is in this sense that neorealism is defined as a problem-solving theory because it takes conflict as a problem to be solved, while critical theory is a theory for emancipation which welcomes conflict as the necessary catalyst for such emancipation. Perhaps Cox is most correct in pointing out the difference between neorealism and critical theory in terms of the functions of conflict in their respective depictions of development of international relations. However, it is also true by his comparison that the two theories both take conflict as ontologically significant, whether it is a constant of human life or a crucial cause of social change, or whether it is a problem to be solved or a driving and progressive force for social transformation.

The conflict and conflict-driven progress of humankind has been further developed by Christian Heine and Benno Teschke, who, having criticized the mainstream IR for marginalizing the dialectical approach and denying it a legitimate place in the discipline, argue that the

---

[29] Ibid., 215.   [30] Ibid.

appropriate method to comprehend reality is dialectics, for social reality is itself contradictory and dialectics is the best way to understand social contradictions. In Albert and Lapid's words, they believe that dialectical thinking is able to deal with the contradictory nature of reality.[31] Contradiction, with ontological significance, needs a dialectical mind to understand and to transcend. When Brincat develops his "social-relational dialectic" for world politics, the core of the Hegelian dialectics is even more emphasized.[32] The ontological significance of contradiction and conflict in social life in general and international relations in parti-cular is emphatically and systematically explored. Epistemologically, dia-lectics provides a useful way to understand the world; ontologically, it sees a world full of dynamics because of contradictions; and methodologically, it is the right way to explore change and transformation in the world.[33] For him, significant contradiction and serious conflict produce social crisis and it is such a social crisis that makes social transformation possible.[34] Thus, for the dialectical approach, the central principle is contradiction, the central theme of social life is conflict, and the central aim of theory is to identify crucial contradiction and conflict and fully exploit them to achieve social transformation. Although those authors in IR who follow the dialectical thinking and build upon the dialectical tradition, from Cox to Brincat, do not agree with one another in many respects, they all abide by this fundamental tenet of the Hegelian dialec-tics – conflict as ontologically significant and as the driving force for social transformation.

It is generally recognized that the Hegelian dialectics is a powerful tool for organizing thoughts and analyzing realities and historical develop-ments. As such, it is, consciously or unconsciously, applied widely in social studies. Marxist understanding and interpretation of the staged development of human history and society is a telling and most cited example in this respect. Kuhn's thesis on scientific revolution has an obvious imprint of the Hegelian dialectical thought when he argues that the clash of two immensurable paradigms leads to such revolution.[35] But in IR, scholars of the dialectical school often argue that the dialectical approach is absent or at least marginalized in the mainstream theory, and that IR is the sleeping beauty yet to be awakened by the kiss of the dialectical prince.[36] It is perhaps true that the dialectic approach, as an

---

[31] Albert and Lapid 1997, 406.   [32] Brincat 2011.   [33] Ibid., 681.   [34] Ibid., 683.
[35] In Kuhn's scientific revolution theory, the struggle of the normal science against the anomalies constitutes the key contradiction, which is to be solved by a revolution staged by the scientific community to destroy the established theory and to establish a new one. See Kuhn 1962. Also see Heine and Teschke 1996.
[36] Heine and Teschke 1996; Brincat 2011.

intellectual tool, has not been explicitly employed by mainstream IR theorists. It is also true that dialectics is even explicitly criticized and denied. But, as Mathias Albert and Yosef Lapid have commented, the dialectical tradition has been with IR for years.[37] In IR theories, it seems to me, there are numerous examples that reflect the influence of the Hegelian dialectics in understanding relations among actors. Although the influence is multidimensional and sometimes fragmented, IR theories, especially the mainstream ones, reflect a conspicuous Hegelian tendency in terms of conflict and conflict resolution: The international relations world is one where conflict is ontologically real and objectively normal. Accordingly, self-other conflict is normal and the resolution of such conflict is then either elimination or homogenization of the other. Explicitly or implicitly, difference is to be cancelled out.

Let us consider the three international cultures. Alexander Wendt discusses three international cultures, namely the Hobbesian, the Lockean, and the Kantian. In fact, he describes three types of relationships in the international system: of enmity, of rivalry, and of friendship. The logics of all the three anarchies imply a deeply seated assumption of conflict in the international system, but at the same time reflect three different ways of conflict resolution. Conflict is of ontological significance in international political life as well as in life anywhere. In other words, the self-other relationship is essentially conflictual. It means not only the actor-actor relationship, but also the actor-environment relationship, for the environment can also be taken as the other and is in constant conflict with the self. Wendt argues that the Hobbesian culture is a complete self-help system, which means first that the international relations environment, or the international system itself, is a place of conflict; and second, conflict resolution is unlimitedly violent. It is a wrestling ring where might is right and where the fittest survive. The Hobbesian jungle is perhaps a vivid description of such an international system where there is not only anarchy but also chaos with "war of all against all." In such a culture, the logic is that "actors operate on the principle of *sauve qui peut* and kill or be killed."[38] In a somewhat moderate form of this self-help system, it is a place where violence, though not happening all the time, may occur any moment. In such a culture, the elimination of the other through violence is not only a means to the realization of the value of the self but also an end in itself.[39] In other words, the *realpolitik* world of international relations is one full of conflict and one worshipping conflict resolution through fire and blood.

---

[37] Albert and Lapid 1997, 414.   [38] Wendt 1999, 265.   [39] Ibid., 274.

The way of conflict resolution in the Lockean culture differs from that in the Hobbesian culture. Both situations imply that the self-other relationship is conflictual. They may act in a revisionist and even violent fashion toward each other. But in a Lockean culture, the nature of the self-other relationship has changed: The state as the self takes other states as rivals but not enemies. The difference lies in the fact that in the relationship of enmity the other does not even recognize the right of the self to live and therefore may use unlimited violence toward the self, while in the relationship of rivalry the other may recognize the self's right to exist and the use of violence is limited. It is the same with the self. However even in the rivalry situation use of violence continues to be a legitimate means to achieve one's objectives.[40] It is beyond doubt that violence is still an important way of conflict resolution, but its use is limited, depending very much on whether its user is willing to exercise self-restraint. Since the self and the other both recognize each other's sovereignty, it is a system of "live and let live," rather than one of "war of all against all." Wendt believes that Waltz's international world is a Lockean one rather than a Hobbesian one. It is true because if we consider the relationship between the self and the other, it is no longer a life-and-death struggle, for the establishment of sovereignty as a primary principle of the international system means that the recognition of the right of both the self and the other to exist has been a common practice. However, even though violence is reduced in the Lockean culture, it is more so in quantity rather than in quality, for violence still constitutes the most threatening but, perhaps to some, the most effective way to solve conflict. The two world wars, both of which occurred after the sovereignty principle was established, or in the Lockean culture, did have unprecedented intensity and violence. As Waltz comments on international anarchy: "The state among states, . . ., conducts its affairs in the brooding shadow of violence. Because some states may at any time use force, all states must be prepared to do so – or live at the mercy of their militarily more vigorous neighbors. Among states, the state of nature is a state of war."[41] In such an international system relations among its members, the nation-states for example, have to be conflict ready in the first place.

Moving from enmity and rivalry into friendship is perhaps a qualitative change, marking the third culture, the Kantian one, which is basically a culture of a collective security community and where disputes and conflicts are solved without resorting to force. In the framework of the self-other relationship, "states identify with each other, seeing each other's security not just as instrumentally related to their own, but as

---

[40] Ibid., 280.   [41] Waltz 1979, 102

literally being their own. The collective boundaries of the Self are extended to include the Other."[42] NATO is given as an example of this kind of collective security community and the European Union is often taken as an inspiring model. However, in the IR literature, "substantial literature exists on enemy images, but little on friend images, on enduring rivalries but little on enduring friendships, on the causes of war but little on the causes of peace."[43] Friendship as a concept has so far been marginalized in the study of international relations and the dominant discourse continues to be hostility and antagonism.[44] If it is discussed, it is limited to a very small part of the international system where a Kantian culture dominates. Furthermore, it is particularly noteworthy that the Kantian culture constitutes a system where conflict is resolved without war, but such a collective security community, as many prominent scholars have identified, has an important precondition, that is, the same value system. Kant himself argues that perpetual peace is achieved through a federation of free states. Democratic peace theory makes it clear that war continues to occur between democracies and non-democracies and the former are usually the winners.[45] Emanuel Adler makes an explicit explanation of this precondition for a security community:

Members of pluralistic security communities hold dependable expectations of peaceful change not merely because they share just any kind of values, but because they share *liberal democratic* values and allow their societies to become interdependent and linked by transnational economic and cultural relations. Democratic values, in turn, facilitate the creation of strong civil societies ... which also promote community bonds and common identity and trust through the process of the free interpenetration of societies.[46]

In other words, the Kantian culture exists only within a sphere of value homogeneity, where conflict exists, but it is not value-related and can therefore be resolved through peaceful means. Between nations within and outside this sphere international actors continue to follow other logics of anarchy and conflict may well be resolved violently. If the same value system is the precondition, then the problem is that a homogeneous system of values all over the world is hard to materialize. Then, naturally, we have a distinct divide of the in-group/out-group dichotomy in terms of value systems.

If the Hobbesian, Lockean, and Kantian anarchies are largely reflected in mainstream IR theories, the above discussion has revealed an interesting resemblance of those theories in terms of the self-other relations with

[42] Wendt 1999, 305.   [43] Ibid., 298.   [44] Berenskoetter 2007.
[45] Reiter and Stam 2002.
[46] Adler 1992, quoted in Acharya 1998, 198–199, emphasis in original.

the binary structure of the Hegelian dialectics. Once international actors are structured in a self-other binary where the other is often an antagonistic, negative antithesis to the self, conflict becomes the objective fact and tends to be non-reconcilable. Such conflict exists between capitalist states and proletarian states,[47] between democratic states and authoritarian/totalitarian states,[48] and between different civilizations.[49] It also exists between established and emerging powers.[50] The non-reconcilable nature of the conflict between the self and the other, then, tends to make the disappearance of the other as the solution to conflict. Although Hegel is perhaps not so radical in his formal and logical dialectics, it is easy to go to radical solutions in reality, especially in the international relations world where the established belief is that anarchy rules. Furthermore, there are two ways to make something disappear: One is to eliminate it and the other, to assimilate it. Radical theoretical perspectives may see destruction and elimination as the most effective way of conflict resolution, while moderate ones may seek homogenization through assimilation and believe that it is more suitable and practical.[51] In this respect, realists are the pessimists, believing the conflict is fundamentally insoluble as long as anarchy is the defining feature of the international system and states are the principal units in this system; institutionalists are half-optimistic because they, though believing that conflict rather than harmony exists in the anarchic international system, tend to be more confident in the role of international institutions in reducing the intensity of conflict and facilitating international cooperation for the common good;[52] and constructivists are more opportunistic, trying to nurture a collective and shared identity to build a Kantian culture of ideational uniformity, which in fact is to ideationally eliminate or assimilate the difference and realize a higher degree of homogeneity.

Fundamentally the Hegelian dialectics is about relations, and moreover, it is about the conflictual self-other relationship. Also, this self-other binary in terms of the thesis and antithesis in the Hegelian dialectic framework constitutes a prominent theme and discourse in the mainstream IR theory, very often implicitly. Although some studies have pointed out that the self does not necessarily depend on a negative and antagonistic other for its existence, for the realization of its values, and for the fulfillment of its life,[53] the structure of thesis and antithesis, as well as

---

[47] Lenin 1939.   [48] Russett 1993.   [49] Huntington 1993.
[50] Organski and Kugler 1980.
[51] This may resemble Brincat's interpretation of Hegel, which argues that the Hegelian dialectics does not aim to eliminate the other and in fact embrace difference: Brincat 2009.
[52] Keohane 1984.   [53] Lebow 2008.

the conflictual nature of their relationship, seems to continue to be a dominant discourse in the mainstream IR theoretical literature. It is true that Acharya's study of ASEAN indicates that homogeneity of values may not be a necessary condition for a community of collective security;[54] the dominant presumption continues to be that a security community is possible only when it is composed of nations that have shared value and belief systems. If this view should stand, then in today's world a global security community would be possible if and only if all states should be changed into something similar to one another in terms of religious beliefs, political systems, and social norms. In other words, in the self-other binary structure, peaceful resolution should be possible only among members of the "us" category, and violent resolution should, as always, continue to be an important choice between members of the "self" and the "other" categories.

I do not intend to deny the argument that the difference between the dialectical approach and the mainstream IR is real. And I agree also with Cox that their difference lies mainly in the fact that the former aims for emancipation through changing the existing order while the latter for its maintenance. What I want to point out is that the crucial difference lies in their disagreement on whether contradiction and conflict are negative or positive. Mainstream IR theories generally see conflict as negative although it is real and objective, so that they try to solve this problem, through balance of power, international institutions, or security communities. On the other hand, critical theorists that explicitly adopt the dialectical tradition cheer for social conflict, believing that hope for social change and transformation lies exactly in such conflict. It is positive conflict which makes human progress possible. Despite their differences, however, the dialectical approach and the mainstream share one important view: Conflict lies in the nature of life and has therefore an ontological status that is real and significant.

Zhongyong Dialectics and Harmony of Polarities

The *zhongyong* dialectics is drawn from the practices of the Chinese cultural community and constitutes a key component of both the Confucian and Daoist philosophical views about the universe.[55] It is also embodied in Sunzi's art of warfare, in *Yijing*, or the *Book of Changes*, and in later Confucian schools of thought.[56] Chinese philosophical traditions believe that the world is one of relations and hold that the most significant relationship, or the relationship of relationships, is the

---

[54] Acharya 2009.   [55] He et al. 1991, 90.   [56] Song 1998.

relationship of *yin* and *yang*. This is what I term the "meta-relationship," resembling, more in form than in content, Hegel's being and nothing. This relationship represents the fundamental nature of the totality of relationships in the Confucian cosmos. The appropriate way to understand the nature of this correlated *yin-yang* relationship is the Chinese dialectics, *zhongyong*, which is often translated into "the golden mean," or "the middle course." It means in fact much more than the meaning contained in its English translations.[57] *Yin* and *yang*, therefore, constitute the ontological foundation of everything and their interaction the beginning of every form of life. Furthermore, the *zhongyong* dialectics has been the primary epistemological device for the Chinese to understand the relational universe in general through its interpretation of the *yin-yang* relationship and the basic methodology for finding solutions in world affairs, natural and human alike.

As a worldview and the way of thinking of the Chinese cultural communities, the *zhongyong* dialectics and its understanding of the *yin-yang* relationship started from ancient times, have continued to the present, and still influence today the understanding, interpretation, and behavior of the Chinese as well as the Confucian cultural communities. It is particularly relevant to the discussion of relations in the social world. In this section I will discuss the *zhongyong* dialectics, focusing on its three key elements: inclusivity, complementation, and harmony, which are interrelated and logically come from one another and because of one another. A comparison with the Hegelian dialectics is also made through the discussion to identify their significant differences.

Inclusivity

The first principle of the *zhongyong* dialectics is inclusivity. It means that the two interacting items, objects, or forces are immanently inclusive and therefore inclusively related. Like the Hegelian tradition, the Chinese also see the world as composed of interacting polarities. The two terms or forces, *yin* and *yang*, in fact are the simplest but the most fundamental forms of such interacting polarities: They are the two halves that constitute an organic whole and the diagram indicating their relationship is called the cosmological diagram, for it demonstrates the basic conceptualization of the universe by the Chinese (see Figure 6.1). Any other polarity can be seen as being derived from this meta-relationship. A possible pair, such as male and female, fortune and misfortune, strength and weakness, nature and culture, continuity and change, or East and West, consists of

---

[57] Ames and Hall 2001.

Figure 6.1: Chinese cosmologic diagram

such parts in a whole. They are polarities in unity as well as parts of the whole.

This kind of holistic understanding of polarities requires that the inclusivity should be immanent. In other words, the two halves are within and of each other. Zhu Xi (1130–1200 AD), a leading neo-Confucian scholar in the Song Dynasty (960–1279 AD), says: "*Yin* is within *yang*, and *yang* is within *yin*." It is also vividly depicted by the folk saying, "you in me, and me in you." The pair, *yin* and *yang*, is not only related, for two independent entities can also be related as the thesis and antithesis in the Hegelian dialectics, but also and perhaps more importantly immanently related: They are inclusive of each other and depend on each other for life.[58] The Chinese cosmological diagram expresses exactly this relationship. The two fish-like swirls, one black and the other white, designate *yin* (the black half, indicating the female force) and *yang* (the white half, indicating the male force) and together they constitute an organic whole. However, the immanency is emphatically indicated by the diagram:

---

[58] It is argued that the Hegelian dialectics does stress intersubjectivity, that Being and Nothingness are mutually related and remain absolutely distinct, that the opposites are inseparable, and that together they complete a totality (Brincat and Ling 2014, 13). There is no doubt about the mutuality and relatedness of the opposites in the Hegelian dialectics. The *zhongyong* dialectics shares with the Hegelian dialectics the intersubjectivity, the relatedness, and the holistic view of the opposites. What makes the *zhongyong* dialectics distinct, however, is this inclusive mutuality expressed in *yang*-within-*yin* and vice versa. *Yin* and *yang* tend to be becoming each other because of this immanent inclusivity.

The black swirl contains a white dot and the white swirl contains a black dot. The two dots look like the eyes of a fish, showing that the two swirls are within each other. If they were taken as discrete entities, they would be lifeless or non-existent, for the eye means life in the Chinese tradition. This relational and immanent mutuality is expressed clearly in Laozi's idea as Pang Pu identifies an important view of Daoism: The self is the other and the other is the self. He further argues that it constitutes a primary principle of Daoism.

In Chapter 20 Laozi asks, "How much difference is there between what is deemed beautiful and ugly?" meaning that there is little difference between the beautiful and the ugly. The beautiful is the ugly and the ugly is the beautiful . . . This idea of the sameness of polarities is seen in many places in Laozi, such as "Radiant way-making seems obscured; advancing way-making seems to be retreating . . . The greatest square has no corners; the greatest vessel is last to be attended to (Chap. 41)" . . . "It is upon misfortune that good fortune leans; it is within good fortune itself that misfortune crouches in ambush (Chap. 58)."[59]

Laozi's own examples illustrate this inclusiveness as he says:

> The thirty spokes converge at one hub,
> But the utility of the carts is a function of the nothingness (*wu*) inside the hub.
> We throw clay to shape a pot,
> But the utility of the clay pot is a function of the nothingness inside it.
> We bore out doors and windows to make a dwelling,
> But the utility of the dwelling is a function of the nothingness inside it.[60]

Something (*you*) and nothing (*wu*) therefore are inclusive of each other, as shown by the relationship between the house walls and the emptiness inside. If we did not have the tangible and physical walls, how could we have the intangible space/emptiness inside? Or, if we did have the tangible and physical walls, how could we not have the space/emptiness inside? *Yin* and *yang* exactly refer to all these polarities that reside in everything, and furthermore, *yin* includes *yang* and *yang* includes *yin*. All the seemingly opposites, thus, are mutually in and of each other. Similarly, continuity and change are in each other, for the past and the present are also polarities inclusive of each other. The nation-state, for example, is not a discrete entity, standing alone and coming from nowhere. It is the product of the immanent mutuality of the past and the present. It must be something that can be traced back to some other things, just

---

[59] Pang 1986; 1987. The translation of the sentences in *The Analects* is from Ames and Hall 2003, 140–141 and 166.
[60] Ames and Hall 2003, 91.

as a child can be traced back to her parents. Thus both spatially and temporally, opposites are inclusive of each other.

In this sense it is qualitatively different from the principle of identity explicit in formal logic and implicit in the Hegelian construction of thesis-antithesis dichotomy. In other words, the Chinese do not have the dualistic way of thinking in the first place and do not tend to separate interacting objects into two distinct categories and non-transformable entities. Rather, from the very beginning they have been taken as immanent and immanently inclusive. *It is co-embedded inclusivity*. As for formal logic, the *zhongyong* dialectics clearly violates the identity principle by taking inclusivity as the key to understand the *yin-yang* relationship. It assumes that each of a pair is inclusive of the other, despite and because of the fact that they are different. In other words, A is not a pure, definite, and absolute A, with fixed properties and attributes. A is inclusive of its opposite B and implies B with the potential of becoming B. It goes also against the non-contradiction theorem, which stipulates that a contradictory pair, A and non-A, cannot be both true and both false. The fundamental assumption of the noncontradiction theorem thus typifies the "either-or" logic, either true or false. Two statements, for instance, cannot be both true and false. When a true/false question is given, you can either choose true or false, but you cannot choose both. When a multiple choice question is given, only one of the four or five answers is correct. The *zhongyong* dialectics, on the other hand, prefers the "both-and" alternative and provides a radically different approach: A and non-A, despite the fact that they appear contra-dictory, are immanently inclusive of each other: Good luck, for example, may contain misfortune, and strength is at the same time weakness. Two seemingly contradictory arguments may both have something reasonable inside. As the Peng-Nisbett psychological experiment shows,[61] when two clearly contradictory arguments were presented, the Chinese respondents tended to believe that there is and can be something true in both while the American respondents often chose one as true and dismissed the other as false. Any two interacting cultures or civilizations are taken as mutually inclusive too, each containing elements of the other even though they are different in many respects or even though they seem as opposite to each other in what it is believed are their defining attributes.

The *zhongyong* dialectics shares more with the Hegelian dialectics than with formal logic. The Chinese also conceptualize the universe in a polar way, believing that change, progress, and evolution take place by interac-tion of the two opposite poles in transformative processes. However, the inclusive immanency distances it from the Hegelian logic in a crucial way:

[61] Peng and Nisbett 1999.

In terms of polarities, the Hegelian logic is dualistic while the *zhongyong* dialectics is immanent. In other words, the Hegelian whole consists of two independent poles interacting with each other, while the whole of the *zhongyong* dialectics is a whole with two mutually penetrating halves. As I argued in the previous section, the Hegelian dialectics in this respect follows formal logic in that it presumes the polarities as discrete entities independent of each other and engaging each other as such in their interaction. The Hegelian signifiers of "thesis" and "antithesis" explicitly indicate the assumption that the polarities are independent categories structured in a dichotomous way. On the contrary, the Confucian tradition understands them in an immanent way. They interact not as the thesis and antithesis, but as *co-theses*. In other words, the opposite poles represented by *yin* and *yang* are not two discrete entities standing as the independent self and other and interacting with anterior properties. Rather they are two correlated parts of an organic whole in the first place. Neither is independent of the other, and both depend upon each other for life. They participate and join in each other. It denies the Western dualism that separates the two poles, and establishes a worldview grounded on the concept of correlativity for any pair of opposites. Inference about the nature of other relationships starts from this basic understanding of the meta-relationship. As Hall and Ames argue: "The epistemological equivalent of the notion of an immanental cosmos is that of conceptual polarity. Such polarity requires the concepts which are significantly related are in fact symmetrically related, each requiring the other for adequate articulation."[62] Such an articulation is not through the help and assistance of an exterior other, but by the immanent mutuality of the two as an organic whole. This inclusiveness distinguishes the *zhongyong* dialectics from formal logic in its violation of the principle of identity and from the Hegelian dialectics in its insistence in immanency.

We may think about the self-other relationship from the perspective of immanent inclusivity. It is no longer a relationship of two dualistically structured, self-organizing entities, each with distinct properties and attributes. Rather they are penetrating each other and within each other. They depend on each other for life and for the generation of new life, for identity, and for production and reproduction of identity. But what is more than a mere dependence is that they are within each other and their interaction is one from within rather than one from without. The simplest way to understand this immanent inclusivity is to personify *yin* and *yang* as mother and father. "It should be noted," as Roger Ames

---

[62] Ames and Hall 2003, 17.

and David Hall argue, "that mother is the impregnated female and father is the siring male. Each of them entails the other."[63] It is this immanency that distinguishes the *zhongyong* dialectics as conspicuously immanent and inclusive, for it is perhaps illogical by formal logic and undialectical by the Hegelian dialectics. But it is the way of thinking and doing by the Chinese. As Ling comments:

Daoist dialectics, however, differ in one key respect: internal co-implication, ... Whereas Hegelian-Marxian dialectics may posit that polarities – for example, "master" and "slave" – are mutually created, Daoist dialectics place this co-implication within polarities as well: that is, the "master" within the "slave" and the "slave" within "master."[64]

It is the immanent inclusivity that offers a different understanding of change. It holds that change takes place through inclusive intersubjectivity, or, in the terminology of the *zhongyong* dialectics, through the immanently dynamic relationship between *yin* and *yang*. That change is a becoming process by the *zhongyong* dialectics means that *yin* and *yang* are always engaged with each other in the process of each becoming the other. Becoming the other is a genuine change. It is change within and from within, for the interactive relationship between the two poles, *yin* and *yang*, are genuinely embedded and inclusive. In other words, A is becoming non-A, and vice versa. "*Yin* does not transcend *yang*, nor vice versa." *Yin* is always "becoming *yang*" and *yang* is always "becoming *yin*," as in the natural world day is always becoming night.[65] Similarly, East and West are mutually becoming and there are no fixed and eternal identities that are not transformable in the becoming process. This process of becoming is therefore more important than any being with distinct properties of its own because it explains the dynamics of continuity and change, of continuity through change and change through continuity. Life itself is such an endless process of becoming with the constant co-creation and co-evolution of *yin* and *yang*.

Take identity change as an example. It is not the interaction discussed by social constructivists, which requires the two poles with anterior properties and focuses on the change of their variable attributes through interaction.[66] This kind of identity change emphasized by mainstream constructivism, by the standard of the *zhongyong* dialectics, is at most change at the superficial level, for, as Jackson and Nexon have pointed out, what changes are some of their variable attributes rather than the entities themselves, whose constitutive properties and requisite attributes

[63] Ibid., 109.   [64] Ling 2013, 559.   [65] Hall and Ames 1987, 17.
[66] Emirbayer 1997, 285–286.

remain unchanged.[67] The change seen by the *zhongyong* dialectics implies coevolution in nature: Both poles change during the process of becoming, where there appears the new synthesis that combines the two but equals neither. Thus the *zhongyong* dialectics envisages a kind of "coevolution-ary" change. It is genuine change, but with a strong historical or anthro-pological sense. Therefore it is processual by definition. It constitutes a sharp contrast to the dichotomously structured concept of "thesis vs. antithesis." Rather, it is a coevolution of the "co-theses."

Complementarity

The second principle of the *zhongyong* dialectics is complementarity. It means that the two inclusively interacting items, objects, or forces complement each other. In terms of the relational theory, the meta-relationship, or the *yin-yang* relationship, is a dynamically complemen-tary process. In other words, *yin* and *yang*, or any pair of seemingly contradictory poles, such as cold and hot, weak and strong, nothing and something, etc., are complementarily related to each other so that they together create life and lead to a balanced form of life. The balance is not static, for it is always maintained through the dynamic comple-mentation of the two extremes. The strength of one pole implies simultaneously its weakness, which is necessarily made up for by the strength of the other pole, and vice versa.

Complementarity denotes that each relies on the other for existence and development. Dialectics is about polarities and contradictions, and thus we may start from the Chinese word "*maodun*," which is in transla-tion the equivalent of "contradiction" and indicates a typical Chinese pair of opposites. The Chinese word "*maodun*" is the combination of two characters: *mao* (spear) and *dun* (shield), representing respectively the weapons of offense and defense. The spear is good at offense while the shield is better for defense. For a battle both are needed though function-ing differently, just as in a war both offensive and defensive tactics are necessary: There is no defense if there is no offense. They are mutually assumed, for each requires the other for its own identification. Moreover, they do not stand for two concepts that exclude each other, because offense and defense are the two related sides of a war, exactly like the polarities represented by *yin* and *yang*. Defense makes up for offense and offense makes up for defense. Thus Chenshan Tian is right as he says, "*[m]aodun* is incapable of being an equivalent to the concept of contra-diction, for it precludes the concept's assumption of disjunction,

---

[67] Jackson and Nexon 1999, 293.

negation, or exclusion (p and non-p). The two side of *maodun* are rather seen in complementarity constituting a totality."[68] It is exactly this complementary mutuality that defines the *zhongyong* dialectics. It is also this complementary relationship of the polarities that makes the Chinese word of *"maodun"* differ from its English equivalent – "contradiction."

The Chinese language contains many more words which consist of polarities than English[69] and all the polarities in the repertoire of the Chinese language, as the word *"maodun"* indicates, have a similar complementary relationship. It is also a common practice among average people in their daily life. A good sword should be both piercingly sharp and unbreakably pliable, indicating that the hard and the soft should complement each other in terms of the material so that it is able to make a good sword. For marriage, Chinese tend to believe that if one of the couple is inflexible and aggressive by temperament, the other should be basically peaceful and mild, so that the complementation of the two will make up for each other's weakness and result in a happy and sustainable married life. People on a team should complement one another in terms of abilities and dispositions so that they can develop a more favorable team spirit. It is also important to have both hawkish and dovish people in the process of foreign policy-making, otherwise the state would be either too much of a bully or too chicken. In short, many Chinese proverbs reflect this complementary understanding of polarities, for example, *gangrou bingji* (temper toughness with gentleness, be both tough and gentle), *fuhuo yifu* (from sorrow comes happiness, and in happiness lurks sorrow), and *bubei bukang* (be neither haughty nor humble), indicating that a complementary balance leads to a better condition for life.

Seemingly opposite polarities, thus, are not treated as a black-or-white fairy tale or a true-or-false choice on an examination paper. The Chinese concept of contradiction itself contains two fundamentally complementary rather than conflictual sides, both having merits and demerits. The Chinese proverb *"chiyou suochang, cunyou suoduan* (Sometimes a foot may prove short while an inch may prove long – Everyone has strengths and weaknesses)"* expresses exactly this understanding of contradictory polarities. Zhuangzi argues that there can be no victorious side in a debate because neither side may have a universally recognized reasonable argument and both sides may have something reasonable.[70] The psychological experiments by Peng

---

[68] Tian 2005, 79.   [69] Peng and Nisbett 1999.

[70] It is argued by some that Zhuangzi is wrong, because his view goes against the law of excluded middle and therefore it is fallacy. It seems to me that Zhuangzi's "no victor" argument follows the Chinese *zhongyong* dialectics, which in the very beginning values the middle rather than excludes it. See Sun 2014, 108; see also Zhuangzi 2012.

and Nisbett vividly indicate the tendency to value the complementation between polarities of a seeming contradiction in the Chinese tradition, indicating a "both-and" way of thinking in contrast to the "either-or" pattern of thought. They presented to Chinese and American students, for example, a case in which the mother and the daughter, with conflicting values, each holds an argument reflecting her value and their arguments are obviously opposite to each other. It was found that Chinese students tended to address the issue from both sides and believed that there was something right and also something wrong in the values of both the mother and the daughter, while American students tended to find exclusive fault with one side or the other.[71] Other experiments, including completely contradictory scientific statements, indicate similar results: The Chinese students tend to find merits and demerits in both, while the American students are more likely to accept one and reject the other categorically. Peng and Nisbett did not go further to explore the implications of such behavior. In fact, the complementary treatment of contradictions tends to produce something like a compromise between two statements, two policies, two institutions, two attitudes, and two values. However it may not be a passive compromise, but a compromise for a dynamic reproduction: By combining the strong and reasonable elements of both polarities, a more balanced and therefore better solution will be worked out and a better situation created. It is the "appropriate middle." In the mother-daughter value conflict case, Chinese tend to think that there is some reason in both the value of the mother and that of the daughter, so that the appropriate resolution of the conflict is to combine those reasonable elements from both and abandon those unreasonable elements so that a new and more reasonable value can be produced. It is expressed in the Chinese idiom, *quchang buduan* (learn from each other's strong points to make up for their own weak points), an important precept of the *zhongyong* dialectics and a wise attitude in the Chinese practice.

The active and dynamic complementation does not only produce the "both-and" way of thinking, but, perhaps more importantly, leads to co-generation. It is the basic understanding of life and change. "*Dao* begets the one; the one begets the two opposites (*yin* and *yang*); the two begets

---

[71] The text of the mother-daughter conflict is "Mary, Phoebe, and Julie all have daughters. Each mother has held a set of values which has guided her efforts to raise her daughter. Now the daughters have grown up, and each of them is rejecting many of her mother's values. How did it happen and what should they do?" 74 percent of the American responses, such as "Mothers have to recognize daughters' rights to their own values," are coded nondialectical, while 72 precent of the Chinese responses, such as "Both the mothers and the daughters have failed to understand each other" are coded dialectical. The difference is significant. Peng and Nisbett 1999, 746.

the three; and the three begets all things in the universe."[72] The one is Dao itself; the two refers to *yin* and *yang*; and the interaction of *yin* and *yang* generates the three – something new that indicates the direction of the generation in which all things in the world are produced. The *zhongyong* dialectics thus holds that opposite polarities generate new life, thus defining the *yin-yang* relationship as a vigorously co-generative process in which new life is produced through complementary interaction and interpenetrating mutuality of the polarities. This complementary interaction of *yin* and *yang*, inclusive in nature, is the origin of life. One of the Confucian classics, *Yijing* or the *Book of Changes*, and the Daoist classic, *Daodejing*, both believe that the *yin-yang* mutuality begets life. They constitute life for each other and tend to co-evolve into a new, harmonious synthesis, which, in the form of a new life, contains elements of both the poles and is unable to be reduced to either, just as a happy couple gives birth to a new baby. In other words, the polarities generate life through their immanent interaction. It means that the *yin-yang* complementary interaction is the source of life, which does not need a transcendental prime mover to give the first push. Chenshan Tian argues that Westerners tend to view the world as "the one world", or "this Cosmos" in the tradition of Plato and Aristotle, whose static nature makes a prime mover logically necessary. The Chinese have a different view, as he says:

Instead of being moved by any transcendental Being, the Chinese world is *ziran* or *self-so-being*, and *ziwei* or *self-so-going* or *self-so-doing*. The moving forces, . . . come from the interactions of the complementary and contradictory polarities, from the ten thousands of things themselves all under the sky rather than from an external mover.[73]

Thus all things are generated by themselves and the generation itself is through the penetrating mutuality and inclusive complementation of the polarities. As Hellmut Wilhelm has commented, "The explanation of the creative process in terms of the interaction of complementary oppositions is fundamental to the Chinese tradition."[74] Back to the origin, it is this

---

[72] This is my own more word-for-word translation, which vividly describes the co-generating sequence. The translation by Hall and Ames is "Way-making (*dao*) gives rise to continuity,/ Continuity gives rise to difference,/ Difference gives rise to plurality,/ And plurality gives rise to the manifold of everything that is happening (*wanwu*)." See Ames and Hall 2003, 142. Very often people are puzzled by this "three." If "one" refers to the Dao, and "two" means *yin* and *yang*, then what is the "three" between the *yin/yang* and all things? I would refer to Professor Pu Pang's explanation. He explains that the word "three (*san*)" in the ancient Chinese language is the same as the word "participate or join (*can*)," thus, "three" in fact means co-participation or co-joining of *yin* and *yang* for combination, for unity, and for co-generation of all things under the sun. See Pang 1980, 94–95.

[73] Tian 2005, 34.   [74] Quoted in Tian 2005, 10.

creative process of *yin* and *yang*, the simplest form of all other pairs of polarities, that starts the movement and dynamic life of all in the universe. The co-generative process works as co-becoming dynamics along both the temporal dimension and the spatial dimension. The past and the present, and the present and the future, are taken as such polarities. Overall it is a temporal continuum. *Yin* and *yang* represent any particular points on this continuum, such as day and night, winter and summer, the pre-modern and the modern, etc. In this sense, the *zhongyong* dialectics is also historical and genealogical, for the complementation of polarities places emphasis on their inclusive mutuality as the necessary condition for their existence and coexistence. An interesting example perhaps is the ancestor worship in the Chinese tradition, which is still very popular today. There is no single and dominant religion in China but the Chinese always worship their ancestors, because they believe that their ancestors in the nether world continue to be related to themselves in this world. Today is thus a continuity of yesterday even though they are different, and for this reason today has always inside it something of yesterday and tomorrow will always have inside in it something of today. Spatially it is similar. The typical example in this respect is the complementary relationship between heaven (nature)[75] and humans. In the Chinese tradition, humans are an integral part of nature and constitute a continuity of nature. As such humans and nature are inclusively interdependent on each other and in the general sense humans and nature live and die together.

Furthermore, they co-generate each other. *Yin* and *yang* are always engaged with each other or entangle each other in a co-becoming process and the co-becoming process itself is from within. As Laozi says:

> As soon as everyone in the world knows that the beautiful are beautiful,
> There is already ugliness.
> As soon as everyone knows the able,
> There is ineptness.
> Determinacy (*you*) and indeterminacy (*wu*) give rise to each other,
> Difficult and easy complement each other,
> Long and short set each other off,
> High and low complete each other,
> Refined notes and raw sounds harmonize (*he*) with each other,
> This is really how it works.[76]

In other words, *yin* and *yang* do not only combine to create a new synthetic life, but also tend to be becoming each other. It is called *xiangfan*

[75] Here the "heaven" refers to the natural world and has no religious implications.
[76] Ames and Hall 2003, 80.

xiangcheng, or the opposite polarities generating each other through complementation. Laozi sees that in the becoming process one of the polarities tends to change to become the other. This view is expressed by the Chinese proverb *"wuji bifan* (Things turn into their opposites when they reach the extreme.)" *Daodejing* says:

> Crimped then whole,
> Warped then true,
> Hollow then full,
> Worn then new,
> Modest then satisfied,
> Demanding then bewildered.[77]

In many places in *Daodejing*, Laozi points out this law and argues that things gain when they seem to lose or lose when they seem to gain (Chap. 42); that the more you store up, the more you lose (Chap. 44); that the prime time is the beginning of getting old (Chap. 55); that weal comes after woe, and woe lies under weal (Chap. 58); and that a strong army will be wiped out, as a tall tree will be cut down (Chap. 76). Polarities are thus always moving toward their opposites in the ever-becoming process. If we take a human being as a life system, it consists of many polarities in itself. Selfishness and selflessness are one of such polarities. Both are inside the human being and constitute the two sides of the human nature that are inseparable. By the principle of co-becoming, she is always experiencing the tough interaction of the two. The selfishness tends to become the selflessness and vice versa. Similarly, the material and the ideational are such polarities, too. For Laozi himself, his key concept of *Dao* is at the same time material and spiritual, as he says that *Dao* is a thing that is vague and indefinite; and that *Dao* seems both to be and not to be and both to exist and not to exist.[78] Brincat argues that Daoism prioritizes the abstract over the real and the thought over the social relations. The fact is that in the very beginning there has been nowhere to find such a dualistic structure of the material and the ideational or of the abstract and the real, as Brincat has imagined perhaps through a deeply internalized structure of dualism. Such dualism, however, is never in Laozi's menu for choice. Of course what is more important is that the emphasis of the *Daoist* dialectics is always placed on the process of becoming from one to the

---

[77] Ibid., 110.

[78] Laozi says: "As for the process of way-making,/ It is ever so indefinite and vague./ Though vague and indefinite,/ There are images within it./ Though indefinite and vague,/ There are events within it./ Though nebulous and dark,/ There are seminal concentrations of *qi* (vital energy) within it./ These concentration of *qi* are authentic,/ And have within them true credibility." See Ames and Hall 2003, 107.

other. This is the "Daoist process cosmology," on which Hall and Ames have commented as follows:

Insight into this process cosmology and the interdependent character of the correlative distinctions used to interpret it provides a kind of sagacity in dealing with the world. The sages do not take sides, but are catalytic in facilitating the flourishing of the process as a whole. To favor one distinction over another – for example, the beautiful over the ugly – would make it exclusive and thus impoverishing. Given the continuity assumed within process cosmology, these categories are correlative and mutually entailing. Not only do you get one without the other but, simply put, every constitute is necessary for every other constitute to be what it is.[79]

This transforming process, or the tendency toward becoming the other, reflects the essence of the Daoist dialectics and also constitutes a defining assumption of the *zhongyong* dialectics. We say that it is a defining assumption because it distinguishes the *zhongyong* dialectics from the Western dialectics in a crucial way. The Hegelian tradition understands dialectics as one in which "one observes a logic of higher agreement, which presupposes and accomplishes a synthetic unity of opposites, in which contrasts, or multiplicities, and in which partial, abstract views are subsumed and reconciled –whether aesthetically, actively, or propositionally – in an emerging whole."[80] If we say that the polarities combine to produce a new and higher level life, it still bears a resemblance with the Hegelian tradition, which does not assume that polarities move and become each other. This Daoist view that the polarities are begetting and becoming each other is distinctively unique. It is exactly here that the generative relationship of *yin* and *yang* through complementation reflects a different epistemology to understand the world.

Harmony

The core of the *zhongyong* dialectics is harmony. It sees polarities in everything, but argues that change and progress are not ignited by conflict and crisis, but rely on the harmonizing process of the *yin-yang* trans-subjective mutuality. The above-discussed two characteristic features of the *zhongyong* dialectics, inclusivity and complementarity, cannot lead automatically to harmony, even though they provide the necessary conditions for harmony. It is noteworthy that when the Chinese dialectics is discussed, usually *Daodejing* by Laozi is the main text for reference,[81] and Confucianism is considered as similar in its dialectical way of thinking.[82]

---

[79] Ames and Hall 2003, 80.   [80] Tian 2005, 13.   [81] Ling 2013; Brincat and Ling 2014.
[82] Cheng 2006.

It is true that Daoism provides the foundation for the Chinese dialectical tradition, and it is also true that Daoism and Confucianism share a pattern of dialectical thinking, and together they provide the core of the Chinese dialectics. However, their foci are not perfectly identical.[83] If we say that Laozi places more emphasis on the polar structure of everything and the inevitable transformation from one pole to the other, that is, from *yin* to *yang* and from *yang* to *yin*, or on the process during which *yin* is becoming toward *yang* and vice versa, Confucianism stresses more the principle for the becoming polarities to be in a dynamically harmonious state, that is, *shangzhong*, or simply put, "towards the due centrality." Using Tu's translation, it can be conceptualized as "central harmony." Daoism believes that harmony is to return to the state of nature while Confucianism holds that harmony is the state of nature to be reached through practicing centrality in society. Therefore, even though Daoism implies the importance of centrality, Confucianism makes it an explicit and defining feature of the Chinese dialectics, especially for social purposes, that is, harmony among humans. Harmonious human relations are managed by practicing the centrality principle. I term the Chinese dialectics *zhongyong* dialectics exactly because of this important development of Confucian dialectics with its accent on harmony in terms of centrality through human agency. It is also this centrality that critically distinguishes the Chinese dialectics from the Hegelian dialectics.

"Central harmony" is a distinct dialectical concept of Confucianism. The first chapter of the classic book of *Zhongyong* (*The Doctrine of the Mean*) gives an illustration for understanding harmony and centrality:

Before the feelings of pleasure, anger, sorrow, and joy are aroused, it is called centrality. When the feelings are aroused and each and all attain due measure and degree, it is called harmony. Centrality is the great foundation of the world, and harmony is its universal path. To cultivate centrality and harmony with thoroughness is the way to bring heaven and earth to their proper place and all things their proper nourishment.[84]

---

[83] Zhu 2005, 120–128.

[84] Tu 2008, 2. It is interesting to compare Tu's translation with that of James Legge. Legge's goes as: "While there are no stirrings of pleasure, anger, sorrow, or joy, the mind may be said to be in the state of EQUALIBRIUM. When those feelings have been stirred, and they act in their due degree, there ensues what may be called the state of HARMONY. This EQUILIBRIUM is the great root from which grow all the human actings in the world, and this HARMONY is the universal path which they all should pursue. Let the states of equilibrium and harmony exist in perfection, and a happy order will prevail throughout heaven and earth, and all things will be nourished and flourish." *The Doctrine of the Mean*, trans. by James Legge (Confucius et al. 2014, 255, (emphasis in original)). I use Tu's translation because his is more direct and word for word.

Thus, we can see that centrality and harmony are inseparable and in Chinese the word "*zhonghe*" is often used to illustrate the meaning. The concept of *zhonghe*, "centrality and harmony," or "central harmony," expresses this immanently related pair representing the foundation and the path. Since it believes in the non-conflictual nature of the meta-relationship, harmony is then the state of nature and the universal principle of order. However, harmony in human society is not achieved mechanically or statically without a sustaining mechanism. The mechanism is "centralizing." In other words, the *zhongyong* dialectics can be taken as "the practical application of the principle of central harmony."[85] Centrality and harmony are indivisible. Or if we say that harmony is the state of nature, then centrality is what enables and sustains this state. Furthermore, when something or someone is going to the extreme, it is the mechanism that brings it or her back to central harmony.

By the *zhongyong* dialectics, everything that tends to be dynamically positioning itself in or moving toward the due middle implies appropriateness, reasonableness, and auspiciousness. Otherwise it tends to be inappropriate, unreasonable, and inauspicious. Pang illustrates this view that values "centrality" by pointing out that all the combinations of the *bagua* (Eight Trigrams), which come in turn from the various combinations of *yin* (symbolized by a broken line "- -") and *yang* (symbolized by a solid line "–"), indicate that central positioning implies auspiciousness.[86] Throughout *Yijing* or *Book of Changes*, it is common to see such a central positioning in a trigram that means good luck in life, such as successful career development or flourishing business. As we have discussed, *yin* and *yang*, or any other polarities they represent, complement and supplement each other by using one's strength to make up for the other's weakness. The greatest effect of this mutually complementary process occurs when they are moving toward the due middle. It recognizes the mutual transformation of polarities, which is very much stressed by Daoism, but argues that going too far in the transforming process is as bad as not going far enough.[87] The meaning of centrality was illustrated by Confucius himself when he told people what should be the manner of a true gentleman. He says:

Where the solid qualities are in excess of accomplishments, we have rusticity; where the accomplishments are in excess of the solid qualities, we have the manners of a clerk. When the accomplishments and solid qualities are equally blended, we then have the man of virtue.[88]

---

[85] Tu 2008, 16.   [86] Pang 1980.   [87] Confucius et al. 2014, 108.   [88] Ibid., 56.

The Confucian doctrine recognizes the coexistence of polarities, the complementary nature of such polarities, and the process of their co-transformation. At the same time it also stresses the dynamic process of moving toward the middle and argues that it is this dynamic centralizing and the due blending of the polarities that bring about harmony. In this sense, the "middle" is neither an indicator of the physical location, nor the mathematical median. It is the "due" middle in terms of appropriateness and reasonableness. Or, centrality means the constant process of harmonizing, the process of polarities moving toward each other with due measure and degree. It is a dynamic process, a process that is continuously reaching harmony by adjusting all the differences appropriately toward centrality. Professor Pang thus argues that in Confucianism: "The dynamic centrality is harmony."[89]

The immanent inclusivity and complementarity of *yin* and *yang*, the process of their transforming toward each other, and the dynamic centrality that stresses the transforming movement unfolding with due measure and degree, constitute the essential elements of the *zhongyong* dialectics and reflect an important worldview of the Chinese: The *yin-yang* relationship, or the relationship of any polarities in this sense, is fundamentally harmonious and is always in the process of reaching harmony. The state of nature is harmony, which is also the home of any polarities. In other words, the *zhongyong* dialectics assumes that the *yin-yang* relationship is a constantly and continuously harmonizing process. It is important for the relational theory because it assumes the fundamental non-conflictual and harmonious nature of all relations, supporting the belief that harmony is not only desirable, but also reachable, for it is the state where the world is in and of its true self.

Dahrendorf has made a well-accepted statement which argues, "society has two faces of equal reality: one of stability and harmony and one of change, conflict and constraint."[90] It is undoubtedly a true description of the real social world, but the question is which is more ontologically fundamental. The harmony assumption argues that harmony is more fundamental. This fundamental assumption of harmony leads to two related concepts, especially in international relations: difference and conflict. They are related because it is quite often believed that differences bring about disharmony or lead to conflict. In IR, as has been discussed, George Kannan holds that the conflict between the United States and the Soviet Union was real mainly because of the irreconcilably different ideologies;[91] realism of various strands basically believes that different interests of nation-states are real and objective, leading to conflict of

[89] Pang 1980.   [90] Dahrendorf 1958, 127.   [91] Kennan 1947.

interests and possibly to war;[92] Samuel Huntington argues that the post-Cold War international conflict comes mainly from the difference among different civilizations, Islamism, Confucianism, and Christianity;[93] and democratic peace theory sees that similar political systems and value systems are a precondition for international peace.[94] These theories and views perceive the world in their own ways with different foci, but it seems that they all imply a deep-seated belief or inarticulate worldview: Homogeneity is the premise for harmony and difference leads to disharmony. To use the same logic, we may easily reach a conclusion, very much a Hegelian one, that polarities are different and therefore they tend to conflict with each other, bearing in mind that dialectical/critical theories see conflict as positive and progressive while the mainstream takes them as negative and problematic.

It is this antagonistic and irreconcilable nature of the Hegelian contradiction that necessarily brings about social conflict and crisis, which in turn creates the condition for social transformation. Contradictions and conflicts, as Heine and Teschke have commented, are of ontological significance because "reality is itself contradictory," and the dialectical contradiction expresses "the real antagonism," operating "precisely on the opposite principle – the principle of contradiction." It is exactly the dialectical approach that "captures the real historically- and socially-constituted antagonism in the world."[95] In other words, social progress always depends upon revolution ignited by social crises accumulated over time from social conflict among social forces. In fact human/inter-subjective engagement is a persistent and constant struggle to overcome contradiction and conflict. By this logic, social conflict, defined in terms of antagonistic and irreconcilable contradictions which constitute "the central principle of dialectics",[96] gains ontological significance and becomes the driving force for social transformation and revolution. As Brincat has cited McTaggart: "It is only when contradictions are perceived as being contradictory, incompatible and antagonistic in their unreconciled form that the dialectical processes of change and potential sublation can begin to take place."[97] Cox makes the contradictory conflict an outstanding feature of his critical theory of world politics, which seeks emancipatory change as its ultimate purpose.[98] Using the Hegelian/Marxian dialectics as his main methodological device, Cox places particular stress on social transformation through social conflict by saying,

---

[92] Carr 1964.   [93] Huntington 1993.   [94] Doyle 1997.
[95] Heine and Teschke 1996, 412.   [96] Brincat 2011, 685.   [97] Ibid., 687.
[98] Cox 1986, 217.

The framework or structure within which action takes place is to be viewed not from the top in terms of the requisites for its equilibrium or reproduction (which would quickly lead back to problem-solving), but rather from the bottom or from outside in terms of the conflicts which arise within it and open the possibility of its transformation.[99]

For the *zhongyong* dialectics, on the contrary, difference is exactly what makes harmony possible. In other words, harmony rests on difference. Harmony exists when *yin* and *yang*, the two very different elements, are moving toward each other and duly blended along with the process and when they complement and supplement each other by using one's strength to overcome the other's weakness. It therefore does not seek to cancel out or eliminate differences, but believes that differences exist naturally as the existence of *yin* and *yang* does. It is the opposite of difference, similarity or homogeneity, that denies the premise of and need for harmony. For any piece of good music, it is the result of different sounds, appropriately adjusted and combined. Imagine the world in which we are living. It is naturally a place of multiple cultures, societies, and peoples, which are different and which cannot become homogeneous. By the *zhongyong* logic, it is this difference and heterogeneity that create the necessary condition for a harmonious order. Therefore, the process of cultivating centrality and harmony with thoroughness is both a practical process of doing things and a lofty ideal for "synchronicity of heaven and earth and the symbiosis between different modes of existence."[100] As such, the *zhongyong* dialectics recognizes the existence of conflict. Fundamental harmony of relations does not mean that there is no conflict in the natural and the social worlds. It is well known that harmony and conflict are two key words in social life, international relations in particular, and they are often taken as opposites just like the polarities in dialectics. Chung-ying Cheng frames harmony and conflict in a polarity structure and his definitions of the two terms provide a useful starting point for a meaningful discussion. It goes as follows:

From an intuitive view, harmony means the following: For any two distinctive coexisting or succeeding forces, processes, or entities, if there is mutual complementation and mutual support between the two, so that each depends on the other for strength, actuality, productivity, and value, then we can say that these two form a harmonious whole and an organic unity. In contrast, conflict means the absence of harmony between two distinctive, different or not different forces, processes, or entities, to the extent that each tends to cancel out the other, contradict the other, harm the other, or even perhaps destroy the other. As a consequence, there is no unity or harmony underlying the conflict elements.[101]

---

[99] Ibid.   [100] Tu 2008, 22.   [101] Cheng 2006, 27.

This definition distinguishes between the two concepts of harmony and conflict. In IR, as well as in philosophy, a fundamental question is: Which is the state of nature: harmony or conflict? To hold that the basic state of the world is harmony or to believe that it is essentially conflict divides the two different worldviews and often leads to different answers to social cooperation and conflict. While the Hegelian expressions in IR theoretical literature see the international relations world as conflict ridden, the two major Chinese schools of thought – Confucianism and Daoism – share the worldview of harmony. Applied to the *yin-yang* relationship, it means that the nature of such a relationship is harmony. "For the Confucian, harmony is the basic state and underlying structure of reality, while conflict does not have roots in reality, but rather represents an order of unnatural imbalance or a disorder of no lasting significance."[102] Conflict is thus resolved in the process of harmonizing. It is again the *zhongyong* dialectics that provides an interpretive tool for understanding this basic state of life and relationship. It means that the state of nature is harmony and the proper order of society is also characterized by harmony. The reason is fairly simple: Since *yin* and *yang* are immanently inclusive and since they are two halves in unity and therefore in fact they are one, the proper state of their relationship should be harmony. Conflict or disharmony is primarily a deviation from the state of nature and a violation of the "due-degree" principle in the dynamic unfolding of interactive relationships.

While the *zhongyong* dialectics sees harmony as the basic state of nature and human affairs and the overall tendency of development as moving toward harmony, the Hegelian dialectics sees conflict as a normal way for the formation of a new synthesis.[103] While differences are seen as the premise for harmony by the *zhongyong* dialectics, they are the sources of conflict as reflected by the difference between the thesis and antithesis and progress can be achieved only through eliminating such differences no matter whether they are manifested as logical or social contradictions – by sublation perhaps in the former and social revolution in the latter. By the logic of the Hegelian dialectics, for example, conflict is conceived as a necessary condition for progress and evolution. Humans and nature are conceived as conflictually interrelated, with one conquering the other as the sign of progress. Socioeconomic classes are structured as two opposite poles and struggle against each other in a zero-sum game until one eliminates the other and a new synthesis emerges in the form of a new society and new social relationships. Then historical progress is accomplished and even history ends. As mentioned above, the concept of

---

[102] Ibid., 28.   [103] Cheng 1991, 184–186. See also Cheng 2005.

essential conflict is also embedded in much of mainstream IR theories: Conflict of interests is unavoidable among nations, clash of civilizations is inevitable among different civilizations, and conflict of norms leads to differentiated regional international societies, standing independent of one another.

Thus, beliefs and assumptions concerning conflict and harmony constitute perhaps the most important difference between the Hegelian and the *zhongyong* dialectics. Although the *zhongyong* dialectics and the Hegelian dialectics share assumptions on mutuality, process, and change, their difference is also conspicuous. The Hegelian dialectics believes that human interaction involves inevitably contradictions and such contradictions are antagonistic and irreconcilable. As Brincat argues, "a dialectical methodology of world politics is, and must be, thoroughly intersubjectivist as it is through human interaction that contradictions and social antagonism are generated, wherein lies the dialectical catalyst of social transformation."[104] It differs qualitatively from the *zhongyong* assumption that harmony is where social order rests and harmony-based transformation is what evolution is oriented toward. The world through the lens of the *zhongyong* dialectics is thus a world that differs from the Hobbesian jungle, where everyone fights again everyone else. It is a world where differences make harmony and where conflict has no ontological significance. Change, for example, is not seen as a challenge to stability as Dahrendorf believes; rather change is necessary for a dynamic stability. Change, therefore, is always change through continuity, and continuity is always continuity through change. The *zhongyong* dialectics sees two opposites interacting in an immanently inclusive way, depending on and complementing each other for full expression and for life, and co-evolving into a new synthesis through dynamic processes which keep maintaining, adjusting, and managing complex and fluid human relations so as to reach the ideal as well as the basic state of harmony. It is for this reason that Cheng correctly calls it the harmonizing dialectics.[105]

The argument that conflict has no ontological status concerns also human agency. Although the *zhongyong* dialectics and the Hegelian dialectics both stress the importance of human agency, believing that without it there could be little change. However, their causal directions differ. For the Hegelian dialectics the causal direction is almost completely externally oriented. The self looks, thinks, and takes action outwardly toward the other. For example, human agency is needed to identify critically the most antagonistic and irreconcilable social contradictions produced by different social forces.[106] Furthermore, sublation, change,

---

[104] Brincat 2011, 681.   [105] Cheng 1991, 182–184.   [106] Cox 1986.

and social revolution exist as potentials and possibilities, and their materialization is not automatic and inevitable, for actors may well choose not to identify such contradictions and maintain the status quo.[107] The dialectical theory for emancipation tells us that active and positive humans are able to reach out so as to identify such contradictions, find opportunities in antagonistic conflicts, and make the crisis-brewed potentials materialize for a thorough social change. This external orientation of agency bears a lot of resemblance to that in the mainstream IR theory and the only difference is that the latter seeks to solve problems faced by the establishment rather than to identify crucial contradictions to overthrow it.

Since conflict exists despite the fact that it does not have roots in reality, to resolve conflict and bring back harmony, then, is indeed an important question for the *zhongyong* dialectics. In fact, as I have discussed, inclusivity and complementation of the polarities provide the necessary conditions for harmony, and human agency provides the sufficient condition, which decides whether harmony can be reached and maintained in the due middle. Human agency is thus the crucial factor. Confucianism makes human agency an outstanding factor in the first place that provides the key support for harmonious relations and the crucial push for the movement toward the appropriate middle. It is human agency that may lead toward harmony or astray to disharmony.

However, this human agency is not the same as it is embodied in the Hegelian dialectics. It is what can be first termed inward-oriented human agency, or self-cultivation, through which the self realizes its harmonization with the other, with the social world, and with nature. It is true that Confucian scholars may not agree with one another how to practice self-cultivation. Neo-Confucian scholars like Zhu Xi argue that self-cultivation should first of all follow the moral principles taught by Confucius and other sages, while others such as Wang Yangming hold that self-cultivation should follow more one's natural goodness through penetrating deeply into the inner self rather than being distracted by outside disturbances. Despite the disagreement on ways of practicing self-cultivation, what they all stress is that self-cultivation is the main channel to realize harmony, because it is virtuous persons that can maintain good relationships among people and good order in society. Any harmonious and fiduciary community, as Tu argues, is based upon the virtue of profound/virtuous persons trained with and self-disciplined by morality.[108] In other words, any harmonious relationship rests on the cultivation of the self which in turn brings about

---

[107] Brincat 2011.   [108] Tu 2008.

self-constraint and self-discipline. If two people or two sides both practice this way, the resulting relationship between them must be harmonious. Or in Confucius' words, two people are in good relations if they both want to make the other successful while making themselves successful.

However, if the self-cultivation is taken as a mere inward activity, and a complete withdrawal to oneself, as Hegel has criticized Daoism,[109] it is seriously misleading. Even though Daoism encourages keeping a distance away from society and practicing meditation in isolation, self-cultivation, largely a concept of Confucianism in social contexts, aims to harmonize human relations, especially the self-other relations, in society so that society as a whole may be harmonious. Thus it is inward-oriented in the sense of going deep into the inner self for cultivation and it is also outward-oriented in the sense of appropriately relating the self to others. In other words, its purpose is to establish and maintain harmonious human relationships. The inwardness is for the outward-ness. The Confucian practice of self-cultivation is, as expressed in the well-known motto, to "cultivate oneself, put one's house in order, run the state well, and let peace and prosperity prevail in the world." It is therefore first of all relational and social. All the standards for self-cultivation orient the self appropriately toward others. *Ren* (virtue, benevolence), for example, the first and most important norm of Confucianism, teaches an appropriate attitude of the self to others, that is, the care and love one should have toward others. In fact the character "*ren*" itself in the Chinese language is the combination of two characters – "two" and "people,"[110] indicating that *ren* is practiced only among people rather than for oneself. Confucius' famous teaching – "do not do to others what you would not have them do to you" – reflects the fact that the virtue is expressed in one's relations with others and is clearly social in meaning. Mencius holds that *ren* is to "care one's family, be benevolent to one's people, and be friendly to all things," none of which can be achieved purely through self-meditation in complete iso-lation. Thus *ren* means loving others. *Li* (rite, ritual), another important norm of Confucianism, expresses this relational and social nature even more clearly. By definition, it is to respect others and implies that harmony is achieved if everyone respects everyone else in society. The *Analects* says: "Let the superior man never fail to order his own

---

[109] Brincat and Ling 2014, 3.
[110] Xu Shen 2006, 423. Xu Shen's explanation of the character *ren* is benevolent love between two people. (Xu Shen's *Etymological Dictionary* is the first Chinese character dictionary compiled between 100 and 121 AD in the Han Dynasty, explaining the ideographical origins of 9,833 Chinese characters.

conduct, and let him be respectful to others and observant of propriety:–
then all within the four seas will be his brothers."[111] Ritual is the social
expression of the due centrality, and therefore is the regulating mechanism for harmony, for "if harmony itself is not modulated by ritual, things
will go amiss."[112]

Conclusion

The above discussion aims to explain the *zhongyong* dialectics as the
intellectual lens through which we understand the complexity of relations
in the social world and as a practical tool by which we know the appropriate way of dealing with human relations. The *zhongyong* dialectics,
primarily a Confucian philosophical notion and general worldview,
assumes harmony as the basic state of the world and denies an ontologically significant status of conflict. Although Confucianism and Daoism
agree with each other on this important assumption, it is Confucianism
that explicitly applies it to the social world, especially in terms of social
relations. It is also Confucianism that has found the "due middle" as the
ideal state for harmony. The natural state of human relations is harmony;
any conflict that arises is a deviation from such a state and can be
corrected so that harmony is returned and maintained.

The relationship of any polarities is characterized by inclusivity and
complementarity. Inclusivity in the *zhongyong* dialectics is not mere interdependence, mutuality, and intersubjectivity. It does not only mean that
two independent objects or people interact with each other. Rather it
places particular emphasis on embeddedness and immanency.
The polarities of *yin* and *yang*, which represent all the pairs of polarities
in the cosmos, are life in, of, and for each other. An important assumption
of the *zhongyong* dialectics is therefore "*yin*-within-*yang* and *yang*-within-
yin." It is this character of embedded inclusivity that provides a necessary
condition for the state of fundamental harmony, because the polarities are

---

[111] Confucius et al. 2014, 119.

[112] This is the translation by Arthur Waley (see Confucius 1998). For the whole passage his
translation goes as follows: "Master Yu said, 'In the usages of ritual it is harmony that is
prized; the Way of the Former Kings from this got its beauty. Both small matters and
great depend upon it. If things go amiss, he who knows the harmony will be able to
attune them. But if harmony itself is not modulated by rituals, things will still go amiss.'"
The translation by Ames and Rosemont goes as "Master You said, 'Achieving harmony
(*he*和) is the most valuable function of observing ritual propriety (*li* 礼). In the ways of
the Former Kings, this achievement of harmony made them elegant, and was a guiding
standard in all things large and small. But when things are not going well, to realize
harmony just for its own sake without regulating the situation through observing ritual
propriety will not work." (See Ames and Rosemont 1998, 74.) James Legge's translation
is somewhat ambiguous. See Confucius et al. 2014 (translated by James Legge), 9.

one in the very beginning. In addition, this assumption precludes any effort to form a dualistic structure, which has always been a problem in the social sciences in general and in IR in particular. Furthermore, complementarity provides a second necessary condition for harmony of the polarities. It is assumed that the two poles complement each other, each using its strength to make up for the weakness of the other. Together they facilitate and strengthen life, a life for both. The complementarity assumption gives the *yin-yang* dialectical relationship the generative power: They generate life through inclusive interaction and the new life inherits from and through both of them without being reducible to either of them. Moreover, the new life is healthy and vigorous only when the relationship of *yin* and *yang* is a harmonious one.

Human agency provides the sufficient condition for harmony. Harmony is the basic state of all relations, but harmony is not automatically maintained and self-preserved. It requires human agency for its materialization and maintenance. The general principle for such human agency is "moving toward the due middle," or, simply put, it is the centrality principle. Centrality requires human agency, which orients relations of the polarities, or relations of the self and the other, toward the central harmony. Otherwise, the relationship of the polarities may go to the extreme, where conflict can easily appear. When both the self and the other have learned through education and self-cultivation how to behave appropriately, their behavior is neither too aggressive nor too humble. Furthermore, the self does not impose on the other what she does not want imposed on herself, but wants to make the other successful as she herself succeeds, and together they use their own strength to make up for the weakness of the other. As a result, the relationship between the self and the other is harmonious and society is harmonious, too.

However, human agency in the *zhongyong* dialectical tradition is not exactly the same as the explicitly outward-oriented human agency generally understood in the social sciences in the West. It is neither the purely inward-oriented type misunderstood and criticized by Western scholars. Rather, it is a process of "inward-outward" agential activities. Human agency in the Chinese cultural tradition, therefore, is first inwardly oriented, i.e. going deep into the inner self for reflection and cultivation; and then it moves outward embodied in a cultivated person's managing her relations toward others. It is first inwardly oriented, requiring that one should practice self-cultivation by using either the moral and normative standards or the essential virtue embedded in human nature, or both, to make one a really virtuous and profound person (*junzi*). But this self-cultivation is not just for mere self-purification or self-satisfaction. It aims to go outside and reach out in society. Thus, human agency in the *zhongyong* dialectics requires that one, through self-reflection, should apply what one gets from self-cultivation to one's relations with others. Inwardly, it is to overcome one's own weakness, and outwardly, it is to use one's strength to make up for the weakness of the other. Going inward is for reaching outward. Once the self and the other both behave this way, the centrality principle is spontaneously applied and a harmonious relationship prevails as a natural result. It is this type of human agency that carries within itself the seeds of inclusivity and complementarity. Together they bring about or simply return to the state of harmony.

A philosophy based upon such dialectics differs from the Hegelian tradition, which puts far more emphasis on contradiction and conflict. In terms of relations of polarities, the Hegelian dialectics gives contradiction and conflict a conspicuously significant status of ontology, endeavouring to discover the crucial contradictions that are antagonistic and irreconcilable. Applied to social studies, the Hegelian dialectics takes irreconcilable contradictions as the driving force for change in general and as the prime mover for social transformation in particular. Human agency is important in that contradiction and conflict do not automatically lead to social transformation and revolution. It requires human agency to identify them and make them the catalyst for change. Such human agency is fundamentally outwardly oriented. Compared with the *zhongyong* dialectics, the Hegelian tradition is much more transformative, revolutionary, and perhaps radical. It rests on a philosophy of conflict and seeks progress through confrontation. It is particularly suitable for theories of emancipation. On the other hand, the *zhongyong* dialectics is more order-oriented, evolutionary, and perhaps conservative. It is more about maintaining the basic state of harmony through effectively thwarting conflict, an abnormal and deviant social phenomenon. It therefore is more suitable for mediation and reconciliation, especially in terms of human relations.

I do not intend to say which tradition is superior, for each has its historical and cultural background and each has its strengths and weaknesses. For the relational theory of world politics in this book, the *zhongyong* dialectics is the main epistemological and methodological device. It provides a different worldview and a different philosophical and interpretive system. My curiosity is what the international relations world would look like if we use such a worldview and such an interpretive system. However, since the *zhongyong* dialectics holds that any polarities are mutually complementary, the two dialectical traditions may well complement each other to produce a promising synthesis for a better understanding of the international relations world.

7   The Logic of Relationality

What motivates human action has always been a fundamental question for social exploration. In the IR literature there have been different points of view around logics of action. The logic of consequences and the logic of appropriateness are the two that have been most often discussed and cited.[1] In addition, Thomas Risse explores the logic of arguing,[2] Vincent Pouliot studies the logic of practicality,[3] and Ted Hopf goes into the logic of habit.[4] These logics of action in the IR literature, in fact, can be divided into two broad categories. One is the logic of rationality and the other the logic of practicality. The former includes the logic of consequences and the logic of appropriateness. The logic of arguing can be also put into this category because its fundamental claim resembles the logic of appropriateness. These logics assume individual rationality: instrumental rationality for the logic of consequences and normative rationality for the logic of appropriateness and the logic of arguing, for they all require individual rationality to sustain their respective logics. The other category includes the logic of practicality and the logic of habit, for both require practical and background knowledge for the logics to stand. Furthermore, these logics are interrelated rather than separate from and independent of one another. In the following lines I will discuss these logics. Then I will develop the logic of relationality, and explain why the logic of relationality provides both a different and a complementary base for human action.

The Logic of Rationality

The logic of consequences and the logic of appropriateness are logics of action based most explicitly on rationality. James March and Johan Olsen discuss the bases of action and point out quite correctly that mainstream IR theories actually explore two kinds of logic for action:

---

[1] March and Olsen 1998.   [2] Risse 2000; see also Kornprobst 2007.   [3] Pouliot 2008.
[4] Hopf 2010.

the logic of consequences and the logic of appropriateness. The former reflects the rational choice proposition, arguing that human actors "choose among alternatives by evaluating their likely consequences for personal and collective objectives, conscious that other actors are doing likewise."[5] It assumes that actors are instrumentally rational, with prior preferences and well-defined self-interests. They are capable of comparing and calculating policy alternatives and choose the one that maximizes their interests. Fixed interests and prior preferences are the fundamental driving forces for action. Mancur Olson's logic of collective action fits well into this type, for every actor in Olson's collective-action problem is instrumentally rational, self-interested, and ready to sacrifice the interests of others as well as of the collectivity.[6] Free-riding is thus a characteristic feature of collective action. In IR, structural realism and neoliberal institutionalism are typical examples of this logic: The crucial mechanism for international structures and international institutions to influence actors' behavior is the instrumental rationality of the actor herself. Only through working on such individual instrumental rationality is the structure of power distribution and international institutions able to have impacts on the behavior of the actors. For what Keohane terms "the rationalistic approach" to the study of international relations,[7] instrumental rationality is the key word.

March and Olsen hold that the logic of consequences ignores the identities of the actor and the roles of rules and norms. Social constructivists then offer an alternative argument that action is driven by a logic of appropriateness and a sense of identity. "Human actors are imagined to follow rules that associate particular identities to particular situations, approaching individual opportunities for action by assessing similarities between current identities and choice dilemmas and more general concepts of self and situations."[8] In other words, the logic of appropriateness is the sense of doing the right thing, or following the right social norms in a particular situation. It is what Hopf terms "value rationality," which "implies reference to some norms when making a choice."[9] Since the study of international norms has become a prominent research agenda of mainstream social constructivism, rules and norms have been considered as both constitutive of the actor's identity and regulative of the actor's behavior,[10] serving the purposes of both the rationalistic emphasis on behavior and the constructivist exploration of identity. To date, the logic of appropriateness mainly focuses on norm-guided behavior: from

---

[5] March and Olsen 1998, 949.   [6] Olson 1995.   [7] Keohane 1989c.
[8] March and Olsen 1998, 951.   [9] Hopf 2010, 540.   [10] Ruggie 1999.

accepting norms to their internalization and then to the norm-following behavior. Martha Finnemore, for example, places special emphasis on the teaching of good norms by international organizations to international actors: It is the mechanism of teaching that enables such actors to understand what their interests should be and what behavior is therefore appropriate.[11] When many newly established states had a similar definition of their national interest almost simultaneously, it was the teacher, UNESCO in her case, that played the crucial role in shaping the identity of the states concerned. It is said that the logic of appropriateness focuses on norms and identities, but individual rationality works almost throughout the process of norm learning and following, because, as Finnemore's study shows, following the norms taught to them is beneficial in the first place and then comes the acceptance of such norms. As Thomas Risse correctly points out, the logic of appropriateness, which gives full play in the third stage of norm suasion in Checkel's study,[12] reflects a presumption of "normative rationality."[13] If we say that instrumental rationality means that actors take action according to their calculation of gains measured against their fixed interests, then normative rationality purports that human action is considered rational if and only if it follows the right norms.

The logic of arguing, to a large extent, goes with the logic of appropriateness.[14] Essentially it is about rules and norms, especially about better rules and norms. Drawing on Habermas' communicative action theory, which stresses the importance of argumentative rationality, with perhaps a focus on arguing for truth, it holds that "human actors engage in truth-seeking with the aim of reaching a mutual understanding based on a reasoned consensus (*verständigungsorientiertes Handeln*), challenging the validity claims involved in any communication."[15] There are norms, but which norms to follow is the question. It is necessary to follow good norms, but it requires people to argue so that they can know what norms are good and reasonable. Automatic acceptance is misleading and even dangerous. Crawford's study on argumentation shows the important role arguments with ethical and moral contents played in the abolition of slavery, decolonization, and humanitarian intervention. Moral arguments clarify what norms are good and progressive, bring about changes in norms, and therefore changes in practice.[16] Thus, "let's argue," find nice norms through our arguing, and then follow them.

---

[11] Finnemore 1996.   [12] Checkel 2005.   [13] Risse 2000, 4.
[14] It may be argued that the logic of arguing differs from the logic of appropriateness in a crucial point: While the latter implicitly assumes that rules and norms are nice, the former holds that convincing norms are selected only through argumentation.
[15] Risse 2000, 1–2.   [16] Crawford 2002.

Fundamentally it is about the relationship between norms and social action and, furthermore, it supports the constructivist argument that norms not only regulate behavior, but also shape identities and interests. However, the constitutive effect of norms goes with the belief that the norms are taken as good and reasonable only through argumentation, which is considered as the effective way for truth-seeking. What it stresses is in fact a higher stage of an evolutionary process of socialization.

Staged processes are discussed in some detail by Jeffery Checkel,[17] who proposes three generic social mechanisms – strategic calculation, role playing, and normative suasion, which can also be understood as stages of an evolutionary process of socialization starting from instrumental rationality through bounded rationality to normative rationality. Strategic calculation is about the actor's self-interests and therefore is instrumentally rationalistic; role playing is also rationalistic but follows more the logic of bounded rationality, indicating the beginning of a switch from the logic of consequences to that of appropriateness; and the normative suasion stage is indeed done by communicative rationality, internalizing norms through reasoned arguments. (Kornprobst provides an interesting case study of the value of argumentation.[18]) From such discussion, it is easy to see that instrumental rationality, though not necessarily an element within the logic of appropriateness, constitutes a necessary stage of norm socialization in international politics and international socialization starts with it. The logic of arguing simply tells the story of a critical stage of the process of norm compliance, the stage from knowing that there is the norm to knowing why there is the norm, why the norm is good, and why following it is appropriate. In between the knowing-that stage and the knowing-why stage individual rationality is crucial. As Risse points out, "argumentative rationality appears to be crucially linked to the constitutive rather than the regulative role of norms and identities by providing actors with a mode of interaction that enables them to mutually challenge and explore the validity claims of those norms and identities."[19] In other words, social actors follow rules and norms, but they do not follow them blindly. It involves "a reflexive process whereby agents need to figure out what behavior is appropriate to a situation."[20] They need first to make sure that the rules and norms are good through argumentation. Argumentative rationality works to make nice norms the guidance for individual behavior and thus makes normative rationality even more rational. Better arguments select.

Rationality, therefore, constitutes the basis for all three logics whose difference lies merely in what kind of rationality is the most important.

---

[17] Checkel 2005.   [18] Kornprobst 2007.   [19] Risse 2000, 2.   [20] Pouliot 2008, 262.

For neorealism and neoliberal institutionalism, it is instrumental rationality; and for mainstream social constructivism, it is normative rationality. Whether it is the material international structure or the ideational international structure, it must play on the individual rationality so as to influence the behavior of the actor. The contribution of the logic of arguing is to recognize the existence of various and perhaps competing norms, whose validity is determined through argumentation, but it does not go beyond normative rationality. Rather it reinforces such rationality. Thus, in the final analysis, these IR theories are theories based upon the rationality of individual actors in the system. It is exactly in this sense that I argue that the metaphysical component of their theoretical hard core is individualistic rationality.

The Logic of Practicality

The logic of practicality starts with a criticism of the above-discussed logics of action. It draws on the practice approach in sociology which has established the ontological priority of practice, arguing that what actors do counts most in social life.[21] As Vincent Pouliot holds, both the logic of consequences and the logic of appropriateness (including the logic of arguing) "suffer from a representational bias in that they focus on what agents think about instead of what they think from."[22] For the logic of practicality, human activity, largely unreflective and automatic, is rooted in practices and social action is based upon background knowledge rather than representational knowledge. It is more a knowledge-driven model of social action, arguing that:

most of what people do, in world politics as in any other social field, does not derive from conscious deliberation or thoughtful reflection – instrumental, rule-based, communicative, or otherwise. Instead, practices are the result of inarticulate, practical knowledge that makes what is to be done appear "self-evident" or commonsensical.[23]

Clearly, the most important claim of the international practice approach is that practical knowledge or background knowledge constitutes the driving force for social action. As it is argued, many actions cannot be explained by rational choice or rule-based or communicative action theories. Security communities are made such because people there think

---

[21] Pierre Bourdieu's theory of practice greatly influences the practice approach in IR. His key concepts, such as *habitus* (background) and *doxa* (tacit consensus), have provided scholars of the IR practice approach with intellectual inspirations by establishing the significance of practice and practical knowledge. Bourdieu 1977; 1990; 2012. For the practice turn in social theory, see Schatzki 2001.
[22] Pouliot 2008, 257.   [23] Ibid., 258.

from diplomacy and there is no place for violence on their menu of practice. Diplomacy as a typical example cannot be a "mathematical calculation; it is not an exact science; it remains a matter of human skills and judgments."[24] "Peace exists in and through practice when security officials' practical sense makes diplomacy the self-evident way to solving interstate disputes."[25] It is emphatically repeated that practice rests on background knowledge rather than representational knowledge. Most of what people do is the result of inarticulate and unreflective knowledge that makes what is to be done appear "self-evident" or commonsensical. Thus the logic of practicality, as international practice theorists have defined, is the logic that takes background knowledge as the basis of action. A strong case is made by using Bourdieu's concept of *habitus*, which is "a system of durable, transposable dispositions, which integrates past experience and functions at every moment as a matrix of perception, appreciation, and action, making possible the accomplishment of infinitely differentiated tasks."[26] As Bourdieu's personal experience shows, it is the background that disposes actual action.

There is little doubt that background knowledge is extremely important and it is also even very true to argue that human action is most of the time driven by such knowledge. In this respect, the logic of habit is similar. In his article entitled "The logic of habit in international relations," Ted Hopf argues that human action is made from an "unreflectively utilized viewpoint," or habits which are "automatic cognitive processes," and are, very much along the line of Searle's definition of Background, "unintentional, unconscious, involuntary, and effortless."[27] While the logic of habit differs explicitly from any of the logics of rationality, Hopf also believes that it differs in important respects from the logic of practicality and he accents that the logic of habit eliminates three fundamental premises of IR theory: rationality, agency, and uncertainty. Clearly, mainstream IR theories rely variably on these factors, while agency, in particular, still plays a crucial role in practice theory.[28] In addition, rationality has little role in the logic of habit, which holds that action comes out of habits rather than deliberate calculation. But he also agrees that the two, that is, the logics of practicality and habit, share some important views such as the negation of deliberate calculation and the emphasis on doing rather than speaking, on thinking "from" rather than thinking "about." However, if practice implies the actualization of the past at present so that agents know what is to be done in the future without conscious reflection or reference to explicit and codified knowledge, it seems that the two logics bear much more resemblance than

---

[24] Ibid.   [25] Ibid., 259.   [26] Ibid., 272.   [27] Hopf 2010, 541.   [28] Ibid., 544–547.

difference, because they both rest on background knowledge and both turn to *habitus* for inspiration. In other words, the foundation of their theoretical assumptions is the same. If "all forms of practice are rooted in habits,"[29] then, habits in turn rest on and at the same time reinforce background knowledge. It is therefore background knowledge that constitutes the key to both the logic of practicality and the logic of habit. They differ in degree rather than in essence.

A most important contribution of the international practice approach is its emphasis on the ontology of practice, which places human practice and the knowledge thus produced as the foundation for other logics of action. A serious problem for the approach, however, is that they place the two types of knowledge, representational knowledge and background knowledge, into a dichotomous structure of knowledge with one standing against the other. This dualistic way of thinking has more or less become a habit, betraying itself whenever it is possible. It is a serious misunderstanding and it is also highly misleading. In fact, Pouliot has correctly and repeatedly pointed out that the logic of practicality has ontological priority over both the logic of consequences and the logic of appropriateness.[30] In other words, the former constitutes the ontological underpinning for the latter. But in his discussion of practicality and perhaps for the purpose of making the two types of knowledge appear conspicuously different, he actually parallels the two kinds of logic – the logics of consequences and of appropriateness on the one hand and the logic of practicality on the other. They are thus understood as mere alternative logics of social action. Compared with the logics of both instrumental and normative rationality, practicality is ontologically at a more fundamental level indeed. If we consider it simply as another logic of action in a narrow sense, or a newly discovered alternative to the two other logics of consequences and appropriateness, we may confine ourselves to the more superficial levels rather than the ontological level. In this respect, we need to clarify the relationship between background knowledge and representational knowledge, for in the difference between these two types of knowledge lies the difference between the logics of rationality and the logic of practicality.

The problem is rooted in the interpretation by Pouliot of the two types of knowledge.[31] He structures them in a dualistic way and construes background knowledge as an alternative to representational knowledge, which can also be called foreground knowledge because it is articulate and explicit. In the course of seriously criticizing the representational bias, he places almost exclusive emphasis on background knowledge, which, compared with representational knowledge, is a fundamentally different

[29] Ibid., 547.   [30] Pouliot 2008.   [31] Pouliot 2008; see also Adler and Pouliot 2011.

type of knowledge playing the most important role in orienting human action. Representational knowledge, constituting the foundation of the logics of consequences, appropriateness, and arguing, concerns "thinking about" rather than "thinking from." Therefore, if we use representational knowledge rather than background knowledge as the key to logics of action, it is putting the cart before the horse. Pouliot's ontology of practice is no doubt most reasonable, but what he does not realize and actually negates is the fact that representation itself is practice. As such it rests on the background knowledge of those who do the representation. It is not only diplomats or Red Cross workers that are practitioners. Theorists and knowledge producers are practitioners, too. The foreground knowledge they produce in their practice reflects the background knowledge embedded in the community of practice where they think and do and where they are embedded. The logic of practicality is one for both the way of doing and the way of thinking, for thinking is also doing just as speaking is doing.[32] Practical or background knowledge orients people's doing and thinking and combines the two together. Pouliot, too, perhaps unconsciously, separates the body and the mind, as Descartes did, through the implicit argument that a thinking mind is not a doing body.

Background knowledge is, I argue, not an alternative to representational knowledge, but provides the foundation or the background for it, because knowledge production itself is practice and therefore rests on the background of a community of practice, of which a cultural community is most representative. Think about an academic community. It resembles a diplomatic community in most respects: Its members come together, discuss and deliberate, form rules and norms, and do as practitioners in knowledge production and reproduction. If we say that a community of diplomats or a community of Red Cross workers is a community of practice, there is no reason to say that a community of academicians is not a community of practice. Representation is practice. If this view stands, representational knowledge is closely related to background knowledge. On the one hand, background knowledge lays the foundation on which representational knowledge grows; on the other hand, representational knowledge actualizes and manifests the background knowledge. The key is still the producer of knowledge, who is at the same time immersed in the background knowledge of a cultural community and the representational knowledge she produces rests at the deeper level on the background knowledge of the community. It is hard to imagine that a social scholar immersed in a certain community of practice and shaped

---

[32] Austin 2002. Onuf also says: "Indeed, saying is doing: talking is undoubtedly the most important way that we go about making the world what it is." Onuf 1998, 59.

by the background knowledge thereof may produce some representational knowledge absolutely alien to such background knowledge.

The mainstream American IR community provides a telling example. Its members are knowledge producers and their daily activities are producing knowledge. They think, speak, write, and publish. They are also engaged in discussion, dialogue, and debate. They generate useful and inspiring representational knowledge, which goes to other places and passes on to coming generations. Their academic activities are no doubt practices and they are practitioners, too. At the same time, they are embedded in the American cultural community. Their background knowledge is exactly the background knowledge of the community at large, for they are living it, shaped and disposed by it. If we say that they produce representational knowledge and if we agree that such production is practice, then their representational knowledge is based in the first place on their background knowledge. The triumph of the behaviorist revolution and obvious "scientific" characteristic of American IR is by no means an accident. Representational knowledge and background knowledge are the two sides of the same thing and they are mutually supportive and complementary. While the background knowledge orients and disposes the producer of the representational knowledge, the representational knowledge reflects and reinforces the background knowledge; while the former constitutes the ontological foundation for the latter, the latter is the manifestation and the articulation of the former.

Thus, as soon as practice theorists structure representational knowledge and practical knowledge into two distinct and discrete categories, they fall into the familiar Cartesian dualistic trap. Even though they aim to overcome dichotomies in social theory, dichotomies between the material and meaningful, the agential and structural, the reflexive and background, and continuity and change,[33] their practice of putting representational and practical knowledge into two distinctive categories makes their mission impossible from the very beginning, because it not only negates the fact that representational knowledge production is itself practice, but also betrays the fundamental dualistic structuring of the mind and the body, of ideas and things out there. It follows what it criticizes. Since representational knowledge and practical knowledge are treated dichotomously, anything based upon and derived from them is necessarily dichotomous in nature. It is misleading if the exploration should focus on the question of which type of knowledge, representational or background, constitutes the base for action. It is even more misleading if the two types of knowledge should be taken as two distinct bases for different

---

[33] Adler and Pouliot 2011, 12–18.

logics of social action: the former for the logics of consequences and appropriateness while the latter for the logic of practicality. The reason is that the two types of knowledge are fundamentally and immanently inclusive and inseparably complementary. Reflecting the background and the foreground, they together define the logics of action and enable certain actions to take place. While individualistic rationality is deeply embedded in the background knowledge of Western communities, it disposes academicians to explore what kind of rationality constitutes the prime mover of human action, instrumental or normative. In other words, academic practices are also reflections of background knowledge, just as are diplomatic or other practices.

Traditional Chinese philosophy largely holds that knowledge and practice are the two sides of the same thing and that they cannot be separated as two discrete categories. The Chinese word for "learn" or "study" is "*xuexi*," a compound word with two characters. Literally, the first character means "learn" and the second, "practice," indicating that the two are understood as fundamentally inseparable. In the very beginning of the *Analects*, Confucius says: "Is it not pleasant to learn with a constant perseverance and application?"[34] Confucius attaches equal importance to both and stresses the fact that the two go hand in hand. For him, knowledge is from, for, and through practice. The *Analects* contains a story, telling people that even some trivial practices such as sprinkling and sweeping the ground imply great learning.[35] This line of reasoning applies to practical knowledge and representational knowledge, too. Any representational knowledge reflects background knowledge at a particular temporo-spatial point where they are mutually and simultaneously activated. Rationality, usually considered as an essential part of the representational knowledge, is in fact the reflection of the practical knowledge and the sediment of the practice of the more individualistic Western communities at the historic moment when human individuality was inspiringly activated and glorified with the Renaissance. It is representational because it is embedded in and inseparable from the background in the first place. It is widely accepted by Western academic communities because it has always been there in their background and disposed them even without their realizing it. Thus, practical knowledge and representational knowledge, just as practice and theory,[36] are immanently related and inclusively complementary rather than separate and discrete as two distinct forms of knowledge competing against each other.

[34] Confucius' words: "*Xue er Shi Xi zhi, Buyi Yuehu* (学而时习之不亦说乎)" (Confucius et al. 2014, 3) are also translated into: "Is it pleasant to learn with constant practice?" See Li Zehou 2004, 24.
[35] Confucius et al. 2014, 209.   [36] Qin 2016b.

In this sense the logic of practicality goes naturally with the logic of consequences and the logic of appropriateness in Western societies because people there carry out their practices that way. In other words, it is wrong if we separate thinking and doing and take "corporeal knowledge" and mental knowledge as profoundly different. Thinking is doing, and thinking and doing are two inseparable parts of practice. Together with speaking (and speaking is doing, too), they form the trinity of practice.[37] Representational knowledge relies on and at the same time reflects background knowledge, inseparable just as the body and the mind.

In the following section I will discuss in detail the logic of relationality, which, accordingly, also rests on the logic of practicality, for it is the sediment of long practice of Confucian communities – their view of the world and their way of life. Practices over hundreds of years have crystalized certain ways of thinking, speaking, and doing, constituting members of the community of practice and the representational knowledge thereof. Science and technology did not develop in China and representational knowledge in the fields of the natural sciences did not grow prosperously in Chinese cultural communities because their practices had seldom involved scientific exploration and exploitation.[38] For millennia the Chinese simply did not do and think that way. On the other hand, their practices had been biased conspicuously toward human relations, having invented much more nuanced terms for people of differential relationships in their language while borrowing only in recent times directly from abroad terminologies in the natural sciences. It is therefore not surprising to see that in their practical knowledge relationality has been a distinct, characteristic feature, and accordingly in the teachings of the Chinese master thinkers, such as Confucius and Mencius, the most representational is the understanding, clarification, and management of human relations. Practice, rather than the material or the ideational, provides undoubtedly the ontological foundation on which representational knowledge develops and evolves. Practical knowledge and background knowledge are thus inclusive of each other in a dialectic and dynamic process of complementation and coevolution.

Thus, rationality and relationality both rest on the background knowledge of communities of practice, of which civilization-based cultural communities are the most spontaneous and therefore the most stable. The logic of rationality and the logic of relationality both perhaps fit more into the category of representational knowledge,

[37] Austin 2002.   [38] Feng 1991.

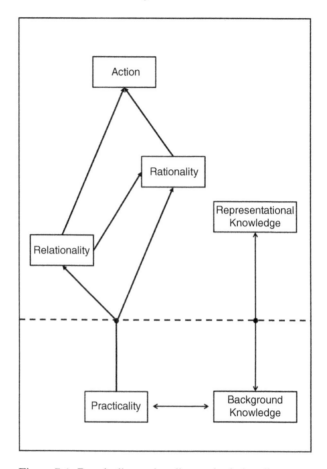

Figure 7.1: Practicality, rationality, and relationality

but, according to the theory of unity of knowing and doing, they are representational because they are practical in the first place, embedded in their background and represented in thinking, doing, and speaking. Thus, the map of logics of action in international relations may be drawn according to the following reasoning: The logics based upon background knowledge provide a foundation and have ontological priority, while the logics based upon representational knowledge reflect the ways of thinking, doing, and speaking, growing out of and resting on the background knowledge and having practice as their ontological underpinning. The former includes the logics of practicality (and perhaps of habit); while the latter, the logics of rationality and relationality.[39] Western IR theories, including the logics of consequences, appropriateness, and arguing, basically follow the key concept of rationality, for all of them can hardly deviate far from individualistic rationality, no matter whether it is instrumental, normative, or argumentative rationality. The logic of relationality, as I have proposed, rests on a different type of background knowledge, that is, the background of the Confucian cultural communities, members of which not only think about relationality, but also think from it. Figure 7.1 indicates the relationship between background and representational knowledge as well as among these logics of social action.

The Logic of Relationality

Relationality is a key concept abstracted from the world of relations. It comes from the cultural and social practices centered round relations and becomes to a large extent the most important element of the background knowledge of Confucian cultural communities. The relational theory focuses on human relations and holds that relationality is the key to understanding social phenomena and meaningful human actions. It is reasonable to say that relationality is the counterpart of rationality in Western cultural traditions in the sense that rationality as a key concept has also been developed and abstracted through practices in more individualistic society and more object-oriented cultures. On the other hand, however, rationality has become the core of many mainstream social theories while relationality is an underdeveloped concept and its logic has not been systematically explored. In this section, I will sketch the logic of relationality as both a neglected and a complementary base for human action.

Relationality as a Basis for Social Action

Relationality means that a social actor bases her actions on relations. In other words, the logic of relationality holds that an actor makes judgments and decisions according to her relationships to specific others, with the totality of her relational circles or the relational context as the

---

[39] Hopf may argue against this point of view, for he has found that it is unhelpful at this early stage of theorizing about habit and practice if the logics of habit and practice are taken as foundational for other logics. However, in his discussion he seems to take this position already as he says: "While the logic of practice treats unreflective practices as the taproot for all other logics of action, the logic of habit assumes, at this early stage of theorization, that all logics have their place in everyday life." Hopf 2010, 544. Ontologically, the position is reasonable.

background. In any social setting, what action an actor is to take depends very much on her relationships with specific others and her relations with the relational context in which she is embedded. In other words, her interests, desires, and preferences, which motivate her action, are not fixed. Rather they change as the nature of a relationship changes. In short, relations select.

There are some concepts crucial to understanding the logic of relationality. The first is "relators." Social actors, or human beings, are relators and the term "relator" is used to stress the fact that social actors relate by nature, by instinct, and by design, which indicates that they are fundamentally different from actors assumed by individualistic rationality as discrete and independent atoms. In fact, in an interrelated cosmos, everyone is a relator, incessantly relating and being related during her entire life cycle. If one refuses to relate and to be related, she is considered an autistic patient. As relators, they are aware of the reality of coexistence, knowing that their existence depends on their connectivity with others. They are also conscious that their action depends on their relations with others, understanding that interest is best achieved by joint efforts and through social relations. A social actor is born into a relational web-like complexity, tending to establish more relational ties; and at the same time, every "other" is also a relator and therefore the actor is simultaneously and constantly related by others during her lifetime. Moreover, relators are not mere passive reactors, simply responding and adjusting to the environment. They are also active agents, purposefully making use of their relations and relational contexts for self-advancement. Similarly, in international relations states are relators (so are non-state actors, even though our focus is more on the state), relating and being related as long as they live in international society. Even the most isolated state, such as North Korea, is a relator, for its action is based upon the nature of its relationships with others in international society and the self-interest it has defined is automatically shared with the interest of the specific others. Its drastic and seemingly irrational actions aim to realize its interest through playing with the complex relationships between itself and others and among all other relators, especially the major ones, relevant to it.

The second is relational circles. As previously defined, the self's relational circles refer to the totality of her relationships, starting from the self *per se* who perceives herself at the center of the multilayered concentric relational circles, and indicating the self's relationships with others. It is the self that is the origin and the starting point, from which her relational circles are extending, outreaching, and ramifying. Through those relational circles she connects herself and others. It is exactly what Fei's ripple analogy depicts. The self's relational circles indicate the degree of intimacy of her relationships with others, constituting her relational sphere of influence. Those within the innermost or the core ring are the most intimate others. The degree of intimacy decreases as the circles move farther away from the center, from the primary circle through the secondary and then to the tertiary. The more intimate the circle is, the more influence she has over those within this circle. In a general society, the most intimate circle of a person is her family. Similarly, in international relations, for example, a more intimate relational circle of the United States in the Asia-Pacific region is its military alliance system, on which it has more influence. Another example is ASEAN. If we take ASEAN as a relator, its relational circles may at least include three interrelated concentric circles. The first and the core circle is ASEAN as a regional organization at the center, consisting of ten Southeast Asian nations; the second includes neighboring actors or ASEAN's dialogue partners such as China, Japan, and South Korea, gradually extending to include more actors like India, Australia, New Zealand, Russia, and the United States; the third is the outreaching one and may involve any other state in the world, which comparatively speaking is less close and less relevant. ASEAN tends to make a balanced consideration of its relationships with actors within its relational circles before it makes a collective decision, but the priority is reaching a consensus among the members of the core circle first.

The relational circles are not a constant and they vary with the passage of time and the change of the situation. For example, ASEAN initially had only six members, which constituted its primary circle. It successfully expanded to include four more states, Vietnam, Laos, Cambodia, and Myanmar, during its course of development. ASEAN 10 has now become the core circle. Immediately after the 1997 Asian financial crisis, the Asian integration plan was quite ambitious. The East Asian Vision Group (EAVG) made the proposal for building an overall East Asian community with the thirteen countries of ASEAN plus China, Japan, and South Korea as its members (EAVG I).[40] It was to replace ASEAN and meant something like the European Union, forming a core relational circle of thirteen countries with equal membership. However, it has never come true. EAVG has recently made a second proposal (EVAG II), modifying its original goal and encouraging the thirteen Asian nations (ASEAN 10 plus China, Japan, and South Korea) to first build an East Asian economic community by 2020 instead.[41] The relationships among various actors have become much more complicated with China's rise and the US rebalancing East Asia strategy. Now there are two different relational

<hr />

[40] East Asia Vision Group 2001.   [41] East Asia Vision Group II 2012.

circles at work. One is in the economic field, where ASEAN nations continue to develop economic relations with China; and the other is in the security field, where they rely more on their relationship with the United States. Moreover, the two circles are overlapping and interpenetrating. For ASEAN, how to maintain a balanced relationship between China and the United States seems to have become its priority, and perhaps a relator's dilemma, too.[42]

The third is the relational context. Each relator is a self, and her relational circles overlap with and penetrate into those of others, connecting herself with others in various ways. All these relational circles together compose a multidimensional and multilayered relational complexity. This complexity, or the totality of the relational circles of all relevant relators, constitutes the relational context. It is like a cubic web with nodes and ties, indicating the relators and their relationships in a specific temporal space. It is not like one spider's web, but many spiders' webs put and piled together. If one should view the world as a time-space field with ramifying and entangling relations, it would be a world substantially different from one composed of atomistic actors. In such a web-like world, each relator is the center of her relational circles and at the same time a node within another relevant relator's circles (as Figure 5.2 indicated). Someone, as the self, is the son of his parents, the husband of his wife, a colleague of his fellow professors, and a member of a professional association. France is a key member of the European Union and at the same time a member of the US-led NATO alliance. Similarly, the Philippines is a member of ASEAN and also an ally of the US hub-and-spoke alliance system in East Asia. China is the largest country in East Asia, relating itself to the BRICS group (Brazil, Russia, India, China and South Africa) and at the same time being related to by ASEAN as one in the 10+3 and 10+1 processes. Each relator tends to perceive her social world from a relational perspective and, in a more Confucian society, to think from relations. At the same time she naturally sees the relational web from her own angle as how to maintain and manipulate it. In contemporary international relations, as mentioned above, this relational context is fairly limited and more clearly defined, for states continue to be the most important players though they no longer monopolize world affairs. If we take states as relators, therefore, in the space of the relational context there are about 200 relators, and their respective relational circles, put together, constitute the relational context which is the international social world today. Of course it is extendable by

---

[42] I will discuss "relator's dilemma" in detail in Chapter 9, where cooperation is the major topic.

the addition of non-state actors and highly complicated by the numerous combinations of various relationships.

Relations and Actions

The logic of relationality argues that social action is based upon relations. In other words, "relatedness" is an important mover of social action. Some significant factors pertaining to relationality bear heavily on a relator when she makes a decision. In this section, I will discuss several variables that matter for the logic of relationality, especially for a social actor who is in a decisional situation.

Significance of Relationships: Intimacy and Importance The significance of relationships is first and foremost reflected by the concept of identity relationship, for it reveals the nature of relationship which clarifies how the self is related with a specific other or others. Before one takes an action, she should understand clearly toward whom the action is to be taken. In other words, what action she is to take is based upon what relationship she has with the specific other and identity relationship is perhaps the most relevant concept in this respect. In general society, it may refer to someone that is a blood relative or a complete stranger while in international society it may refer to a dead enemy or a close ally, or using the three-layered-circle model there are friends, enemies, and neutrals referring to those who are neither friends nor enemies. Without clarifying the nature of a relationship, the relator simply does not know what her interest is, let alone whether the action is rational or not.

There are many indicators to clarify the nature of personal relationships, but intimacy is the most significant and perhaps the simplest single factor to specify the self's relationships with others. In a Confucian society, intimacy is key to the understanding of all the five cardinal relationships, father-son, emperor-minister, husband-wife, brothers, and friends. The father-son relationship provides the foundation for other relationships because it is the most intimate, and all other relationships are derived from this basic one, for the family constitutes the smallest and primary unit in a Confucian world and its features are extendable to general society. Thus, the fundamental rule in a relational world is the rule of intimacy.[43] Confucian society starts from the smallest and core unit, the family, mainly because family members are most intimate in terms of their relationships. It is true that family members may become enemies, but compared with other groups in society it always

---

[43] Li Zehou 2011, 52–53.

constitutes the most intimate circle of the self. Moreover, Confucianism believes that other social relationships should model themselves on those among family members so that society will be harmonious. The Confucian ideal is that the intimate family relationship will extend to friends, to society, and to the world so that the whole world would be "one family" with everyone being intimate with everyone else.

The concept of "intimacy" or "intimate relationship" has long been neglected by the mainstream IR theory due largely to the overwhelming theme of survival and the dominant assumption of the state as an averter of a security threat.[44] "Alliance," a key concept in international affairs, is studied more from the aspect of power struggle and security enhancement. It is more about dealing with a common threat than about establishing and building up friendship. The improvement of Sino-US relations in the 1970s, for example, has been taken as a measure not to establish friendship but to deal with a common threat, that is, the Soviet Union. The Confucian discourse of social relationships, interestingly enough, tells a different story. It stresses those elements of relationships more readily found among family members, such as affection, amity, and altruism, and discusses much less the enmity type. It recognizes enmity, but believes at the same time that enmity can be changed into amity. It focuses therefore more on how to establish amity and how to harmonize relationships rather than how to deal with hostile threats. None of the five cardinal relationships imply hostility and threat. Starting from the family, the Confucian discourse of relations pays natural attention to the intimacy of relationships and lays special emphasis on brotherhood and friendship. It comes from the practices of an agricultural society over millennia and constitutes the simplest rule of thumb for a relator to evaluate her social relationships. Figure 7.2 shows the nuanced differences in terms of intimacy of human relationships.

Figure 7.2 demonstrates the degrees of intimacy of one's relationships. *Liuqin*, who are included in the primary circle of intimacy, including the six blood relations, including the father, mother, elder brothers, younger brothers, wife, and children, are the most intimate and it is taken for granted that those relatives offer generous and even selfless help to one another. *Liuqin Buren*, or refusing to offer any help even to one's closest relatives, is an idiom derogatorily depicting those who do not have human emotions and sympathy at all. Another Chinese idiom, *Liuqin Wukao*, or having no close relatives to turn to, describes a situation in which one gets

---

[44] Berenskoetter holds that IR pays exclusive attention to survival and leaves "friendship" out of the mainstream discourse. He attempts to bring back this concept and to account for the friend as the "significant other." See Berenskoetter 2007.

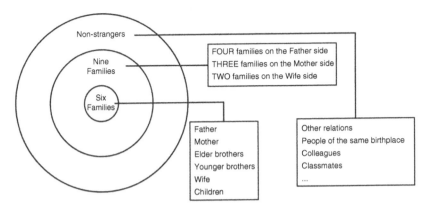

Figure 7.2: Intimacy of relationships in traditional Chinese society

no help at all. *Jiuzu*, the nine families, refer to four families from the father's side, three families from the mother's side, and two families from the wife's side. In other words, they include the families which are closely related to one's father, mother, and wife; for example, the family of one's father's brother and the family of one's mother's brother. They are less intimate than the six blood relations, but more intimate than average friends. Even less intimate are those relatives outside these families and those who are not relatives such as co-workers and other acquaintances. In ancient China, it was a common legal practice to punish those who were related with somebody committing an offense and the punishment for the most serious crime was *Mie Jiuzu*, or death penalty not only for the criminal himself, but also for all the members of the nine families he was related to. Intimacy of relationship is always the most important factor in every aspect in social life.

Thus, sociologists, especially those who study Chinese and oriental societies, tend to focus on "intimacy" to indicate the nature of relationships and very few lay particular emphasis on hostility. Fei discusses the differential structure of Chinese rural society with intimacy as a key factor[45] and the model of three-layered concentric circles is used to describe the degrees of intimacy. Yang Kuo-shu believes that personal relations can be divided into three types according to their respective degree of intimacy: The first is the blood tie, the second is relations among non-strangers, and the third refers to the world of strangers.[46] Bian Yanjie also uses three circles to indicate intimacy of relationships: the core circle, the acquaintances' circle, and the strangers' circle.[47]

---

[45] Fei 2012.   [46] Yang Kuo-shu 1993, quoted in Luo and Wang 2011, 213.
[47] Bian 2011, 3.

Hwang Kwang-kuo provides a more sophisticated typology and divides one's relations into three different categories: the expressive tie, the instrumental tie, and the mixed tie.[48] The expressive tie refers to highly stable relationships, including the blood relations, and the family is seen as the most intimate and the primary group of the self, especially in Confucian societies. The instrumental tie is the opposite to the expressive tie and refers to relationships with others who are not intimate, usually with people who are almost strangers, and who are often used for the self to realize instrumental purposes. The third one, the mixed tie, stands in between the expressive and the instrument ties. It is the tie among acquaintances or non-strangers, such as co-workers, co-professors, or teachers and students.[49] From the self's perspective, the express tie indicates the most intimate, the mixed tie is less intimate, and the instrumental is the least intimate. In society, the mixed tie represents the most common relationship. All these scholars use intimacy to indicate the nature of the self's relationships with others. It is by no means an accident. Rather it is the unconscious reflection of the practice of Chinese society.

In general society most people are strangers. International society, however, is an exception in terms of social ties, because, in a strict sense, there are no blood ties and no strangers, thus confining it to what Hwang terms a world of mixed ties and a world without strangers. Although the relational context is confined to a non-strangers' social world, intimacy is still the crucial indicator. Allies are naturally considered more intimate than average states in the system. Members of a regional organization, such as the European Union or ASEAN, feel that they are closer to one another than to non-members. An interesting example is that when there is a meeting of ASEAN plus China, Japan, and South Korea (10+3), ASEAN member states often have closed-door meetings first to coordinate their positions while leaders or delegates from the Plus Three countries are sometimes waiting outside the meeting room. ASEAN is not only highly conscious of the greater intimacy among its member states, but also intends to make their dialogue partners know the difference. China has carried out "partnership diplomacy," having established respectively with other countries "partnership," "comprehensive cooperative partnership," "strategic partnership," and "comprehensive partnership," among which "partnership" is the least intimate and "comprehensive strategic partnership" the most intimate. Similar situations happen quite often on international occasions.

Although intimacy is a key indicator, it does not mean that an intimate relationship is at the same time or automatically important. It is therefore

---

[48] Hwang 1987. See also Hwang 2006.   [49] Ibid.

necessary to add the second dimension – "importance" as an indicator together with intimacy to demonstrate the self's relationships with others, for it is a significant factor that can interfere, even decisively sometimes, with intimacy when an actor calculates in terms of relationships before taking action. Among the five Confucian cardinal relationships, that between the father and the son is both the most intimate and the most important, as discussed above. The emperor-minister relationship is extremely important, but less intimate than the father-son relationship. In international relations, various types of relationships exist. During the Cold War years, the most important bilateral relationship in the eye of the United States was its relations with the Soviet Union although the degree of intimacy was extremely low as the two powers were deadly enemies. The United States takes the United Kingdom as the closest ally and maintains a special relationship with it, but may not take this relationship as the most important among all the bilateral relations it has in the world. Since the end of WWII, the United States has taken Germany and Japan as its important pivotal countries in Europe and Asia respectively for maintaining the order of American imperium, though the two countries had been deadly enemies of the United States during WWII, and though the degree of intimacy between the United States and those two countries was less than that between the United States and Britain.[50] It is said that China and Pakistan are "all-weather strategic partners." Although there is no such rank among the four types of partnership relations, it indicates the relations between the two are most intimate. However, China-Pakistan relations may not be considered as important as the China-US relations in China's overall international strategy and foreign policy. In fact, the latter is often defined as the most important bilateral relationship.

It is thus necessary to add the factor of "importance." "Intimacy" plays the crucial role if "importance" is taken as a constant. However, once it is in the picture, it may even shape the outcomes more conspicuously than intimacy. The US decision to establish diplomatic relationships with the mainland of China and sever its official relations with Taiwan indicates that its relationship with the mainland was considered more important than that with Taiwan, although the long-time and heated debate before the US decision was made shows how sometimes intimacy struggles with importance when an actor is weighing her relationships with specific others.

Relational analysis is particularly relevant to international relations because there are a limited number of states as relators, which still constitute the leading international actors, usually persist for a long time, and

---

[50] Katzenstein 2005.

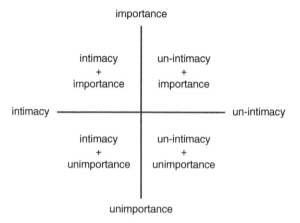

Figure 7.3: Intimacy and importance of relationships

are specifically and tangibly located.[51] In international relations, as illustrated in the previous paragraphs, these two dimensions of intimacy and importance do not go hand in hand most of the time. Both the dimensions, however, are significant for the actor, who needs to consider the intimacy and the importance of a certain relationship before a decision is made. By these two dimensions of intimacy and importance we can get four types of relationships between the self and the others, that is, important and intimate, important and un-intimate, unimportant and intimate, and unimportant and un-intimate, as shown in Figure 7.3.

Relators may use this simple two-dimension yardstick to consider their relationships with others, taking into consideration both intimacy and importance. Intimacy indicates how the self and the specific other identify themselves. An actor uses intimacy as a baseline according to which a decision is made and an action planned. In other words, all other things being equal, an international actor may base its action on how intimate its relationship is with the specific other or others. The more intimate the relationship is, the more the self is likely to cooperate, including altruistic, unilateral cooperation. As the ripple analogy indicates, the actor is at the center of concentric and overlapping relational circles: Each ring signifies a degree of intimacy and between the rings there are no clear boundaries but connecting small water waves. In international relations, for the self, there can be friends, rivals, and enemies, indicating the degrees of

---

[51] Brantly Womack reminded me of this point in our correspondence about the relational theory.

intimacy of their respective relationships to the self, and each of the categories can be further divided into more subcategories such as key allies, allies, close friends, and average friends within the category of friends. A state may use different terms to express intimacy of relationships with other states. For example, the United States has a special relationship with the United Kingdom, which is also a US ally, and is an ally with other NATO member states; China has partners, strategic partners, comprehensive strategic partners, and all-weather strategic partners. Such definitions of the nature of relationships largely indicate the degree of intimacy between the actor and specific others. An actor tends to take different actions in these different types of relationship. She treats her friend differently from what she may do to a rival, and similarly a state provides a special policy toward its allies which it would not offer to other countries.

How important a relationship is also constitutes a crucial factor for an actor to make decisions. In general, power is the primary factor to indicate the importance of a relationship. China takes its relationship with the United States as the most important bilateral one mainly because of its consideration of the power of the latter. Interdependence is of great significance too, for asymmetrical interdependence itself produces power.[52] It is believed that in East Asia ASEAN nations usually turn to China for economic benefits and the United States for security assurance, indicating the economic influence of China and the political and military capabilities of the United States, both being highly powerful in the region. Smart ASEAN strategic actions should therefore be based upon decisions that enable it to benefit from both while offending neither. Quite often, an actor uses her most important relationship as the benchmark against which she adjusts her other relationships. The triangular relationships among China, the Soviet Union, and the United States during the 1970s provide a classic example. The United States took its relations with the Soviet Union as the most important bilateral relationship. In order to maintain the upper hand in this most important but highly hostile rivalry, it adjusted its relationship with China, a long-time enemy of the United States since the late 1940s, to make it more intimate or even a quasi-ally. As a result of the engagement policy, the United States gained a strategic advantage over the Soviet Union by winning China over to its side.[53] The frequent occurrence of proxy wars during the Cold War years is another example to demonstrate the constant adjustment of relations with specific others against the backdrop of the self's most important relationship.

[52] Keohane and Nye 2001.   [53] Zhang 2009.

Relational Rationality We do not argue against the proposition that social actors are rational, but we do argue that they are rational because they are relational. In other words, the logic of rationality does not negate the proposition that a social actor is rational, but argues that her individualistic rationality is necessarily mediated by her relationships with others in the first place. Rationality is thus defined in terms of relationality. Before the self is clear about the nature of the relationship between herself and the specific other, she does not know what action is rational, arational, or irrational. It is generally understood that rationality is about gaining self-interest, but self-interest is shared, defined, and gained through social relations. This is what I term relational rationality – whether or not your action is rational depends on how you are related to the specific other toward whom the action is taken.

A Chinese story tells why rationality is relational in the first place. In a kingdom of ancient China, there was a well-known handsome man called Mr. Xu. Another quite handsome man, Mr. Zou, lived in the same city. Zou once asked his wife, "Who is more handsome, Xu or I?" His wife answered, "Definitely you are. How can Xu compare with you?" Then he asked his concubine, who gave the same answer. The next day he asked a visitor who answered exactly the same way. He knew that he was not as handsome as Xu and, after reflecting on the three answers, he commented, "My wife said that I was more handsome because she loves me; my concubine said so because she fears me; and the visitor said so because he was asking me to do him a favor." All three were rational and behaved according to their understanding of the nature of their respective relationship with Mr. Zou. Thus, social relations define the background for rational choice. As Axelrod says, professors in a department do not treat a visiting professor the same way they treat a tenure-tracked colleague, exactly because the nature of their relationship with the former differs from that of the latter.[54] Thus Gu Hongming (Ku Hung-Ming) has advised people to understand how norms and principles are "applied and carried out in complex social relations and family life" of the Chinese people. Without such relations, rules and norms would have no context at all.[55]

It is true of instrumental rationality. Maximization of self-interest is what an economic person seeks and it has become the widely accepted principle of individualistic, instrumental rationality. From the perspective of relationality, however, the so-called self-interest, as assumed by the rational choice model, is in fact arationally constructed because it is defined as the interest of and by the self without taking into account

[54] Axelrod 1984.   [55] Gu 2006, 212–213.

what kind of relationship the self has with the specific other. Consider the classical PD game. It is presumed that each of the prisoners has her own interest and thinks about how most rationally she can realize such interest in a strategic interaction with the other prisoner. These kinds of "'rational strategies' pursued by two players in a situation of pure conflict ..." as Thomas Schelling has commented, "should not be expected to reveal what kind of behavior is conducive to mutual accommodation, or how mutual dependence can be exploited for unilateral gain."[56] Interestingly enough, the rational strategies pursued by two players in an individualistic world should not be expected to reveal what kind of behavior they will show in a relational world where relations select. Relational rationality differs exactly in that from the very beginning the players know that their interest is defined and achieved in terms of relations and therefore rationality is always defined in terms of relationality. Defection, for example, is a natural choice in a single-move PD game, but may not be so when the players have known each other and expect to play the game repeatedly in the future. It is simply because they are no longer strangers, or they have begun to get somewhat related.

A story tells that Haldane, a well-known scientist of genetics, was asked whether he would risk his own life to save some drowning people. He replied: "No, but I will jump into the river to save two brothers or eight cousins."[57] As a selfish rational actor, he was ready to save his blood relatives to increase the possibility of genetic reproduction. It is the nature of the relationships that decides what action he would take. Similarly, the United States would have been completely irrational if it had required an ally such as Britain to destroy its nuclear weapons during its strategic rivalry against the Soviet Union while it is quite rational if it puts forward the same requirement to an enemy. Pouliot has made similar comments: "[W]hile it makes sense for a Westerner to be instrumentally rational when planning investment in the economic field, it is quite nonsensical (and social[ly] reprehensible) to constantly calculate means and ends with family and friends."[58] Pouliot owes this to practicality, for "[i]n certain social contexts but not others, instrumental rationality is the 'arational' way to go thanks to the logic of practicality."[59] In fact, it is easier for people to understand that it is the nature of the relationships that defines what action is rational, arational, or irrational. What is rationally done to strangers can, again, be arational to your friends and even irrational to your family. In this sense, it is the nature of the relationship that informs what is instrumentally rational and what is not.

---

[56] Schelling 1980, 84.   [57] Nowak with Highfield 2011, 95.   [58] Pouliot 2008, 276.
[59] Ibid.

It is also true of the logic of normative rationality, which means that an actor follows social norms when taking action. Again, without a clearly defined nature of a relationship, the actor, while in a decisional situation, does not know what, which, and whose norms should be followed. It is the nature of the relationship that defines the appropriateness of an action. In Confucianism, "*ren* (virtue)" is the most important moral and social norm.[60] However it is difficult to use a general term to express its real meaning. On the contrary, it is expressed in different forms for different relationships. For instance, the father-son relationship determines that the norm to be followed by the son is filial piety and the friend-friend relationship stipulates that the norm to be followed by friends is sincerity. Filial piety in the former and sincerity in the latter are both expressions of the moral norm of "*ren*." As Hwang argues: "[A]n individual will employ different rules of social exchange to interact with people of different types of relationships or different degrees of intimacy."[61] Fei also holds that, in a Confucian society, "general standards have no utility. The first thing to do is to understand the specific context: Who is the important figure, and what kind of relationship is appropriate with that figure? Only then can one decide the ethical standards to be applied in that context."[62]

Such a phenomenon is conspicuous in a Confucian society, but it is found in other societies as well. Edward Keen's study of the British treaty-making against the slave trade in the early nineteenth century also points to the fact that the British followed different norms when signing treaties with actors Britain had different relationships with. Reciprocity was followed in signing treaties with countries within the "family of civilized nations," of which Britain was a member, but little reciprocity was considered in dealing with "barbarous peoples" who were outsiders.[63] It was the nature of relationships that defined the rules and norms Britain was to follow when dealing with the slave trade issue. Acharya argues that ASEAN nations privilege ASEAN norms over norms that are more international: If an international norm fits into the normative framework of ASEAN, such as "common security," ASEAN will accept it; but if a norm goes against the local normative structure, such as "humanitarian intervention," ASEAN will not follow it. The key factor that enables a norm with global prominence to spread is the "congruence" between

---

[60] As has been said: "The idea of *ren* (human-heartedness ðr benevolence) formed the most important constituent in the thoughts of Confucius and one from which all his ethical teachings were derived." He, Bu, Tang, and Sun 1991, 26. Feng Youlan also said: "*Ren* is the principle that goes throughout the Confucian teachings and the core of Confucian thoughts." He believes that *ren* is a comprehensive term that represents all the virtues in the Confucian teachings. Feng 1962, 100–102.

[61] Hwang 1987, 949.   [62] Fei 2012, 68.   [63] Keene 2007.

this norm and the local normative structure. "Norms that can be made to fit local conditions and traditions spread more easily than those that cannot."[64] There are no absolute norms, because there are no discrete actors. Thus, for any individual actor to make a decision, the precondition is always that she is an actor in relations, or she is a relator. Whether her action is rational or not, instrumentally or normatively, depends on what type of relationship she has or defines with the specific other toward whom the action is taken. It is the nature of social relationships that defines what is rational. In this way, the logic of relationality precludes abstract, *a priori* individual rationality and self-sustained agency, which assumes the ability of the isolated and discrete individual to make decisions on the basis of exclusive self-interest. In an interrelated world, the relational context is very much like an invisible hand that informs and guides an actor as to what action to take.

It is important to reiterate here that relationality does not mean to deny or negate rationality. It is also necessary to repeat that rationality is meaningful in a social setting if and only if it is defined in terms of relationality. In other words, rationality, instrumental or normative, is relational rationality rather than individualistic rationality and works when and only when it is put in a relational context. Exclusive self-interest does not exist in society. To relate is human. Once related, one's interest is shared. In this sense relationality has ontological priority over rationality.

Relational Contexts and Agential Relators The relational cosmos forms a social context, which both constitutes and is constituted by, both enables and is enabled by, and both constrains and is constrained by relators therein. As a base for social action, the logic of relationality therefore works along two directions. The first is the contextual effect, meaning that the relational context helps shape the relator's behavior. It is the top-down approach, focusing on the relational context in which a relator is embedded that enables and constrains her behavior. Since a relator takes action with the relational context as the background in the first place, the logic of relationality tends to be highly context-oriented and furthermore the context is human in nature. It argues that any relationship does not gain meaning merely from the more conspicuous specific other to which the self is related, but also from the totality of relationships that constitute her relational context. The meaning thus gained leads the self toward appropriate actions accordingly.

---

[64] Acharya 2009, 5.

Imagine a simple relational space where three actors A, B, and C coexist and are related. We take A as the self. Her relations with B and C respectively constitute her relational circles, meaning that she is related with B and C. Her relations with both B and C, as well as the relations between B and C, make up her relational context. While the nature of her relationship with B and C respectively may shape her decision to take action toward them, the totality provides a more complex decisional domain. A is to take some action toward B, but she has to think about the relations between herself and C and the relations between B and C too. This relational context, or A's relational sphere, constitutes the background for A's action. It is both constraining and enabling. For example, China was to fight against Vietnam in 1979, but had to consider its relations with the United States, who was a most important actor for China at the initial stage of China's reform and opening up, and whose acquiescence was crucial. If China's action against Vietnam would not worsen its relations with the United States, China would go ahead. ASEAN tends to take action toward the United States with careful consideration of its relationship with China, trying to avoid reaching a tipping point beyond which one relationship dominates. In the six-party talks, North Korea played with the five powers of China, the United States, Russia, Japan, and South Korea with careful manipulation of its relationships with each of the five for the best realization of its own core interest defined in terms of the regime's security. It is sometimes quite complicated. Duvall and Chowdhury have pointed out this complication and, following Saussure, they argue: "[S]ignifiers derive their meaning in relation to other signifiers: a cat is a cat because it is not a bat, for example. Yet, because the other signifiers are infinite in number, meaning is perpetually differentiated, and hard to fix finally, depending on which signifiers are in play at any time."[65] Due to the complexity of relationships, it is sometimes extremely hard indeed to clarify the real meaning of entangling relationships. Even though for today's international relations, where relators are more or less fixed in number, the combination of the various relationships may mean much more than the number indicates.

The second direction is the agential effect, meaning that a relator tends to make use of the relational context for some purposes of her own. It is the bottom-up approach and shows the more instrumental and more agential dimension of relationality. This respect has been widely discussed by social psychologists and cultural scholars. As Lucian Pye has pointed out: "The Chinese tend to see the manipulation of human relationships as the natural and normal approach for accomplishing

---

[65] Duvall and Chowdhury 2011, 344. See also Saussure 1959.

most things in life," for they perceive "society as a web of human relations and associations."[66] It is not only the Chinese, but also most of the nations in the world, who behave similarly. Like the rational choice theory, the logic of relationality assumes that relators pursue their self-interests and seek tangible and material gains through the relational circles by asking for and exchanging favors. What differs is that their interests are located often in relations and their pursuit of interests tends to be through managing, manipulating, and expanding their relational circles. In other words, actors make their decisions and take their actions to achieve self-interest, utilizing relational circles to facilitate the achievements of instrumental objectives and to influence the outcomes.

Xie wrote an article in *Science*, entitled "It's whom you know that counts."[67] It discusses a phenomenon that hometown ties help Chinese scientists get ahead, saying that "*guanxi* (ties or relationships)" plays an important role in electing members to the two most prestigious scientific organizations in China (the Chinese Academy of Sciences and the Chinese Academy of Engineering). The article starts with the Chinese situation, but argues that *guanxi* is not a unique thing to the Chinese scientific community. "In American science, social networks, especially those developed in graduate programs, affect attainment of academic positions and achievement recognition."[68] It is a violation of universalism, which is such an overwhelming norm in scientific communities, but scientists are human and cannot be devoid of human sociability.

We may imagine a more general situation in a company where three relators A, B, and C coexist. A and B are equally competent and both want to be promoted to a managerial position. C is the key person who can decide which one will get the promotion. It is more likely that the one who is good at managing relations with C will win. It is not only whom you know that counts, but whom you know better that counts. In international relations, a small country located between two giants should think carefully about manipulating its relations with both so that it may achieve the best result in that it gets benefits from both or at least avoids offending either. China decided to improve its relations with the United States in the early 1970s because it considered carefully its position in the relational web where the Soviet Union was a key node, and so did the United States. For China at that time, neither the United States nor the Soviet Union was intimate at all, but both were quite important. It was judged after serious discussion by the decision-makers that the threat by the Soviet Union was more acute and the relationship with the United

[66] Pye 1968, quoted in Gold, Guthrie and Wank 2002, 11.   [67] Xie 2017.
[68] Ibid., 1023.

States was, accordingly, more important to thwart such threat. China, therefore, chose to side with the United States against the Soviet Union and warmly received Richard Nixon, the then US president, even before the two countries established official diplomatic relations. The improvement of China-US relations in the early 1970s thus shows a strong instrumental consideration through manipulation of relationships by China for national security and by the United States for rivalry against the Soviet Union.[69] It was a classic example that China and the United States gained through a successful manipulation of their bilateral relationship as well as of the triangular relationship with the Soviet Union.

It is worth noting that not only tangible and material benefits count. Intangible and non-material gains are an important aspect of the instrumental dimension of relationality. More often than not, a relator's instrumental activity may not be reflected by seeking immediate payoffs in maintaining and manipulating relations with others. Instead, she thinks about returns in longer terms and even merely does it for such social capital as reputation and prestige. During the Cold War years the Soviet Union had tried its best to maintain its special relations with East European nations by providing resources, offering tangible benefits, and even resorting to force to guarantee that the regimes there were pro-Soviet. The investment was enormous, and the tangible and material gains on the part of the Soviet Union were largely negligible. The most significant meaning for the Soviet Union, as the self at the center of its relational circles, was to gain, through its special relationship with other East European countries, such social capital as the leader of the socialist world and the reputation as the marshal of the forces for just causes against the counterrevolutionary force led by the United States. Moreover, a long, stable relationship itself implies interest, which may not be immediate and readily tangible. Huang and Shih call it "nonapparent national interest," which refers to long-term interest acquirable through stabilized relationships.[70]

The logic of relationality therefore argues that a relator seeks to realize her objectives through manipulating her relational circles, with the enabling and constraining relational context as the background. On the one hand, the context draws the boundary where the actor's relations can

---

[69] Kissinger shows that the Chinese decision-makers compared the nature of China's relationships with the United States and the Soviet Union and believed that the latter constituted the major threat. He discusses the situation at that time: "In the face of increasing Soviet troop concentrations and a major battle at the border of Xinjiang, on August 28 the Central Committee of the Chinese Communist Party ordered a mobilization of all China's military units along all China's borders. Resumption of contact with the United States had become a strategic necessity." Kissinger 2011, 213.

[70] Huang and Shih 2014, 6.

reach and shape her identities and roles. It may be termed as the extensity of one's relationships. Imagine a family of three – father, mother, and a teenage son. We take the son as the relator and assume that his primary relational sphere or the extensity of his relational circles is this family of three. If he wants to get some interest, he has to deal with his parents. He gets more if his parents love him. Furthermore, if his mother loves him more than his father while the latter has more say in family decisions, then he may realize his objectives by indirectly influencing the outcome through his mother. Without the parents he has no interest even to talk about and by manipulating the relationships between himself and the mother and between the parents he can better realize his interests. The relational sphere is, however, not a static fix. As he is growing up, he is making and enlarging his relational circles beyond his family to reach more people, through whom he realizes his objectives. The more intimate the people and the more important the people in his relational circles, the more he may gain. Especially when we consider the two dimensions, intimacy and importance, a smart strategy for a relator is to make the less intimate intimate and make the more important intimate too. China's strategy in the early 1970s, in terms of the triangular relationship of China, the United States, and the Soviet Union, was first to extend its relational reach to include the United States and then to make the important and un-intimate superpower at least more intimate.

Having discussed the logic of relationality and the motivation of action, we need to point out another aspect of relations, which seems to be more sentimental than material or instrumental. Although it is not what we place emphasis on, it is worth noting, for it happens from time to time. It means that "the ultimate motive of *guanxi* (relationship) is to reinforce, sustain, and deepen relationships, rather than the instrumental goals that they serve so well. In this instance, *instrumental action becomes the means, and 'guanxi' becomes the end.*"[71] To some extent, it seems as if it is relations for relations' sake. Sentimentality means, for example, that two actors take action simply to maintain and strengthen their ties without any desire of material gains, and therefore it is not instrumental. The sentimental aspect of relations is more likely to occur among actors in relational circles of the express ties, where affection often dominates and actors may not even think of and from self-interest. In Chinese families, parents are even willing to do whatever their children want for no expectation of return at all, sometimes to the extent that the children are completely spoiled. A couple deeply in love may be willing to do anything for each other without the slightest idea of gaining material or non-material returns.

---

[71] Lin 2001, 161, emphasis in original.

They even sacrifice their life for each other, just as Romeo and Juliet do in the Shakespearean play. In international relations, express ties are rare, but similar practices can be seen from time to time between close allies, countries of the same religious or ideological belief, or between a major power and its protégés.

Management of Relations

Human relations are most complex, but they are not unmanageable. Management of relations is the most important skill for any actor embedded in the complex relational context. If we view the social world as one of relations, it is reasonable to say that relational management is the essence of politics. To some extent, only the harmoniously related prosper, and prosper together. Relational mismanagement means political failure. It is also or even particularly true of international politics. We have just discussed the two distinct features of relations in international society: immovability and durability. In general societies, these two features may not be so conspicuous, for most people are strangers to one another, and even for non-strangers their social relations can be terminated when the two people really want to do it and physically move far away from each other. The two features are thus particularly relevant and meaningful in international society, where states, the leading international actors, cannot move one another away and have to live together in long-lasting relational webs. There are now, for instance, about 200 nation-states in international society, none of whom can choose their neighbors and almost all of whom have to interact for life with the rest of the other nation-states. It is indeed a global village, a world of non-strangers. As actors in the international system they can only be actors in relations, and as relators they have little choice but to relate and be related.

In some sense, the most important practice in world politics is to manage relations among various international players. In a relational cosmos, power and institutions, important as they are, may both be instruments for relational management. More often than not, order means a state of balanced and harmonious relations among members of a community, while disorder is the reflection of failure to manage relations in society. The emphasis on relational management, in addition, does not mean that interests are not important. Rather it argues that interests are embedded in relations and can be gained more through a skillful management of relations. A state cannot choose its neighbors and cannot break off relations with any other members in international society. What a state cannot do is cut off its actual relations with other states, whether the relations are good or bad. What a state can do, then, is to manage relations for its benefit. Following Mencius, we assume a harmonious relationship is beneficial for the relevant actors to gain self-interest. Management of relations is to maintain and enhance a relationship that is concordant and to change the nature of a relationship that is discordant. In international relations, every state faces such management. Hence an important question for the relational theory of world politics is how to manage relations among actors.

Two Philosophies of Relational Management

Since relations are everywhere in human society, no social theory can completely ignore their management. There are two different philosophies of relational management, the essence of which concern the maintenance or change of the nature of the relationship between the self and the other. One is to achieve homogeneity and the other to respect heterogeneity. The former holds that once all social actors become fundamentally the same, their relations will be simultaneously good. Thus, to manage relations among actors is primarily to change the other and make her more like the self. The latter argues that it is never possible and never feasible to achieve homogeneity among social actors. Diversity is normal and cannot be eliminated. To manage relations among them is first of all to recognize and respect the diversity, only on this basis can actors successfully and skillfully manage their relations.

Mainstream IR theories explicitly or implicitly argue that homogeneity is the solution for relational management and its underlying assumption is that differences bring about conflict. Hegemonic stability theory, for example, holds that coercive power may turn a disobedient other to do what the self wants and enable a community to stay in order. If all other members of international society should follow rules made by the hegemon who has overwhelming power, international order would be maintained. Immediately after the end of the Cold War, the United States wanted to change the nature of its relationship with some important Middle East countries and the approach to the management of such relations was resort to force, hoping that those states, once becoming democracies, would change from enemies to friends of the United States. In the history of international relations many states have taken this approach and the East European policy of the Soviet Union during the Cold War years was to keep the political system the same as the Soviet one and never let any East European country "change color." Institutionalism and constructivism prefer rules and norms to coercive force. The former believes that international institutions are able to regulate the behavior of actors. Once they follow the rules, they will behave in a similar and expectable way. As a result, cooperation will be facilitated and order maintained. The latter holds that norms have an even more fundamental function, for they make actors not only follow the rules, but also follow them willingly and rationally. In other words, they do not only have similar behavior but also have similar identity and therefore mindset.

Force, institutions, and norms are employed for maintaining more orderly and more favorable relations, trying to turn a foe into a friend, a rival into a cooperator, and a rebel into a good citizen. Their approaches, based upon their different theoretical assumptions, seem to differ a lot at the substantial level, stressing different factors as the most important for relational management. However, they have one thing in common: Good relations can be established and maintained only among homogeneous actors who show similar behavior, similar belief, or similar ways of thinking. Other Western IR theories have also shown such a feature. Hobson's theory on imperialism, for example, argues that the capitalist system leads to overproduction and underconsumption domestically, resulting in imperial competition overseas for raw materials and commodity markets.[72] Lenin further develops the theory and believes that imperialism is war and that elimination of war internationally requires a change of the capitalist system domestically within the capitalist state into the socialist system.[73] The 1917 Bolshevik revolution in Russia could be seen as an experiment of Lenin's theory to change the regime type from a bourgeois government to a proletarian dictatorship. George Kennan's long telegram also holds that the Soviet ambition is to materialize its ideology and realize the Soviet-type of socialism over the world. With a similar line of reasoning, the theory of democratic peace holds that peace or even perpetual peace would materialize if all states should become democracies.[74] These theories believe that once nation-states are homogeneous in nature, they will become friends and their conflict will be solved once and for all. Very often relations among members of the European Union are taken as an example, for war is both impossible and unthinkable for them as a means to the realization of self-interest and national objectives. Such theories do not believe that actors with differences, especially differences in terms of their important attributes, may live peacefully and prosperously together. What is outside their menu of choice is the manageability of relations among actors with very different attributes and dispositions.

---

[72] Hobson 1965.   [73] Lenin 1939.   [74] Doyle 1997; Russett and Oneal 2001.

The second approach recognizes the diversity and argues that relational management among actors should be based upon the recognition and respect of such diversity. In international society, it is impossible to change all international actors to an enlarged homogeneous self. The fact that the world is so complex and the members of international society are so diversified means that the messianic mission for homogenization tends to fail. International society is a social space where no one is able to escape the diversity and everyone has to manage the complex relationships. Even in domestic society, diversity is a fact. Peter Katzenstein discusses civilizations in world politics, emphatically pointing out the diversity both across civilizations in general and within one civilization in particular.[75] The diversity is so conspicuous that prosperous coexistence depends very much on how relations among greatly diverse actors are managed. In our world, especially in the post-Cold War years of globalization, it is even more so. In general, therefore, in any complex systems, management of relations is of utmost importance if the system is not to collapse and members of the system are able to live in peace and stability.

Management of relations often means management of complex relationships among social actors with diversity and difference. If we should take the homogeneity approach, it would be necessary to do away with them. Since it is in fact not possible to eliminate diversity, it is often argued that "tolerance" is important – tolerance of diversity and difference. But for the relational theory, it is not sufficient to merely bear something that you dislike or to allow others to say or do something you disagree with. The relational theory stresses more "respect." It means that one should not only tolerate diversity and difference, but also respect diversity and difference. For example, if someone has some ideas or behavior very different from yours, you should not only tolerate them, but also assume that there is something reasonable in her ideas and behavior, something you can learn from, rather than merely tolerate her simply because she does not physically do harm to you. To illustrate the concept of respect, we may use the experiment by Peng and Nisbett again.[76] When you hold a statement completely contradictory to another statement held by someone else, you may categorically rebut it, or turn a deaf ear to it, or try to find some reasonable elements in it, reflecting your intention to eliminate it, tolerate it, or respect it, respectively. Confucius says: "When I walk along with two others, they may serve as my teachers."[77] You learn exactly from the way they differ from you. But

---

[75] Katzenstein 2010a.
[76] Peng and Nisbett 1999; See also Nisbett, Peng, Choi, and Norenzayan 2001.
[77] Confucius et al. 2014, 68.

before you are ready to learn, you cannot merely tolerate the difference. You must respect it. Recognition of diversity and difference is important for relational management, and respect is even more important, for a good relationship requires mutual respect.

International society seems to resemble more a traditional agricultural village. There are villagers and villagers: Some are stronger and some weaker; some richer and some poorer; some more selfish and some more selfless; and some well-behaved and some rebellious. Even in a small village the diversity is obvious. In addition, movability is out of the question: The villagers have no way to leave their land and have to stay there perhaps for life. The only practical thing they can do is to manage the various relationships and the most skillful politics is to manage such relationships well. Tolerance is necessary, cooperation indispensable, and respect vital. It is not an exaggeration to say that Confucianism focuses most on management of social relations, for its practical and cultural basis is the traditional Chinese agricultural society consisting of villages and villagers. Rituals, norms, educational principles, and codes of behavior are all designed to manage the complex relationships for a more stable political and social order. Individual villagers all work hard to maintain and manipulate relations for personal gains and for communal order.

With the village analogy in mind, we may examine briefly the case of ASEAN. It is a regional organization aiming at integration and it has maintained basically peace and stability among its members in the region since its initiation in 1967. When we look at the members of ASEAN, they are highly diversified – different religious beliefs, different regime types, different social systems, different cultural traditions, and different levels of economic development. Compared with the European Union, it is more inclusive, especially concerning different political systems, implying that befriending is possible among all members of society. They have stayed together for such a long time and completed the ASEAN community by the end of 2015. Moreover, ASEAN has played a central role in regional affairs even when major powers such as China, India, Japan, Russia, and the United States have joined in the regional processes.

There is little doubt that the impressive achievements of ASEAN are due to many factors, but one important experience is that it does not base its integration on homogeneity, and it has not worked for homogeneity, which is never possible in its part of the world. Rather it bases the regional coordination and integration on management of relations, within and without. The relational circles are multilayered concentric ones: The core is ASEAN, which plays the leading role and sits at the driving seat; the second layer is the Plus 3 dialogue partners, including China, Japan, and South Korea, with whom ASEAN established the 10+3 regional cooperative process; and the circles have expanded to include India, Australia, and New Zealand, with the United States and Russia joining in later; and finally the world at large. It is very much like the ripple analogy, geographically, politically, and socially. Management of the complex relations and maintenance of a balance of the differentiated relationships in favor of ASEAN has always been a strategic priority. Norms and rules are more often than not designed to manage relations among actors. The "comfort level" norm, for example, is quite a unique norm of ASEAN, which seeks complete consensus by making every participant comfortable. It is not mere tolerance. It is respect, respect for the position even if all the others do not agree with it. Only after everyone feels comfortable can a decision be made.[78] Voting tends to impose some people's position on other people and thus make some uncomfortable. It is therefore usually not an ASEAN choice. Instead, long and even tedious deliberations and consultations are a common practice so as to reach a complete consensus which every participant feels comfortable with. Serious concessions are made perhaps to take into consideration only one participant's comfort level. Although it is done sometimes at the cost of effectiveness and efficiency, it is not a sacrifice of principle, but a way of maintaining cooperative relations among actors. Maintaining a good relationship among all the participants and avoiding breaking up the cooperative processes seem to be more important than achieving immediate and tangible results. To manage relations is, therefore, an important element of the ASEAN way. It may not be as effective as the European Union, but it is also less easy to break up the regional process of integration, because more often than not it focuses on maintaining the relational process rather than achieving immediate results, on finding out common grounds rather than debating over differences, and on taking care of everyone's comfort level rather than imposing a majority decision. As an organization of nations with great diversity, its life is more resilient and durable, and the cooperative process it maintains is more difficult to break up.

Practical Measures for Relational Management

For the Chinese, stable, harmonious, reciprocal, and long-term relations between the self and the other/others are the most desirable situation for both social order and personal advancement. Establishment of such relationships is important, for to relate is not only for the realization of self-interest, but also constitutes part and parcel of self-interest.

---

[78] Qin and Wei 2008.

In dynastic China, marrying daughters of the Han imperial family to rulers of minority nationalities was an important policy for pacifying such groups and maintaining good relations with them[79] and the belief was that once the ruler of the minority group and the Han emperor became relatives through marriage, the norms for family members were able to apply to the relationship between the Han empire and the minority group. It was also a policy for some empires in other parts of the world. The presumption of such a policy is that once you are related, you may not fight each other; and once you are intimately related, you may help each other when needed.

Once a relationship is established, its maintenance is a most outstanding feature of relational management. The relationship among family members is often taken as an example of positive relationships, where the blood ties provide the most solid connection among them and where such ties continue for life. The ideal relationship among members in a community, say an agricultural village, is one resembling the family, for Confucianism tends to believe that the nature of the family relationship is able and desirable to extend to that among members of a community. To maintain a stabilized and long-term relationship is often more important than achieving tangible and immediate interests. Furthermore, a social actor, as an active agent and relator, works to expand her relational circles by widening them to include more actors, who may offer help when it is needed. Usually, the more friends you have in your relational circles, the more benefit you may gain. In other words, relational extensity matters. In international society, it is natural that a state wants to make more friends and fewer enemies. To some extent, partnership diplomacy, alliance formation, and regional integration are all means to establish and widen one's relational circles, either for the gain of the self or for the maintenance of a more stable social order, or both. In general, as one's relational circles get bigger and ramify farther, one's influence and interest are also widening, reaching to a larger relational sphere where one acts and interacts.

One not only widens one's relational circles, but also deepens relationships with others. A deepening of one's relationships with others, as discussed above, means first of all that one makes efforts to get one's intimate friends more intimate. China's partnership diplomacy provides an example in this respect. The partnership can be upgraded from average, to strategic, to comprehensive, and to all-weather, indicating the increasingly more intimate relationship between the self and the other. The relational theory argues that the more intimate the relationship

[79] Shang 2015.

between the self and the other is, the more they tend to cooperate and help each other. A deepening of one's relationship also means making the more important partners more intimate. Although an important relationship may not be intimate, one will be better off if one can make such a relationship intimate. The détente during the Cold War years was an effort by the United States and the Soviet Union to make their relationship more intimate so that they might have at least some rudimentary trust and mutual assurance, no matter how fragile it was, upon which tension could be reduced. A more desirable situation is that one can make some important partners more intimate so that one can get the necessary help when one needs it. This skill of relational management is in fact a wide-spreading phenomenon. After the end of WWII, the United States, rising irreversibly to globalism and aiming to be the leader for a global liberal order, established several important alliance systems. With NATO in Europe, SEATO in East Asia, the Rio Pact in Latin America, and the Baghdad Pact in the Middle East, the United States had established intimate relationships with allies through those groupings. Furthermore, it successfully turned Japan and Germany, two important countries respectively in East Asia and Europe, into intimate friends and pillars for the US-dominant order in these regions.[80] By 2016, China has established more than eighty partnerships with countries and regional organizations and is continuing to find "pillar" partners in important regions in the world. Efforts to continue a positive relationship, especially through widening and deepening, are seen everywhere in international relations. It is generally true that one is more powerful and more influential if one has more intimate friends and more important intimate partners in a community.

Relational management also involves change in the nature of a relationship. In the Confucian worldview, there are some important assumptions that provide an optimistic understanding of relational complexity and its management. The first is the fundamental harmony of human relations as well as relations between humans and nature.[81] This

---

[80] Katzenstein 2005.

[81] It is important to point out that harmony in traditional Chinese philosophy means harmony of relations rather than harmony of interests, as Confucius says, 君子和而不同 (Virtuous persons seek harmony not sameness). It is a situation where members of a community maintain good relations despite the existence of different ideas, opinions, and interests. Furthermore, it is exactly the different ideas, opinions, and interests that come together and make a good society and an energetic living habitat. Harmony is, for Confucianism, a situation where different and even conflicting interests are managed to the extent that they all have their right places and that they complement one another exactly because of their difference. It differs from Keohane's harmony, which "refers to a situation in which actors' policy (pursued in their own self-interest without regard for others) automatically facilitates the attainment of others' goals" (Keohane 1984, 51). Keohane's interpretation of

point was discussed in the previous chapter when we were analyzing the *zhongyong* dialectics. The second is change. Traditional Chinese philosophy believes that change is normal and always possible. It is also true of relationships among actors: Positive and negative relationships can change toward each other. A and B are enemies, but their relationship can be changed and the two can become friends. Of course the reverse is also possible and two friends can become enemies. However, the first assumption about the fundamental harmony indicates that the overall relations in the social as well as natural cosmos should evolve for the better. The third is that such change is not automatically realized and relations should be managed so that the change for the better can be materialized. Skillful management enables the relationship to become better, while mismanagement leads to its worsening and even to a hostile environment where one has no friends at all.

Since traditional Chinese philosophy believes that harmony is not only desirable but also achievable, change in the nature of a relationship often means change from negative to positive, for example, from enmity to amity and from conflict to cooperation. It is possible and even necessary to use coercive force to change the nature, but it is not the desirable and advisable way. Even for victory in the military field, Sun Zi, one of the greatest military strategists in ancient China, thinks that actually fighting to take a city is the most undesirable way, while the best strategist always seeks to take the city by winning over the hearts of the people in the city rather than to occupy it by force.[82] L. H. M. Ling uses the well-known story "seven times caught, and seven times released," which tells how Zhuge Liang (181–234 AD), another master military strategist in ancient China, dealt with an enemy king. After the Shu State was founded, it was repeatedly attacked by neighboring small kingdoms along the southern borders. In the fighting against an enemy kingdom, which was also the most powerful among many of the small kingdoms, Zhuge Liang, the prime minister of the Shu State and commander of its military forces, captured the enemy king seven times, but the king was not convinced and

---

harmony is more about interests, a situation where "pursuit of self-interest by each contributes to the interest of all"(Ibid., 51). Thus, for Keohane, where there is harmony, no effort for cooperation is necessary. What Keohane has explored is how to achieve cooperation when there are common interests without harmony. For Confucianism, however, harmony first of all refers to a type of relationship among people. It is not about interests of individuals. Harmonious relations are facilitated by cooperation and at the same time promote cooperation among members of a community. What Confucianism focuses on, therefore, is how to maintain good and cooperative relations among people who have different ideas and interests. See also Chapter 9.

[82] Sun Zi's original words go as follows: "So to win a hundred victories in a hundred battles is not the highest excellence; the highest excellence is to subdue the enemy's army without fighting at all." See Sun Tzu (Sun Zi) 2015, 29.

would not surrender willingly each time he was captured. Each time he complained, and each time Zhuge Liang released him. When he was released the seventh time, he was very much moved and surrendered whole-heartedly. Ling holds that it is an example of balancing the *yin-yang* relationship, for Zhuge Liang combined "the *yin* of 'hearts and minds' with the *yang* of warfare as a military strategy."[83] Moreover, the story also shows that the balance of immediate interest (to capture the enemy king) and long-term relationship (to win over the heart of the enemy king so that he would never make trouble) was a serious consideration of Zhuge Liang, who, as the prime minister of the Shu state, had to maintain a long-term relationship with the neighboring kingdom. To kill the king and occupy the territory of his kingdom was easy, but to let the king and his people willingly become part of the Shu State was much more difficult. In other words, to eliminate the other is easier than to transform the other and make the other part of the self. After he was released the seventh time, the enemy king submitted himself willingly and became an intimate friend of Zhuge Liang and even a high-ranking official of the Shu State. Furthermore, no offensive attack ever occurred along the southern borders of the Shu State until Zhuge Liang's death. Thus, the best way to change the nature of a relationship from negative to positive is persuasion and conviction rather than coercion and compulsion. It is also true of maintaining a positive, long-term relationship. It is possible because of the belief that there is always something in common between two opposites, including between enemies. If the Hegelian tradition stresses the need to find out the differences and the most crucial contradictions so that they will be overcome for evolutionary and perhaps revolutionary progression, the Chinese tradition and the *zhongyong* dialectics tend to give less prominence to differences and contradictions and make great efforts to find common grounds so that a better relationship can be achieved and cooperation carried out.

The basic principle of the logic of relationality is intimacy. Intimate relatedness, therefore, is the golden rule of relational practice. To make more intimate partners in one's relational circles, to make the less intimate more intimate, and to make the important more intimate – this is the practical approach by the logic of relationality. It does not categorically reject and exclude the use of coercive measures, which are also quite important for maintaining or changing the nature of a relationship. However, the emphasis is on persuasion and conviction and the most desirable approach is to find and exploit common grounds rather than to accent and enlarge differences, for self-interest is always shared with

[83] Ling 2013, 561–562.

others and can always be better realized through joint efforts. In addition, coercively established social order is never stable and coercively maintained social order never sustainable, while a fiduciary community based on genuine intimacy, like that in a family, provides both the best social order and the best environment for the realization of self-interest.

Conclusion

The motivations of human action have been investigated extensively in the social sciences. Two kinds of logic for action have been seriously discussed in IR literature. The first is the logic of rationality, arguing that human action is based upon instrumental rationality or the normative rationality of individual actors. The logics of consequences, appropriateness, and arguing go in this category. The second is the logic of practicality, holding that human action is based upon background knowledge, which has been formed through long practice and is not articulate and reflective. The logic of habit can also be included in this category, for it is a logic based also upon background knowledge and continual practice rather than on representational knowledge and rational calculation.

What I suggest is a different kind of logic: the logic of relationality. It argues that human action is based more upon relations: It is the relational web in which the actor is embedded that regulates the behavior and constitutes the identity of the actor. It is also the relational web that the actor tries to make use of so that she can better realize her self-interest. Thus, on the one hand, the relational web both enables and constrains the behavior of the relator; on the other hand, the relator both manipulates and is manipulated by the relational web. To take an action, a relator has to consider along two dimensions – the intimacy and importance of her relationships toward the specific and significant others, which serve as the yardsticks for the actor to make her judgment. She tends to take different actions toward her friends and foes, and toward the important and unimportant others. Intimacy, however, is the basic rule in the logic of relationality and relatedness, always a most important independent variable for the explanation of human behavior. What action a relator is to take depends very much on how she is related to the specific other. A customer is much less likely to be cheated in the small convenience shop in her neighborhood because she and the shop owner have known each other for years, that is, they are not strangers and they are socially related.

Relationality, as a logic of action, comes from practice, especially the practice of oriental agricultural societies like China, just as rationality is the sediment of long-time practice in the more individualistic Western societies. However, relationality is not limited to Confucian or Eastern societies and can be seen almost everywhere. From a different perspective, individualistic rationality, instrumental or normative, rests on relationality, because without defining what relationship the self has with the other in a social situation, it is impossible to define what action is instrumentally and normatively rational. In other words, it is important to take seriously self-interest and social norms as movers of action, but it is also important to recognize that either self-interest or social norms work if and only if one is clear about how one is related to the specific other/others toward whom the action is taken. If we say the logic of practicality enjoys ontological priority over both the logic of rationality and the logic of relationality, then it is also reasonable to argue that in social settings the logic of relationality has ontological priority over the logic of rationality. In society one can only be relationally rational.

It is also important to point out that the presumption of the logic of relationality is that background knowledge and representational knowledge are inseparable and the former constitutes the basis on which the latter grows while the latter reflects what is deeply embedded in the former. Relationality is the sediment of practice especially of Confucian culture and society and has been conceptualized through representations of intellectuals for generations, just like the concept of rationality strongly influences the mainstream social sciences in the West. I have placed special emphasis on the logic of relationality not because the logic of rationality is wrong, but it is so overwhelmingly dominant that other logics of action, such as the logic of relationality, are marginalized though they exist and work in practice. As a result, they have not been well represented in the study of international relations and continue to stay dormant in theoretical constructions. Furthermore, relationality is a conspicuous feature of the Confucian society, but goes far beyond its geo-cultural boundary. In all societies it works, although it may not be the focus of intellectual representation. Foregrounding relationality is therefore necessary, for, after all, to relate is human.

Part III

Power, Cooperation, and Governance

8   Power and Relation

Power is a most important concept in international politics. Since the current international system has been largely defined as an anarchy, power tends to be taken as the ability to control and command, for in such a system you are either secure or insecure, either order or are ordered, and either dominate or are dominated. According to the generally acceptable definition of power by Robert Dahl, in terms of one's ability to make others to do what they otherwise would not do, power is considered something exclusively owned by the individual actor – as her attribute, her possession, and her characteristic feature. In the international system, no matter whether it is a Hobbesian jungle or a Waltzian self-help habitat, power, owned and used by the individual actor such as the nation-state, is the only means to enable one's survival and prosperity. "Sovereignty" symbolizes the exclusive and inalienable power of the modern state. In this sense it is a crucial private property. As such, it is sacred and inviolable.

It is not deniable that in today's international system power continues to exist conspicuously as a private property, an important attribute of the nation-state or other international actors (international organizations or private corporations, for instance), and an ability to realize one's own interests by overcoming resistance when necessary. While recognizing that the conceptualization of power by the mainstream IR literature reflects some most important aspects of power, especially its nature as sacred private property and its function as controlling, commanding, and domineering, we may also ask whether some other significant aspects are left out of the IR literature's vision and therefore to a larger extent neglected. From the perspective of a relational theory, power, or at least some forms of power, are not absolutely privately owned in the first place and do not aim to dominate from the very beginning.

In this chapter, I will first propose a new typology of power based on two indicators: the location of and accessibility to power resources. Since it will be discussed in more detail below, suffice it to say here that by such a standard there are three basic types of power, namely agential, structural, and relational. The mainstream IR literature has paid great attention to either the agential or the structural power, but largely overlooked the third type, or what I term "relational power," whose resources reside with relations among agents and are accessible or usable through relations. In a social world of relatedness, such power is at least equally significant as power owned by the individual actor or embedded in the systemic structure. As such, relational power has some distinct features. It is *sharable*. Since it comes from relations among actors, it is shared and sharable in various ways. Once a relationship is established, power is no longer absolutely private. It is also *exchangeable*. In other words it reflects an exchange relationship, in which actors related with each other take turns to be the power wielder and the power recipient through time-honored social practice. Furthermore, relational power may well constitute a *co-empowering process*. A power relationship can be unilaterally commanding and domineering as mainstream IR theories tend to believe, but it can also be mutually empowering, making both actors engaged in a power relationship more powerful, as the Chinese dialectics tends to hold.

To illustrate alternative ways to conceptualize power through comparison, I will review the basic power literature in mainstream Western political and IR theories and see how they have both privatized power and made it a unilateral and command relationship. Also I will discuss the implications and consequences of such conceptualization of power in IR. My purpose, of course, is to work out a reconceptualization of power from a relational angle, or at least to reinterpret some dimensions of power in a different way. I argue, in particular, that in terms of resources relation is power and that in terms of influence power is the ability to manage relations. It is true of human relations, and it is also true of international relations.

A Typology of Power: Agential, Structural, and Relational

Power, as one of the most elusive words, has been conceptualized and categorized in various ways. To make things simpler, we may use an easy criterion including two dimensions. The first is the location of power resources, or where power resides. If a power resource is located at the agent's level, it is agential power. Examples may include a nation-state's territory, military forces, economic wealth, or leadership. If it is located at the structural level, it is structural power. Distribution of capabilities or of ideas in the international system is considered a systemic factor that influences actors' behavior. It is therefore structural power. But we do find some power whose resources reside neither exclusively with the agent nor exclusively with the structure. They reside in relations among agents. If a power resource is located with relations among agents, it is relational power. For example, complex interdependence as an intersubjective relationship produces power. It is not possessed by any actor in such a complex relationship. Although the mainstream IR power literature has little in-depth discussion on this third kind of power, it is of great importance for politics in general and international relations in particular, especially from the perspective of the relational theory.

The second is accessibility to power resources: If a power resource is accessible exclusively by the owner who is an independent agent, it is agential power; if it is accessible exclusively by the owner who is an impersonal structure, it is structural power; if it is accessible by another actor who is not the owner but related to the owner, it is relational power. For instance, through an alliance arrangement, the agent's power resources are available to its allies; or, through a special relationship, an agent may have privileged access to the decision-making power of an international institution. Such power can be categorized as relational power, for its actual usability is through relationship rather than owner-ship. In an increasingly interdependent world, power may come from connectivity among actors. It means one's ability to have access to power resources even though one does not own such resources. Connectivity is power.[1]

In scholarly discussions and analyses of power, the most traditional and convenient way is perhaps to take power as agential. Power is commonly defined, for example, as an agent's ability to influence the outcomes of an event and the behavior and conditions of others. In international relations it means "a state's ability to control, or at least, to influence other states or the outcomes of events."[2] It can, there-fore, be seen as some attributes or capabilities possessed by an agent, or as an influential relationship through which an agent is able to make another do as she wishes.[3] There have been a lot of analyses as well as controversies concerning these two aspects of power. It is, however, reasonable to argue that power as resources and power as relations are merely two aspects of power and neither can exist without the other. Together they constitute the power of a particular agent. Nobody can imagine that influence would be made without power resources while power resources stay dormant if not mobilized and used for purposes of

---

[1] See Slaughter 2009.   [2] Griffiths and O'Callaghan 2006, 253.
[3] A popular IR textbook, for example, defines power as "the ability to overcome obstacles and influence outcomes." It continues to say that "power is the ability to get what you want and to achieve a desired outcome through control of your environment, both human and nonhuman." See Russett, Starr, and Kinsella 2006, 104.

influence in a relationship. Power resources that reside with the agent constitute the base on which influence is exercised. The state that owns more power resources is likely to have more influence, such as the United States, even though it cannot do whatever it likes. On the other hand, the Vatican is often cited as an actor with few power resources but which enjoys strong influence. It is a rare case and, more importantly, its non-material power resources are enormous. Definitely, power as resources is potential power. Only when power is exercised in a relationship does it become the actual power of influence. Dahl's classical analysis of power defines it most explicitly as a "relation between people."[4] It involves a power wielder and a power recipient and describes a relation between them. The United States was already the most powerful in terms of capabilities even before WWI, but did not have influence proportionate to its capabilities because it was not willing to use its potential power in world affairs. "If there is one point on which most power theorists have come to agree, it is the utility of treating power as a relation rather than as a possession."[5] It is true, but a power relationship does not exist if there are no power resources in the first place. In fact, power as resources and power as relations sustain and complement each other though they are not the same thing. Any discussion of power cannot escape the concept of power as resources and at the same time needs to focus on power as relations, for after all power exists in and through relations. In fact, the concept of power used and discussed in the mainstream IR literature explicitly or implicitly contains these two aspects, that is, power as resources and power as relations. It is justifiable.

Power takes many forms. The US example indicates the importance of material capabilities while the Vatican case tells us that non-material power is equally significant. Since power is such a central concept in international relations, efforts to differentiate its various forms have often been made and different types of power discussed. To describe the nature or characteristics of power – for instance, material and non-material power; hard and soft power; coercive and enabling power; power over and power to – such terms are often used in speeches of political leaders and articles on international relations. Kenneth Boulding puts forward his typology of three kinds of power: coercive, exchange, and affective.[6] An insightful study divides power into what can be termed "good" and "bad" power. In this study, Mark Haugaard discusses in detail the two faces of power and holds that power is commendable if it does not take the power recipient as a means to an end. Otherwise, it is reprehensible.[7] The easiest is perhaps to see power

---

[4] Dahl 1957, 201.   [5] Baldwin 1971, 585.   [6] Boulding 1990.   [7] Haugaard 2012.

in two forms – hard and soft, as Nye's discussion has shown in all clarity.[8] He tries to place much more emphasis on the importance of soft power, perhaps because most IR literature has an explicitly or implicitly biased fever for hard power, but at the same time he does not deny the role of hard power and the connection between the two forms of power.[9] Whatever typology is used, all these forms of power are seen as agential because the power resources are located at the agential level and used by the agent for exercising influence.

These studies have therefore a common feature: Implicitly or explicitly, they take power as possessed and used exclusively by the individual agent for her purposes. The power wielder is an agent, using her power resources to influence other agents in terms of the latter's behavior and circumstances. Usually it is the nation-state in international relations, but it is not limited to it. Other studies, however, have found that power may not reside merely with the agent. A more recent and highly sophisticated approach to categorizing power is provided in an analysis of power by Michael Barnett and Raymond Duvall.[10] Criticizing the mainstream IR's biased focus on controlling power, they distinguish among four types of power: compulsory, institutional, structural, and productive. Influenced perhaps by their constructivist orientation,[11] they see power as both regulative and constitutive. Compulsory power, for example, is more a power to control and change others' behavior, directly by one agent over another, while structural power and productive power are both able to constitute the identities of agents and consequently shape their interests. What they also do is to identify explicitly another level where power resources rest, that is, the structural level. They divide the two roles of regulation and constitution for power to work: One refers more to the

---

[8] Nye 2002; 2004.

[9] Nye expresses it clearly when he says, "The distinction between hard and soft power is one of degree, both in the nature of the behavior and in the tangibility of the resources. Both are aspects of the ability to achieve one's purposes by affecting the behavior of others. Command power – the ability to change what others do – can rest on coercion or inducement. Co-optive power – the ability to shape what others want – can rest on the attractiveness of one's culture and ideology or the ability to manipulate the agenda of political choices in a manner that makes actors fail to express some preferences because they seem to be too unrealistic ….The forms of behavior between command and co-optive power range along a continuum: command power, coercion, inducement, agenda setting, attraction, co-optive power. Soft power resources tend to be associated with co-optive power behavior, whereas hard power resources are usually associated with command power behavior." Nye 2002, 176.

[10] Barnett and Duvall 2005.

[11] Ruggie, for example, distinguishes between two international rules, one regulating actors' behavior and the other constituting actors' identities, using it as a standard to discuss the different treatment of international regimes by rationalists and constructivists. See Ruggie 1999.

interactions of specific actors, where they take an individual agent as the power wielder; and the other is identity constitution, where they take structural forces as the power wielder. Their productive power, which is able to produce subjects, is diffuse and exists everywhere, as Foucault has interpreted. However, from what they say about productive power, "the bases and workings of productive power are the socially existing and, hence, historically contingent and changing understandings, meanings, norms, customs, and social identities that make possible, limit, and are drawn on for action."[12] We can re-organize these elements roughly into a system of meaning and call it a normative or discursive structure. Therefore such power resources are at the structural level rather than at the agential level. The interpretation that identifies the structural location of power resources is perhaps a most inspiring insight in their study.

It is true that the Barnett-Duvall study is clear about the two major levels, agential and structural, where power is located. Whereas it is not sufficient to use only agents' power in the study of politics in general and international politics in particular and whereas power at the structural level has obvious effects on behavior and circumstances of agents, it is natural to extend the concept of power to structures. Mainstream IR theories have identified the structure of capabilities, of institutions, and of ideas as systemic variables that influence, but are short of taking them directly as power elements at the systemic level. Barnett and Duvall have done this. Stefano Guzzini has also pointed out the inadequacy of agential power and added structural power to his typology. He argues:

Agent power is no longer the sufficient means to understand international power or rule. It is probably not unexpected that scholars in International Political Economy, dealing with capital markets and their systemic effects, have been particularly interested in rescuing the understanding of international power or rule from the analysis of sheer capabilities ... they kept the focus on three components usually overlooked in the established power analysis, namely, power in terms of unintended effects, indirect institutional power affecting outcomes by changing the rules of the (institutional) games, and in terms of the impersonal power structures which mobilize a bias constituting individual opportunities. The thrust of these analyses is to take the focus away from direct power-to-power relations towards power structures and the more institutionalized settings in which social relations occur. In doing this, they either kept an agency concept of power in which they added the indirect institutional or unintended effects of agency (agency through "structural effects"), or they moved to an understanding of power located at the structure ("the power of structures" to effect).[13]

---

[12] Barnett and Duvall 2005, 56.   [13] Guzzini 2013, 7–8.

To see power reside either with the agent or with the structure provides a brief and perhaps a simplistic summary of IR literature on power, especially mainstream Western international theories. It is useful. In academic discourses, structural power and agential power are probably the two categories that most IR theorists explicitly or implicitly recognize and consciously or unconsciously employ in their studies. We can see from the mainstream IR literature that structural power refers to forces at the macro or systemic level, while the agential power to forces at the micro or individual level. Usually such forces refer first to potential power or power resources. It is undeniable that these two types of power are highly significant. Individual level discussion tends to focus on agential power for shaping the conditions and consequences. On the other hand, system-level analysis usually assumes the existence and effectiveness of structural forces that influence, emphasizing the top-down effect.

While it is important to pay attention to the two types of power, that is, agential and structural, we need to consider a third type: power whose resources are located at neither the agential level nor the structural level or power whose resources can be accessed by someone who is not the owner. It comes from relations among social actors. It may be possessed by a particular agent, but usable by others related to the agent. At the same time it is similar in terms of roles and functions to both structural and agential power. It requires power resources to start with, and it exercises influence in a relationship. Focusing on an atomistic world one may easily overlook power resources located in human relations, because human beings are taken as independent atoms whose power resources are from themselves, that is, their muscles and their minds, or from their environments, their foods and their nutriments. However, if we change our angle of observation and see the world as one of relations, then it is not difficult to see that power may well come from relations.

We have already mentioned complex interdependence as an example for jointly owned relational power. It is also illustrative to see another example proposed by Barnett/Duvall and Guzzini. Barnett and Duvall in their taxonomy undoubtedly imply the two levels, but at the same time they discuss what they term "institutional power." Guzzini is somewhat similar, using a similar term, "indirect institutional power," to express it. Barnett and Duvall take institutional power as agential in nature, believing that it is an agent's ability to indirectly control socially distant others through international institutions. An example they provide is that the United States before the Bush administration relied more on institutional power to exercise its influence, but that the policy of the Bush administration was "a shift from a grand strategy revolving around institutional power to one founded primarily on compulsory power."[14] It was this change that made the United States more of an empire. However, the term "institutional" is not appropriately defined. It obviously means a power resource that resides with an international institution but is made use of by agents. When Guzzini discusses this "indirect institutional power," he is also similarly unclear about its meaning. He seems to follow Barnett and Duvall and thus adds to the ambiguity of this institutional power as agential. It is in fact defined as agential only because it may be used by the agent. To clarify this point, we may simply see where the power resource resides and whether its usability is shared. It is not a power resource residing with or possessed by any particular international agent. It is embedded in the institution. However, it may at the same time be usable by an agent. If such power is defined as agential power, it is misleading. On the one hand, institutional power can be made use of by privileged members, but it gains an ontological significance by being able to stand away from the agent and stay alone at the structural level. On the other hand, it is accessible by some privileged agents. The word "privileged" in fact indicates a special relationship between the agent and the institution. For me it is relational power, because the accessibility to such power resources depends on the relationship. It is usable through relations.

If this power resource, that is power from relations and accessed through relations, exists, we need to add a level, one largely missing in the mainstream IR power discourse. It is the relational level. It shows that social relations or relations among social actors are an important power resource. Overall, we may use Figure 8.1 to illustrate these three types of power.

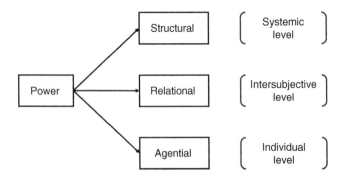

Figure 8.1: A typology of power

[14] Barnett and Duvall 2005, 63.

Power as Resources

Power as resources provides a convenient concept which is still very much in use despite the fact that it has been criticized and even denied by some political scientists and IR theorists. But what they are against is taking power as mere resources and what they cannot deny is taking power resources as an important aspect of power. It is reasonable because power cannot be deprived of its base, which refers exactly to resources an actor, personal or impersonal, may have and mobilize for the purpose of influencing. Moreover, what constitutes power resources and where power resources are located – these are fundamental questions. Answers to such questions reflect how the nature and function of power are understood and interpreted. Thus to use the location of power resources to categorize power and understand power forms is not only a simple method, but also a reasonable way of revealing the nature of power.

A common sense example may well illustrate this point. Average people are neither a Foucault nor a Bourdieu and the simplest way for them to understand the concept of power is to see who has more power resources. In dynastic China, people believed that the emperor was the most powerful because all under the sun, including ministers and soldiers, people and property, and whatever you could see under the sky, was his. People on the street today tend to think that the US president is powerful because he/she is not only the most important administrator of a state, but also the supreme commander of the US military forces. It is true that common sense is misleading sometimes, but it is highly reasonable most of the time. For political leaders and decision-makers, it is such common sense that often works simply because it provides the rule of thumb for them to consider what they are able to do and to compare which actor is more powerful. If an actor is compared to a chef, she can only cook something with the materials she has at hand. As a Chinese proverb goes: "Even the cleverest housewife cannot cook a meal without rice." It is the same as James Bond suddenly giving up his effort to fight back when he sees the enemy is a giant with iron teeth, twice as strong as he is. If politics is the art of the possible, then, potential power provides the actor with capabilities of performing the art. After all the more resources one has, the more things it is possible to do.

In this section, I will discuss first how power as resources is described in the mainstream political science literature. Then I will propose a different power resource, that is, relation. In other words, relation is a significant power resource. Simply put, relation is power.

Agential Power as Resources

By agential power, I mean the forces owned and accessed by an actor that are able to influence the behavior of other actors and the outcome of an event. Its most conspicuous feature is that it is possessed by the agent, as the widely used definition indicates. At the agential level, hard power is the most conspicuous. In fact, power as resources in many Western theories more often than not refers to something linked to hard power, which happens often to be material, too. It is the power that can overcome through coercion and eliminate through violence. Overcoming and eliminating often imply hard and violent might and it is usually oppressive and destructive force. For realists, teeth often speak louder than tongues; for radicals, a new world is always built on the ruins of the old.

In international relations, it frequently means the power to wage and win wars. Morgenthau argues that in international politics, "armed strength as a threat or potentiality is the most important material factor making for the political power of a nation."[15] Joseph Nye points out that a traditional test of a great power in international politics was "strength for war."[16] After WWII, since the Allies had defeated the Axis, the former was more powerful. Power elements given by IR authorities and well-known databanks often include those that can be converted to military capabilities. E. H. Carr lists three types of power: military power, economic power, and power over opinion, and Morgenthau also includes such hard power elements as geography, natural resources, military preparedness, and population.[17] The Correlates of War (COW) Project, for example, uses three dimensions and six indicators for calculating the capabilities of a state. They are the military, industrial, and demographic dimensions, measured respectively by military expenditures and personnel, iron-steel production and energy consumption, and total and urbanized populations.[18] These indicators are included because they are the power elements that can be converted into actual destructive forces in war. To overcome, to defeat, and to conquer describe a mindset about power, the mindset envisioning power exclusively in winning in a conflict by conquering the rival and opposite forces, or in a situation where zero-sum games prevail. It has been reminded from time to time by various military exercises where situations get tense and where disputes rise. It has for a long time dominated the study of international politics. To a disproportionately large extent, it is still so.

---

[15] Morgenthau 1961, 29.   [16] Nye 2004, 3.   [17] Carr 1964; Morgenthau 1961.
[18] See Organski and Kugler 1980, 36–37; Russett, Starr, and Kinsella 2006, 114.

Hard power is the easiest to observe. In international relations, agential power is often measured by the power resources one possesses or the capabilities one has. Simply put, what one needs to do is to count how much money an actor has or how many nuclear warheads she owns before one decides who is more powerful. Although it is generally acknowledged that power resources are potential power at the best and cannot be equal to power as influence, for potential power, if not activated, cannot influence the outcome and cannot affect the behavior of another actor. Some argue that power resources have been paid special attention, especially since the behavioral revolution, mainly because they are easier to see and quite objective to measure.[19] It is true, but the most important reason is that they provide a more visible base on which influence is exercised. It is quite easy to tell unambiguously what a country's gross domestic product (GDP) is and how much it spends on the military.[20] In addition, it is easier to say the United States is number one in the world because it has the largest GDP and the largest military expenditure. China is number two in terms of economic strength because it has the second largest GDP after the United States. In the academic literature of IR, in particular quantitative studies, such tangible power elements are often used to indicate the relative power of a nation-state. For the purpose of being rigorous, scholars have even proposed using only one indicator, GDP for instance, to indicate capabilities of a state.[21] Relative power, or power gaps between states in terms of material capabilities, provides the potential and likelihood to win in a conflict.

Of course agential power is not limited to material or hard power, even though IR seems to prefer defining it first of all by looking at such factors. Nye has developed the concept of "soft power," which is said to be non-coercive and non-destructive. Moreover, it is more ideational or value-related than material. As "the second face of power," it is the power to "get others to want the outcomes you want," or the ability to co-opt people rather than coerce them.[22] It is attractive and seductive power,

---

[19] For example, Karl Deutsch holds that power resources are easier to measure, acknowledging that actual power cannot be exactly measured, but that "it can be estimated in proportion to the power resources or capabilities that are visibly available, such as numbers of countable supporters, voters, or soldiers available or required in a particular political context" (Deutsch 1963, 120). David Baldwin agrees that power resources are not difficult to measure, though political power itself is not easy because there is no consensus on a standardized measuring rod for it (Baldwin 1971, 595 and 596). Most behaviorists use power resources as substitutes for power itself largely because they are easier to measure and quantify. Baldwin in fact is quite correct to point out that the money-power analogy "can be harmful if it tempts to single out a particular base value in terms of which to express the value of others" (1971, 597).

[20] See Organski and Kugler 1980, 36–37.   [21] Kugler and Arbetman 1989.

[22] Nye 2004, 5.

possessed by one and appealing to others. Values, cultures, institutions, and policies are all considered resources of soft power. To measure American soft power, such indicators are used: the largest economy in the world, the overwhelmingly large proportion of American firms in the top 500 global companies, and the impressive number of foreign students and scholars who study in American educational institutions.[23] However these elements are not taken for their face values by the logic of soft power. The economy factor is included because it is a reflection of the good economic system that others will willingly follow; the large number of foreign students indicates the quality of education and the superiority of the educational system. No matter how soft power is defined, Nye's discussion and detailed interpretation of the concept reveals the fact that soft power is possessed and exercised by an individual actor aiming to control others' behavior and circumstances. It is the power to win and to conquer, of course by means, perhaps, other than coercion. Nevertheless, it is also unilateral, reflecting influence flowing from the power wielder to the power recipient and what it tries to change is not merely the recipient's behavior, but more importantly, to reconstruct others' minds, thus making them willingly do what you want them to do. Compared with hard power, the form of power changes, but the nature is the same.

Structural Power as Resources

Power resources can rest at the structural level as well, or we may call it structural power. To discuss structural power is an important move along the development of power analysis in IR. Power was basically an agential concept in the formative years of IR as a discipline, but has been considered in a broader way since scholars found that such a conceptualization is not sufficient. In fact, most of the mainstream IR literature has explicit or implicit connotations and implications of power. Some may distinguish between power on the one hand and norms and institutions on the other, believing that the latter are not "power."[24] If we define power as force to influence outcomes or actors' behavior, then the three mainstream IR theories, neorealism, neoliberalism, and constructivism, all have strong power connotations inside, for all of them aim to find some factors at the systemic level that influence the behavior of the units inside, though they

[23] Ibid., 33.
[24] For example, Helen Milner criticizes realist scholars' biased focus on "power," arguing that a concern with norms and institutions should be added to this focus on power. It sounds as if norms and institutions were not "power," but something parallel to power. In fact, norms and institutions influence actors' behavior and have obvious and very often strong power implications. See Milner 1993, 162.

aim to find some power element different from the realist's hard power. Their discourse involves power as resources, but such resources are not conspicuously and clearly possessed by a particular agent. Rather they are embedded in a systemic structure, which is, to some extent, personified and individualized. Power is no longer the property of a particular actor, but of an impersonal structure. For me, the three mainstream IR theories are systemic theories exactly because they locate the power resources at the systemic level. In some sense, they are all about "power politics."

Structural power thus refers to the forces at the systemic level that are able to influence the behavior of international actors and to constitute preferences and identities of such actors so as to influence the outcome of an event. It is not possessed by any individual actor, for structural power comes from the structure itself and does not depend on any particular unit in the structure. Waltz sees exactly this type of power in his discussion of the international structure, the configuration of which is the distribution of actors' capabilities in the international system. It is systemic in nature. "Power is estimated by comparing the capabilities of a number of units. Although capabilities are attributes of units, the distribution of capabilities across units is not. The distribution of capabilities is not a unit attribute, but rather a system-wide concept."[25] It is, as Wendt comments, "a property of the system as a whole with effects that cannot be reduced to the unit-level."[26] Although structures are made by agents, once a structure is established and existent, it has power of its own, influencing the behavior of all the units rather than the other way round.[27] The market is a typical example, for its invisible hand controls sellers and buyers in it. The invisible hand is power. Structural power is very much the invisible hand in international relations. It is not as visible as the tangible power elements at the agential level, but it is everywhere in one's life. The bipolar structure during the Cold War years, for example, influenced almost every aspect of international life and almost every international actor. In IR the three mainstream theories all connote power, which is defined as influence unilaterally from the systemic structure and over outcomes or agential behavior.

Structural power is recognized by locating its resources at the structural level and by identifying the structure itself as the power wielder. Like

---

[25] Waltz 1979, 98.   [26] Wendt 1999, 99.
[27] Waltz 1979, 97–98. Keohane and Wendt have both followed this Waltzian logic. International institutions and international cultures are established or constructed by agents, but once they are established, they are highly independent and exercise influence over systemic units, that is, nation-states in international relations. See Keohane 1984; Wendt 1999.

agential power, it can be material, institutional, or ideational. In IR theories, structural power of the material type has been given great importance by realists, especially neorealists. The concept of balance of power has long contained structural implications, though it is often interpreted in mixed terms involving agential strategies. Sometimes, structural power is not discussed in lucid terms. For American mainstream IR theories which follow the scientific tradition, the common practice is to find a particular force and see how it influences the behavior of units in this structure. Waltz's structural realism provides a most pioneering and systematic piece of work in this respect.[28] Drawing on the market analogy and using microeconomics as an inspiration, Waltz establishes his neorealism with the structure of the international system as the main locale of power to influence. The greatest influence on the behavior of units in the international system is thus the systemic structure. He further defines the international structure in terms of the distribution of capabilities among major players in the system, especially among the very few strongest states. For Waltz, once the distribution of capabilities is clear, the structure of the system is clear and the behavior of the states also determined, certain and predictable. Since the most important factor that determines the behavior of states is the distribution of capabilities, the power of the international system rests with the systemic structure and is material in nature. It is not what one state owns, and it is neither what one state can exercise of and by itself. Furthermore it is fairly steady as a structure and can be easily measured by calculating the material capabilities of the major players that constitute the power oligarchy. Unipolarity, bipolarity, and multipolarity are all used to describe what the structure of the international system is and empirical studies have been done to explain which structure produces more peace-oriented or more warlike behavior. If you want to know what behavior international actors tend to have then, what you should do is simply make clear what kind of power distribution exists in the international system. Distribution of capabilities among the major states in the system constitutes the resource of the systemic power. It provides the potentiality for influence to flow from the systemic structure to the circumstances of units inside. It does involve a power wielder and a power recipient, but the former, as Barnett/Duvall and Guzzini have pointed out, is impersonal, or for me, it is impersonal but personified. The relationship between them, however, tends to be causally regulative.

Since neoliberal institutionalism and structural constructivism both follow the Waltzian logic of theorizing at the systemic level, they tend to stress

---

[28] Waltz 1979.

structural power as well. Keohane defines his theory of neoliberal institutionalism as a systemic theory because he too tries to find what factor constitutes the most significant force at the systemic level that influences the behavior of the actor. He has found international institutions.[29] He first takes international institutions as a dependent variable because they are established often by hegemonic power due to the initial high cost. Perhaps what Barnett and Duvall understand as institutional power is reasonable in this respect,[30] because institutions established by the hegemon may serve its objectives more than other member states due to its privileged position to the institutions. However, Keohane differs essentially from Barnett and Duvall because his intention is not at all to consider institutions as agential power. With a macro-level logic of theorizing, which places power always at the systemic level, he continues to argue that once international institutions are established, they acquire an independent existence, having their own life and being able to influence the behavior of states. They constitute an institutional space where actors' behavior is regulated by the structure of the international institutions. Nye has defined processes at the systemic level and pointed out that processes are about how international actors play the game with patterned behavior by obeying rules embedded in institutions.[31] But they are also, and even more so, structural because once established international institutions have themselves become a stable and structural framework, influencing the behavior of actors who are in this institutional space. Behavior is patterned because the institutional structure makes it so and it is therefore a system-arranged outcome under the structural force.

Wendt places neoliberalism in his map of IR theories across the materialism-idealism quadrants.[32] For me, institutions by neoliberal institutionalism are very much reified and therefore materialized as structures of established institutions in the international system. Numerous empirical studies have, for example, simply taken international institutions as an independent variable, quite steady and stable, and tried to find how they influence the behavior of state actors within this institutional framework. Even though institutions continue to contain non-material elements, they become a physically palpable edifice. They draw a tangible sphere of international regimes and constitute an institutional structure within which rules rule.[33] Once they are established, they are something out

---

[29] Keohane 1989b.   [30] Barnett and Duvall 2005.   [31] Nye 1993, 30–31.

[32] Wendt 1999, 32.

[33] See Onuf 1989. Both the terms of "rule" and "rules" have strong power implications. He accepts power as influence and defines rule as effective exercise of influence (238), and stresses the mutual transformation between them, or, in his own words, rules are "to enable or effectuate rule," and rule "works through the medium of rules" (29).

there. They are corporeal entities with their rules and regulations, their values and standards, and their independent self-existence and own life. Think about the international trade regimes. Members of the trade regimes have more patterned interactions, which, however, are first of all the result of the institutional structure in this area, with its value-laden rules that influence member states and make their behavior patterned. They constitute something of a logical-legal structure. They are powerful because they influence. They encourage some behavior, discourage some behavior, and change some behavior. What to encourage, discourage, or change depends on rules designed and implemented by institutions. Institutional power is power embedded in the structure of the system of international rules. In this sense institutional power is structural power, too, and rules made by institutions constitute the resource of power.[34]

Wendtian constructivism also seeks to identify power at the systemic level. Following the Waltzian logic, Wendt focuses on the systemic level. But he uses the ideational structure to replace the material structure and international culture is the key word in his discussion of the international system. His Kantian, Lockean, and Hobbesian cultures are in fact all normative spaces that inform people what they should do and what they should not. Fighting with all means is the norm of the Hobbesian culture, "live and let live" the norm of the Lockean realm, and friendship the norm of the Kantian world. His structure is thus very much a normative structure and his power normative power: The normative power rests with the ideational structure of the international system that influences the behavior of the actors inside. What Wendt seeks in fact is more than Waltz and Keohane, for his normative power is capable of not only influencing behavior, but also shaping identity. It is neither as conspicuously coercive as Morgenthau's and Waltz's nor as materially attractive as Keohane's, but it can be much stronger and runs much deeper, for it is to change not only the behavior, but the actor *per se*. "Indeed, is it not the supreme exercise of power to get another or others to have the desire you want them to have ... to secure their compliance by controlling their thoughts and desires?"[35] Or, is it not a supreme exercise of power to bestow an identity on or change the identity of an actor?[36] It is in this respect akin to

---

[34] Barnett and Finnemore 2004. Also Michael Byers in his study of the relationship between law and power says: "The customary process and other fundamental rules, principles and processes of international law, in terms used by Keohane, 'persistent and connected sets of rules ... that prescribe behavioral roles, constrain activity, and shape expectations.' ... in other words, they are normative structures which regulate applications of what international relations scholars usually refer to as 'power.'" Byers 1999, 4.

[35] Russett, Starr, and Kinsella 2006, 106.

[36] Finnemore in fact argues that developing countries are taught to have a "correct" identity and then learn to define their interests accordingly. See Finnemore 1996.

Nye's soft power, because the power is exercised through influence that is subtle and even imperceptible. But the purpose is the same. For mainstream constructivists, international norms are the main resource of power at the systemic level.[37]

In addition to the mainstream, other theories discuss the concept of structural power, too. From the radical camp, we may use the world system theory and Gramsci's cultural hegemony argument as two typical examples. The world system theory sees more a material economic structure that underlies the unequal and exploitative economic relations in the world.[38] The resources of the systemic power derive from the distribution of wealth, together with the corresponding division of labor, or the structure of the world capitalist system. It makes the world into three distinct and also related parts: the center, the semi-periphery, and the periphery. Advanced capitalist states have created and tried to perpetuate the division of labor in the world, with the periphery as the supplier of raw materials and the market for their products. It is a kind of structural and material power with economic wealth as its most important resource. The other side of the story is told by perhaps Gramsci's cultural hegemony theory.[39] His cultural hegemony in fact is a structure of ideas and values which become dominant through the forced consent of the ruled and dominated. In a capitalist system, for example, this ideational structure is fairly stable, static, and steady, providing a kind of invisible power to maintain the existing order. The resource of this power is the ideology of the dominant class, based upon which supremacy is achieved and domination maintained. To extend it to the international arena, it performs somewhat similar functions with the normative structure via constructivism. Although the world system theory and Gramsci's hegemony argument are both highly critical of the existing system, their way of theorizing is not very much different from that of the mainstream theories, with an economic structure (distribution of wealth) or an ideational structure (cultural hegemony) as what they believe to be the most important power element at the systemic level.

The above discussion shows that resources constitute an integral part of power at the structural level, defined in terms of influence on outcomes and behavior. Within the three mainstream American IR theories, we may

---

[37] To some extent, Kratochwil's more legalistic rules and norms and Onuf's more linguistic rules play a similar role. They also have both the regulative and constitutive power to influence actors' behavior, preference, and identity. Kratochwil structures a normative context in which decisions are made and Onuf believes that rules, institutions, and unintended consequences form stable patterns called structure. See Kratochwil 1989; Onuf 1998.

[38] Wallerstein 1974.   [39] See Gill 1993.

find that power as resources refers to distribution of capabilities for neorealism, to institutional rules for neoliberalism, and to international norms for constructivism. As with power at the agential level, we can see hard and material resources on the one hand and soft and non-material resources on the other. While agential power is power possessed or enjoyed by an agent, materially or ideationally, as Mearsheimer's hard power and Nye's soft power represent respectively, structural power is power located at the systemic level. It is not owned by any particular agent and it is exercised by the structure as an impersonal power wielder.

Relational Power as Resources

The discussion of power as resources in the Western IR literature focuses either on a particular agent or on a structure where power is located and from where power is wielded. Whatever it is, it must be something of an entity, personal or impersonal. Mainstream IR power analysts seldom think about a different form of potential power, that is, relations as a power resource. Perhaps relations are not as tangible and entity-like as a nation-state or systemic structure. Rather relations are a factor much more fluid and elusive, thus being largely left out of the discussion. The relational theory, however, takes human relations as a crucial factor in political analysis and therefore conceptualizes power more from a relational perspective. It does not deny the fact that hard, material power elements such as military forces, economic wealth, population, and size are indispensable base values and recognizes at the same time that soft power such as leadership and culture are equally important. It also recognizes that power resources can be embedded in structures, either material or ideational. However, it argues that a different form of power as a resource exists in every society and has been used by social actors to exercise influence and achieve desired outcomes. It is human relations.

The relational theory, therefore, argues that, as far as resources are concerned, relation is power. I use the term "relational power" to refer to power whose resources come from relations and can be accessed through relations. It is power that resides with relations among actors rather than with an independent and discrete entity. Since the term "relational power" may have been used and understood for other meanings and led to other interpretations, I need to define it here for the purpose of this study. It differs both from "relative power," which is used to compare two actors in terms of their respective resources to see who is more powerful, and from power as relations, which reflects only one aspect of the relational dimension of power by indicating power as a relationship between two actors with the power wielder influencing the power recipient. What

I propose as relational power has three interrelated meanings. First, relation is a power resource. It means that relational power as a resource may be neither possessed by a particular agent nor by a systemic structure. Relation itself is a power resource. In other words, human relations *per se* constitute a valuable power base, performing similar functions as military forces, economic wealth, or effective leadership. Relational power resides with relations among actors and therefore no single entity can have an exclusive possession of it. Second, relational power is sharable. It is sharable and shared in the first place. It may mean that the ownership of relational power is shared or that its accessibility is shared. In other words, sharability constitutes a most distinct feature of relational power. Third, relational power increases by use. Most power resources possessed by an agent, especially the material ones, are limited and exhaustible. The more one uses them, the less remains. Relational power resources are maintained and may increase by actual use. If relations as a power resource are not used, they tend to become weaker and weaker. Let me discuss these three features in the following sections.

Power Comes from Relations Relation as a power resource means that an actor's power can come from her relations with others. As we have discussed before, the social world is one of relations and each actor is a relator. She has her relational circles, where there are other relators connected with her. Her relational circles overlap with those of others, together constituting a relational space in which she acts and interacts with other relators. Her relational circles and other relators in such circles, due to the connectivity she has with them, produce power for her in the form of a resource or base value. It is not hard power, because it is neither material, nor quite tangible. It appears closer to the concept of soft power. Nye once used an interesting indicator, for example, to compare the soft power of China and the United States. He argued that more countries in the world are friendlier to the United States than to China, and therefore the former's soft power is greater.[40] This argument implies at least that soft power may come from the relationships one has with others. But relations as a power resource differ from soft power resources in some important aspects. By definition, it is not owned exclusively by any individual actor while soft power is. Relational power resources are shared among actors who are related with one another. In addition, it is neither attractive nor co-optive in nature, for it does not mean to attract or to co-opt. As a power resource, however, relations function similarly as both hard and soft power resources because they may enable an actor to affect

---

[40] Nye 2015, 17.

others' behavior and the outcome of an event. We may imagine a person in difficult circumstances, both material and psychological. More often than not she will turn to her friends who may provide her with money and/or solace. In other words, she is empowered in and through her relations with others. What she gains from such relations affects the circumstances of her life as well as her behavior.

A practical example in international affairs is ASEAN as a regional actor. It is often said that ASEAN has few power resources. It is true according to the traditional IR conceptualization of power. The ten members of ASEAN are almost all lesser states; its GDP is a little more than one-tenth of the East Asian total, which includes ASEAN 10, China, Japan, and South Korea; its military expenditures account for about one-tenth, and its population is less than half that of China. If we consider its power from a traditional perspective, it lacks resources indeed. However, ASEAN has been playing a leading role in East Asian regionalism in the last three decades, and it has been quite successful. If an international actor plays an important role in some respect, it must have power one way or another, or it must be able to exercise influence in international affairs. The Vatican relies on its soft power in the form of religious authority to produce influence in the Catholic world and beyond. What then constitutes a particularly important power resource of ASEAN as a regional player? It does not have the material resources the United States possesses and the soft power resources the Vatican enjoys. What comes first to one's mind is more often than not the power that comes from either the relationships among ASEAN members or from ASEAN's relationships with other actors. Internally, it gains power from a cohesive relationship. ASEAN members have close relations with one another and maintain a unity with diversity, announcing the completion of the ASEAN community in 2015. Externally, it gains power from its role as a relational hub to connect outside players. ASEAN has maintained fairly balanced relations with the major powers within and without the region and such relations have been workable enough to exercise influence. In the first decade of the twenty-first century, it played a leading role in bringing China and Japan together, maintaining a good working relationship with both and managing to become the platform on which both China and Japan not only recognized the centrality role of ASEAN, but also competed with each other to get the support of ASEAN. From the mainstream IR's power conceptualization, ASEAN was much weaker than either China or Japan, but its management of relations with both generated power for itself, influencing the behavior of the two major regional powers as well as the regional processes. Virtually it has become a connecting center that converges, adjusts, and manages relationships of various kinds in the region, and the hub of relationships itself then has become a major source of power. Today it faces another competition, the strategic competition between China and the United States. It produces tough problems for ASEAN, but it also provides opportunities if ASEAN can successfully manage its relationships with both. Since a power resource residing in relations is not like a power resource possessed by a single entity, it is generated and maintained to a large extent by the management of relations.

Relational Power is Sharable A resource of relational power has a most distinct feature: It is sharable. It means both shared ownership and/or shared accessibility. The former refers to the fact that power resources are owned jointly by actors who are related with each other. Such resources disappear once the relationship is severed. The latter means that power is no longer an exclusively and absolutely owned property of a particular individual agent. Once a relationship is established between Actors A and B, for example, power resources originally possessed by A and B respectively become sharable through their relationship. In other words, both A and B have accessibility to each other's power resources through the fact that they are related. By the same logic, as the relationship is cut off by any one of the related parties, both lose such power resources.

Think about the situation where there exists a complex interdependence situation between two actors. Robert Keohane and Joseph Nye define interdependence as "situations characterized by reciprocal effects among countries or among actors in different countries."[41] There is no doubt that such a situation describes a relationship. In fact they use again and again the term "interdependent relationship" consistently throughout the book. Furthermore, they argue that an interdependent relationship is not necessarily symmetrical. In other words, asymmetrical interdependent relationship means power. They have made the following comments:

It is *asymmetries* in dependence that are most likely to provide sources of influence for actors in their dealing with one another. Less dependent actors can often use the interdependent relationship as a source of power in bargaining over an issue and perhaps to affect other issues. At the other extreme from pure symmetry is pure dependence (sometimes disguised by calling the situation interdependence), but it too is rare. Most cases lie between these two extremes. And that is where the heart of the political bargaining process of interdependence lies.[42]

---

[41] Keohane and Nye 2001, 7.   [42] Ibid., 9, emphasis in original.

Asymmetrical interdependent relationships are thus taken as a power resource.[43] Actor A is more powerful than Actor B because it is less dependent and therefore less subject to vulnerability interdependence. While Keohane and Nye focus their attention mainly on the power A gains from this interdependent relationship, they perhaps forget that A's power is not what it possesses by itself as its property, but what it derives from its relationship with B. If power comes from a relationship, then it is not owned by one actor as its inherent attribute. Only when this asymmetrical relationship is formed and exists can power be produced. A's power is because of B, or because of the relationship that exists between A and B. Once such relationship ends, A's power disappears. It is thus not agential power, for it involves at least two people and no single actor can possess such a power resource. Nor is it a structural power resource, for it is located not at the structural level, but at the intersubjective level. For A, it is more a relational asset, but definitely one with some opportunity cost. In IR, for example, we may define military forces and economic wealth as agential power which is at the disposal of the agent who has the ownership. We may define distribution of capabilities, of institutions, and of norms as structural power because they are located at the systemic structure, which, impersonal as it is, works as the power wielder. Relational power, however, neither belongs to the individual agent nor rests with some impersonal structure. It resides in relations among agents. It is neither personal nor impersonal power. It is intersubjective or relational in nature.

Shared accessibility is equally meaningful. Social capital studies have shed light on this point, in particular through a consensual viewpoint among scholars in that area that social capital is derived from social relations. They not only argue that social capital is not located in any particular actor but is located in relations among actors,[44] but also stress the shared accessibility to relational power resources. Aldrich identifies three forms of social capital, namely, bonding, bridging, and linking, all of which refer to relationships of various kinds (respectively, among family members, friends, and between citizens and government officials) through which power resources are shared.[45] "No one player has exclusive ownership rights to social capital. If you or a partner in a relationship withdraws, the connection dissolved with whatever social capital it contained."[46] Although social capital scholars have seldom used the

---

[43] Brantly Womack has discussed asymmetrical relationships in detail, arguing that such relationships can create misperceptions for international actors engaged in an interaction. His theory of asymmetry implies that power may come from such a relationship. See Womack 2006; 2016.
[44] Coleman 1988; Adler and Known 2002.   [45] Aldrich 2012.   [46] Burt 1992, 58.

word "power" in their studies, they have inspired us in terms of how resources are owned and used. At least it indicates that some forms of power are not absolutely and exclusively owned by an individual actor due to their shared accessibility.

An interesting word to express this shared accessibility is "borrowing." It means that relational power is borrowable. Power resources that used to belong to a particular agent are no longer exclusively used by the owner once some relationship with another actor is established. They are usable by those who are connected to the agent and share with her a relationship. Nan Lin, who has contributed to the development of social resources theory, uses the word "borrow" and defines social resources in the following way:

Social resources are resources accessible through one's direct and indirect ties. The access to and use of these resources are temporary and borrowed. For example, a friend's occupational or authority position, or such position of this friend's friends, may be ego's social resources. These resources are "borrowed" and useful to achieve ego's certain goals, but they remain the property of the friend or his/her friends.[47]

The word "borrowed" indicates that such resources can be possessed by the agent but at the same time are also sharable in actual use. Shared accessibility reflects this important feature of relations as a power resource. They may be possessions of an agent, but can be borrowed by another or others for use. Others' resources are usable by you because you are related to them. The ability to "borrow" itself thus implies power. It is power generated from relations, and, to some extent, shared through a relationship, without which there would be no "borrowing" at all. "Borrowing" also indicates that sharing a resource is more likely if there is more intimate and intensive relatedness between the borrower and the lender and that the specific act of borrowing is likely to strengthen such relatedness. Military alliances are in fact the legal expression of a relationship by which one actor's military forces can be "borrowed" by another for the use of protecting the latter from being attacked or invaded. No military alliance would ever be established between two actors who were not intimately related. It reflects a shared accessibility through relational connections and social ties.

In this respect, Portes' discussion of social capital is quite inspiring. He uses Bourdieu's definition of social capital, which is "the aggregate of the actual or potential resources which are linked to possession of a durable network of more or less institutionalized relationships of mutual

___

[47] Lin 1999, 468.

acquaintance or recognition"[48] and interprets it as "decomposable into two elements: first the social relationship itself that allows individuals to claim access to resources possessed by their associates, and second, the amount and quality of those resources."[49] In other words, such resources exist in the relations between the self and the others she is related with. Once relations are existent, such resources exist as sharable power. Furthermore, there is a point worth mentioning here: If relations are to be maintained, it requires both or all the relators to invest in them and no single actor is able to accomplish it. Relations are thus always of a sharing nature. The maintenance of a relationship means continual shared accessibility. Thus, relations as a power resource, in the first place, imply sharing and co-accessibility.

This sharing nature of relational power is not limited to the inter-agential level. It is also reflected in an agent-structure relationship. It is interesting to recall that Barnett and Duvall in their typology of power discuss the concept of institutional power, which refers to the capability of an agent to influence outcomes through institutions. An agent's special positioning in relation to the institutional arrangements means that she enjoys privileges others do not. The privileges are hers. We may imagine an extreme situation where a hegemon almost completely controls an institutional framework and its positioning in this institutional structure enables it to influence others more than the other way round. Barnett and Duvall believe that such a power resource is agential in nature, because it is usable and actually used by an agent. For me it is more relational power. Institutional power is not the possession of any individual agent. Rather it is embedded in the institutional structure. An agent is able to use it not because she owns it but because she has a special relationship with the institution where it resides. The United States is able to use the institutional power of the International Monetary Fund (IMF) because it made a special arrangement with the institution when its own power played the most important role to establish the IMF. It is through this special relationship that the United States is able to "borrow" power resources from the international institution more than other members.

The concept that relation is power thus differs from the mainstream IR theory most conspicuously in the ownership of and accessibility to power resources. Agential power is owned by a particular individual actor. Since the international system has been largely defined as an anarchy, power tends to be taken as the ability to dominate and control, for in such a system, power, owned and used by the individual actor such as the nation-state, is the only means to enable one's survival and prosperity.

---

[48] Portes 1998, 3.   [49] Ibid., 4.

In this sense it is a crucial private property. As such, it is inalienable and inviolable. Structural power is similar. It is true that structural power is not owned by any particular actor, but it is owned by a systemic entity or a superstructure with its power diffusing, in Foucault's words, "everywhere."[50] It is impersonal, but it is an impersonal super-being, or a transcendental entity that is very much personified in terms of exercising influence over agents inside, whether it is material, institutional, or ideational. It is not sharable. Its ownership is exclusive.

This fundamental assumption of power by the mainstream IR theory is in fact a conspicuous exception which is taken for granted. In other fields, that power resources embedded in relations are sharable and should be shared has long been an accepted view. Political theorists have pointed out that power should be shared and is shared in domestic politics. In practice, democracy presupposes a separation of power, or power sharing, to prevent the possible abuse of power that is monopolized. Power cannot be owned exclusively by one actor. Power belongs to all the citizens of a democratic country, who willingly lend or delegate their power to an elected government. In other words, power is owned and shared by all, and is at the same time "borrowed" by the government for exercising it on their behalf. But, it seems that the mainstream Western IR theory deliberately draws a clear dividing line between domestic and international politics.[51] In the former, power is and should be shared, while in the latter, power has been largely understood and interpreted as the inviolable property of an independent actor, either the state or the international structure. Power is thus artificially privatized in the international setting, justified by the anarchic nature of the international system and repeatedly reinforced by the survival theme. Power politics is, to a large extent, backed by the logic that only privately owned and used power is able to protect the power owner from insecurity and uncertainty.

---

[50] Foucault's power is said to be neither structural nor agential. It is diffuse power that pervades society; power whose embedded norms are so internalized by people through surveillance and education systems that they discipline themselves to behave and think in expected ways. It is therefore power that constitutes agents. In fact the effect is very much like that of a normative structure. International norms, for instance, permeate in international society through a teaching and learning process and become the regimes of the good and appropriate. Once norms are internalized by international actors, they enable such actors to discipline themselves in their thinking and doing, without overt coercion from any naked form of violence. For this reason I put Foucault's power into the category of structural power. See Foucault 1991.

[51] Morgenthau argues that the morality of the state is different from that of an individual, thus making international politics a realm fundamentally different from domestic politics. Waltz holds that domestic politics and international politics are two distinct domains, with the former structured in hierarchy and the latter in anarchy. See Morgenthau 1961, 10–11; Waltz 1979.

If Waltz's anarchy assumption distinguishes (wrongly?) between domestic and international politics,[52] then private power provides the chief mechanism to sustain his international anarchy. However, if we agree that from a high degree of power concentration such as a dictatorship to power sharing in a democracy history has witnessed great progress in human society, then why does it seem to be so reasonable to see power as private property in international society?

Relational Power Increases by Use Another distinct feature of relational resources is that such power increases by use. Since the origin of such power resources is human relations, the more you invest in such relations by keeping communications through use, the greater your relational circles will be and the more intimate your relationships will become. On the other hand, if you stop using your relations and reduce the frequency of contacting other actors in your relational circles, the relationship between you and those others will turn out to be estranged – a process of estrangement through which your friends or acquaintances are becoming strangers. The practice of using relations is in fact a way of strengthening relationships and hence increasing relational power resources.

Imagine a situation: You have just arrived in a foreign city where you are a complete stranger and where you need to stay for a one-year teaching commitment. You have a few friends who have stayed there for quite some time. If you contact them and seek advice as to how to live a better and more convenient life in this strange city, you begin to use your relations, which by itself is an investment in your relationship with your friends. You may get various kinds of help, making your life there easier. On the other hand you may choose not to contact any of them, or you do not want to use such relations; this decision itself constitutes a move to estrange your friends there and you will actually have no relational resources to use because you do not want to use them in the very beginning. In international relations, national leaders visit one another to establish or strengthen the relationship between their countries, showing that they are ready to share some resources with one another.

We may use two indicators to illustrate this point: intimacy and extensity, with the former indicating the quality of a relationship and the latter the quantity. It is posited that the more intimate your relationship with another relator is, the more reliable the resources you may get from this relationship. An intimate relationship tends to provide you with accessibility to more reliable resources. During the Cold War years the United

[52] Milner 1993.

States and the Soviet Union were both readier to provide assistance to their own allies, and on the other hand their allies were readier to seek assistance from the two superpowers respectively. If a US or Soviet ally stopped using such a relationship to access the superpower's resources, it was in fact a sign to indicate the weakening of their relationship. A telling example is that in the 1960s the Soviet Union withdrew its experts who were helping China's economic development, indicating that they would no longer to use each other's resources and foretelling the end of their alliance relationship, which was in fact to follow quite soon after.

Extensity of one's relational circles is another indicator to illustrate relational power resources. In normal cases, the more extensive your relational circles are, the more resources you may derive from relations. If State A should have all the five permanent members of the UN Security Council as close friends, it would be more powerful than State B who enjoys no friendship with any of the big five. A most tragic anecdote in modern Chinese history is that in 1900 the Qing Court declared war against eight major powers in the world, including the United Kingdom, the United States, Germany, France, Austria, Russia, Italy, and Japan, who formed an allied army to fight against the Qing Empire. Thus on the one hand there were eight major Western powers which were united with one another and shared their resources in the event. On the other hand, the Qing failed to get resources from its relationship with any others. Thus the Western powers' relational circles were much more extensive than the Qing Court. Who was more powerful was most obvious and the outcome of the war was no surprise either. Another example is the Japanese attack on Pearl Harbor and Japan's declaration of war against the major powers in the world. Japan won the sea battle, but pushed the United States into becoming a formal member of the Alliance, thus increasing dramatically the relational power of the Alliance in contrast to that of the Axis.

The concept of relational power places emphasis on the shared ownership and shared accessibility of power resources, for relations as power resources cannot be owned and accessed by any actor alone. Relational power is seen in both domestic and international societies with its conspicuous social and human characteristic. While agential power as resources is the possession by the agent and structural power as resources is the possession by the structure who serves as an impersonal owner of power, relational power is shared in the first place. It goes with the coexistence assumption and the shared interest principle of the relational theory, arguing that in a world of relatedness power resources embedded in human relations are in fact jointly owned and used. This argument paves the way for a reconceptualization of power as relations in a more positive way.

Power as Relations

Power analysis in the Western IR literature has largely agreed that whatever power resources mean, they remain potential until they are activated and become influence, or when potential power becomes actual power. In fact, the mainstream IR theory, when identifying resources of power, has already indicated the dimension of influence. At the moment it becomes influence, it is simultaneously relational. By relational, it often means that power is able to influence because there exists a relationship which involves at least two actors – the power wielder and the power recipient. It is a power relationship if and only if the latter changes her behavior to satisfy the desire of the former. In this sense power exists only in and through relations.[53]

Agential Power as Relations

Hard power at the agential level is often taken as "power over," thus becoming directly relational in nature. When we ask the question "over whom," it immediately refers to one's capabilities to change another's behavior so that one can get the desired outcome. Morgenthau understood power as the ability to control over others' minds and actions.[54] Dahl's greatest contribution in his conceptual analysis of power is to highlight the relational nature of power while paying sufficient attention to the aspect of power as resources. In Dahl's classical definition, it is the capability to make others do what they otherwise would not do. As he says: "My intuitive idea of power, then, is something like this: A has power over B to the extent that he can get B to do something that B would not otherwise do."[55] At least there are two important messages in his definition: One is that power is possessed by an actor, reflecting her capability, and the other is that power is expressed in A's relationship with B, reflecting her ability to influence. It is why Dahl defines power as a relation among actors, but this relation is a direct interaction between two actors each of whom possesses some resources. As a behavioral scientist and with a conflictual mindset, Dahl focuses on who overwhelms in a conflictual interaction by comparing the power resources respectively possessed by A and B and how they use such resources. The one who makes the other follow her wish and who overcomes resistance is the more powerful. The strongest message is no other than "power over."

---

[53] Barnett and Duvall define power as "the production, in and through social relations, of effects that shape the capacities of actors to determine their circumstances and fate." Barnett and Duvall 2005, 42.
[54] Morgenthau 1961, 28.   [55] Dahl 1957, 202–203.

In international relations, it is often a state's ability to change the behavior of another or other states so that the outcome will turn out to be what the state desires. Simply put, it is the ability to get one's way through force or show of force. It strongly implies coercion, and therefore such power is often termed "coercive power" or "compulsory power," and the relationship it involves is a coercive or domineering relationship. Much of the IR literature has focused on this kind of power. The United States was more powerful than the Soviet Union, Iraq, and Japan when it forced the Soviets to withdraw their missiles from Cuba, when it drove the Iraqis out of Kuwait, and when it made the Japanese "voluntarily" reduce their exports to the United States. It is controlling power possessed and exercised by one actor over another. It is relational because it is seen if and only if it is being exercised between the power wielder and the power recipient.

This use of power as a command relationship is implied in the Weberian understanding of power as the force that overcomes resistance. In an interactive process the two opposite poles are entangled in a struggle as the thesis and antithesis. It is assumed that one of them will win out by overcoming the opposite and eliminating the obstacle. Just as with two boxers in the ring, the one who defeats the other until the latter is not able to stand is the more powerful. This mindset tends to emphasize power as the force that overcomes and eliminates. Overcoming and eliminating often imply hard and superior might and it is usually destructive forces. In international relations, it is frequently the power to wage and win wars. After WWII, since the Allies defeated the Axis, the former was more powerful. Indicators of power usually refer to those power elements that can be converted into actual influencing forces in war. To overcome, to defeat, and to conquer describe a mindset about power: winning in a conflict by conquering the rival and overcoming the opposite. Coercive power as relations expresses a command relationship, a power relationship between the victorious and the defeated, the conqueror and the conquered, the winner and the loser, and the ruler and the ruled. The former is the power wielder, while the latter the power recipient. This understanding of power has for a long time dominated the study of international politics. To a considerably large extent, it is still the case.

It may be argued that soft power is much less so because the relationship it expresses is more an attractive one and represents the ability to co-opt rather than to coerce. However, the basic definition of power applies to soft power, too. It is the ability to influence, to change the behavior of others, and to enable the desired outcome to materialize. It is also a control relationship, but it is control of the mind rather than the body; it is influence to change preferences rather than immediate behavior. It requires people to learn to understand what is good and what is bad, and then to take action accordingly. If we define soft power as a relationship, it is one that differs more in form than in content. It uses a different means, intending to reach the same end. By Nye's definition, attraction aims at change – change others' mind and then change of their behavior will inevitably follow, and, as Nye himself says, coercive power and co-optive power differ only in degree.[56]

In this respect, it is worth noticing the "compulsory power" identified by Barnett and Duvall, which can be both hard and soft. Fundamentally, they interpret power as social relations.[57] They argue, for example, that the realist definition of power, relying heavily on material resources and focusing on the effect of coercion, is more compulsory, seeking direct control by one actor over the other. Compulsory power is most explicitly agential, for it is one actor using her resources to shape directly the circumstances or actions of another. Such power is reflected by relations between actors, between the power wielder and the recipient. They point out in particular that "compulsory power typically rests on the resources that are deployed by A to exercise power directly over B,"[58] which are not necessarily material. Non-governmental organizations, for example, "have deployed normative resources to compel targeted states to alter their policies through a strategy of shaming."[59] It is thus very much soft power possessed by an agent and used to shape or change another's preference and behavior. It is reasonable to argue that soft power can be compulsory and coercive, even though it does not employ resources in a violent way. For some, control of the mind means control of the body; for some others, control of the mind is even more coercive than control of behavior, no matter what means is employed.

Structural Power as Relations

Structural power is relational, too. It is not like agential power that constitutes a one-to-one relationship, indicating one actor's influence over the other. Structural power is impersonal, embedded in systemic structures and reflected by influencing processes that regulate and constitute agents. Institutional structures, such as the structure in the international economic domain pillared by the IMF, the World Trade Organization, and the World Bank, are impersonal. They are not owned by any particular actor and it is not easy to identify who possesses them.

---

[56] Nye 2002, 176.   [57] Barnett and Duvall 2005.   [58] Ibid., 51.   [59] Ibid., 50.

But they are powerful through their rules that influence the behavior of actors engaged in world economic transactions.

The three mainstream American international theories in fact are all centered on power as relations, identifying power at the level of the international system and placing emphasis on how such structural ability regulates or constitutes agents, even though what they define as the most important power element differs. Radical IR theories do the same, perhaps even more, but the difference is that they see such power in today's world as more evil than good and should be overthrown perhaps through revolutionary changes. What I term "structural power" here refers largely to power embedded in the international system itself rather than with individual actors, even though it may favor some actors to the disadvantage of others. For structural realism, neoliberalism, and structural constructivism, the force that influences outcomes and shapes identities is systemic in nature, coming from the structure of capabilities, institutions, or norms. Structural power is indeed powerful because most of the narratives, discourses, and actions are derived and justified by and through the given structure, which determines the action, position, and identity of every unit inside through its meaning system. The three mainstream IR theories have in fact treated systemic forces as properties of the system and as the power wielder, and take units as objects of the impersonal systemic structure and as recipients of the structural power. Such structural power may not clearly show itself in specific dyadic interactions, but is able to regulate, sometimes decisively, actors in their behavior and shape and change their mind as well.

Two important features reflect the relational nature of structural power. First, it works in and through the relationship between structures as the power wielder on the one hand and actors in the structure as power recipients on the other hand. It produces an effect on actors and its effect is shown in the process of influencing the actors in question. Power recipients may obviously change their behavior. A bipolar structure may influence the behavior of states in such an international system, for example, to bandwagon with or to balance against one of the two superpowers that constitute the major poles; a liberal international trade regime may encourage free trade policy of member states and discourage and even punish those who exercise mercantilism; and a Lockean ideational structure produces the norm of sovereignty that prohibits a state from invading the generally recognized territory of another state. Moreover, it does not only exercise power over an actor in a behavioral relationship. It also reflects a constitutive relationship in which actors are made what they are with their identities and interests.[60] The Nazi regime had turned Jews into beasts and demons and had effectively taught other people in German society to accept, sometimes quite willingly, this distorted image it had framed for the Jews. It changed the identity of the Jews and the mind of the Germans. The capitalist system structures the relationship between capital and labor, defining the former as the exploiter and the latter as the exploited. UNESCO, as an important international organization, teaches developing countries what their identities are and what their interests should be in accordance with such identities.[61] Power at the systemic level constitutes identities of actors in the system and makes them what they are through a teacher-student or an authoritative relationship. It is control, and it is more than a direct control over others. All the systemic forces in these theories have a strong and loud power tone and the effect of the structural power, no matter how it is defined, is reflected in the relationship between the impersonal power wielder and the personified actors as the power recipients. Power at the systemic level, functioning as an influence and command relationship, does not differ much from power at the agential level.

Second, structural power is relational because it is the structure that defines the relational positions of actors in the system and thus defines the nature of their relationships. The power at the systemic level makes an uneven balance of relational positions a reality. Structural power is the power embedded in the structure of the international system, constituting the social capacities and interests of actors. The distribution of positions of actors in the system constitutes a structure, which in turn defines, enables, and consolidates such positions. In a structural universe, State A exists only by virtue of its relation to State B, or A's position can be defined only by B or B's position in relation to A. Structural power can be either material or ideational. The Confucian description of the Chinese socio-political system illustrates such a distribution of relationships, for example, between the emperor and ministers, father and sons, and so on. The structurally defined relationship gives the former more power because of his positioning in the structure. These relationships in turn sustain and maintain the socio-political order. The structural power defined by world system theory provides another example.[62] It is the global capitalist system that makes possible a center-periphery world and perpetuates its division of labor. As a result, actors' positions toward one another are defined as center, semi-peripheral, and peripheral countries, each having its role identity in the system. Developed capitalist

---

[60] Barnett and Duvall 2005, 46.   [61] Finnemore 1996.
[62] Wallerstein 1974; Shannon 1989. See also Frank and Gills 1993.

states at the center are privileged because of their positioning in this global capitalist system which provides them with power to control peripheral countries more the other way round. To some extent, the power or the lack of power of center, semi-peripheral, and peripheral countries are determined by their different positions, the structure of which in turn consolidates the division of labor, the power relationships, and the world capitalist system *per se*. Global social fabrics sustain the structure in terms of the distribution of relations, which in turn defines the nature of power relationships among its members and privileges some over others. The global system itself is power, directly shaping the conditions and actions of actors and exerting influence on the outcomes of their interactions.

To sum up, agential power and structural power are identified and defined in terms of the location of power resources. They have bases at different levels, but they share common features as to how influence is exercised. Behind this kind of conceptualization there is an ontological position, that is, ontologically, power bears a conspicuous mark of subjectivity and describes a subject-object relationship. It is owned and used by a clearly defined independent and sovereign entity. It can be a specific agent; and it can be a personified impersonal structure. But the ownership is almost always exclusive. This way of conceptualizing power goes with the ontology of self-existence, which stresses the individual being as the starting point of almost everything under the sun. The priority of this ontology naturally sees power as some indispensable attribute of the individual entity and denies other features of power in the first place. Foucault's concept of power is said to be subject-less.[63] It is everywhere and influences everyone, while no specific owner can be identified. It does, however, imply a subject – the overt structure of the dominant ideology and the covert structure of the background knowledge (*episteme*). It is some momentary configuration of historical processes into a structure that permeates and dominates, or some articulate emergence of historical *a priori* that influences and controls because of being taken for granted. Furthermore, since it is taken for granted, it is not seen as a structure, or it is an invisible structure that rules.

Power as Exchange Relations

From the discussion in the previous sections and with this ontological position of subjectivity in the backdrop, we can see that the conceptual treatment of power by the mainstream IR theory has a few specific

---

[63] Foucault 1991.

features. First, power is exercising influence by using resources, both material and ideational. Power is essentially relational, because power exists and is shown in a relationship. It is done in the process involving the power wielder and the power recipient. Power resource is an important aspect and it is true that without resources power is deprived of its foundation. Power resources, however, are potential at the best and their transformation into influence is accomplished only in and through relations among actors. Second, it is largely a zero-sum game. What realists understand as hard power is obviously coercive and the often used example of pointing a gun at somebody's head reveals the zero-sum nature. Soft power, despite the claim that it is not coercive but attractive, also tells of a winner-loser relationship, because the power recipient will change her behavior and mind "willingly" according to the values and desires of the power wielder. It aims to change the mind of the power recipient rather than merely her behavior. It is a zero-sum game at a deeper level and in a more subtle and penetrating way. Structural power is no exception, no matter whether it is to change actors' behavior or mind. Third, it is unidirectional. It always flows from the power wielder to the power recipient. At the agential level, influence flows directly from the former to the latter, and at the systemic level, it comes down from the structural level to units in the system. The three American mainstream theories, for example, all focus on the influence of the systemic forces, capabilities, institutions, or ideas, over actors in the international system. The more structural and abstract the theories are, the more exercise of power becomes a one-way traffic. A structural emphasis necessitates the elimination or assimilation of the agency, both in body and mind, through changing it and remaking it. It is perhaps a more thorough uni-directional power relationship and produces both causal and constitutive effects. It tends to be zero-sum, for it implies the assumption that homogeneity in a given structural space is the ideal living habitat.

The unilaterality and zero-sum character, which are in fact two related assumptions, reflect how the mainstream IR literature conceptualizes power. Simply put, power is a relationship that is a one-way influence and a win-lose game. It is the power possessed by the power wielder as her private property that is used as influence to make the power recipient do what otherwise the latter would not do or to change the circumstances of the recipient so that the latter will follow the will and wish of the former or rules and norms made by the former. Simply put, it is power that goes from the former to the latter. This uni-directionality has been produced through the overall understanding of power as a force of conquering and dominating. It is in the very beginning doomed to be a zero-sum game, implying at the same time an emphasis on outcomes or on results. Even the complex interdependence argument, which implies that power may come from relations rather than from one's own attributes, holds that asymmetrical interdependence gives the less dependent more power, enabling it to influence un-directionally the more dependent, who are obviously trapped in the situation of vulnerability interdependence.[64] Power as relations, a concept reflected in numerous analyses represented by Dahl, is exactly such a unilateral and zero-sum relationship. Even though power as exchange relations has been discussed and quite widely accepted in domestic politics, it is not an argument as widely accepted in IR. On the contrary, the mainstream IR literature on power takes it essentially as a private property, sovereign, sacred, and ready for the exclusive use by its owner in order to gain benefits, either through violent or non-violent means.

The relational theory, while recognizing all the negative aspects of power, also posits that power is an exchange relationship with great potential as a positive factor. Relational power exists in a power relationship, involving the power wielder and the power recipient. In this respect, it is not much different from hard or soft power. But since the resources of relational power are shared in the first place and cannot be absolutely possessed by the actor who may serve as the power wielder at the moment, it reflects by nature as well as by necessity an exchange relationship. In other words, at the moment the actor uses the power she shares with or "borrows" from another actor in her relational circles to achieve her personal objectives, she is ready, as well as expected, to return this favor in the future. If one owns something exclusively by oneself, one may use it without thinking about repaying. But if one uses something that is jointly owned and even borrowed, a kind of exchange is already there inherently in one's action of using or borrowing it. It is not like the power relationship described in the mainstream IR literature, with one wielding power and the other receiving it, or one influencing and the other being influenced. Relational power as relations excludes unilaterality. From the very beginning it is a two-way traffic with exchange as its defining characteristic.

Price as the Mechanism for Power as an Exchange Relation

Power as an exchange relationship is not a new concept in political science despite the fact that it has not been widely accepted in IR studies. In his 1971 article "Money and power," for example, David Baldwin unambiguously argued that power is a kind of exchange.[65] If power is an

---

[64] Keohane and Nye 2001.   [65] Baldwin 1971, 592.

exchange relationship, it requires a mechanism to make the exchange possible. Power analysts have tried to identify such a mechanism and there are mainly two views in the Western power narrative, price and institution. The former relies on the cost-benefit calculation inspired by economics, arguing that it is the price that enables power as an exchange relationship, while the latter stresses the role of the institutionalized rule. Such rules, which perform the function of general governance, guarantee that each time the power wielder influences the power recipient gives the latter an opportunity to become a power wielder in future and sees to it that the overall opportunities of influencing and being influenced are fairly distributed and exchanged.

David Baldwin stands for the price mechanism. He discusses from an economic perspective the mechanism that enables power to be an exchange relationship and his focus is price. He posits that power as exchange is accomplished if the price is right. There are two successive steps in his argument. First of all he agrees with the viewpoint that power is an exchange relationship. He has discussed this dimension of power in detail, starting from his careful analysis of the analogy of power as money. He criticizes the statement by Karl Deutsch and Talcott Parsons that power to politics is what money is to economics, arguing that money is only a medium for exchange while power is itself what is exchanged.[66] Power is the essence and substance of politics. It is not a mere medium like money in economics. For Baldwin, therefore, power is neither the means nor the currency of politics. Power is more like purchasing power. It is not a symbolic medium of exchange; rather it is the substantial thing to be symbolized. He says, "power is not a symbol of the ability to change results; it *is* the ability to change results."[67] He also compares power to direct barter trade in economics, because this type of trade is an exchange without a medium. It is "probably more useful to consider power as a kind of exchange rather than to consider it as a medium of exchange."[68] Through criticizing the argument that power is a medium for exchange he has reinforced the view that power itself is an exchange relation.

That power itself is an exchange relation is perhaps the most insightful and crucial insight in Baldwin's discussion of power, for power is exchangeable if and only if it is something to be exchanged rather than something to symbolize exchange. It seems to him that political science, unfortunately (or perhaps fortunately), lacks exactly a standard measure, a generally accepted medium like money in economics, but it does not change the nature of power as exchange. Exchange does not necessarily mean a symmetrical one. The actor who is wielding power simultaneously

[66] Ibid.   [67] Ibid., 589, emphasis in original.   [68] Ibid., 592.

provides the power recipient with a choice and should take an opportunity cost if the recipient is reluctant to do what is required. It is because of this economic understanding of power that Baldwin argues that in such a situation "A influences B to do X, but B's reluctance to do X also affects A's behavior."[69] In other words, even in an asymmetrical power relationship exchange exists because both the power wielder and the power recipient have a cost to pay. For this reason, all exchange relationships can be described in terms of power concepts and most power relationships can be described in exchange terminology.[70]

Having made a strong argument for conceptualizing power as an exchange relation, Baldwin precedes to identify the main mechanism for power to be an exchange relation. He argues that price is the main mechanism that makes power as exchange possible. If power is an exchange relationship, such a deal is done if the price is right. He compares political power to purchasing power in economics, arguing that purchasing is an exchange relation, involving both a buyer and a seller and can be done if the highest price the buyer is willing to pay overlaps with the lowest price the seller is willing to accept.[71] Exchange of goods or services is another example, for direct barter trade is an exchange deal which is done if the two sides feel the price is right for the exchanged goods or services. It constitutes an exchange relation because the price mechanism determines that it rests largely on a voluntary basis. Baldwin says:

In other words, the likelihood that B will perform X may depend on the sanction (positive or negative) provided by A. Supply and demand schedules may thus be considered as describing a kind of power relationship. To ask whether B is "willing" to do X is like asking whether General Motors is "willing" to provide you with a car. Neither question can be answered satisfactorily until the price is specified or implied.[72]

It is in this respect that Baldwin considers power relations completely in terms of economic exchange: With the right price the transaction is done and cooperation accomplished. An extreme example may be what realists often use: You do whatever you are asked to do when a gun is pointed at your head. Even in that situation where realists see more coercion and reluctance, Baldwin sees more volition. It is again the price that decides the exchange. The realist assumes that every human being takes her life before everything else, for life is priceless and survival is the most fundamental human desire. But Baldwin holds that if one thinks her life is worth little, she may not obey even if a gun is being pointed at her head.

[69] Baldwin 1978, 1237.   [70] Baldwin 1978.   [71] Ibid., 1232   [72] Ibid.

If a religious person believes that her sacrifice will bring her an eternally glorious life in the next world, she will prefer to die for her belief. Political and social exchange is similar in essence to economic exchange and they differ in only one thing: The former does not have a generalized medium. But it does not affect the essential similarity. The demand and supply pattern decides the price and the price decides whether or not power can be an exchange relation. Thus, for Baldwin, the "apothegm that 'every man has his price' is no doubt false, but it represents an analytical perspective that is more useful than the perspective that depicts people as 'acting against their wills'."[73]

Baldwin provides valuable inspiration on the conceptualization of power. His main contribution is to change the dominant view which takes power as a unilaterally relational practice. It refutes mainstream IR theories which tend to take power as a domineering relationship, as a force that makes others do what they do not want to do, and as a zero-sum game in which only the power wielder gains. The argument of power as exchange relations implies the positive side of power. Power as exchange is fundamentally different from power as domination, for the former may well imply a gain-gain situation while the latter always sees a gain-loss game. If we consider power as the use of what one possesses to get what one wants by overcoming the resistance of the other, or in Dahl's words, by making the other do what she is not willing to do, then power is no other than a process in which one conquers the other. Any power game then is necessarily a zero-sum game. In this respect, Baldwin's argument is remarkable, for he sees the positive and non-zero-sum nature of power if it is taken as exchange rather than domination. Power as exchange, therefore, is based on a voluntary basis, implies the potential for cooperation, and provides for social actors to gain mutual benefits through a power relationship. But, as any exchange in a market, power is first of all the possession of an individual actor. Baldwin's theory has further reinforced this argument.

Institutionalized Rules as a Mechanism for Power as an Exchange Relation

Baldwin's price mechanism inspires efforts to conceptualize power as an exchange relation. At the same time, however, the price rule has a serious flaw. It implies that power as relations may well be used for a single deal while it fails to see power as exchange relations in a more lasting and sustainable way. As in barter trade, the two sides have done a deal with

[73] Ibid.

both offering the right price, but they may never meet and do business again. The price rule can work as a mechanism that enables power to be an exchange relation, but may not sustain power as such. The argument that power is an exchange relation does not necessarily mean that power is maintained sustainably as exchange relationships. What is the factor or mechanism that is able to keep power as an exchange relationship? There must be something that works to play this function. It seems that Baldwin's more purely economic perspective cannot explain this puzzle well. It seems that he has not even considered this question.

It is most inspiring here to think about Haugaard's discussion about power, although it is not in the field of international relations. For Haugaard, the institutionalized rule is the key mechanism that guarantees a power game as a repeated and long-lasting exchange relationship. He starts with a distinction between domination (power over) and empowerment (power to), or simply put, good power and bad power.[74] He holds that power can be used to dominate or to empower, for during the process of exercising power both positive-sum and zero-sum results can be produced. Normatively desirable power exists side by side with power to dominate, though power as domination has been the focus of discussion in political studies. He further argues that any form of power, power over or power to, can be normatively commendable or lamentable, depending on whether the process will eventually lead to positive-sum or zero-sum results. Even power of domination, defined as Dahl has done in terms of making others do what otherwise they would not do, cannot be reduced simply to coercion of domination, for it may produce positive-sum results. For Haugaard, good power is non-zero sum or positive-sum power, which empowers both the party that exercises power and the party that is the recipient.

At the deeper level, what tells good power from bad power is whether or not the power wielder takes the recipient as a means to an end. It concerns a fundamental question of our discussion here. If Baldwin's discussion on power as exchange relationships is more in terms of specific outcomes, such as the analogy of purchasing power and barter trade, Haugaard's analysis focuses more on institutionalized and internalized rules. He borrows Wong's and Clegg's typology of power as episodic and dispositional, pointing out that dispositional power "constitutes the structured rules of the game, defining the dispositions of actors over time."[75] General elections, for example, are so structured that this time Candidate A wins, only to indicate that the next time Candidates B or C may win. If each episodic power exercised is a reinforcement of the

---

[74] Haugaard 2012.   [75] Ibid., 37.

dispositional power, the power recipient then is not taken as a means. Rather both the power wielder and recipient are empowered. In other words, the structured institutional rule guarantees power as a sustainable exchange relationship.

Haugaard takes power as an exchange relationship, too, but places more emphasis on the mechanism of institutionalized rules to sustain such exchange. Each power wielder is at the same time a future power recipient and her exercise of power this time empowers the recipient to wield power next time. The emphasis on this dimension of power as normatively desirable has indeed value added, compared with Baldwin's argument for power as exchange relations. It refers no longer to a specific exchange situation. Rather it structures a general game that underlies and sustains the exchange nature of power relations. In addition, it adds to Baldwin's argument that taking power as exchange relations may help people realize the positive dimension of power rather than merely the negative effects, as he argues: "Exchange is often depicted as mutually rewarding and beneficial, while power relations are often portrayed as based on negative sanctions and detrimental to the object of the influence attempt."[76] Haugaard tells us clearly why exchange power relations can be good and produce win-win results.

"Renqing" as a Mechanism for Power as an Exchange Relation

Baldwin's mechanism is economic and Haugaard's legal-political. The relational perspective, while recognizing that the price and institutionalized rule can both serve as mechanisms to enable or perpetuate power as an exchange relationship, argues that there is another factor, a more processual and human factor that works as an important mechanism to maintain power as an exchange relationship. It is what the Chinese call "*renqing*," which constitutes an inseparable part of relationality. In Chinese communities, *renqing* is the main mechanism to maintain the exchangeability of power relations and constitutes a significant practice that maintains relations among social actors.[77] It is human and social.

Renqing literally means "human feelings" or "human sentiments." However, it is a most elusive term and has much richer meanings in a relational society.[78] Three of them may be particularly noteworthy when we discuss the social aspect of power. First, *renqing* is a resource for

---

[76] Baldwin 1978, 72.
[77] Hwang 1987; see also Hwang Hu et al. 2004; Gold, Guthrie, and Wank 2002.
[78] Zhai 2005, 84–90.

exchange.[79] It can be material. If a friend falls into a serious illness and lacks money for hospitalization, one may well offer the money in need. If a country suffers from a huge natural disaster such as an earthquake or a tsunami, other countries may offer assistance in cash or kind. Usually more friendly countries may offer more assistance. It can also be non-material. One may offer solace to the friend in illness to show one's care and sympathy. However, no matter what kind of help one offers, the case is usually one in which the helper and the recipient are related and the purpose is usually to maintain and strengthen the relationship. It differs from purely economic understanding that exchange is being carried out between things that are appropriately priced. It is human in the first place, as the semantics of the word "*renqing*" shows. In addition, it can be quite instrumental. One may ask somebody to do her a *renqing* (meaning here "do her a favor") for purely instrumental purposes, getting oneself a good job, for example. It can also be done without instrumental purposes. You help a friend simply because she is your friend. In most cases it is mixed, combining instrumental and sentimental purposes. Thus the debate among sociologists over whether *renqing* is instrumental or sentimental is meaningless, for it is a mixture of feelings and obligations in most cases. Human feelings, including sympathy, care, and love, need to be expressed in concrete and sometimes material ways, and similarly obligations seldom involve no human feelings.[80] For me, the most important is that human relatedness is the context where *renqing* is practiced. Even if a *renqing* is for some obvious instrumental purpose, it is more likely to be required by and done to someone who is somewhat related rather than a complete stranger. Whatever the intention or effect is, *renqing* is done usually between actors who are related with each other. The more intimate they are, the more likely a *renqing* is done between them.

Second, *renqing* is a social practice, characterized by reciprocal human feelings and obligations through the norm of "*bao* (roughly meaning 'reciprocity')." In fact it is more like the *habitus* in Bourdieu's terminology and embedded deeply in the background knowledge of Chinese communities. "Do a *renqing*" and "return a *renqing*" is what members of a Chinese community do without even thinking about it. It is their way of exchange. *Bao* means that the act of "*zuo renqing* (doing a *renqing* or doing somebody a favor)," is expected to be returned or "*huan renqing* (returning or repaying a *renqing* or favor)." In this respect it has long become a practice-based social norm, that is, the norm of "*bao*" constitutes the key part of

---

[79] For example, Hwang argues that *renqing* is a resource for one to present to another. But he also believes that *renqing* is a medium of exchange. In fact, *renqing* is something to be exchanged rather than something as a medium for such exchange. See Hwang 1987, 954.

[80] Kipnis 2002.

renqing. It is in general quite similar to reciprocity, even similar to the "tit-for-tat" strategy in game language. But it differs from the exact meaning of reciprocity in the fact that it has much less emphasis on an exchange relationship in the economic sense, for *renqing* is not something one can make a precise evaluation of in monetary terms and therefore cannot be returned with something of equal values. Nobody can correctly evaluate the right price of a *renqing*. The reciprocation of *renqing* can be material. If somebody helps you with some money, for example, you can return this with equal amount of money. It is different from borrowing money from a stranger or a financial institution. As the borrower and the lender are friends or related in some way, you do not have to repay the money with interest if you are the borrower, and you do not need to specify when the money should be repaid if you are the lender. One even does not have to return the money at all but repay this *renqing* in some other ways. It can also be an exchange of feelings or sentiments. This reflects even more the original meaning of *renqing*, because its basic meaning is human feelings. Your friend has offered you some help when you need it, then you may return it with a gift, which may not be as valuable in monetary terms, but reflects your thanks in a sincere way. As the Chinese idiom goes, "*liqing qingyizhong* (The gift is trifling but the sentiment is profound)." Thus the exchange is not on an equal-value basis, nor is it carried out according to a contract, but on a basis that takes human relations into serious consideration. The *renqing* in an exchange relationship therefore can be exchange of feelings, of material things, or feelings and material things mixed together. It is a resource that indicates the exchange nature of power relations through the norm of *bao*.

Third, *renqing* is the maintainer of relationships among actors. A favor as a resource may not be returned if it is expected that the doer and recipient will never meet again. Reciprocation of *renqing*, however, is carried out only when both sides expect that they will meet again and their relationship will continue in the future. This way *renqing* is done and returned as a maintainer and enhancer of relations between the doer and the recipient through reciprocation. It is exactly this function of *renqing* that makes it the main mechanism for keeping human relations. In Confucian or Confucian-influenced communities, as discussed above, *bao* is an important social norm, which itself indicates the mechanism for maintaining relations. There are three important measures concerning *renqing* for maintaining and strengthening interpersonal ties. The first is "*zuo renqing* (do a favor)," indicating the establishment of a relationship. Imagine a situation where there are two actors, A and B, who do not know each other before a *renqing* is done. Once a *renqing* is done, both the doer A and the recipient B are no longer strangers and they are related by this first *renqing* deal. When A is offering the favor, B simultaneously owes A a "*renqing zhai* (a debt of *renqing*, or a debt of gratitude)." Then it is "*huan renqing* (return the favor) by B." Thirdly, once a *renqing* is done and then is repaid, the cycle of *renqing* reciprocation starts. It is this cycle of *renqing* reciprocation that makes this *zuo renqing* and *huan renqing* a lasting process in which the doer and recipient take turns and change roles constantly. In other words they both do and return *renqing*, a process which can consolidate and enhance their relationship continually. It is neither a clearly institutionalized rule nor a legally enforceable contract. It is a practice.

Think about this mechanism in terms of power as an exchange relationship. There are two actors A and B, who do not know each other at the beginning. Actor A has a power resource X, and Actor B needs to use A's power resource X. B first tries to get to know A and thus completes the initial step which aims to relate oneself to A in some way. Once they get to know each other, B may ask A to do her a favor by letting her use A's power resource and she gets it, then A and B start a power exchange relationship. B shares A's resource and realizes her material or nonmaterial purposes. The moment she uses B's resource, she implies an agreement that she will return B in the future by, for example, letting B use her resources. B is prepared to lend her power resource Y and makes it available for A to use. This reciprocal exchange of power resources between A and B not only satisfies both of their interests, but also enhances their bilateral relationship through power exchange. In this respect, it is somewhat similar to "gift economy." In an interesting article entitled "The Cornucopia of the Commons," David Bollier says, "Capital is something that is depleted as it is used. But a gift economy has an inherently expansionary dynamic, growing the more that it is used."[81] Relational resources always increase by use, decrease by infrequent use, and are depleted by non-use.

Power as a Co-empowering Process

We have just compared the three different mechanisms for enabling power as an exchange relationship. Baldwin's price mechanism rests more on the economic basis, arguing for the likelihood of exchange with an appropriate price. Haugaard's mechanism is an institutional mechanism, stressing the institutionalized rule that guarantees power as a sustainable exchange relationship. What I have proposed from a relational perspective is the *renqing* practice that sustains power relations

[81] Bollier 2001, 2.

as a process of reciprocal exchange. If the price mechanism is based more on economic consideration and the institutional mechanism more on legal-political authority, the *renqing* mechanism is more human, involving both material and non-material, and both obligatory and sentimental. It is embedded in practice-produced background knowledge and appears as a taken-for-granted social norm.

Whatever difference lies among the three mechanisms, taking power as exchange relations tends to see more the positive side of power. It forms a sharp contrast to the mainstream IR power literature. One of the most distinct features of power conceptualized in the mainstream IR literature, as we discussed in the previous sections, is its negative connotations, such as forces to conquer, to command, and to overcome resistance. It is unilateral and unidirectional, tending to produce a zero-sum result. It is the power possessed by the power wielder as her private property that is used as influence to make the power recipient do what otherwise the latter would not do or to change the circumstances so that the latter will follow the rules and norms made by the former. Simply put, it is power that goes from the former to the latter. This unilaterality has been produced through the overall understanding of power as a force for conquering and dominating. It implies an emphasis on outcomes or on results. Even the complex interdependence argument, which implies that power may come from relations rather than from one's own attributes, holds that asymmetrical interdependence gives the less dependent power so as to be more able to influence the more dependent who suffers from the situation of vulnerability interdependence.[82]

The conceptualization of power as an exchange relationship denies most of the mainstream arguments about power. The highly inspiring aspect is what I term the co-empowering process of power relations. If the traditional and dominant interpretation of power as negative sanctions by the self to overwhelm the other, as the ability of the self to overcome the other's reluctance, and as the force of the self to reach a zero-sum result at the cost of the other's interest, power as a co-empowering process aims to empower the self and the other and to realize a positive-sum result. Of course, co-empowering is not necessarily good, for the two parties that co-empower each other may well be engaged in something quite evil. Government officials and businesspersons can, for instance, empower each other through rent-seeking and bribing to bypass laws and realize self-interest at the cost of the public. And a co-empowering process can also be morally desirable by making both parties more powerful. What it

---

[82] Keohane and Nye 2001.

denies is a unilateral and zero-sum game usually assumed by the mainstream IR theory in its conceptualization and interpretation of power.

From the perspective of the relational theory, power is a co-empowering process due more to the exchange nature of power. In traditional Chinese philosophy, power is not only seen as a relationship. Rather power relations are taken as a process in which the two parties co-empower each other. It is not a single-move game, but a multiple and iterated interaction between the two which are immanent in the first place. The simplest illustration is again the meta-relationship between *yin* and *yang* in the Chinese *zhongyong* dialectics. This relationship contains three important messages in terms of power. First, power is shared. *Yin* and *yang* are opposites in unity and their interaction is not only intersubjective but also immanent, for they are by definition within each other, that is, "*yin*-in-*yang* and *yang*-in-*yin*." They are mere two sides of the one and same phenomenon. Since they are one, any power the self (*yin*) has is at the same time shared by the other (*yang*). Their relationship has a strong implication of power sharing, or power owned jointly by both of them. Any single pole is powerless for it is not able to make a life possible, and even cannot have life of its own. Together they are powerful. Second, *yin* and *yang* are engaged in an endless process of co-empowering each other. Since each has little power of itself, they derive power from each other in their immanent and dynamic interaction. The Chinese *zhongyong* dialectics believes that *yin* and *yang* complement each other and make up for each other's weaknesses. Thus each time they interact, they are empowered from such a dynamic relationship. Furthermore, this co-empowering process is a mutual, reciprocal, and natural give-and-take one with the influence going both ways. Both are simultaneous power wielders and recipients. Third, the final test of power is whether it is able to produce new, healthy life. It is not a domineering force that conquers and it is not a force that destroys. It is a force that produces fresh and dynamic life through a harmonizing interaction. The liveliest illustration is the relationship between a couple, who produces a new, healthy life through a co-empowering process of love. *Yin* and *yang* constitute and articulate life for each other and together they make new life through inclusive cooperation. The processual production and reproduction of life continues with activities of the two, who complement and empower each other throughout. In other words, this process is a dynamic one of co-empowering, making each other powerful enough to create new life together. It is positive, dynamic, and conducive to a win-win result.

In general, we derive from the meta-relationship of *yin* and *yang* understanding of the process as simultaneous and mutual reciprocity.

Overall across time and space, it is such a process. In specific situations where two relators interact, we may posit that co-powering activities can be in sequence. At any particular point of time and space in the process it may appear as one influencing the other. This is similar to Haugaard's understanding of episodic and dispositional power, with the former focusing on a specific outcome and the latter on the overall structures by which the rule of the game is sustained.[83] His discussion on such a process is particularly inspiring.

In a normatively legitimate structurally constituted exercise of *power over*, the gain of B is relative to future agency. Wrong (...) and Clegg (...) distinguish between the *episodic* aspect of power, which focuses upon specific outcomes, and *dispositional* power, which constitutes the structured rules of the game, defining the dispositions of actors over time. When A and B prevail over each other in a structured contest, the episodic exercise of *power over* B, contributes to the creation or recreation of the future dispositional power of both actors. In the episodic moment that A exercises *power over* B, structures are reproduced that constitute the democratic game, which gives both actors the dispositional *power to* replay. Structural reproduction entails the possibility of B exercising *power over* A at a different future episodic moment. In that sense, the dispositional power which is created in the moment of successful structural reproduction re/creates subject positions of empowerment. While the episodic power may be zero-sum (A wins and B loses), at a dispositional level the relationship is positive sum (structures are reproduced which guarantee future agency).[84]

Relational power is similar in this respect, but it is more a fluid process than a somewhat fixed structure. Imagine a situation where A uses the power resources it gains from its relationship with B and influences the outcome to be what A has desired. Thus A gains through the episodic use of relational power. Haugaard uses the example of democratic elections, which promise a winner in each general election but guarantee the possibility of all being winners. Use of power in international affairs can be similar. For example, State A, a lesser player in an international relations game, uses its relations with State B, a major power in the international system, to influence the outcome of its dealing with State C. It is no doubt that A realizes its objective at this episodic moment. However, seldom can we find that power relationship is a mere episodic occurrence, or a single-move game. It is more a repeated game, or more a continuous process of power relationships, which to some extent locks the two players in a long-term engagement. The episodic moment is thus reciprocal if it occurs among human players. In other words, the moment that A is exercising episodic power to gain its objective, it promises B to have a similar use of power in the future. The actual gains of a state in

[83] Haugaard 2012, 37.   [84] Ibid., 38, emphasis in original.

economic and financial aids may well be returned, for example, in terms of its support for the donor country in the voting in the UN General Assembly. It is the joint ownership and accessibility of relational power that disposes it to have a reciprocal nature and makes this kind of power relationship a repeated give-and-take process that may empower both.

Conclusion

Having discussed the main approaches to conceptualize power, this chapter has proposed a new way from the perspective of the relational theory. It first posits that relation is power, arguing that in terms of power as resources relations among actors constitute an important locale where power resides. While recognizing the mainstream's views of power as an individual actor's inviolable property and power as structurally embedded forces, the relational theory shifts the attention to social relations as another significant resource of power. Then it suggests that power is a reciprocal exchange relationship maintained and sustained by the *renqing* mechanism through the social and moral norm of *bao*. It agrees with the argument that power is an exchange relationship, but differs in terms of its mechanism. The *renqing* practice with *bao* as its core differs from an exclusively economic mechanism such as the price for exchange and from a more legal and institutional mechanism such as the rule for general elections. The *renqing* is more a practice deeply embedded in the background knowledge of a cultural community with human feelings and personal interests comingling together. It is sentimental and obligatory reciprocity. Power taken from relations and exchanged among relators tends to form a reciprocal cycle, which develops into a continual process in which both parties to power are engaged in a "power-from and power-to" game. Power therefore is a co-empowering process. It is most conspicuously expressed in Confucian societies, but exists in various degrees in all types of human societies.

The three interrelated arguments concerning the reconceptualization of power from the perspective of the relational theory may well lead to a redefinition of power in a world of relatedness. If power as a resource may come from relations among actors and is sharable in the first place, if power as relations indicates a reciprocal exchange relationship, and if a cycle of reciprocation of material and emotional credits and debts constitutes a co-empowering process, then power is no longer merely the ability to control the behavior of others and to influence the outcome of an event. Power is not expressed in the self's ability to produce influence over a particular other, to overcome resistance, and to dominate. It is the ability to enable the co-empowering process to go smoothly on so that all parties involved are empowered in one way or another. It is the ability to orchestrate and cope with relations.

Thus I define power as the ability to manage relations. That relation is power refers to power resources or potential power, while management of relations signifies influence or actual power. You need to manage relations as a power resource so that you can have an ample supply of power resources ready for use; you need to manage power as relations so that you have more positive relationships with others to produce influence and desirable results; and you need to manage the most complex human relations so that the reciprocal cycle of benefit giving and taking is able to empower all parties, including yourself in the process. Defining power this way, I try to add an important aspect to the existing conceptualization of power, which, I admit, has identified some most significant aspects of power, such as its resources and its effect as influence. What I add is that relation is power, an aspect the mainstream tends to overlook. Moreover, I want to open the concept of power to a wider horizon. Power can be quite repellent and repressive, but can also be quite positive and productive. Power can be quite unilateral and unidirectional, but can also be mutual and reciprocal. Power can be the ability to overcome and dominate, but can also be the ability to empower and energize. Power destroys life but produces life as well. Life-producing power is more powerful. Since all these functions happen in a world of relations and relatedness, a most significant ability is the ability to manage relations, where power resides and from where it comes.

9   Cooperation in a Relational World

What promotes cooperation among social actors? What constitute formidable obstacles to such cooperation? These are questions that have persistently puzzled scholars of the social sciences who have tried directly or indirectly to provide some answers. It is particularly true in international relations, for the international system is assumed as an anarchic world where self-help is a characteristic feature.[1] Self-interest has thus become the eye-catching concept in discussing international cooperation and the cost-benefit ratio a key term for any individual and rational actor to weigh before taking action. Whenever the perceived benefit is less than the cost, cooperation fails, even at the expense of the collective good.

This line of reasoning is based on a deeply embedded worldview, which presumes the world as an atomistic one, composed of independent and discrete individual actors. The self-organizing nature of such actors decides that they can independently and rationally decide their own interest. Survival, for example, is defined by most realist IR scholars as the fundamental interest of a nation-state. Game theory, prisoner's dilemma (PD) in particular, exemplifies how rational selfish players interact. Exclusive self-interest constitutes the most formidable obstacle to cooperation. It is perhaps true that in such a world "evolution competition is based on a fierce competition between individuals and should therefore reward only selfish behavior."[2]

However, if we take a different worldview, what shall we see? What facilitates cooperation and what constitute serious obstacles to cooperation? To answer such questions, I am turning back to the relational theory of world politics, which sees the international relations world not as one of discrete individual actors, but as one of relations.[3] Relatedness, rather than individualistic rationality, is thus the keyword in this relational world. Accordingly, I argue that the more positively related human actors are, the more likely it is that they cooperate. Then I proceed to discuss the

[1] Waltz 1979; Keohane 1984; Oye 1986. See also Buzan, Jones, and Little 1993.
[2] Nowak 2006, 1560.   [3] Qin 2016a.

289

key question concerning barriers to cooperation from the perspective of my relational theory. I will argue that the kinsperson's dilemma (KD) or an extended form of it, that is, relator's dilemma (RD), is a real and one of the most serious problems in cooperation and it can hardly be solved through rational calculation of self-interest or through legally defined rights and obligations.

Cooperation Construed by the Mainstream IR Theory

The mainstream IR theory has discussed cooperation, which constitutes one of the most important concepts, together with conflict, in the IR discourse up to date. Many IR works have tried to reveal how cooperation can be possible in an anarchic international system and the three major theories in the United States, namely, neorealism, neoliberal institutionalism, and constructivism, have all identified some important mechanisms for international cooperation to be materialized. In sum, they advocate force, institutions, and norms as promoters of cooperation.

Forced Cooperation

Forced cooperation is what realism largely believes in in the anarchic international system. Realists are pessimistic about international cooperation, arguing that the most fundamental need of the state is survival, which is constantly threatened in anarchy. Conflict of interest among states is normal, very often seen as a zero-sum game due to the dominance of the survival theme. In the debate between realism and liberalism over the "relative vs absolute gains" problem in the 1980s–1990s, realists held that actors seek relative gains rather than absolute gains because only relative gains matter in terms of survival in the international system. As a most articulate realist, Joseph M. Grieco in the debate argues, *"the fundamental goal of states in any relationship is to prevent others from achieving advances in their relative capabilities."*[4] In other words, it does not matter to only talk about how powerful you yourself are. What really counts is how powerful you are if compared with other actors. Even if you gain absolutely in the interaction, others may gain even more than you do. In the long run, they will be more powerful than you and take advantage because of their power edge, dominating and even eliminating you. International politics is a tragic power game and out-powering your competitor is what a nation-state should seek and has in fact always sought.

---

[4] Grieco 1988, 127, emphasis in original. Also in Baldwin 1993.

Representative of this realist argument, Kenneth Waltz holds that cooperation in anarchy is difficult because the relative gain consideration is a genuine problem produced by the structure of the international system. As he pointed out as early as in his 1959 work, "relative gain is more important that absolute gain."[5] He makes some detailed comments on the relationship between relative gains and international cooperation as follows:

In a self-help system each of the units spends a portion of its effort, not in forwarding its own goods, but in providing the means of protecting itself against others ... When faced with the possibility of cooperating for mutual gain, states that feel insecure must ask about how the gain will be divided. They are compelled to ask not "Will both of us gain?" but "Who will gain more?" If an expected gain is to be divided, say, in the ratio of two to one, one state may use its disproportionate gain to implement a policy intended to damage or destroy the other. Even the prospect of large absolute gains for both parties does not elicit their cooperation so long as each fears how the other will use its increased capabilities. Notice that the impediments to collaboration may not lie in the character and the immediate intention of either party. Instead, the condition of insecurity – at the least, the uncertainty of each about the other's future intentions and actions – works against their cooperation.[6]

Realists thus hold that the key question is survival, which depends on the capabilities to defend oneself from domination and destruction in the anarchic international system. In addition, even if one's survival and physical elimination is not at issue, gaps in gains may also cause the actor to worry, because over time they will make the disadvantaged side more dependent on the advantaged side. "A state may also worry lest it become dependent on others through cooperative endeavors and exchanges of goods and services."[7] Both destruction and loss of independence are real concerns of a state in the anarchic international system. For this reason, realists cast serious doubt on international cooperation. In domestic politics, there is the political authority that promotes cooperation through coercive measures if possible. In international anarchy, however, there is no such authority. Therefore, for players in the game of international politics, cooperation, though not completely impossible, may well increase the relative power of the specific other and put the self in a weaker position. Since the "relative gains" problem occurs very often in international relations, it is thus reasonable to argue that cooperation is "harder to achieve, more difficult to maintain, and more dependent on state power than is appreciated by the institutionalist tradition."[8]

[5] Waltz 1959, 198.   [6] Waltz 1979, 105.   [7] Ibid., 106.   [8] Grieco 1988, 302.

Following the realist argument, we may imagine three situations where an international actor is willing to cooperate. First, it is when both actors have equal gains from their cooperation.[9] It stands in theory, but can hardly be found in reality. Even if there is some agreement that promises equal gains, as Powell points out, "one state can achieve relative gains by defecting from the agreement."[10] In addition, even if the gains are equally distributed indeed between the actors, they may not be perceived as such. Perception is always more important than the genuine reality, which has no meaning without the observer.[11] One tends to be uncertain in a self-help system and tends to believe that the other side gets more.

Second, it is when the actor is not sensitive to relative gains. For example, the sensitivity level is extremely high between two states at war but quite low between two friendly states. However, according to realism, there are no permanent friends and today's friend may become tomorrow's enemy; sensitivity to gaps in gains from cooperation always exists. Moreover, despite the variance, "states worry about gaps in gains from cooperation to some degree with virtually all partners and in virtually all domains."[12] Mastanduno's study indicates that the United States and Japan, despite the fact that they were allies, were sensitive to relative gains in their cooperation, because "over the long run, such developments could pose a threat to America's economic welfare, political autonomy, and perhaps even to its military security,"[13] especially when Japan was on the rise as a state that was recovering from WWII.

The third is when an actor realizes that she will have relative gains in the cooperation. The argument that relative gains motivate an actor to cooperate is in fact the most important constituent of the realist theory of cooperation. It is, however, a mere logical fallacy. It sounds quite reasonable and realist scholars may well support this argument. Unfortunately, they neglect an interestingly tricky spot implied by this condition. Cooperation needs at least two actors who could both have relative gains in an interaction. By logic it is not possible. The concept of "relative gains" means by definition and assumption that one actor gains more than the other, indicating the other actor gains less. In other words, relative gains for one is at the same time relative losses for the other. By the realist logic of cooperation then, that is, one cooperates only when one gains more than one's partner, so no cooperation can ever materialize: The other actor will not cooperate because she tends to gain less even though she may also gain in absolute terms. In an interaction, if only one wants to cooperate and the other refuses to do the same, no

---

[9] Stein 1982.   [10] Powell 1991, 229.   [11] Jervis 1976.   [12] Grieco 1988, 324.
[13] Mastanduno 1991, 251.

cooperation can be realized. Since international anarchy is an objective and constant fact, and fear of being destroyed by or dependent on others is a reasonable response to it, and since relative gains for one means relative losses for the other, unwillingness to cooperate by the actor who gains less is natural. In this sense, the relative gains argument is also an argument that cooperation in the anarchic international system is extremely difficult if not completely impossible.

Then, how can the side that has relative losses cooperate? Or what can motivate the reluctant actor to cooperate even though she suffers from relative losses? This question leads us to the most familiar domain of realism: power. The egoistic international actor with negative gains is never willing to cooperate unless she is made to do so. It is not a question of willingness, but a question of power. Cooperation under hegemony, alliance systems, and balance of power contains strong power elements. This is, I argue, what realism really holds: Cooperation in international politics is more often than not forced cooperation. Consider Dahl's definition of power: the ability to make others do what they otherwise would not do,[14] and consider also the numerous definitions of power as a coercive, dominant, and conquering relationship discussed in the previous chapter. The realist theory of international cooperation is indeed a theory of forced cooperation, a theory that takes cooperation as a function of power. Stephen Krasner's study exemplifies this point.[15] Based on the analysis of the cases of radio and television broadcasting, electromagnetic spectrum allocation, telecommunication, and remote sensing, he points out that power is the most important factor that decides "how the payoff matrix was structured in the first place, how the available options are constrained, who can play the game, and, ultimately, who wins and who loses."[16] For Krasner, there are two kinds of problems concerning cooperation. One is market failure, which can be solved through institutions that provide information and reduce transactional costs. The other, which occurs more frequently in international life, refers to those with distributional consequences, or relative gains. This second kind of problem can be solved primarily by power rather than institutions. There are many points along the Pareto frontier, as he argues, and which point will be the actual outcome is decided by the relative power of the actors involved. In other words, power provides the final say in international interaction, and, therefore, "power needs to be given pride of place."[17] The connotation is quite clear: The more powerful is willing to cooperate because she knows that the outcome will favor her more, and

---

[14] Dahl 1957, 202–203.   [15] Krasner 1991, 234–249.   [16] Ibid., 246–247.
[17] Ibid., 246.

the less powerful has to cooperate because she has no other choice once the more powerful decides. Thus, the more powerful cooperates as she wants and the less powerful cooperates as she is told. Even Robert Keohane, the leading scholar of institutional liberalism, in summarizing the twenty years' dominance of neoliberal institutionalism, recognizes the value of the realist view that "institutions depend on structures of power and interests," while continuing to reject realism as "a good moral or practical guide to world politics."[18] He emphasizes, "a core lesson of Realism needs to be learned and relearned: *Institutions rest on power and changes in power generate changes in institutions.*"[19] Like Krasner, he believes that power is the foundation whereon cooperation rests, even though institutions have persistent life and facilitate cooperation.

Institutional Cooperation

Neoliberal institutionalism has a more sophisticated and systematic theory on international cooperation. By design, it is also a theory on cooperation in anarchy, but much more optimistic than realism. It is assumed that actors are willing to cooperate, knowing that they will both gain from cooperation and suffer from non-cooperation. Cooperation between egoistic states therefore is not only desirable but also possible in the anarchic international system without the force of the hegemonic power. As Keohane argues:

> If the egoists monitor each other's behavior and if enough of them are willing to cooperate on condition that others cooperate as well, they may be able to adjust their behavior to reduce discord. They may even create and maintain principles, norms, rules and procedures – institutions referred to in this book as regimes ... Properly designed regimes can help egoist to cooperate even in the absence of a hegemonic power.[20]

Neoliberal institutionalism thus makes an unconventional assumption that cooperation among egoists may well be carried out without the exercise of power. In his monumental work, *After Hegemony*, Keohane develops a systematic theory of institutional cooperation. He accepts the main assumptions of realism: anarchy as the essential character of the international system, states as the primary and rational actors in the international system, and interests as non-harmonious among states. Nevertheless, he argues that cooperation among rational states is possible even in the absence of common government.[21] He defines the major obstacle to cooperation in a very different way. Realists see fear by states

---

[18] Keohane 2012, 125.   [19] Ibid., 135, emphasis in original.   [20] Keohane 1984, 84.
[21] Ibid., 13.

of their survival as the most serious and real obstacle because a disproportionate increase of capabilities in favor of one may someday make it much
stronger so that it may threaten the survival of the rest. Keohane, as well as
other liberals, sees inadequate information and high transactional costs as
the major obstacles to international cooperation. It is more therefore
a market failure problem rather than a concern about the distribution of
power. In addition, free-riding is a frequent issue, and cheating or fear of
being cheated tends to occur in an anarchical system. The underlying
assumption clearly differs from that of realism. While realists assume the
fundamental reluctance of egoistic states to cooperate, liberals believe
that states are willing to cooperate in the first place, however, because
"cheating and deception are endemic" in an anarchic international
system,[22] increasing the transactional cost dramatically, they have to
give up. Thus, if the cooperation problem is to be solved, there must be
measures to increase access to information and reduce the transactional
costs so as to effectively decrease the chances of cheating and fear of being
cheated. International institutions satisfy such functions and therefore
can "facilitate mutually beneficial cooperation."[23] To simplify Keohane's
sophisticated theory on international cooperation, then, the most serious
barrier to international cooperation is lack of access to information and
high transactional costs incurred by the anarchic international system,
causing cheating to frequently occur and reducing the probability of
cooperation even for actors who know cooperation will bring them benefits and are willing to cooperate. It is international institutions that
constitute the most effective way to solve such problems and facilitate
international cooperation. It is an optimistic view of cooperation, for it
sees actors are willing to and also need to cooperate to be better off.

The question, however, narrows down to "mutual beneficial cooperation." Realists hold that mutual beneficial cooperation itself is not
enough, as we have just discussed, and the most important thing is who
gets how much, that is, the relative gain. Liberal institutionalists, on the
other hand, argue that if an egoistic actor is sure that she will gain, then
she will cooperate regardless of the gains her partner is to make from the
cooperation. Keohane makes it clear by saying:

Firms are assumed as rational egoists. Rationality means that they have consistent, ordered preferences, and that they calculate costs and benefits of alternative
courses of action in order to maximize their utility in view of those preferences.
Egoism means that utility functions are independent of one another: they do not
gain or lose utility because of the gains or losses of others.[24]

[22] Axelrod and Keohane 1985, 85.   [23] Keohane 1984, 13; 2012, 126.
[24] Keohane 1984, 27.

It is thus the absolute gains that matter in an egoist actor's decision as to whether she is to cooperate or not. Simply put, a hypothesis based upon Keohane's theory of cooperation is that an egoist is likely to cooperate if she can make absolute gains from the cooperation. Many studies during the debate over the "relative or absolute gains" problem have shown that liberal institutionalism is either valid or at least partially valid. Neoliberal institutionalism has emerged from the debate as the most influential challenge to realism and, as Keohane has summarized recently: "The world has now experienced what could be regarded as 20 years of Institutional Liberalism: the dominance of the view that cooperation in world politics can be enhanced through the construction and support of multilateral institutions based on liberal principles."[25]

Neoliberal institutionalism provides a much more optimistic picture for international cooperation. However, it limits institutional cooperation, more or less, to some special spheres and areas, that is, among more advanced economies, in less sensitive areas, and with *a priori* mutual interests. Conditionality is an important factor in neoliberal theory on cooperation. In a reply to the realist challenge to neoliberal institutionalism, Keohane says that institutional theory "is explicitly conditional."[26] Existence of mutual interests is taken as the most important condition. Actors' intentions, numbers of actors, etc., also constitute conditions for cooperation. For example, in some areas where the sensitivity level is high and use of force is at issue, or between some actors who are enemies, cooperation is recognized as difficult indeed if not absolutely impossible.

Interestingly enough, the twenty years of institutional liberalism happen to be the time period during which the Soviet Union collapsed and international liberalism in general was on the rise. Optimism spread rapidly. It goes beyond the limit drawn initially by Keohane. It is not only optimistic about cooperation among actors on the average, but also confident that the international institutional structure, established mainly by the United States since WWII, is able to incorporate any rising power into its orbit and the rules embodied in these institutions are expected to be universally applied once the East–West divide is gone.[27] The international order, designed by the West, takes the establishment and maintenance of effective, legitimate, and long-term liberal international institutions as its core, stressing the combination of liberal values and rule of law, and envisaging wide international cooperation under such an institutionalized system for global governance. John Ikenberry defines this liberal world order as: "Open markets, international institutions, cooperative security, democratic community, progressive change,

---

[25] Keohane 2012, 126.   [26] Keohane 1993, 275.   [27] Ikenberry 2008.

collective problem solving, the rule of law."[28] Once such an order is established, international actors will jointly maintain a liberal world order with cooperation among nations as the new normality. War-driven change has been abolished as an out-of-date practice and rising powers such as China will cooperate because as new entrants they can get into and benefit from this system and have "ways of gaining status and authority to play a role in its governance."[29] This enlarged optimism for international cooperation and for incorporating major actors and rising powers in the institutional order based upon liberal institutions has been expressed, to various extents, in the major strategic projects in the United States during the first decade of the twenty-first century.[30]

Normative Cooperation

If neoliberal institutionalism takes mutual interests as the most important condition for international cooperation, the constructivist agenda on international norms seems to offer at least an equally optimistic picture for international cooperation. Since this agenda has become highly attractive in the study of international relations, learning, teaching, and internalization of international norms have been focuses of much of the research in the field. There is not much systematic and explicit theorizing particularly about cooperation within the framework of social constructivism and Wendt says that there is no relationship between shared ideas and cooperation because "culture may constitute cooperation or conflict."[31] However, cooperation is a kind of behavior. Since constructivism is an evolutionary theoretical approach, believing that the international system will go from the Hobbesian culture through the Lockean culture to the Kantian culture, it is not difficult to infer its understanding of international cooperation.

The study of international norms provides a more explicit interpretation of cooperation. Constructivism holds that interest is not given. Rather it is defined by one's identity, which, in turn, is not given either, but is socially constructed.[32] How the identity of a social actor is formed and how her interest is shaped become questions in constructivist research. When international norms became a conspicuous research

---

[28] Ikenberry 2009b, 71; see also Ikenberry 2001.
[29] Ikenberry 2008, 32. See also Thornton 2008.
[30] This is reflected quite thoroughly and optimistically in three strategic reports around the time when Barack Obama became the president of the United States. See Ikenberry and Slaughter 2006; Slaughter et al. 2008; Jones, Pascual, and Stedman 2009.
[31] Wendt 1999, 251.
[32] Wendt 1999. See also Wendt 1994; Hopf 1998; Checkel 1998; Copeland 2000.

agenda, a mainstream argument is that such norms and the international institutions where the norms are embedded help shape the identity and therefore the interest of the actor. In her pioneering analysis of norm spreading, Martha Finnemore argues that international organizations such as UNESCO, IMF, and the International Red Cross teach actors what their interests are and how they can realize the interests thus defined. Norms sustaining these international organizations are accepted by the learning actors and gradually internalized, making them follow the norms as if these norms were their own.[33] Then they simply follow the norms even without realizing that they were taught and inducted into the norms.

The material incentives for actors to cooperate, constructivist scholars argue, work most at the first stage of cooperation. Shared identities and norms are taken as the most important factors related to stable cooperation, as seen in a security community.[34] If the institutional design, for example, "constitutes a social environment within which actors are socialized to internalize new preferences, norms and roles," there will be more robust cooperation than that merely based upon material incentives.[35] In his design for the study of socialization and norm spreading, Checkel defines socialization as a process of inducting actors into the norms and rules of a given community and takes international institutions as the most important independent variable for socialization.[36] He points out that neoliberal institutionalism involves no socialization because it is only about calculation of gains and losses by instrumentally rational actors. Only when actors complete with conviction the process of social internalization of social norms can we say that they are socialized. Socialization through persuasion, which he terms norm suasion, leads to high quality cooperation. Then social behavior by the actors who have internalized the norms is what they do consciously, naturally, and spontaneously. By this approach, cooperation based upon neoliberal assumptions can only be behavioral adaptation, involving nothing about identity and interest formation. On the other hand, however, cooperation based upon the actor's internalization of social norms is lasting and sustainable because their identities, preferences, and interests fundamentally and perhaps unconsciously facilitate cooperation. Traffic lights, for example, are rules that encourage people to cooperate. If drivers should run their cars without obeying the traffic lights, then they would either risk their life or pass the crossroads extremely slowly. Following traffic lights is a cooperative behavior that fits into neoliberal institutionalism's more

---

[33] Finnermore 1996.   [34] Adler and Barnett 1998, 10.
[35] Acharya and Johnston 2007a, 24; 2007b, 264.   [36] Checkel 2005; 2007.

functional argument. However, once the cooperative norms are internalized, drivers cooperate spontaneously even without any traffic lights, just
as the practices in some Scandinavian countries have already shown.

Relatedness and Cooperation

From the discussion by mainstream Western IR theories on international
cooperation, we can see that their major interest is in the role systemic
factors play in promoting cooperation. More specifically, they have tried
to find what structural factors most significantly influence individual
actors' decision to cooperate. If we take cooperation as the dependent
variable, then what they have done is to find the independent variables
respectively from their theoretical perspectives. The above discussion
indicates that this independent variable is power for realism, institutions
for neoliberalism, and norms for constructivism.[37]

The worldview that sustains the proposed relational theory of world
politics is that the world is one of relations. It further presumes that the
social world is one of human relations. It is not a world in which individual
and independent entities interact with each other, but a world where
every self is related with significant others. From such a perspective, the
promoter of cooperation is not some force outside the intersubjective
relators, for power, institutions, and norms are all structural factors over
actors. I argue, therefore, that it is their relatedness that matters.
A relational worldview tells us that the focus of social studies in general
and international studies in particular should be on relations among
actors rather than on individual actors *per se*. Furthermore, it argues
that actors follow the logic of relationality, basing their action on social
relations in the first place. In other words, all other things being equal, an

---

[37] If we move steps further, cooperative behavior may be explained by practice and habit.
In a security community, for example, cooperative security is a common practice of its
members. If mainstream institutionalists and constructivists take a more top-down
approach, focusing largely on the design of institutions for solving cooperation problems
(Acharya and Johnston 2007a), the practice theory reverses it by taking a bottom-up
approach, stressing the spontaneous and unreflective nature of human action. Practical
knowledge, or the inarticulate, unreflective, and background knowledge, shapes what
action one is to take (Pouliot 2008). Adler's (2005) community of practice places
particular emphasis on such background knowledge as the prime mover of human action.
For Hopf (2010), even human agency is not relevant because most of human behavior is
out of habit. Out of repeated practice, actors do things simply following their habit.
Agency, rationality, uncertainty, and other rationalistic assumptions are basically irrelevant once habit is at work (Hopf 2010, 540). If this is the case, cooperation depends more
on the cooperative habit of actors. Hopf argues, "the United States cooperates with
Britain in the WTO automatically, without any reflection at all about costs and benefits
or norms" and "[a]utomatic cooperation between any pairs of states in international
regimes should be very robust ..." (550).

actor makes judgments and decisions according to the degrees of intimacy of her relationships to specific others, with the totality of her relational circles or the relational context as the background.[38]

The relational theory is sustained by three interrelated arguments, as discussed before: the principle of coexistence, the argument of relational identity formation, and the assumption of shared interest. The first sees coexistence or relational existence of social actors as the basic form of life in the social world; the second holds that identities of an actor are formed and reformed through relations with others; and the third assumes that interest is always shared and that exclusive self-interest is hard or even impossible to define. If the relational theory and its underlying assumptions stand, it may well provide explanations for cooperation. Following Nowak,[39] I define cooperation as an altruistic act that causes one to pay a cost for someone to receive a benefit.[40] For Nowak, the question is "Why should one individual help another who is a potential competitor in the struggle for survival?"[41] while for me it is important not only to think about the self-other dyadic strategic interaction, but also the relational world in which actors play. If the social world is one of coexistence, if one's identity is shaped by relations, and if self-interest is at the same time interest shared with others, then a key factor in studying cooperation is "relatedness." I therefore hypothesize that relatedness promotes cooperation. To be more specific, the more intimately actors are related, the more they will cooperate with each other.

It is what Confucianism tells by the intimacy (qinqin) principle, which means loving and serving one's parents and family members. Mencius explains this principle most systematically and clearly. He believes that the greatest service is to serve one's parents and the richest fruit of benevolence is to serve one's parents, too. "Filial affection for parents is the working of benevolence. Respect for elders is the working of righteousness."[42] I call it the intimacy principle because it suggests that family members are the most intimately related and cooperation among them is therefore the easiest. Furthermore, Confucianism teaches that relational intimacy among family members should be extended and is extendable to society. Confucianism believes that one can be sincere and

---

[38] Qin 2016a.   [39] Nowak 2006.

[40] Nowak's definition goes beyond the understandings of mainstream IR theories. Unlike realism, which stresses the role power plays in cooperation, for example, he describes a situation where one cooperates with a potential competitor; unlike neoliberalism which presupposes common or mutual interests for cooperation, he assumes that no such common interests exist. Nowak's cooperation goes without coercive force and does not take immediate common interests as a precondition. That is perhaps why he defines cooperation even in altruistic terms.

[41] Nowak 2012, 1.   [42] Mencius 2014, 332.

benevolent to other people if and only if one can serve one's family members well first. "Treat with the reverence due to age the elders in your own family, so that the elders in the families of others shall be similarly treated; treat with the kindness due to youth the young in your own family, so that the young in the families of others shall be similarly treated."[43] The extended family image shows that the ideal Confucian society is one resembling a family where everyone is intimately related to everyone else and where cooperation is a normal state. I therefore argue that "relatedness" is a most significant variable for the study of cooperation. Cooperation is dependent on whether or not people are related and how intimately they are related. In other words, the more intimately related the actors are, the more likely they are to cooperate. I do not intend to test this hypothesis, but rather discuss three mechanisms for such cooperation, that is, kin selection, reciprocity, and Mencius optimality, to illustrate how relatedness is a most significant factor for cooperation.

Kin Selection

The Confucian argument that family members tend to help one another seems to be supported by contemporary studies of evolutionary cooperation. W. D. Hamilton's theory of inclusive fitness discusses cooperation among genetic relatives, pointing out that in such situations restraining selfish competitive behavior and limited self-sacrifices are possible.[44] Genetic relatedness therefore indicates that even the extreme form of cooperation, that is, unilateral altruism, is possible if the players are "sufficiently related."[45] Axelrod and Hamilton in their study of cooperation in biological systems describe the mechanism of kinship in the following way:

A gene, in effect, looks beyond its mortal bearer to the potentially immortal set of its replicas existing in other related individuals. If the players are sufficiently closely related, altruism can benefit reproduction of the set, despite losses to the individual altruist. In accord with this theory's predictions, almost all clear cases of altruism, and most observed cooperation – apart from their appearance in the human species – occur in contexts of high relatedness, usually between immediate family members.[46]

Hamilton's rule, well known also as kin selection, means that "natural selection can favor cooperation if the donor and the recipient of an altruist act are genetic relatives,"[47] even though it may favor defection between

---

[43] Ibid., 19.   [44] Hamilton 1964, 7.   [45] Axelrod 1984, 96.   [46] Axelrod 1984, 89.
[47] Nowak 2006, 1560.

players who are not related.[48] When the cost-benefit ratio of an altruistic act is less than the coefficient of relatedness (the probability of sharing a gene), the altruistic act is likely to occur. The closer the relatedness is, the more likely it is for cooperative acts to occur. The rule of kin selection is written as "$r > c/b$." In this formula, r is the coefficient of relatedness and c/b the cost-benefit ratio. What is most relevant to my relational theory is the significance of this coefficient. It is the coefficient of relatedness, expressing that relatedness matters and matters significantly to the extent that it will overcome the egoistic nature to cooperate as an altruist. For example, $r=1/2$ for two brothers and $r=1/8$ for two cousins. Nowak cites the reply by J. B. Haldane, who, asked whether he would risk his own life to save some drowning people, replied: "No, but I will jump into the river to save two brothers or eight cousins." Nowak therefore makes the comment that "the more viscous the blood tie that links us to another person, the more we might strive to cooperate with them."[49] It means that the more intimately related the players are, the more likely they are to cooperate. The argument goes well with the Confucius-Mencius proposition.

The mechanism of kin selection reveals at least two important dimensions in terms of cooperation between actors. First, it supports the relational existence assumption. In fact, it is a relational thinking even though it starts from an individualistic perspective. Relatedness has become a key factor in the decision as to whether or not to cooperate and constitutes a crucial condition, based on which interest is calculated. Second, it supports the intimacy rule in particular. An altruistic cooperative act, which is almost impossible if the recipient is a stranger, is quite possible among closely related people. In other words, the greater r is, the less important c/b becomes. Although evolutionary literature takes Hamilton's rule as primarily motivated by the self-interest for prosperous reproduction, it is quite likely that when the self is jumping into the river to save her brother, she has little time to consider such a long-term and serious issue. Knowing that the recipient is her brother is sufficient for her to make the decision.

Feng, a late Chinese philosopher, discusses a similar situation described by Mencius. It is when a person suddenly sees a child about to fall into a well. Since Mencius believes that human nature is fundamentally good, he argues that people "will without exception experience a feeling of alarm and distress."[50] While Mencius tries to tell us that people's first impulse tends to be good because their nature is essentially good, Feng, commenting on Mencius' saying, raises an interesting

---

[48] Simon, Fletcher, and Doebeli 2012; Veelen et al. 2012.
[49] Nowak with Highfield 2011, 95.   [50] Mencius 2014, 78.

question: "If, however, the man does not act on his first impulse, but . . .
pause[s] instead to think [the] matter over, he may then consider that the
child in distress is a son of his enemy, and therefore he should not save it,
or that it is the son of his friend and therefore he should save it."[51]
It indicates that whether to save the child or not depends very much on
how the would-be donor is related to the child/recipient in danger.
To save an enemy's son is morally noble, while to save a friend's son is
relationally natural. To save a brother rather than a cousin, to save
a cousin rather than a stranger, and to save a friend's son rather than an
enemy's son – all these cooperative acts rest on the relatedness of the
donor to the recipient.

Reciprocity

The second important mechanism is reciprocity. In a world of coexistence, interest is shared and best gained through shared efforts. In such
a context, the principle behind the dominant strategy of the single-move
PD game does not work. If each of the two players only wants to maximize
her self-interest without realizing that there is in the very beginning no
exclusive room for such interest to stand, they naturally and rationally end
up in the Nash equilibrium in which both end up in a situation of sub-
optimality. In other words, the Nash equilibrium is reached because of
the pre-assumed exclusive self-interest of the two discrete and independent players. An individualistic society, based firmly on the ontology of
existence, tends to teach its members and socialize them to such an extent
that they all assume the primacy of self-existence and the individualistic
rationality therein. As a result, the starting point is naturally to seek to
maximize the self-interest by ego. But the way of thinking and doing in
a Confucian society is different. While recognizing that the self has her
interest, reasonable and legitimate, Confucianism also stresses that such
interest is shared always and throughout, and therefore to achieve such
interest needs joint efforts. Reciprocity is thus the golden rule for the
realization of self-interest.

Since Confucianism never sees an individual as a discrete being,
self-interest is not exclusively defined and advancement of self-interest
happens only in a relational context. In fact, Confucius believes that self-
advancement needs other-advancement and that self-interest, perhaps
paradoxically, requires altruistic cooperation for its realization. The
Analects says: "Now the man of perfect virtue, wishing to be established
himself, seeks also to establish others; wishing to be enlarged himself,

---

[51] Feng 1991, 490.

seeks also to enlarge others."[52] Confucius is thus clear about the best principle for the realization of the self-interest: Since interest is always shared from a relational perspective, increasing others' interest is to increase your own interest. In other words, if you want to succeed, make others succeed, for your success depends on the success of others. The corollary of the same principle is the well-known axiom in the *Analects*:

Tsze-kung asked, saying, "Is there one word which may serve as a rule of practice for all one's life?" The Master said, "Is not reciprocity such a word? What you do not want done to yourself, do not do to others."[53]

Zhao Tingyang summarizes this idea of Confucius, especially the rule of reciprocity, as the "Confucian improvement."[54] Take the self-other relations as an example. The Confucian improvement holds: When the self (X) and the other (Y) coexist and are related to each other, having respectively x as X's interest and y as Y's interest, X can maintain x if and only if Y can simultaneously maintain y; X can improve x to x+ if and only if Y can improve simultaneously y to y+. For X, therefore, to maintain x, she must help Y to maintain y; to realize x+, she must help Y improve y to y+. It is the same for Y. If the self and the other both follow this principle and do it in their interaction, then the result tends to be the realization of both x+ and y+. Zhao's summary is, "be established iff let established; improved iff let improved."[55] Gaining interest in a context of coexistence, therefore, should follow a path different from that in a context with an ontology of existence.

The Confucian improvement agrees to a large extent with the rule of reciprocity in the literature of evolutionary cooperation. Axelrod's best strategy for cooperation is tit-for-tat. For those who are not genetically related, Axelrod goes to reciprocity as the main strategy of evolutionary cooperation.[56] He starts from the individual, that is, the selfish individual who wants to realize her own self-interest. This starting point of his allows him to examine "the difficult case in which cooperation is not completely based upon a concern for others or upon the welfare of the group as the whole." He has found that in an iterated PD game the tit-for-tat strategy, by which one starts with cooperation and thereafter does what the other player did on the previous move, is the most successful strategy and the most robust rule. His findings are based upon the iterated PD game. It is well known that in a single-move PD game, natural selection always favors the defector. The payoff structure changes when it comes to

---

[52] Confucius et al. 2014, 60.   [53] Confucius et al. 2014, 167.   [54] Zhao 2009, 27.
[55] Zhao 2016, 117.   [56] Axelrod 1984, 6.

a repeated PD game because the two players have a chance to meet and play with each other again.

Axelrod uses the discount parameter w to indicate "the weight (or importance) of the next move relative to the current move" or the probability of the players meeting again.[57] He defines an evolutionarily stable strategy (ESS) as one which prevents any population of individuals using it from being invaded by a rare mutant that adopts a different strategy. His experiment tells that if w is sufficiently large, cooperation will be more likely to occur. The parameter w is thus crucial, for the tit-for-tat strategy is evolutionarily stable "if and only if the interactions between the individuals have a sufficiently large probability of continuing."[58] If the players do not value the future or their continual interaction, as they should do in the iterated PD game, then they tend to choose defection instead of cooperation, for in a single-move PD game, temptation to defect (T) is greater than the reward for cooperation (R). Axelrod cites Mayer: "The great enforcer of morality in commerce is the continuing relationship, the belief one will have to do business again with this customer, or this supplier ..."[59] He further argues that a long-term relationship helps stabilize cooperation and that in small towns or ethnic neighborhoods reciprocity is easier to maintain than in a strangers' world.

From the perspective of the relational theory, the crucial factor w that promotes cooperation indicates relations. If two strangers meet only once in a single-move PD game, it is a zero relationship. But two players are socially related once they have met, played with each other, and known that they will meet again. The shadow of the future works only in the situation where a relationship exists and is expected to continue between actors. Axelrod's example of the visiting professor goes with the intimacy rule, for the relatedness of the visiting professor to the faculty members in the department is less than that among the permanent faculty members. For me, the repeated PD game makes cooperation possible because a relationship between the players is established and expected to continue. Thanks to this relationship, the payoff structure and the pattern of behavior change. It is easier for people to cooperate in small towns because everyone is somewhat related to everyone else, and they all know it. It is also illustrated by the case of trench warfare during WWI, which Axelrod has discussed in detail and which indicates that "this is a case of cooperation emerging despite great antagonism between the players."[60] The live and let live system in fact was established on the understanding that their very survival was interdependently related and

---

[57] Ibid., 13.   [58] Ibid., 96.   [59] Ibid., 60.   [60] Ibid., 74.

their security interest was shared. The US–USSR relationship during the Cold War years was similar: They coexisted or co-deceased.

We may revisit the debate between neorealists and neoliberals over relative or absolute gains. Grieco developed a theory on cooperation with his famous k, the coefficient of an actor's sensitivity to relative gains.[61] Following his basic assumption of the fundamental goal of states in anarchy as survival, he believes that this k is always greater than zero. In other words, all states in all times are sensitive to gaps in gains. At the same time, he recognizes that k may vary, depending on what relationships the actors involved have with each other. "In general," as he says, "k will increase as a state transits from relationships in what Karl Deutsch termed as a 'pluralistic security community' to those approximating a state of war."[62] It is interesting to notice that Grieco realizes that relationships matter in determining the value of the sensitivity coefficient, even though he places emphasis on the general application of k for all states, for the uncertainties even make allies sensitive to relative gains from cooperation. We may rephrase Grieco's hypothesis as follows: Actors' sensitivity to relative gains varies, depending on how they are related and how closely they are related while engaged in cooperation.

Keohane gives a somewhat different interpretation of the sensitivity coefficient. He makes the following argument:

Professor Grieco holds that relative gains concerns (his "k") are always positive – that is, they inhibit cooperation – and often large ... My view, by contrast, is that this coefficient can be positive, negative, or zero. It can be negative, contrary to Grieco's statement, in the case of stable alliances, where one ally seeks to reinforce the other's strength. Early in the Cold War, for instance, the United States deliberately built up the economic capabilities of its allies in Europe and Asia, while striving hard to limit the technological competence of the Soviet Union and China.[63]

Both Grieco and Keohane believe that it is a variable rather than a constant, but where they differ is the range of its variance. For Grieco it is always positive, while for Keohane it can be positive, negative, or zero. Even though Keohane expands the range of varying, he is even clearer that sensitivity depends on relationships, varying from being positive to negative. Thus, for both, relatedness is an important factor for the sensitivity to relative gains to vary.

The significance of relatedness is made further explicit by the discussion of some important promoters of cooperation. Axelrod and Keohane have identified three such promoters, that is, mutuality of interest, the

---

[61] Grieco 1988,129.   [62] Ibid.   [63] Keohane 1993, 279.

shadow of the future, and the number of players.[64] Let me focus on the shadow of the future as an example to illustrate that relatedness is in fact the key factor for the shadow of the future to work. As the PD game shows, defection is the choice if the game is played only once and cooperation is more likely when the game is iterated. What does iteration mean? It means the establishment and continuation of a relationship between the players in the game. Once they begin to play the second time, they are no longer strangers and they are already somewhat related. Axelrod and Keohane use the 1914 Germany and the inter-bank as well as bank-debtor negotiations as examples to illustrate their point.[65] There was a cult of offensive in Germany which believed that the preventive offensive would destroy the capabilities of the enemy while in the contemporary inter-bank and bank-debtor negotiations the banks knew that they needed to maintain a long-term relationship with each other and with the debtor countries. A careful look may tell us that the cult of offensive believes in the annihilation of the enemy and annexation of their land, thus severing the relationship once and for all. The banks know, on the contrary, that they cannot eliminate other banks and have to continue to be related to them. It is, as Axelrod and Keohane argue, the "continuing interbank relationships," and the "continuing relations between banks and debtor countries" that give banks incentives to cooperate.[66] Once similar situations happen in the economic areas where relationships can be cut off, there will be similar behavior. A seller is more likely to cheat tourists than old customers, for tourists buy perhaps only once and old customers have a relationship with the seller through repeated shopping. Even though the seller knows that she cannot eliminate the tourists, she also is pretty certain that the chance for them to come back and buy again is very small. They will be no longer related. It is, therefore, the establishment and continuation of the relationships that condition the shadow of the future and make it work. The longer and more intimate the relationship is, the more incentive there are for the players to cooperate.

Both the Confucian improvement and Axelrod's tit-for-tat strategy resemble what Martin Nowak terms "direct reciprocity," which is an important mechanism for evolutionary cooperation. Nowak, believing that cooperation is the third principle for evolution after natural selection and mutation, has emphasized the importance of this type of reciprocity necessary for an evolutionary process.[67] Among the five rules he has listed, reciprocity is a key factor in at least three of them. Direct reciprocity is like what happens in an iterated PD game in which the same two

---

[64] Axelrod and Keohane 1993.   [65] Ibid.   [66] Ibid., 93.   [67] Nowak 2006, 1563.

individuals have repeated encounters.[68] As Nowak says: "By this [direct reciprocity], I mean simply the principle of give-and-take. When I scratch your back, I expect you to scratch mine in turn."[69] An act of cooperation by one player will be returned by the other with an act of cooperation too. It reminds us of the "*bao*" norm in Chinese society and is also like what the general principle of Axelrod's winning strategy of "tit-for-tat" tells us. Nowak's "generous-tit-for-tat" and "win-stay, lose-shift" strategies are improvements based on "tit-for-tat," and are more likely to maintain cooperation.

Nowak's rules are most interesting because they are rules not only for evolution but also for the development of relationships among actors. Although his theory starts from individual interest of the egoistic self, as game theorists always do, and holds that "selfish interests promote cooperation," such interest is discussed in a relational context indeed, always involving others and taking into consideration cooperative behavior, because for the evolution of life, "chromosomes are communities of genes whose fortunes are intertwined."[70] It is the intertwining of fortunes that make the self-interest and other-interest shared and inseparable. The two mechanisms, direct reciprocity and indirect reciprocity in particular resemble the Confucian improvement, pinpointing that a better realization of self-interest depends on the facilitation of the realization of other-interest. As Tu has pointed out: "The well-known statement in the *Analects*, 'Wishing to establish oneself, one establishes others; wishing to enlarge oneself, one enlarges others,' enjoins us to help others to establish and enlarge themselves as a corollary of our self-establishment and self-enlargement. Strictly speaking, to involve the other in our self-cultivation is not only altruistic; it is required for our own self-development."[71]

Mencius Optimality

Mencius optimality means that cooperative reciprocity facilitates harmonious human relations, which constitute the optimal condition for realization of self-interest. It argues that reciprocity is not only a means to better materialize tangible self-interest, but also a crucial way to create

---

[68] Axelrod (1984) has an extensive and emphatic discussion on the iterated PD game. An interesting question is: Why is cooperation impossible in the single-move PD game but possible in the iterated PD game? From a relational perspective, in the iterated PD game, the players have established a relationship. In other words, there appears a factor – "relatedness," – which does not exist in the first encounter of the players. It is this relatedness that works to make a difference.
[69] Nowak with Highfield 2011, 22.   [70] Ibid., 133.   [71] Tu 1985, 114.

more favorable and harmonious relations in a community in which the interest of its individual members can be better realized. It may be understood at two levels: At the dyadic level, it means that positive reciprocity improves the relationships between two actors and thus facilitates their cooperation; at the macro-level, it means that positive reciprocity among multi-actors improves harmonious relations among members of a community so that cooperation across the community is promoted.

The evolutionary cooperation literature focuses on the strategic choice of the individual: How does she make a strategic move to facilitate the realization of her interest. Axelrod, Zhao, and Nowak point out the important role altruistic acts play in achieving self-interest. But they all start from a particular question: How can the self better achieve her interest in a more or less strategic dyadic situation? Although they emphasize cooperative reciprocity as the most important rule and that self-interest can be better achieved through cooperative interaction, they focus largely on situations where two or more individuals interact strategically for gaining self-interest. Zhao's mechanism is the Confucian improvement and his description, expressed in terms of X and Y, is largely a dyadic situation. Nowak's rules are somewhat more complex, but mechanisms such as kin selection, direct reciprocity, and indirect reciprocity are about interaction between individual players. Both seem to focus on situations where one gains interest from the other and neither has discussed how a community as a whole helps its individual members realize their respective self-interest.

It is interesting to look into the mechanism of group selection, which shows that a group of cooperators is more successful than a group of defectors.[72] Group selection is based on the interest of a collectivity, in contrast to rationalistic models based purely on individual self-interest. Nowak himself in fact criticizes those evolutionary theorists who "insisted that all adaptations had to be explained in terms of individual self-interest."[73] Throughout his research Nowak has criticized the argument that individual self-interest best explains adaptations and evolutions and thus argued against the primacy of the ontology of existence. In short, Nowak's rules facilitate cooperation and therefore promote evolution because he believes, as the subtitle of his book *Super Cooperators* expresses, that we need each other for success and furthermore a group may need the sacrifice of its individual members for the prosperity of the collectivity.

Szabó and Szolnoki seem to tell a similar story by introducing a spatial evolutionary game. A particularly valuable innovation is the discussion of

[72] Nowak 2006, 1561.   [73] Nowak with Highfield 2011, 86.

the "fraternal player."[74] Their model compares the egoistic player, whose only purpose is to maximize her own interest without taking into consideration the interest of others, and the fraternal player, who considers not only her own interest but also the interest of her neighbors. The most significant characteristic feature of the fraternal player is that she "has taken into consideration all of her neighbor's payoff together with her own payoff with equal weight …."[75] The other-regarding preference motivates her to choose a strategy different from that used in the classical game of PD and constitutes a significant improvement. Most importantly, if people share their benefits fraternally, then it will provide "optimum payoff for the whole society" and make the whole society better off.[76]

It is important to notice that both the group selection mechanism and the fraternal player's game discuss cooperation from the individual player's perspective, starting from her *other-regarding behavior* and revealing the resulting beneficial interest for the collectivity as a whole. My question is just the opposite: What kind of collectivity best facilitates the realization of its members' self-interest? Group selection tells us how the sacrifice of the self can contribute to the interest of the group and the fraternal player's game reveals the fact that other-regarding behavior provides better payoff for the collectivity. Their attention is on how a group can successfully carry out its evolution through more prosperous production rather than how an individual gains interest from such a group. Neither considers the question of what kind of community can best help its members to advance themselves through the realization of their individual self-interest.

It is Mencius who provides an answer to this question. If coexistence is a necessary form of self-existence in society and shared interest is therefore a necessary form of self-interest, then what is the best possible condition for the self to realize her interest in a community? Or what kind of coexistence is optimal for self-advancement? The answer lies very much in the well-known saying of Mencius. In the Chinese cultural tradition, Heaven, the Earth, and Men are believed to be the three powers that are both enabling and constraining. They represent the environment where one lives. Things can be successfully done if one gets the support of these three powers. As Xunzi (313–238 BC), a Confucian philosopher during the late Warring States Period, says: "If farmers and husbandmen remain simple and hardworking and limit what they are able to do, then above the natural sequence of the season is not lost in Heaven, below the benefits of the Earth are not lost, and in the

---

[74] Szabó and Szolnoki 2012.   [75] Ibid., 82.   [76] Ibid., 81.

middle the concord of humanity is obtained, so that the Hundreds of Tasks are not frustrated."[77] He stresses the important role played by the natural sequences of seasons or good timing (*tianshi*), the benefits of the Earth or geographical convenience (*dili*), and the concord of humanity or harmonious human relations (*renhe*) in the successful fulfillment of all the tasks. Mencius offers the most succinct teaching: "Good timing is important, even more so is geographical convenience, but the most important of all is harmonious human relations."[78] Mencius thus compares the three and singles out harmonious human relations as the most important condition for one to succeed. It is one of the greatest mottos in the Chinese culture and is taken as a norm to guide one's behavior in many Eastern Asian societies. Although it was first used by Xunzi and expressed explicitly by Mencius as they were advising the ruler in terms of governance and order, it is widely used in everyday life in all fields today.

I summarize this view and call it "Mencius optimality," which gives the ideal condition for the maximization of self-interest. Good timing (provided by Heaven) and geographical convenience (provided by the Earth) are non-human factors, while harmonious human relations (provided by people) are completely human. In other words, it is harmonious human relations that provide the best possible situation for one to realize one's self-interest. Taken as one of the most important principles for the relational theory, it is termed the harmony principle, that is, reciprocity facilitates harmonious human relations, which constitute the contextual condition best possible for interest materialization of the individual therein. It recognizes the importance of reciprocity between individual actors, but at the same time stresses the overall environment that is most favorable for the individual to realize her interest. Thus it has strong macro-level implications: Altruism and reciprocity are mechanisms not only for the realization of self-interest, but also for the establishment and maintenance of harmonious human relations as a whole, because the better one can maintain a harmonious relational habitat, the more one can gain from it. Mencius optimality therefore does not only see other-regarding and reciprocity as a means to achieve personal gains, but also a mechanism to maintain good human relations so that

---

[77] Xunzi 1999, 371.

[78] This is a more direct translation of Mencius' saying. James Legge's translation is "Mencius said, 'Opportunities of time vouchsafed by Heaven are not equal to advantages of situation afforded by the Earth, and advantages of situation afforded by the Earth are not equal to the union arising from the accord of Men'" (Mencius 2014, 84). My more word-for-word translation is based on *New Age Chinese-English Dictionary* (Wu and Cheng 2000, 1519).

one's relational circles are kept in an optimal state through which one may gain the best possible interest.

Mencius optimality is an extension of the Confucian improvement to a more general, multiplayer situation, and to the collectivity as a whole. If cooperative reciprocity in a dyadic situation provides the simplest model for good relations between two players, cooperative reciprocity in a multiplayer situation creates a harmonious relational totality that constitutes the habitat where the players live. Thus, reciprocity is not only a means for the self to gain interest, but also a path to a harmonious relational environment. If the Confucian improvement stresses the one-to-one reciprocity, Mencius optimality focuses more on the overall relational harmony with reciprocity as the mechanism for its achievement and maintenance. Furthermore it pinpoints this overall relational harmony as a most important condition for the success of any individual therein. Thus the logical reasoning in Mencius optimality is that cooperative reciprocity facilitates harmony, which in turn is most likely to make each and all better off. It is quite common to see that self-interest and collective interest are antithetical and therefore there must be some equilibrium beyond which improvement of one's interest necessitates the worsening of the interest of others, as the Pareto efficiency shows. Group selection and the fraternal player's game both require the sacrifice of the individual for the collectivity. They both take a bottom-up position. Mencius optimal, as a top-down approach, tells us that all can be better off if there is a community of harmony, which facilitates other-regarding and helps to make the pie bigger with joint reciprocity.

The primary unit in society, according to Chinese traditional culture, is the family, which is a spontaneous collectivity and relationship whose members are used to understand and interpret relationships in general in society. Nowak's rule of kin selection indicates that cooperation is easiest among family members because the family is where the sense of egoistic self-interest is at the minimum and therefore cooperation is most likely to occur. In fact, the Confucian improvement is also most likely to occur in a family because the members are more willing to facilitate the realization of one another's interest. Chinese parents, for example, are willing to spend every penny and even to shoulder a heavy debt to support their children to receive the best possible education, simply because they believe that their children's success is their own success and perhaps is more important than their own success. Mencius optimality, however, is not from the perspective of each member of the family, but from the family as a whole. It tells that a family with the most harmonious relations among all its members provides the best possible condition for the maximization of the interest of each of its members. As a well-known Chinese saying goes: "Harmony in the family leads to prosperity of all under-takings." The Confucian family is the prototype of all socio-political units and, by the Confucian inference, rules for the family work also for other units such as a community, a nation, or the world. In fact, an ideal Confucian society is simply an extended family, where everyone takes care of parents and children of others as her own.[79]

Consider also the case of China's rise in the past three decades. Before 1978 when China's reform and opening-up strategy was taken, China had believed that the world was one where the dominant tendency was war and revolution, a famous judgment by Lenin of what he called the era of imperialist war and proletarian revolution. In such a world harmony was not only impossible, but also unthinkable. Such was the perceived inter-national environment for China at that time. In fact, China's own econ-omy was on the brink of collapsing by the end of the 1970s. Since China opened up to the outside world and began to improve relations with other countries, things have changed dramatically for the better. China has benefited from the international system and its self-interest has been largely realized, becoming the second largest economy in the world today. As a member, any country gains optimal interest in an interna-tional society where relations among members are harmonious, as Mencius optimality tells us. The opposite is also true. Of course such a harmony is not a God-given. Rather it is the result of the joint belief that harmony is possible and desirable and of the joint effort that builds up the harmony.

Kinsperson's Dilemma

Then what constitute serious obstacles to cooperation in a relational world? The single-move PD game reveals that in a situation where actors are selfish and a central authority is absent, a positive cost-benefit ratio is the main obstacle to the actors cooperating. Evolutionary cooperation studies have shown that relatedness of actors may change the payoff pattern of the single-move PD game and encourage cooperation. Kin selection indicates that the greater the relatedness is, the more likely the actors are to cooperate. The iterated PD game, similar to direct recipro-city, focuses on the expectation of a continuing relationship between actors. In such situations it is clear that an intimate relationship facilitates cooperation.

In a relational world, however, an intimate relationship may also create problems for cooperation. Consider Haldane's answer. If it should

---

[79] Mencius 2014, 19.

involve more actors – three brothers, for example, what would he do and who is he to save first? Haldane's answer tells explicitly who one should save when it is clear who is a genetic relative and who is not, or who is a more intimate relative. But he does not answer a more intriguing question: Who will you save if two brothers of yours are both drowning? You want to help both, but you can only cooperate with one and defect from the other. This dilemma appears no less than the PD in everyday life as well as in international relations.

There is a similar and very popular Chinese puzzle. Chinese society starts with the family, in which the thorniest relationship is the triangle among the son, his mother, and his wife. In many Chinese families, they continue to live under the same roof and therefore they have little choice but to face one another every day. Coexistence is a fact, but how to manage this coexistence is a real problem for the son. Many stories and soap operas on Chinese television are written about this triangular relationship. There are numerous petty questions for the son, such as: "If you have only one egg, to whom will you give it, your mother or your wife?" But the one most similar to Haldane's is the question: "If your wife and your mother are both drowning and if you have the time and energy to save only one of them, who will you save?" We may express this predicament by using exactly Nowak's rhetoric. "If two of your brothers are drowning and if you have the ability to save only one, who will you save?" The two brothers, of course, have the same coefficient of relatedness with the player, that is, $r=1/2$. Let me term it the "Haldane predicament."

From the perspective of the relational theory, we, starting with the Haldane predicament, may construct a game of three actors, who are related and can therefore be called relators. The setting of the game goes as follows:
1. There are three relators, A, B, and C;
2. r_1 is the coefficient of relatedness for A and B; and
3. r_2 is the coefficient of relatedness for A and C.
In such a situation, the rule of kin selection stands if and only if r_1 does not have the same value with r_2, or $r_1 \neq r_2$. The player jumps into the river to save her brother before she goes to her cousin because the coefficient of relatedness for her brother is undoubtedly greater than that for her cousin. However, situations are not always like that. As the Haldane predicament indicates, if two of your brothers are drowning and if you are able to save only one, who will you save? It has nothing to do with reproduction or prosperity of the species, for the two brothers share equal portions of genes with the player; there is no legal obligation involved either, because there is no legally binding rule to instruct you to save one

but not the other, or to save one before the other. Life is equally precious. It is indeed a predicament. There are numerous such cases in real life in general and in international relations in particular.

Using a more formal term, I call it KD. It arises when $r_1=r_2$, or when one is equally related respectively with two other people and is able to cooperate with only one of them despite one's willingness to cooperate simultaneously with both. Furthermore, cooperation with one is at the same time defection from the other. It can be described as a choice between:

$r_1 >c/b$ and $r_2>c/b$, where $r_1=r_2$; c/b assumed as a constant.

As kin selection, KD can be extended to more general circumstances and is applicable in many situations which involve relations among at least three actors. In other words, it is applicable in social situations where there are no blood ties and genetic relationships. We may use it, for example, in situations involving three equally intimate or roughly equally intimate actors. We may call it "relator's dilemma (RD)," for it is the one who is socially related to others that faces the extended kinsperson's dilemma. Szabó and Szolnoki have discussed briefly what they call "lovers' dilemma," which is illustrated vividly by O'Henry's short story of "The Gift of Magi."[80] The idea behind it is that true lovers can be completely other-regarding, ready to sacrifice everything one has for one's lover. But Szabó and Szolnoki discuss completely altruistic acts again only between two lovers. Shakespeare makes more intriguing plots because he involves more complex relationships in his plays. The tragedy of Romeo and Juliet, for example, results in fact from KD, where the degree of Romeo's intimacy with Juliet and with his parents is largely equal, and, moreover, his cooperation with Juliet means defection from her parents, and vice versa. The Chinese butterfly romantic tragedy tells exactly the same story, where the lovers face their parents' categorical disapproval. KD is indeed an RD, for the difficulty in choice comes not from pure self-interest calculation as the PD game indicates, but from relationships involving the actors who are equally related. In this sense it is not a choice between cooperation and defection, but a choice between two conflicting cooperative acts.

There are numerous cases that resemble KD in world politics. Take Singapore as an example. When the United States sends its navy to cruise the South China Sea, apparently a measure against China, should Singapore follow the US action? When China and Vietnam are locked in territorial disputes, who will Singapore support? Singapore's dilemma

[80] Szabó and Szolnoki 2012, 87.

in making the decision comes less from its judgment as to what is right and wrong but from its consideration of its relationships with the two others.

Conclusion

Why do actors cooperate? Mainstream IR theories have provided different explanatory variables. As Table 9.1 shows, it is force for realism, international institutions for neoliberal institutionalism, and international norms for constructivism. In a relational world, however, it is relatedness that explains much of the cooperative behavior. Kin selection tells us that cooperation is easier among actors closely related to one another. It is almost common sense that in everyday life one networks, establishing and enlarging one's relational circles so that things can be done more smoothly. Confucianism seeks for a man an ideal situation where "all within the four seas are his brothers."[81] Even though in the biological sense there is no possibility of changing the genetic ties, it is quite possible to change social ties, making the coefficient of relatedness r larger or smaller. In international relations, diplomacy, to a great extent, is to make more friends, to enable friends to be even friendlier, and to turn enemies into friends. The dictionary definition of diplomacy is "the management of international relations by negotiation,"[82] "the activity or profession of managing relations between different governments of countries," and "the skill of being tactful and saying and doing things without offending people."[83] A practical proposal therefore is to make, maintain, and strengthen relations with others, even though sometimes it is not so easy. In this sense, diplomacy is a typical example of realizing one's interest through making, maintaining, and managing relations with others.

Table 9.1: *Explanations for cooperation*

Theory	explanans
Realism	Force
Neoliberal institutionalism	Institution
Constructivism	Norm
Relationalism	Relatedness

---

[81] Confucius et al. 2014, 119.
[82] *The Compact Edition of the Oxford English Dictionary* 1971, 385.
[83] *Collins Cobuild English Dictionary* 1995, 461.

There are always obstacles to cooperation, such as KD. As to this KD, there is no best solution, for politics is the art of coexistence and human decisions cannot be accurately scientific. In reality one has to make decisions and take actions. In this simple three-player game, whatever her decision is, it tends to benefit the second player and hurt the third. Of course she may consider her own interest, possible consequences, and moral righteousness, or even act on emotional impulse. Whatever she does, she cannot gain advantage from both sides. Choosing sides, a topic that has been discussed quite extensively in IR literature,[84] is not a big problem if there is a conspicuous difference among the various coefficients of relatedness (*r*). During the Cold War years, Eastern and Western European countries had little difficulty deciding to follow the Soviet Union or the United States. But in many other situations it is a real challenge. You must lean toward someone and thus distance yourself from someone else, but how do you lean and how far do you lean? You must offend someone, but how do you offend, and how much do you offend? These thorny questions constantly trouble decision-makers and await intellectual answers.

[84] Alfred and Bueno de Mesquita 1979.

10 Governance: Rule, Rules, and Relations

In IR, the question of global governance has become a main issue that has given rise to numerous research programs and products on the question of how to govern. IR scholarship, however, has more or less been conducted according to the tradition of regime and institution studies, focusing on how rules govern and how institutions promote cooperation by lowering transactional costs and reduce conflict by increasing predictability and decreasing uncertainty.[1] In the IR discourse, rule-based governance seems to be the right model at international, regional, and global levels.

There is little doubt that rule-based governance is an important approach, both conspicuous and promising in its application, and the European Union is often taken as an example in this respect. Similarly, rule-based multilateralism, in contrast to unilateralism and resort to force, is a distinct feature and policy preference in several important blueprints for US global strategy.[2] Jones, Pascual, and Stedman, for example, having criticized the unilateralism of the Bush administration, drew a blueprint for the future world order: a rule-based multilateral international order based upon the principle of responsible sovereignty. They also made the proposal that US foreign policy should work for such an order by supporting multilateralism rather than going unilateral. The two events in 2016, that is, the withdrawal of Britain from the European Union and the election of Mr. Trump as president of the United States, have made people begin to question whether the rule-based approach will continue. However, there seem to have been only two choices before policy analysts in the West: One is governance with multilateral rules and regimes, and the other, dominance with unilateralism and power.

In certain other regions, however, rules seem not to have the same power. East Asia, for example, has long been engaged in regional

An earlier version of this chapter was published in *The Chinese Journal of International Politics* (2011) 4: 117–145.
[1] Krasner 1983; Keohane 1984; Ruggie 1993; Milner 1997.
[2] See Ikenberry and Slaughter 2006, 3–7; Jones, Pascual, and Stedman 2009.

cooperation and governance. ASEAN was set up in 1967 and other mechanisms have mushroomed since the end of the Cold War, especially since the 1997 Asian financial crisis.[3] But their rules and formal institutions are much weaker; a feature that is considered as the "ASEAN way."[4] Despite the inspiration of European practice in regional architecture-building and determination to establish formal institutions and binding rules, practices in East Asia have displayed a significantly different approach. Important as it is, rule-based governance is not the only approach of governance. Formal rules and institutions are, after all, "at odds with our genetic heritage."[5] "Genetic heritage" means more in terms of human sociality and human relations, because it is quite natural and instinctive to use personal ties among human beings in society.

Relational governance provides an alternative approach. Classical Chinese philosophers since Confucius and Mencius have discussed the importance of social relations and maintenance of relations for effective and benign governance.[6] Although rarely seen in IR literature on international order and global governance, in other areas relational governance has been discussed in detail, producing a rich literature on this different approach. In recent years, prominent achievements have been made in this regard especially in the field of business management.[7]

In this chapter, I will discuss both of these approaches to governance, aiming to answer the question of "how to govern." My tentative answer is that governance requires both rules and relations. I agree that rule-based governance is extremely important to make actors' expectations converge, to encourage institutional cooperation, to maintain order, and to enable governance to be workable and effective, because individual rationality – the premise of rule-based governance – is human. Up to date, rule-based governance is a most reasonable and appropriate order, especially compared with other forms of governance such as imperialism, balance of power, and hegemony. At the same time, however, I place emphasis on the relational model of governance, arguing that relational governance is perhaps equally important in our world today. The reason is also simple: relationality, the premise of relational governance, is human, too. Humans are rational and relational animals, but relational animals first. The unconsciously exclusive emphasis on rule-based

---

[3] Qin 2009b.   [4] Acharya 2001; Acharya and Johnston 2007a, 1–31.
[5] North 2005, 84, quoted in Zhou, Poppo, and Yang 2008, 527.
[6] See Confucius et al. 2014; Mencius 2014. A typical example is the mediation system widely practiced in Chinese society, by which people solve their disputes through the mediation of a third party such as the neighborhood committee without going to court. See Tao 1999, 66–68; Luo 2006, 121–123.
[7] Uzzi 1997; Jones, Hesterly, and Borgatti 1997; Dyer and Singh 1998; Poppo and Zenger 2002; Zhou, Poppo, and Yang 2008.

governance, as the existing IR literature on global and regional governance has shown, might neglect social contexts, relational processes, and
human practices, thus missing significant factors in this area of intellectual exploration and practical exercise of governance. Based upon the
comparison, I will first argue that rule-based and relational models of
governance are both important and present in a governance situation.
I will then put forward a synthetic model, which combines the two
approaches, for more effective governance.

Rules and Rule: An IR Approach to Governance

The typical IR approach to international governance is rule-based.
It emphasizes that governance relies on rules, explicitly designed and
laid down, which specify terms for the actors concerned to adhere to.
Kratochwil assumes that rules and norms are guiding devices for decision-makers, that human action is largely rule-governed, and that rules
and norms influence choices through reasoning processes.[8] Since it is
believed that where there are rules there is rule, formal rules are considered crucial and instrumental for order, although informal rules and
social processes are also recognized as important.[9]

This tradition goes back most immediately to the study of international
regimes in the early 1980s and has flourished ever since.[10] Krasner's
classical definition of regimes includes principles, norms, rules, and
decision-making, and he continues to define rules as "specific prescrip-
tions or proscriptions for action."[11] Thus rules are a most tangible and
more easily enforceable core of international regimes. Ever since, both
standard realists and institutionalists have followed fundamentally the
rule-oriented approach to governance in international relations, a phenomenon clearly reflected in both theoretical studies and empirical
analyses. Although both are based primarily upon Western practices,
the realist emphasis on power is rooted perhaps more in post-War
American experiences, while the institutionalist emphasis on rules and
institutions draws more on European experiences, especially practices for
integration since the end of WWII.[12] Within this framework, scholars of

---

[8] Kratochwil 1989, 10–11.   [9] See Rosenau 2003, 394.
[10] Gilpin 1981; Krasner 1983; Rittberger 1993; Baldwin 1993; Ruggie 1993; Katzenstein,
Keohane and Krasner 1999.
[11] Krasner 1983, 2.
[12] A most interesting development in the study of world politics in recent years is to trace
and compare historical practices to see how different traditions and experiences may lead
to different interpretations of international relations and world politics. Theory growing
out of history and theory growing out of logical reasoning seem to have become two
general approaches to the study of world politics. Experiences outside Western

other strands have also discussed in great detail the issues surrounding rules. For example, rule formation, along with norm formation, has become a more recent topic of interest for certain constructivists.[13] Rules have thus become a most conspicuous factor that informs the governance literature. Effective rules, therefore, are the necessary condition for successful governance at the global or any other level. This is the mainstream understanding of global governance in the existing Western IR literature, and also the prescription for policy-making. Academically and practically speaking, governance has to be problematized primarily and almost completely within the framework of rules and regimes.

Realists take rules as a power-dependent governor. The study of international regimes started with a realist reflection on international order, for many of them believed that US power was on the decline in the 1980s.[14] Hegemonic power is considered the most important force that establishes, maintains, and enforces international regimes in an anarchic world consisting of sovereign nation-states. On the one hand, realist scholars recognize the importance of regimes, acknowledging that international regimes encourage international cooperation, and even play some independent role in promoting cooperation; on the other hand, they believe that international regimes are a dependent or at best an intervening variable, able to promote cooperation and maintain order only when power is behind them.[15] As Keohane and Nye have pointed out, hegemonic order means that "one state is powerful enough to maintain the essential rules governing interstate relations, and willing to do so."[16] When hegemonic power is overwhelming, international regimes work well. The post-WWII international regimes in the economic field have often been cited as an illustrative example. The United States provided the public goods of international regimes, including the establishment of the IMF, GATT, and the World Bank, took the leadership, and made them enforceable, to ensure effective governance in the field of world economy, or the Western part of the world economy.

This is exactly why there was a big debate in the 1980s over the decline of US power. It demonstrated concern over the weakening of the United States *per se*, and also reflected worries about a chaotic world looming large owing to the decline of US power. Without such hegemonic power, the established rules would collapse, for nobody had the power required to make them stand and work. Should rules collapse, there would be no

international relations, especially the Westphalian international system, have been particularly explored. See Hui 2005; Kang 2007; Gao 2010; Ringma 2012; Shang 2015.

[13] Barnett and Finnemore 2004; Avant, Finnemore, and Sell 2010.   [14] Kennedy 1987.
[15] Kindleberger 1973; Krasner 1983, 355–368; Grieco 1988.
[16] Keohane and Nye 2001, 38.

governance in the international system in general, and issue areas in particular, where international anarchy dominated. The only way out, for realists, was to reinvigorate the hegemonic power in order to keep the governing rules in good shape as the guarantee for international order and effective governance.

Thus, for realists it is reasonable that power is the very foundation of and support for international regimes and, therefore, the key to international governance. Power makes effective rules, and effective rules make governance work. Power is the first push and rules are the critical enabling factor. Rules without power are useless, for they cannot be enforced, or even established in the first place.

Institutionalists take rules as an independent governor, able to stand largely alone without hegemonic power. We can see from the debate over international regimes that realists and institutionalists have paid great attention to rules, which both believe constitute the direct means for governance. Their difference lies in the fact that institutionalists give rules a much more significant place within governance. If realists understand rules as an important factor for governance and rules depend upon the support of power, neoliberal institutionalists give rules a more ontologically independent status. Their way of going beyond the power factor is to change the key theory sustaining regime studies from a supply angle to a demand perspective. This is exactly what Robert Keohane did in his monumental work *After Hegemony* in 1984.

It was when everybody was talking about the decline of US power that the related worry about international order and governance became more apparent. For mainstream scholars, especially in the United States, the decline of the hegemonic power could lead to another great depression, as it did to that which started in the late 1920s, and which was caused, as Kindleberger has argued, because there was no effective leadership in world economy.[17] The focus was still on rules and the reasoning was clear – no power, no rules; and no rules, no order. Power vacuum creates chaos. At such a moment, Keohane's argument that rules could stand by themselves was truly thought-provoking. Without the hegemonic power, there still should and could be rules that govern. Rules are essentially demanded by international actors, because cooperation will bring about gains, especially absolute gains.[18] International actors, mainly nation-states, will maintain and abide by rules because they understand that rules help to make information more transparent, lower transactional costs, and

---

[17] Kindleberger 1973.
[18] Keohane 1984, Chapter 5; Keohane 1989d. See also Axelrod and Keohane 1993.

reduce uncertainty.[19] The general demand for rules thus gives such rules an independent standing. International regimes are hence able to stand by themselves without the support of overwhelming power.

Institutionalists are good at employing game rationality. In the payoff structure of any game, for example, independent players can rationally calculate what they should do to gain from cooperation with other actors. Usually, there is a great deal of rational calculation, but little attention is given to the power factor. This is perhaps why Krasner has tried emphatically to draw the power factor back into his analysis of games played by rational actors. But even his argument that power works when there exist several possible outcomes sounds highly rule-oriented, for what power can help to achieve is merely to realize the outcome that is most beneficial to the more powerful. He shows the importance of power in determining the final outcome, but does not effectively refute the independent status of rules, for the several possible results on the Pareto frontier that have existed before the final result is out are made possible exactly by rule-guided behavior. Keohane has moved further because he succeeds in negating power as a necessary condition for rules, and negating, therefore, power as the number one important condition for governance. For him, governing power comes from rules that rational actors support and sustain out of their understanding of their own interests. Thus, in the view of institutionalists, power is and can be absent once rules are established. "After hegemony" may well be interpreted as "Rules work to rule without hegemonic power."[20]

Institutionalism continues and builds on the tradition of regime studies, giving international institutions a firmer ontological status, and making them almost independent of power in their functioning. It is argued that international institutions can encourage international cooperation and reduce international conflict by lowering transactional costs and increasing predictability. International institutions are defined as "persistent and connected sets of rules (formal and informal) that prescribe behavioral roles, constrain activity, and shape expectations."[21] Keohane distinguishes between formal and informal rules – the former referring to international regimes, which are "institutions with explicit rules, agreed upon by governments, that pertain to particular sets of issues

---

[19] Keohane 1984.
[20] It is worth noticing that in a recent article Keohane reemphasizes the important role of power while continuing to stress the significance of institutions. In essence, however, he does not change his view that once power helps to establish institutions and thus serves as the foundation of institutions, institutions may stand by themselves, relying on the demand of institutional members for cooperation. See Keohane 2012.
[21] Keohane 1989a, 3.

in international relations," and the latter to conventions, or "informal institutions, with implicit rules and understandings, that shape expectations of actors."[22] Rules, explicit or implicit, are in fact the soul of both formal and informal institutions and therefore the key to global governance.

Following this tradition, institutionalism has become the mainstream theory of International Political Economy (IPE), and rule-based governance the dominant theoretical discourse for global and regional governance in IR. Since the 1990s, this tendency has been more obvious. It is commonplace that governance is defined as rule, with rules, regimes, institutions, and control mechanisms related to multilateralism. James Rosenau, for example, characterizes global governance as systems of rule at all levels of human activity – from the family to the international organization – in which the pursuit of goals through the exercise of control has transnational repercussions.[23] Keohane and Nye take governance as processes and institutions, formal and informal, which guide and constrain the collective activities of a group.[24]

Furthermore, rule-based governance, especially of the institutionalist strand, is rooted largely in the American cultural tradition and post-WWII European experience. Kurth has summarized, after a detailed discussion of America's culture and religion as typically reflected in the "American creed": "By the early nineteenth century, most Americans had come to believe that the only legitimate form of economics was the free market, ordered by written constructs, and that the only legitimate form of politics was liberal democracy, ordered by a written constitution. Americans have thus adopted a very pronounced belief and practice in the rule of law, and hard law at that."[25] George W. Bush was considered as a violator of rule-based multilateral governance in the international system and was seriously criticized for not being able to establish a world order based on rules.

The 2003 invasion of Iraq casts a long shadow on America's standing in the world and its relations with friends and competitors alike. But it would be wrong to trace all of America's difficulties to the decision to go to war or its conduct of the war. Rather, America's standing in the world today reflects a fifteen-year failure to create the rules and institutions of international order.[26]

The European experience of regional integration has provided more in this respect. Rosenau, for example, in his influential co-edited volume, *Governance without Government*, uses almost exclusively European experiences and practices to discuss governance in an

---

[22] Ibid., 4.   [23] Rosenau and Czempiel 1992.   [24] Keohane and Nye 2000, 12.
[25] Kurth 2010, 53.   [26] Jones, Pascual, and Stedman 2009, 5–6.

international setting.[27] Rule-based governance is highly reasonable in many respects, and has been followed in practice in various multilateral settings with success, with the EU as a most telling example. This is natural, because European societies have a long tradition and practice of the rule of law and of abiding by rules. Moreover, European society is highly individualistic. That individuals are assumed to be egoistic economic persons who conclude formal contracts as a precondition for exchange and interaction is longstanding practice. Even new studies of other theoretical traditions on global governance continue to take rules as the key. Avant, Finnemore, and Sell argue that rule-making and implementation are among the most important tasks in the governing process, even though they acknowledge that governance is more than rule-making and enforcement.[28] In the same book, Prakash and Potoski are more explicit: "Following this volume's theme, by 'governance' we mean the organization of collective action through a set of rule structures, also termed 'institutions' or 'regimes'."[29] Their four-step governance model, that is, agenda-setting and issue creating, rule-making, rule-enforcement, and outcome-evaluating, monitoring, and adjudicating, sufficiently reflects their rule-based mindset even though they argue that governance is more than making or enforcing rules.[30]

It is beyond doubt that rules are important and constitute an indispensable factor of governance. It is for this reason that they are present in any governance situation and in any model of governance. At the same time, such a model is not uniformly universal and cannot be the only model of governance. In other societies, formal rules and contracts might not be all that effective, and even be considered harmful to their close relationship. Even in Western societies, rules are neither omnipotent nor omnipresent. If we take a deeper look at the rule-based model, several outstanding features of it reveal the limitations of the rule-based approach to governance despite the fact that it is a most reasonable model in the history of international relations up to the present.

First, it has a strong essentialist connotation. The theoretical assumption of rule-based governance is that the governed are individual actors with certain lasting attributes, perhaps the most significant of which is that of rational calculation. Rules work through the instrumental calculation of the rational actor, for rules reduce their decisional cost; also, rules, as Kratochwil argues, work through their reasoning process, the process of deliberation and interpretation.[31] It goes well with argumentative

---

[27] See Rosenau and Czempiel 1992. See also Kratochwil and Mansfield 2006.
[28] Avant, Finnemore, and Sell 2010, 14–17.   [29] Prakash and Potoski 2010, 76.
[30] Avant, Finnemore, and Sell 2010, 14–16.   [31] Kratochwil 1989, 11.

rationality. Both instrumental and normative rationality thus will support rules as the foundation for governance. Since rules, including regimes and institutions in a broad sense, are able to provide rational actors in a decisional situation with explicit guidance, telling them the best way to materialize their interests, observation of such rules is the way to mutual benefits, positive cooperation, and effective governance. Whether it is by virtue of the reduction of transactional cost and of uncertainty, or the increase of the weight of the shadow of the future, changes in the decisional setting through laying down rules and institutions tend to cause changes in the rational calculation of the individual actor. This kind of rational-actor and variable-based analysis reflects fundamentally an essentialist understanding of the world and of global governance.[32] To some extent it is the legalistic practice of Western domestic politics being applied in the international arena.

Second, it takes the individual actor as the governed. This is closely related to the first feature, wherein because society is assumed to be a collectivity of discrete individual actors with inherent dispositions, it is reasonable to make rules and regimes to govern individual actors. Rules are thus designed to control the negative attributes of the individual actor (extreme egoism, for example) and to turn them to public good. When rules are made, and as actors' essential attributes are invariable, the interaction among such actors will be governed by the set of rules, and effective management follows. Rules guide individual actors' behavior, and a rule-permeated environment encourages international cooperation and helps maintain global or regional order. Thus, rules make practices, patterned practices, rather than the other way around.[33] Once rules are made, they are taught to individual actors, states, groups, and individuals, thus changing the behavior of these actors as well as their identity, and enabling them to recalculate and redefine their interests according to the rules they have been taught and internalized as their own.[34]

Third, the rule-based approach to governance is result-oriented. The most important function of rules is to produce more expected results by making the expectations of individual actors converge so that cooperative strategies will be adopted. Almost all studies taking the rule

---

[32] Katzenstein 2010a, 6.

[33] Norm studies in the mainstream Western IR literature reflect a similar essentialist logic: It is norms that make practices rather than the other way round. No matter whether norms are at the systemic level or at the unit level, norms guide and even determine the behavior of actors. The independent ontological status of norms is assumed without an in-depth analysis of processes and practices of agents which provide for norm formation, acceptance, and observance. See Finnemore 1996; Keene 2007; Haas 2007; Checkel 2005.

[34] Finnemore 1996; Gheciu 2005.

orientation try to pinpoint the linear causal mechanisms that lead to either behavioral or identity changes, believing that such changes are the tangible results that reflect the direct impact of rules.[35] Once rules cannot cause such changes, their effectiveness is questioned. Numerous treaties that European nations have signed since the end of WWII are believed to have produced the most tangible effects for regional integration.[36] When such rules do not perform as they are expected to do, laments about arteriosclerosis of European regionalism appear. By this standard, East Asian regionalism is often considered as a "spaghetti bowl," with few binding rules but many entangling mechanisms and relationships, poorly designed, less effective, and leading to few tangible results.[37]

Fourth, it contains a non-trust presumption. One of the individual actor's attributes is their egoistic nature and therefore cheating is not an unusual act. By definition, rational actors constantly calculate how best to realize their self-interests, thus making free-riding a normal thing and creating the collective action problem.[38] In the self-other interaction, unilateral action taken to maximize the self-interest may well lead not only to a complete loss of the self-interest, but also a no-gain result for the other, creating a lose-lose situation. Binding rules, therefore, are designed to overcome this human nature and make the calculating actor best realize her self-interests through working for the common good, as the prisoner's dilemma (PD) game clearly illustrates. The rule-based governance model tells that externally imposed rules make cooperation possible and governance effective, while intrinsic human qualities count for little. Thus, in the final analysis, there is little room for social trust in the rule-based model, for without rules every actor is expected to work only to maximize her own gains, regardless of or even at the cost of others' interests. As Esperne points out when discussing formal contracts in business management: "Contract negotiations and reliance on terms create distrust between customer and provider."[39] In fact, the fundamental presumption of the rule-based governance is that since there is no trust among actors who are interacting, there must be something, reliable, non-

---

[35] Barnett and Finnemore 2004.
[36] In fact, the evolution of European integration has been marked by the treaties signed over the years, including, for example, the Treaty Establishing the European Coal and Steel Community, the Treaty Establishing the European Economic Community, the Treaty Establishing the Atomic Energy Community, the Merger Treaty, the Single European Act, the Treaty of European Union, etc. It is a tradition and practice, but it is rarely found in East Asia, where most of the consensus has been expressed by declarations or joint statements without strong binding force. Even an agreement that takes the form of a treaty, for example, the Treaty of Amity and Cooperation in Southeast Asia, is based more on principles and moral values rather than legal terms.
[37] See Wei 2010.   [38] Olson 1965.   [39] Esperne 2010.

human, and independent of both the interacting parties, so that actors may engage in transactions without much worry about cheating on the other side. It is rules and contracts that play this crucial function in governance.

Relations and Rule (I): A Transactional Cost Economics Approach to Governance

The relational governance model is believed to be an alternative to the rule-based approach. Since human relations constitute a key factor in any society, relational governance naturally exists in practices of any community, Eastern and Western alike. Western society, however, is more individualistic and Eastern more communitarian. Relational governance is hence more conspicuous in Eastern societies. It is in fact a matter of practice rather than of logical reasoning.[40]

Both relational governance and ruled-based governance aim at governing and share a strong political connotation. But relational governance differs from rule-based governance in that it depends more on the complex relations that operate in a society to organize social life and maintain order. It is true that rules are important for governance and effective in some situations. Rules to govern rational actors, for example, can achieve the purpose of governance because rational calculation is a distinct feature in and of the agent, for rules do provide the rational agent with guidance for behavior. On the other hand, it is also widely acknowledged that social relations are highly significant for governance because social relations also provide guidance and background knowledge for a social agent to weigh alternatives and make choices. To govern individual actors and to govern relations are both about governance, but they differ a lot, for relations cannot be reduced to any single individual actor.

Rarely can we find in the existing IR literature discussion of relational governance, neither does the model of relational governance attract sufficient attention in the theoretical discourse of world politics. Some may argue that social constructivists have discussed relations between and among agents. It is true that, in the mainstream constructivist literature, intersubjectivity and constructed reality involving the actors' relations is an important topic. The constructivist argument that shared knowledge constitutes actors and shapes their relations, such as enemies, rivals, and

---

[40] This is reflected by Chinese philosophy, which shows a strong holistic understanding of the universe, meaning that everything in the universe is related to everything else. This "correlativity" expresses the basic understanding and practice of the Chinese. No individual stands in isolation, and nothing can be reduced to an atomic entity. See Ni 2010; Munro 1985; Cheng 2005, 24–6; Tian 2005, 9–16.

friends, is defined respectively by the Hobbesian, Lockean, and Kantian cultures.[41] Although it is true that relations among actors and actors' roles in such relations are defined, the focus is still on actors: Actors have a firm ontological status that precedes any social relations. The unit in the mainstream constructivist IR literature, like neorealism and neoliberalism, is the individual actor, who needs to have *a priori* an ontological status as a self-organizing entity before any social relations. Mainstream constructivist IR, like rationalistic IR theories, takes the individual agent as the unit of analysis and sees relations among them as more supervenient. In this respect, mainstream constructivism differs little from neorealism and neoliberalism.

Even though relational governance has not become an important topic on the IR research agenda, it has developed rapidly in other fields. Ambitious research has been done in the literature of business management. Firms do business in society, which consists of complex relations. Although IR can afford to neglect for the time being the importance of social relations, firms do not have such a luxury because relations play such an important role in the success or failure of their business. Rules, once made, are more stable and can be modified or changed only with the consent of all the signing parties. Relations are different: They are fluid and changeable any time. Relational governance, therefore, has understandably become an attractive research topic. It is particularly so as firms in East Asia have been playing an increasingly important role in regional and world economic life and are therefore taken as empirical cases for researchers.

Reviewing the theoretical literature in business management, we can easily find two types of studies: one prioritizing rules and the other arguing for relations. While the former has a much longer history, the latter has become increasingly conspicuous over the past three decades. As John Shuhe Li has pointed out: "It is important to notice that agreements can be enforced only either by rules or by relations, and by nothing else."[42] It is perhaps too arbitrary a statement, for there is always the possibility for some other models and practices. It is, however, indicative of the importance of the two models of governance. Because each wants to show the importance and validity of the preferred model of governance, there have been insightful debates, especially when Japan rose as an economic giant in the 1970s and China in the 1990–2000s. Firms of these societies do share a lot with their Western counterparts, pursuing profits and signing contracts for instance, but they also have shown obvious difference in their governing styles, paying special attention to

---

[41] Wendt 1999.   [42] Li 2003, 658.

establishing and utilizing relational resources. The rise of Asian business firms has made relational governance appear quite attractive, encouraging and informing many empirical studies.

Typical research for business governance is economic in nature and relies mostly on transactional cost economics (TCE), which calculates the relative costs of the two types of governance and tries to find out which is the more cost-efficient model. Some argue that relational governance has its advantages in many respects, and enjoys a sharper cutting edge over rule-based governance. Dyer compares the advantages of Japanese and American companies, and concludes that hybrids/alliances or a combination of relational and ruled-based approaches, often employed by the Japanese, realize virtually all the advantages of hierarchy that the Americans use while avoiding their disadvantages.[43] Dyer and Singh, having criticized both the industrial structure theory that argues for a firm's membership in an industry with favorable structural characteristics as the primary cause for its returns, and the resource-based view that differential firm performance is fundamentally due to firm heterogeneity rather than industrial structure, make a strong case for the relational view, wherein the advantages or disadvantages of an individual firm are often linked to the advantages or disadvantages of the network of relationships in which the firm is embedded.[44] They believe that in many cases complex market exchanges involve high levels of various risks and hazards. Under such circumstances, rule-based governance is far from enough and relational governance as a substitute is both necessary and desirable. Relational norms, such as trust, work as self-enforcing safeguards that are more effective and less costly than formal contracts. Rather than entering into a transaction defined by formal rules, "parties may enter into loosely defined cooperative relationships intended to produce business outcomes like more cost-efficient operations or increased comparative advantage in the market place."[45] A particularly interesting point is that they further argue that formal rules might even undermine relational governance, for they signal distrust and worsen relations among actors. As a result, rules may well increase the transactional cost rather than lowering it.[46]

There are also arguments against the view that relational governance is more advantageous than rule-based governance. Although taking seriously the advantages of relational governance, they hold that its usefulness is limited. In other words, relational governance is useful perhaps for the initial phase and tends to become useless once the phase is over.

[43] Dyer 1996.   [44] Dyer and Singh 1998, 660.   [45] Esperne 2010, 1.
[46] Poppo and Zenger 2002, 707 and 708.

North once argued that governance would eventually shift from personal relations to impersonal institutions, taking the latter as a remarkable progress in business performance.[47] It is believed that embedded relationships can promote economies of time, integrative agreements, Pareto improvements in allocative efficiency, and complex adaptation, but that beyond a certain threshold, such relationships begin to fail in cost reduction, and may even derail economic performance and produce chaos rather than governance.[48] Li, too, argues that economic activities go through stages. Because rules are costly to establish and involve more complicated formal procedures, relations usually have a cutting edge at the earlier stages of economic exchanges, and often work well when the business scale is small. This is why relational governance usually exists in developing economies and newly industrializing countries.[49] As business develops and its scale grows ever larger, however, the relative costs to public institutions of providing information fall, while local and informal information and informal implementation are no longer effective and become more costly. Relational governance, therefore, has an inherently paradoxical dynamic which will destroy itself as economic activities enlarge and expand. Thus as business grows, governance will also evolve from the low-stage relational to the high-level rule-based governance. Li further argues that this stage theory can explain both the success of East Asian economic development at the earlier stage and its failure in 1997.[50] Before 1997 when East Asian nations first started their rapid development, relational governance was the dominant approach, which dramatically reduced the transactional costs and boosted the effectiveness. It introduced thus a high rate of economic growth called the East Asian miracle. The year of 1997 was a dividing line: Relational governance continued to be the dominant model while the business scale had grown much larger. The transactional costs became ever higher and naturally there was a serious crisis in East Asia. Li's theoretical model is indicated in Figure 10.1.[51]

Since the relational and the rule-based governance models both exist in real economic life, research has increasingly discussed the advantages and disadvantages of both, and some scholarship tries to combine the two. Dyer's comparison of Japanese and American companies in their

---

[47] North 1990.   [48] Uzzi 1997.
[49] This may well be a coincidence. Western societies experienced industrialization earlier than other societies, oriental societies, for example. It happens that Western societies are more individualistic than other societies and rule-based governance naturally dominated there. It is, therefore, not a question of which governance model is more advanced, but of which dominates the discourse.
[50] Li 2003.   [51] Ibid., 660, used with permission by *John Wiley & Sons, Inc.*

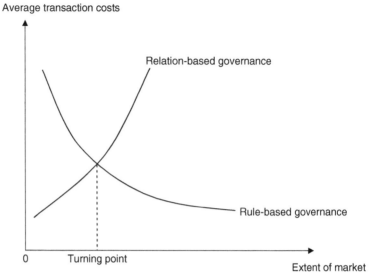

Figure 10.1: Average transaction cost curves

governing styles, as discussed above, has already shown that Japanese companies combine rules and relations in their governing style. Poppo and Zenger said in their 2002 article entitled "Do formal contracts and relational governance function as substitutes or complements?" that although most of the scholarship argues either for relational governance or for rule-based governance, seeing them as substitutes for one another, it is better to develop a model that combines the two. As they argue, "formal contracts and relational governance function as complements."[52] Formal contracts, on the one hand, can promote more cooperative, long-term, trusting exchange relationships because they are able to narrow the domain and severity of risk, thereby encouraging cooperation; to increase penalties so as to promote longevity in exchange; and to provide customized approaches and mutually agreed upon policies and procedures. On the other hand, relational governance encourages continued cooperation, generates contractual refinements that support further cooperation, provides safeguards against hazards poorly protected by contracts, and overcomes adaptive limits of contracts or a commitment to keep-on-with-it despite unexpected complications and uncertainties.

[52] Poppo and Zenger 2002, 707.

A recent study provides more evidence for the mutual enhancement of rule-based and relational governance.[53] It studies Chinese companies and tries to analyze the relationship between specialized assets and uncertainty on the one hand and use of relations on the other. Correlating them in a regression analysis, the authors find that managers rely more on relational ties as asset specificity and uncertainty increase. They also find that there is no association between contracts and asset specificity. In fact, in China, governance relies on both formal contracts and personal ties, that is, a hybrid use of governance models, but relational governance often dominates. Both formal contracts and relational ties are used more as business size increases, a fact contrary to what the stage theory predicts. It is indeed an interesting finding, for it indicates that at least in some important cases the stage theory arguing for the negative correlation between business size and relational governance does not stand. There must be some other factors that encourage the simultaneous increase of both.[54]

For business management scholars, it is important to analyze relational governance, for it is a common practice there in the field of their study. The governance literature in this field largely recognizes the usefulness of relational governance despite the fact that scholars differ as to when and where it is useful. In addition, though there are exceptions, the mainstream literature of business management follows economic logic and uses transaction cost economics as the theoretical framework. The most valuable contribution of such analysis is that it treats relations as an almost equally important element in the practice of business activities. At the same time, rational economics is perhaps the first consideration of such literature. Because of this clear priority, the study of relational governance within the TCE framework is primarily rationality oriented. Irrespective of whether rules or relations are used, the most important motivation is almost always calculation of business costs. Cost reduction is the core of all these arguments. The relation-first theory, for example, argues for relational governance because it believes that employment of relations helps reduce the cost dramatically, and that it is therefore highly rational for actors to choose relational governance instead of rule-based governance. The business stage theory tries to divide business activities into stages and then calculates the cost of each stage. Relations help lower

---

[53] Zhou, Poppo, and Yang 2008, 526–534.

[54] Li's stage theory has also pointed out that East Asian companies continued to use relational governance for business even though their scale has been very much enlarged. It is interesting to ask the question then: Why did they do so? Is it simply that they did not realize the advantage of rule-based governance? Or is it because it is an embedded practice?

the cost at some stages and rules do at others. The rule-and-relation argument then finds that an appropriate combination of the two performs this cost reduction function better.

Trust is considered, not as a social factor, however, but as a means of reducing business costs. Since rule-making and contract-signing aim to prevent cheating, trust has no ontological priority in rule-based governance in the first place. It is based on the presumption of zero trust among actors. Trust therefore is instrumental in nature. To put it simply, trust is a choice of the rational actor for her interests. It is not a norm informed and developed from social practices. In other words, when people feel that trust facilitates the realization of their interests, they will choose it; otherwise they will go to the clear terms designed and defined in explicitly binding rules. Trust is a phenomenon noticed by mainstream business management scholars, but through the lens of instrumental rationality. Trust in such a framework is in fact trust of the contract, of the outside legal authorities that are able to enforce contract terms. It is not trust of humans *per se*. It is, therefore, more a tool or a normative instrument for the advancement of self-interest of the economic person. Calculated in terms of costs and benefits, it is thus deprived of its social and genuinely normative value.

Models of governance in the business management literature, therefore, are mostly informed by economics, for which rational choice dominates and cost-benefit calculation is a most important key to understanding of preference. Preference, in turn, is out of the free will of the actor. Rule-based governance is chosen because it is more cost-efficient, and relational governance is selected also because it is less costly, especially at certain (especially the early) stages of economic activities.[55] The two models, whether considered as substitutes or complements, are both used to reduce exchange barriers and transactional costs, as rational-actor theorists prefer to believe. The literature does, however, shed light on governance, and the most important contribution of the TCE relational model is that it has seriously considered and studied the relational governance approach, thus making it a distinct model of governance parallel to rule-based governance. This is particularly valuable in a field such as IR, whose emphasis has been almost exclusively on rule-based governance.

Relations and Rule (II): A Confucian Approach to Governance

I have discussed and criticized both the IR approach stressing rules and the TCE approach emphasizing the importance of relations in reducing

---

[55] Li 2003.

business costs. The former relies on rules, regimes, and institutions for good and effective governance, while the latter turns more to relations among actors for cost reduction and more efficient governance. I do not mean, however, to dismiss the two governance models, for both have their valuable elements. Rules are indispensable for governance in general and in any particular issue area. An international order relying on rules and institutions has been perhaps the most reasonable, compared with other forms in the history of international relations such as empires, unipolar dominance, and balance of power. But an exclusive reliance on rules represses and marginalizes any other alternative that is seen in actual practice. The TCE approach, while rightly pointing out the importance of relational governance, turns more to economic theory for its explanation to the sacrifice of its social and political dimensions. Its analyses of performance of companies in East Asia have noticed the importance of relational governance, but tried to frame such practices theoretically through the Western micro-economic lens.

What I want to do, therefore, is to present the other side of relations. Relations are born with society and develop with human activities. Relations, as such, cannot be taken outside the overall picture of governance, both domestic and global. Neither can relations be explained away as a mere tool for the advancement of self-interest by egoist rationalists. In fact, relation is and has always been a significant feature when actors take action in society.[56] It provides important background knowledge that guides the actor's action and constitutes a primary factor to be governed and managed. It is necessary, therefore, to develop a governance model based on relations in its due terms, reflecting the socio-political essence of governance. It is the main purpose of this section.

Relational Governance Defined

In order to provide a framework for the discussion of relational governance, we need a general definition. Drawing mainly on the Confucian philosophy, inspired by concepts in sociological theories, and informed by literature about relational governance in business management, I define relational governance as a process of negotiating socio-political arrangements that manage complex relationships in a community to produce order so that members behave in a reciprocal and cooperative fashion with mutual trust evolving over a shared understanding of social norms and human morality.

[56] Qin 2009a.

This definition has several distinct features. First, it does not stress "control" as the essence of governance, as most definitions in English dictionaries do[57] and much of the international relations scholarship implies. Instead, it emphasizes "negotiation." In any issue area, for example, governance requires responsibility on the part of all parties in the community, but must go through negotiations to decide who should do what and how much. It is a common practice in general society, but it is perhaps more a distinct character in international society where there is no highest authority. Second, it takes governance as a process of making arrangements to illustrate its dynamic rather than static nature. Governance is not government. It requires therefore continual negotiation, bargaining, concession, coordination, and balance of relations. It is full of uncertainties and changes, revealing the necessity for constant consultation as well as providing room for human creative thinking and doing. Third, the governed is not the individual actor. Rather, it is relations – relations among actors. Governance aims to manage relations among actors (for example, between the self and the other), who may have different interests and conflictual ideational views, so that a good and harmonious order may be created and maintained. In Chinese culture, it is represented by the idiom of *zhengtong renhe* (good governance and harmonious relations among people), which shows that governance is always linked to relations among people and good governance always reflected by harmonious relations among members of a society. To govern is to govern relations. Governance is done through coordinating and managing human relations and good governance means harmonious relations among different actors living and interacting in a social setting. I will discuss this point in more detail in the following lines. Fourth, trust is the key word. It is not like rule-based governance, which uses rules and regulations to govern the selfish and rational actor. Neither is it like the TCE relational governance model, which takes trust as a means employed merely to realize the end. Relational governance does need trust as a cornerstone. Once a society loses trust based on morality, coercion tends to dominate, eventually leading to a complete governance failure, either through radical reform or violent revolution. A domestic society would be a dangerous place to live in if people do not trust the leadership and do not trust one another and the governance there has only one thing to rely on, that is, force for coercion. An international society is similar. A fundamental question for the relational governance model, therefore, is to establish and maintain trust in their relationships.

---

[57] The Compact Edition of the Oxford English Dictionary, 319; Webster's Third New International Dictionary, 982.

But trust here is trust in its true sense rather that the mere instrumental interpretation. It is trust of the living human being and among human beings.

This definition indicates that relational governance differs from both the IR rule-based governance and the TCE relational governance, even though they share a common goal of making and maintaining order. The key difference between relational and rule-based governance lies in that the former governs relations rather than individual actors and that relational governance requires morality rather than egoistic rationality as the main factor for governance. The difference between the model developed here and the TCE model is that the former takes trust as a genuine norm based on social practices rather than as a rational choice understood by the economic man. Relations based on trust provide the foundation for good governance, and governance, in turn, aims to harmonize relations through enhancing people-to-people trust so that good governance can be lasting and sustainable. It is important to point out here, however, that participation of members in a community is the foundation of relational governance and the premise of moral practice. If there should be no room for moral values and no political soil for social trust, and if there should be no extensive and equal participation of social members, relational governance would become a utopian dream indeed.

Elements of Relational Governance

The relational governance model developed here is primarily based upon classical Chinese philosophy, though it also draws on other literatures. It consists of three pillars or dimensions primarily taken from Confucianism: relation, morality, and trust, expressed already in the definition given above. The first is relation. Governance and order are reflected by relations among social members. Good governance and healthy order are expressed by harmonious human relations in society. The second is morality. Harmonious human relations depend on moral virtues in the final analysis and a society without morality is one of lower animals rather than humans. The third is trust. The backbone of society is *junzi* or virtuous person, who differs from an economic man in that she, fully realizing the importance of coexistence and shared interest, practices the *zhongshu* (loyalty and forbearance) principle, and who differs from a mere social being in that she lives a moral life, refraining from being purely self-calculating. Such people follow moral values and norms conscientiously through education and self-cultivation, thus being reliable and trustworthy. Good governance is an appropriate tripartite combination of these three elements. I will discuss these elements in some detail in the following lines.

Relation. Relations constitute society. It is, as the definition indicates, the key to governance. For any social analysis, an essential strategy is to identify and locate the basic unit for social analysis, which must be the pivot of social life of a certain community. Western society is based more upon individuality; it is therefore natural that Western social theories tend to take individuals as the basic unit and the core of society. Chinese society differs. Confucianism pays great attention to intersubjective relations, giving it the highest ontological status and believing that human relations are what define and shape a society. In fact Confucian society seldom takes the individual as the basic unit. The way of thinking embedded in Confucianism is more based upon groups, that is, "*jia, guo, tianxia* (the family, the country, and the world)." They are social units formed by individuals. Individuality gains meaning only when placed and positioned in a social group. Chinese, therefore, always put emphasis on individuals in a group rather than individuals *per se*.

Since relation is the pivot of the social group, social relations are taken as the key to governance. In other words, governance is to govern relations and good governance is reflected by the state of harmonious relations among members of the community. Thus, rule-based governance governs individual actors, while relational governance governs relations. Quality relations, more than law-abiding individuals, constitute the most significant factor for effective governance. Mediating, coordinating, and harmonizing relations thus become the fundamental means to relational governance. Disorder is first of all a governance failure to appropriately manage the various relations in society. When Confucius himself considered the disorder and chaos in the Spring and Autumn Period (770–476 BC) in Chinese history, he first identified five cardinal relationships in society and argued for good governance based upon appropriate management of these relationships, because he believed that the chaotic disorder had been caused mainly by the mishandling of the five relationships. The Confucian discussion of the five pairs of relationships, namely relationships between father and son, emperor and minister, elder brother and young brother, husband and wife, and friend and friend, are the crucial relationships in society, which is in good order if these relationships are well managed and kept in a harmonious state.

Recent studies in sociology, especially relational sociological theories in the last two decades, have supported, to some extent, the ontological significance of relations in general, thus providing valuable inputs for relational governance. One thing that is particularly important in such social theories is that relations are taken not only as ontologically significant, but also constitute dynamic processes in society. Western mainstream political scientists have drawn heavily on economics, but sociologists have paid much more attention to processes and relations. Mustafa Emirbayer, for example, made an important theoretical endeavor to theorize on "relation." In 1997, he published in the *American Journal of Sociology* his "Manifesto for a relational sociology," which presents at the beginning the two opposing views in sociology, namely, substantialism and relationalism.[58] The former is the way of thinking in economics which holds that an actor is independent, discrete, and rational, able to take self-action of her own free will. These independent units will have to interact with one another in processes. But such interactive processes, involving actors with given identities and calculated interests, merely exist as an empty shell or a non-substantial milieu. The sociology that Emirbayer advocates takes the process itself as a significant unit for analysis. In his view, rather than independent, discrete, and rational, an actor should be social, which means that her social relations are given even before her existence. Although I do not agree with the argument that relations come before states and believe that they are simultaneous, as I have discussed in detail before, I also hold that relations are closely linked with social processes. Moreover, processes are relations. A social process is defined in terms of ongoing interactive human relations.[59] A process is relations in motion, or a complex of interconnected and dynamic relations formed through social practices. In this sense, governance of relations is process-oriented and governance itself is in fact a process in which relational interactions and exchanges take place dynamically, entangling, balancing, and complementing all the time.

I already discussed in detail the significance of relations in the previous chapters and do not intend to repeat it here. Suffice it to point out that relation matters significantly for any society. It is more conspicuous in, but definitely not confined to, oriental societies. Any society, no matter whether it stresses individualism or collectivism, cannot exist without relations. Governance in any society cannot bracket governance of relations and focus only on individual members of a community.

Morality. Morality is the cornerstone for governance. For Confucianism, a society is well governed if what governs it is a system of moral metaphysics, which provides the way for the society to be run as well as codes for all its members to behave. In other words, if governance means governance of relationships, the system of moral metaphysics works as the governing doctrine toward harmonization of relations for

---

[58] Emirbayer 1997.   [59] Qin 2009a.

the society to be a meaningful human collectivity, as well as guiding principles for individual members therein to be worthy human beings. In traditional Chinese ethics, morality is expressed by a system of five cardinal virtues, including *ren* (benevolence/humanity), *yi* (righteousness/ justice), *li* (propriety), *zhi* (reason/wisdom), and *xin* (sincerity/honor) with benevolence/humanity as the core. Together, they describe the system of moral metaphysics. It is not a mere coagulant in society, but more importantly is the reason for the existence, both societal and individual. In Chinese philosophy morality is taken to such a high level that human existence is first of all a moral existence; otherwise it would not differ from the existence of other non-human animals; and that social order is first of all a moral order; otherwise it would be an order of the animal farm. Morality is thus a means to achieve good governance, but it is more an end of good governance as well. Governance, therefore, should be premised upon morality and in turn promote morality. As Tu has pointed out:

the Confucian position asserts that morality is not properly the doctrine of how we manage to gather together, but of how we make our gathering together worthwhile. Morality is not only a means of preserving the community; it is also the very reason why the community is worth being organized in the first place.[60]

This is why the rule of morality is a characteristic feature of traditional Chinese society as the rule of law is one of Western society: Rules govern individuals while morality governs more relations among people. The ideal type of the Confucian approach to relational governance, therefore, is the rule of morality. It requires first of all morality as an essential reason for a worthy social life. While realism either takes morality as utopian or defines it in terms of national interest, and while institutionalism and game theory hold that it is never reliable in social interaction, the Confucian ideal type of governance is always governance by morality and by virtue.[61] Confucius says: "He who exercises government by means of his virtue may be compared to the north polar star, which keeps its place and all the stars turn towards it."[62] Morality, moreover, has *ren* (benevolence/humanity) as its core value. The rule of morality is the highest and ideal model of governance and the rule of benevolence the practical way of performing governance. Human beings are moral beings and human governance should be the rule of benevolence. Mencius in particular defines *ren* in terms of humanity. When criticizing *badao* (coercive, hegemonic rule), Mencius argues that rule based on material and coercive power will be doomed to failure. *Wangdao*, (the kingly way), or rule based

---

[60] Tu 2008, 84.   [61] Xu 2009, 14–16.   [62] Confucius et al. 2014, 11.

on normative power or moral power, is invincible and will lead to sustainable order.[63] When asked by King Hui of Liang, a weaker state than the States of Qin and Chu, Mencius answered:

With a territory which is only a hundred *li* square, it is possible to attain the Imperial dignity. If Your Majesty will indeed dispense a benevolent government to the people, being sparing in the use of punishment and fines, and making taxes and levies light, so causing that the fields shall be ploughed deep, and the weeding of them be carefully attended to, and that strong-bodied, during their days of leisure, shall cultivate their filial piety, fraternal respectfulness, sincerity, and trustfulness, serving, thereby, at home, their fathers and elder brothers, and, abroad, their elders and superiors – you will then have a people who can be employed, with sticks which they have prepared to oppose the strong mail and sharp weapons of the troops of Qin and Chu. The rulers of those states, rob their people of their time, so that they cannot plough and weed their fields, in order to support their parents. Their parents suffer from cold and hunger. Brothers, wives, and children, are separated and scattered abroad. Those rulers, as it were, drive their people into pit-fall, or drown them. Your Majesty will go to punish them. In such a case, who will oppose Your Majesty? In accordance with this is the saying, "The benevolent has no enemy."[64]

This passage indicates that Mencius regards the rule of benevolence as the highest achievement of governance and that a state under such rule is invincible. Underlying such rule is humanity, treating people like people and taking people as the end rather than as the mere means for the ruler. The rule of morality is thus also understood as the rule of humanity. The most important power to realize this is not material power, but moral and normative power. Generally speaking, therefore: "For Confucians normative power is primary, [and] material power is at best, secondary."[65] Morality is thus a cornerstone for good governance. If governance is sustained by morality and the governor and the governed are in a constant process of perfecting themselves through practicing virtue, then relations among them will indeed be harmonious.

Mou Zongsan, when comparing Chinese and Western societies and politics, argues that Western society, because of its religious belief in the original sin, relies completely on the constraint of rules and institutions and on the advancement of science and technology. Its most serious absence is the absence of morality. As he says: "In general, Western culture has many substantial elements, but there is one thing absent – the moral practice that constitutes the core of human society. This absence creates its blind spot."[66] Morality becomes the blind spot, and

---

[63] For a detailed discussion on *Wangdao* and *badao*, see Yan 2011.
[64] Mencius 2014, 10–12.   [65] Paltiel 2010, 41.
[66] Mou 1985, quoted in Li Minghui 2005, 45.

society, therefore, cannot reach its perfection. Mou's comments are perhaps too radical, for any society needs morality as a basic element and it is true of Western societies, too. However, especially since WWII, it has been rare to hear the argument that international order is and should be a moral order. The realist arguments that there is no universal morality and that morality equals national interests are still popular. Scientism, through its performance and domination, has perhaps paradoxically reduced humanity in understanding and interpreting human activity, including governance. Rationalism, placing particular emphasis on self-interest and cost-benefit calculation, has practically reduced the significance of morality in social life almost to the minimum. In the framework of intersubjectivity favored by constructivism there is almost no systematic discussion on morality. Along such lines, rule-based governance largely excludes the role of morality and rests almost exclusively on the egoism of individual actors. It neglects the fact that morality is the conscience and cornerstone of good governance and forgets that the essence of governance is humanity.

The Confucian understanding of the five relationships is often criticized for its emphasis on hierarchy rather than on equality. It is true that four of the five relationships (except the one between friends) are hierarchical in nature. Loyalty and filial piety, therefore, are both considered qualities that facilitate the maintenance and consolidation of this inequality. Hierarchy is indeed a distinct feature of the Confucian philosophy, but there is another dimension that has so far been overlooked. The five relationships can be understood in terms of a hierarchical structure, but at the same time they can also be interpreted in terms of moral metaphysics which govern relationships, hierarchical and non-hierarchical alike. While four of the five cardinal relationships are hierarchical, what is common to all the five is that they are based upon moral norms. Filial piety, loyalty, and sincerity, for example, are not out of self-interest calculation, but out of a moral value system that governs relationships and defines a genuine fiduciary society at work.[67] In Confucianism, it is the moral metaphysics that goes through all governance and management.

Trust. Trust is the guarantee of good governance. Ideal governance of society is based on trust, which is most closely related to morality and

---

[67] Trust and sincerity constitute the principal guidance not only for human and societal relations, but also for heaven–human and nature–human relations. As Tu Weiming has pointed out, "In a strict sense, the relationship between Heaven and man is not that of creator and creature but one of mutual fidelity." (See Tu 2008, 8.) To extend this argument, the relationship between humans and nature is not that of the conqueror and the conquered, but one of mutual fidelity.

virtue. Individuality is associated with contracts and rules, and relationality with trust and sincerity.[68] Confucius himself, as well as his disciples, takes trust as a most important norm in human relations. Social trust rests on sincerity of its members toward one another, which is one of the five most important moral norms for virtuous people (*junzi*). Confucius believes that sincerity is a defining feature of a moral person as he says: "The superior man (*junzi*) in everything considers righteousness to be essential. He performs it according to the rules of propriety. He brings it forth in humility. He completes it with sincerity. This is indeed a superior man."[69] Furthermore, sincerity rests on morality. In other words, virtuous people (*junzi*) are moral people who follow strictly moral norms in their behavior and sincerity toward others is an indispensable quality of such people. People of sincerity trust one another, knowing that they behave by following the moral values, and society composed of such people is a society of trust. Rulers, for example, must be people of sincerity and gain the trust of members of society; "if people have no faith in their rulers, there is no standing of the state."[70] If people have faith in their rulers and if people have faith in one another, the society is necessarily one of trust. By the Confucian standards, a society is well governed if there is a high degree of trust among people, one where every household leaves its door open at night and no one pockets anything found on the road, while a society is misgoverned if betrayal and dishonesty run rampant and people distrust one another, taking others as a means to the realization of one's own desires.

There is a well-known passage in the *Analects*, which indicates Confucius' understanding of the role of trust and confidence in governing.

Tsze-kung asked about government. The Master said, "The requisites of government are that there be sufficiency of food, sufficiency of military equipment, and the confidence of the people in their ruler." Tsze-kung said, "If it cannot be helped, and one of these must be dispensed with, which of the three should be foregone first?" "The military equipment," said the Master. Tsze-kung again asked, "If it cannot be helped, and one of the remaining two must be dispensed with, which of them should be foregone?" The Master answered, "Part with the food. From of the old, death has been the lot of all men; but if the people have no faith in their rulers, there is no standing for the State."[71]

Confidence, therefore, is the fundamental basis of governing, while the material, such as the military equipment and even the food, cannot be as

---

[68] For discussion of the importance of trust in Chinese society, also see Liang 1933/1992, quoted in Li Minghui 2005, 27–28.
[69] Confucius et al. 2014, 165.   [70] Ibid., 120.   [71] Ibid.

important. Faith in the ruler, confidence in government, and trust among members of society go before any other condition for good governance. As William Theodore de Barry argues, trust is a core value of Confucianism. Family members need trust among them and members of society need trust among them, too. Trust among people and trust of people in government are the most important factors for governing. It is also the foundation of the rule of morality. Furthermore, he believes that the most significant meaning of the Confucian *Analects* is that it constitutes some eternal, core values common to all human kind.[72] Indeed, for Chinese thinkers, governance without trust is indeed utopian.

Trust is realized among and through *junzi* (virtuous/profound persons).[73] A virtuous person is a moral human being, whose existence is moral existence, and whose practice is an ever ongoing process of self-cultivation toward moral perfection. Such self-cultivation is meaningful only if it is social or only if it is externalized in her relations with others.[74] Even though such perfection may never be completely realized, the process of self-cultivation perfects her with every passing day and makes her internalize the morality implicit in a well-governed society. As Tu says, since a person in the Confucian tradition is always conceived as a center of relationships, the more one penetrates into one's inner self, the more one will be capable of realizing the true nature of one's human relatedness.[75] Accordingly, "*shendu* or self-watchfulness when alone," as an important standard for spiritual cultivation is far from being a quest for the idiosyncrasy of an atomized individual. Rather, it is intended to reach levels of that reality which underlies common humanity. It is most explicitly expressed in *Daxue* or *The Great Learning* which says:

The ancients who wished to illustrate illustrious virtue throughout the kingdom, first ordered well their own States. Wishing to order well their States, they first regulated their families. Wishing to regulate their families, they first cultivated their persons. Wishing to cultivate their persons, they first rectified their hearts. Wishing to rectify their hearts, they first sought to be sincere in their thoughts. Wishing to be sincere to their thoughts, they first extended to the utmost of their knowledge. Such extension of knowledge lay in the investigation of things. Things

---

[72] Di (William Theodore de Barry) 2011, 64.

[73] There are numerous translations of the Chinese word *iunzi*. I use "virtuous person" in this book. The one translated by Tu Weiming is "profound person." Accordingly, he translated the opposite, *xiaoren*, as "shallow person."

[74] It is perhaps the main difference between Confucianism and Daoism. The former places particular emphasis on the social, for example, relations among social members. The latter also pays great attention to self-cultivation, but prefers to have the cultivation in isolation and live a hermit's life in places far away from human society. It is therefore said that Daoism is the *chushi* (standing aloof from the human world) doctrine while Confucianism is the *rushi* (staying in the human world) doctrine.

[75] Tu 1985, 133.

being investigated, knowledge became complete. Their knowledge being complete, their thoughts were sincere. Their thoughts being sincere, their hearts were then rectified. Their hearts being rectified, their person was cultivated. Their person being cultivated, their families were regulated, their States were rightly governed. Their States being rightly governed, the whole kingdom was made tranquil and happy. From the Son of the Heaven down to the mass of people, all must consider the cultivation of the person the root of everything else.[76]

These opening sentences of *The Great Learning* place particular emphasis on the cultivation of the person and are clear about the purpose of self-cultivation. The virtuous person does not practice self-watchfulness and self-discipline for the intrinsic value of being alone. In fact, she sees little significance in solitariness, unless it is totally integrated into the fabric of social relations.[77] Her conscious self-cultivation is to purify herself so that she is qualified and therefore trusted to govern and to be a decent human being. When a society is peopled by virtuous persons, trust triumphs, relations are harmonized, and good governance prevails.

Governance means establishing and maintaining order, good order is based on harmonious human relations, and harmonious human relations rest on morality and trust, which a virtuous person gains and follows through self-cultivation.[78] Good governance is hence a natural element of a Confucian society that harmonizes relations, practices the rule of morality, cultivates virtuous persons, and has trust as its most important principle for behavior. Good governance depends on three pillars of such society. They are: the virtuous person who is in a continuous process toward ever-deepening subjectivity for moral perfection; a society which is a fiduciary community; and trust which is a primary concept in the construction of a moral metaphysics.[79] A fiduciary society relies on the sincerity of the virtuous person, who in turn constantly self-cultivates the Confucian moral metaphysics and exercises self-restraint. Such a society is "not an adversary system consisting of pressure groups but a fiduciary community based on mutual trust. Only in this sense was Confucius able to make the claim that if the ruler can administrate his state with rites, he will no longer have any difficulty."[80]

---

[76] Confucius et al. 2014.   [77] Tu 2008, 30.

[78] Paltiel 2010, 41. Constructivists may support this idea when discussing "trust." For example, Wendt discusses trust, holding that trust can be realized through both external constraint and self-restraint, the former referring to outside powers and international institutions as realists and institutionalists believe. As for the latter, he argues that a collective identity requires self-restraint. "Ego's self-restraint enables Alter to give up his egoist terms of individuality in favor of identification with Ego. In short, by holding ourselves back we make it possible for others to step forward and identify with us, enabling us in turn to identify with them." Wendt 1999, 359.

[79] Tu 2008, 16.   [80] Ibid., 56.

Since society is relational, governance means proper management of relations in society. It is establishing and maintaining appropriate and harmonious relations among societal members that constitute what good governance is about. In turn, relational management rests on morality and morality-induced social trust. A trustable and trustful society with the rule of morality reflects sustainable governance. It is not out of cost-efficient calculation, but out of humanitarian consideration that goes beyond any naked power and tacit coercion. While the rule-based model places emphasis on rationality, egoism, and contracts, this tripartite scheme of relationality, morality, and trust reflects the essence of the relational approach to governance. The former is more legal, relying on impersonal laws, while the latter is more social, relying on human morality. If we say that rule-based governance rests on the assumption that trust in humans is not reliable, relational governance takes trust as one of its essential pillars and believes that trust is not only possible in human relations, but also cultivatable through education. For the former, the solution is to make law and law-enforcement most effective while for the latter the solution lies with the cultivation of one's inner self so that self-cultivation makes people trustable.

Thus, governance is based upon trust and realized through the inner moral cultivation of socially embedded persons toward balanced and harmonious relations. This is sustainable governance. Here we must realize that the meaning of trust within the Confucian approach to relational governance differs from its interpretation within the economic and business management literatures based mainly on TCE. For the latter, relational governance is a choice; it is a means to realize cost-efficiency. For the former, it is a practice, a practice that is historical and sociocultural, defining a community and shaping the behavior of its members. It is also different from the mainstream constructivist understanding of trust. Wendt believes, for example, that trust can be realized through external constraint and self-restraint. External constraint may include coercive power or international institutions. A powerful state can trust a weaker state for not attacking itself because it has the capability to prevent the weaker from doing so. Two nuclear powers can trust each other for not attacking first because both have the second strike capability where the trust rests. Effective international institutions can make a member state trustable and behave in accordance with the institutions because doing so brings it benefits. Self-restraint, one of the master variables of identity formation, is practiced by internalization of norms, externalization of domestic practice, and/or self-binding. Internalization of norms of a security community leads to self-restraint from use of force and democratic institutions at home may place constraint on a state's external behavior. All these, no matter whether they are external constraints or self-restraints, depend on something impersonal, power of coercion, of institutions, or of norms. They do not depend on humans *per se*. Trust in the Chinese cultural condition depends exactly on humans who are considered as moral beings in the first place. It is exactly this trust on humans that creates confidence in harmonizing relations among humans.

From the Confucian emphasis on relations, morality, and trust we can conclude that relational governance has distinct features compared with rule-based governance. First, it maximizes human creativity in governance. Relational governance tends to be a more flexible approach and less rigid than the rule-based model. It stresses social relations and practices of social agents, which by definition connote complexity and change. It looks more to the uncertainty of the environment and follows a non-programmatic way in which actors interact under an environment of complex relationships.[81] Practices are involved and entangled with the relations among members. Reduction of transactional costs and provision of information tend to be implied in relations rather than explicitly defined in formal rules and contracts. Because of the complexity and changeability of human relations, there is ample room for human creativity in managing and governing such relations.

Second, it encourages positive human qualities for governance. Instead of attempting to control and reduce the negative attributes of the individual actor, relational governance encourages positive human qualities to develop friendly partnerships among actors for the common good, believing morality as a sure foundation for governance and including cooperation and coordination to create an extensive social network for win-win results. Friendship, therefore, is always a most significant word in relational governance, which aims to develop partnership and whose success is evaluated by sincere amity among actors. Alter is no longer framed as a hostile other to enable the self to develop its own identity, but as a friendly other to complete a life meaningful for the self in society. In a certain sense, rule-based governance is governance through dehumanization, using rules and institutions that are increasingly non-human, impersonal, and therefore impartial to control and regulate individual actors' behavior, while relational governance is governance through humanity, taking into full consideration the human and the social, and managing human relations through a fuller development of such humanity.

[81] Qin 2010.

Third, it is process-oriented. Process is defined as ongoing complex relations and has ontological significance. It is not the mere background to or platform for independent actors' interaction and communication. One of the most important features of relational governance is thus the maintenance of dynamic processes, even without tangible results at the moment and even with the glaring disagreement of parties involved in the process. The rationale behind it is that as long as the process itself is maintained, relations among actors will at least not deteriorate to an irreversible point beyond redemption. If their relations are kept rather than broken, there will be opportunities and hopes and the worst scenario for all will not appear. It is more important, therefore, to maintain the process, which means keeping up at least an ongoing relationship, rather than to achieve immediate and tangible results. Asia-Pacific Economic Cooperation (APEC), for example, has been ineffective for years, and many argue that serious reforms must be carried out to make expected results materialize. But the value of APEC can be understood in a different way: Its existence keeps in place a process of participation of the world's most important players, strengthening ties among these actors, and nurturing shared understanding of the salient issues we face. None of these can be defined as tangible results, but all of them – participation, ties, and shared understanding – are conspicuous processual elements that help to maintain cooperative relationships.

Fourth, it takes trust as the most important factor of governance.[82] It is worth repeating here because an interesting assumption in IR is that trust is the most un-trustable. In anarchy, nobody would put her fate and future in the hands of others. Unless there should be a Leviathan, self-help is what one should trust.[83] The TCE arguments hold that trust is an important means to reduce transactional costs and therefore facilitate exchanges. As Uzzi has pointed out, trust is an explicit and primary feature of relational governance. It is "expressed as the belief that an exchange partner would not act in self-interest at another's expense and appeared to operate not like calculated risk but like a heuristic – a predilection to assume the best when interpreting another's motives and actions."[84] For Uzzi and many TCE scholars, relational governance is indeed an effective means to reduce transaction costs. Nonetheless, it is still within the rational-actor framework. For Confucians, trust is a fundamental norm for a fiduciary society. It is not a means to some end, but a way of life for virtuous persons, who trust one another because all of such people constantly engage themselves in self-cultivation toward moral perfection. Trust is not a tool to be chosen and used by the rational

---

[82] Zaheer, McEvily, and Perrone 1998.   [83] Waltz 1979.   [84] Uzzi 1997, 43.

actor merely to reduce transactional costs, but a key element based on social practice and realized through moral cultivation. The economic and sociological arguments do, however, have one thing in common: Both stress the importance of trust, albeit from different perspectives. Such arguments differ from those focusing on the formal rules that are used to enforce cooperation and to exercise effective governance.

Rules and Relations: Toward a Synthetic Approach to Governance

The above discussion has shown several interesting things. First, that rule-based and relational governance models coexist. Mainstream international relations scholars have paid almost exclusive attention to rules and regimes, while business circles and business management scholars have been sensitive enough to relational governance to have carried out comparatively systematic studies on the concept. Empirical evidence, at the first glance, seems also to show that governance needs to be both rule-based and relational. Networking, for example, reflects many features of relational governance.[85] Both approaches to governance exist in reality because both are imbued with certain universally applicable values. For any governance to be effective in practice, rules and relations should be simultaneously at work. Interest and trust, for example, are both indispensable to governance in any society, and results and processes are perhaps equally important for order. Reliance exclusively on one at the cost of the other can be misleading and biased. In an increasingly globalizing world where more nations and cultures are joining the global village, it is necessary to take both into consideration.

The two approaches not only coexist, but can also re-enforce one another. According to the rational choice argument in the management literature, relational governance is more cost-efficient only at the initial stage. As business scale enlarges, uncertainty increases, transactions become more complex, and it is reasonable to use dominantly rule-based governance, which is less costly and more effective. But as discussed above, a recent study shows clearly that the reality in Chinese society goes against this theoretical hypothesis.[86] In fact, as business scale enlarges and exchanges become more complex, relational governance is counted on more, rather than less, for business success. Formal institutions, such as formal contracts to be enforced by law, exist, but relational governance

---

[85] Jones, Hesterly, and Borgatti 1997. See also Keck and Sikkink 1998.
[86] Zhou, Poppo, and Yang 2008.

Table 10.1: *Differences of rule-based and relational governance*

	rule-based	relational
world view	essentialism	relationalism
the governed	individuals	relations
mechanism	enforcement of rules	harmonization of relations
orientation	results	processes
core concept	individual interest	intersubjective trust

coexists. What is witnessed is not that increase in one goes with decrease in the other, but increase in both with the enlargement of business.

Second, rule-based and relational approaches to governance do differ in certain important respects. Having discussed in detail distinct features of each, we want to offer here just a summary, as Table 10.1 demonstrates.

Third, cultures and practices matter. Why relational governance came to attract attention in the study of business management is an interesting question. It seems that the rise of firms, first in Japan, later in other East Asian nations, and now in China, has a direct bearing on attention to the model of relational governance. Firms that have risen in East Asian cultures, especially the Confucian cultural sphere,[87] tend to use more relational governance than do firms in the West. As these oriental firms have become important economic actors worldwide, it is natural that their way of governance should attract academic attention. The TCE model tends to observe the fact from the perspective of the economic person, rightly noticing the importance of relations, but paying inadequate attention to the essence of relations as social practice. It continues to use classical theories of economics without taking into account cultural practices and tries to explain the seeming anomaly within the classic framework so as to save the theories. Because of the significance of cultures and practices, I argue that adoption of relational governance or rule-based governance is not a mere choice; it is a practice embedded and nurtured in culture and society. In other words, both have their roots in social practices. In a more individualistic society, for example, rules have been emphasized because long practices have cultivated and justified such a model of governance. In contrast, a more relational society may have a long tradition of different practices that have nurtured relational ways of governance. Consequently, governance either in a more rule-based or

---

[87] The Confucian cultural sphere refers in a narrow sense to China, Korea, and Japan. Some Southeast Asian nations have been also influenced strongly by Confucianism. See Kang 2007.

a more relation-oriented way is quite often the result of social practice rather than rational choice. It is dangerous to take either one of them as the approach to governance and as the only correct approach at the cost of the other.

It is, therefore, a fact that relational governance coexists with rule-based governance, and that it is more conspicuous in some societies, such as oriental ones, than others. Furthermore, although it is highly reasonable to argue that the transactional cost is a key factor in choice of governance models, it is also important to note that the sociocultural dimension is perhaps at least equally significant in performing governance, for it is not a mere choice of an individual actor but also a practice of a collectivity as a historical *a priori*. It is the perspective that judges governance approaches not only as what they "are," but also as what they "do."[88] This means that we should consider the governance approaches in use as both a choice of the rational individual actor and as a practice of a collective community. It is something between choice and practice, or something that is both choice and practice.

Taking an approach of analytical eclecticism,[89] and particularly applying the *zhongyong* dialectics, I argue that the two can be synthesized into a model that does not see the elements in the two approaches as contradictory. They are not substitutes, but rather complementary. Moreover, they coexist and work together to inform the practice of governance. Thus it is possible to synthesize the important elements of the two, and also to reflect more the reality and real problems of governance. I therefore hypothesize that an appropriate combination of the rule-based and relation-based approaches with due measure and degree is likely to facilitate rather than impede governance.

The above discussion has demonstrated three important factors in governance. First, there are two basic approaches to governance, namely, rule-based and relational. The former governs through providing rules that work on the rationality of the individual actor, making her rationally follow the rules and norms. The latter governs through managing human relations that actors are embedded in, leading to a more harmonious relational cosmos for order. They coexist, and are complementary and mutually reinforcing. Second, the two approaches have different conceptions and assumptions on how governance is effectively exercised.

---

[88] Adler 2010.

[89] As Sil and Katzenstein define, analytical eclecticism means "any approach that seeks to extricate, translate, and selectively integrate analytical elements – concepts, logics, mechanisms, and interpretations – of theories or narratives that have been developed within separate paradigms but that address related aspects of substantive problems that have both scholarly and practical significance." See Sil and Katzenstein 2010, 10.

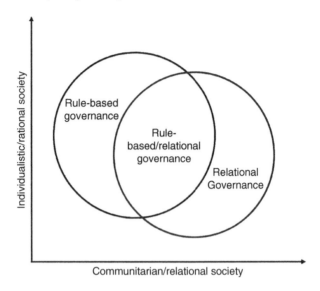

Figure 10.2: A synthetic model of governance

The core of the former is rationality, or rational choice of the economic man, and the latter is relationality,[90] or embedded relationships based on trust among social persons. Third, which of the governance approaches is taken is both a choice and a practice. It is a choice because actors may choose a rule-based or relational model of governance by calculating the cost and benefit; it is a social practice because use of either depends on the longstanding practice of a community in a certain sociocultural setting. It is reasonable to argue that communitarian societies tend more to use relational governance, and individualistic societies emphasize more rule-based governance. But any real governance contains elements of both models, no matter where it is practiced.

On this logic, I develop a synthetic model of governance in general. Rules and relations are both important and significant in this model. They are very often overlapping, as the conceptual Figure 10.2 shows.

Based on the above discussion of this synthetic model, we can derive the following propositions:

Proposition 1: coexistence of the two approaches
It is proposed that coexistence of the two governance approaches is apparent in any regional and global governance area. The present literature in IR

[90] Qin 2009a.

is biased because its overwhelming emphasis is on rule-based governance, almost completely neglecting the relational governance approach that exists in reality and practice. Since we acquire instrumental rationality, we are able to choose whichever is more cost-efficient; and since we are social beings living in a relational web, we do things through distinctive practices embedded in our sociocultural environments.

Proposition 2: complementarity of the two approaches
The two governance approaches complement and reinforce each other. It is a false assumption that as situations get more complex, hazards more serious, and uncertainties more problematic, rule-based governance will replace relational governance as the more advanced, cost-efficient, and sophisticated approach. The existing IR literature focuses on how to establish, strengthen, and improve rule-based governance, the implication being that rules are omnipotent and can be omnipresent. It favors choice over practice.

Proposition 3: cultural contextuality of the two approaches
The conspicuousness of either of the two approaches is associated with the sociocultural settings in which actors are embedded. It is, therefore, reasonable to hypothesize that the more communitarian a society is, the more relational its approach to governance tends to be; and that the more individualistic a society is, the more rule-based approach of governance it will adopt. But what we should remember is that cultural influence is never linear and its effect is through shared background knowledge. At the same time, as the world is getting more and more intermingled in the complex processes of globalization and glocalization, or processes of, in Rosenau's words, "fragmegration,"[91] global governance will involve more Western and non-Western societies and thus will tend to show more elements of both rule-based and relational governance models in a mixed picture. In a more economically interdependent world, business communities of practice are also engaged in a dialogue, communicating with, learning from, and influencing one another. In governance it will be quite unlikely that only one model should dominate when more nations are joining the world community.

Conclusion

I argue for a synthetic approach to governance, because in reality, rule-based and relational elements are both present in any governance,

---

[91] Rosenau 2003, 11.

complementary rather than contradictory to each other; I also argue that governance in different sociocultural settings might demonstrate more elements of one of the two approaches; I further argue that which of the two is more apparent in governance is only partly decided by calculation of transactional costs. It is equally important that social practices play a crucial role. With such arguments, it is hypothesized that a communitarian society tends to take more the relational governance approach, and an individualistic society to take more the ruled-based governance approach. It also proposes that intermingling of elements from the two models will be more conspicuous in future global governance.

Two cases that can be used to test the hypotheses are those of Europe and East Asia. My argument predicts that because of the synthetic nature of governing practice, irrespective of the society in which governance is exercised, features of the rule-based and relational models are both present. For example, the European model of regional governance should show both rule-based and relational-oriented elements in its practice of governance. The same is true of East Asia. Furthermore, the two can be mutually inclusive rather than mutually exclusive. It is predicted that the European governance model should be more rule-based, even though elements of relational governance should also be present. Europe is composed of more individualistic societies and has a long practice of legally binding arrangements, which, according to my argument, tend to be governed more by formal rules and contracts. The European Union is thus a good example to test such a prediction in the context of regional governance.

It is predicted that East Asian regional governance should show more relational elements in its governance.[92] East Asia contains more communitarian societies and therefore should have more elements of relational governance, without excluding those of rule-based governance. ASEAN is perhaps the first example to test such a hypothesis, for its four-decade sub-regional practices provide convincing evidence of its governance, which has shown distinct features Europe may not have. Now it has been declared that the ASEAN community has been established. As a comprehensive community, including the political-security, economic, and sociocultural pillars, it should well pass the initial stage defined by the TCE judgment. It is therefore interesting to observe whether relational governance continues to be a conspicuous factor. East Asia is another test case. Since the 1990s, regional cooperation and governance have been quite a fact in the region, which includes the

[92] Qin 2009b.

ASEAN nations, China, Japan, and the Republic of Korea. This is roughly the Confucian cultural area. It is, therefore, expected that relational governance should be more conspicuous in this region without excluding the usefulness of formal rules.

It is also important to conduct further analyses on the synthetic model. The key to such analyses is how rules and relations are intertwined in actual governance, reinforcing each other under certain conditions. It is clear that each model has its advantages and disadvantages. Rules, for example, are effective where they are supported and enforced by power, where they specify clearly the terms, and where individual actors tend to abide. In addition to the high cost of the initial establishment of rules (say hegemonic power in international relations), however, rules cannot weave a seamless governing web and cannot reach every corner. Furthermore, overemphasis on rules would dehumanize society which is human in the first place. Rules, designed and established to maintain social order for better human conditions, would lead to a dilemma where increasing the role of rules automatically reduces the role of humanity. Society, no matter whether it is international or domestic, is human in the first place as well as in the final analysis, and a dehumanized society, with only abstract rationality embodied in rules, is a non-society, no matter whatever form of governance is practiced. It may even lead to the collapse of a community if rules are too rigid without considering the flexibility of human thinking and doing. A well-governed society is therefore one full of human feelings and human moral values. Mere cost-benefit calculation will not lead to sustainable governance.

Relational governance can create a favorable environment through management and harmonization of relations, wherein governance is based upon mutual trust and is therefore sustainable and lasting. But it requires a much higher degree of self-discipline and self-restraint. Too much emphasis on relationships may even enable actors to make every effort to bypass rules, violate rules, or exploit loopholes in existing rules, especially when rules meet relations. It has been found that Confucianism tends to overstress the importance of morality to the extent that it neglects the use of explicit rules and regulations to define rights and obligations of various sectors in society.[93] Perhaps this is why rules should be particularly stressed in a more communitarian society and relations taken into serious consideration in a more individualistic society. We need to

[93] He and Sun 2015.

understand when they can reinforce one another in a malign way, making cooperation more difficult and governance less effective, or in a beneficial way, facilitating each other in producing better and more effective governance. What conditions, both necessary and sufficient, should be present and created to realize the latter rather than the former will be a question for both analysts and practitioners.

Bibliography

Acharya, Amitav (1998) "Collective Identity and Conflict Management in Southeast Asia", in: Emanuel Adler and Michael Barnett (eds.), *Security Communities*, Cambridge: Cambridge University Press, 198–227.

(2001) *Constructing a Security Community in Southeast Asia: ASEAN and the Problem of Regional Order*, London: Routledge.

(2004) "How Ideas Spread: Whose Norms Matter? Norm Localization and Institutional Change in Asia Regionalism", *International Organization* 58(2): 239–275.

(2009) *Whose Ideas Matter? Agency and Power in Asian Regionalism*, Ithaca: Cornell University Press.

(2014) "Global International Relations (IR) and Regional Worlds: A New Agenda for International Studies", *International Studies Quarterly* 58(4): 647–659.

Acharya, Amitav and Barry Buzan (2007) "Why is There no Non-Western IR Theory: Reflection on and from Asia: An Introduction", *International Relations of the Asia-Pacific* 7(3): 287–312.

Acharya, Amitav and Alastair Iain Johnston (2007a) "Comparing Regional Institutions: An Introduction", in: Amitav Acharya and Alastair Iain Johnston (eds.), *Crafting Cooperation: Regional International Institutions in Comparative Perspectives*, Cambridge: Cambridge University Press, 1–31.

(2007b) "Conclusion: Institutional Features, Cooperation Effects, and the Agenda for Future Research on Comparative Regionalism", in: Amitav Acharya and Alastair Iain Johnston (eds.), *Crafting Cooperation: Regional International Institutions in Comparative Perspectives*, Cambridge: Cambridge University Press, 244–278.

Adler, Emanuel (1992) "Europe's New Security Order: A Pluralistic Security Community", in: Beverly Crawford (ed.), *The Future of European Security*, Berkeley: Center for German and European Studies, University of California, 287–326.

(2005) *Communitarian International Relations: The Epistemic Foundations of International Relations*, London and New York: Routledge.

(2008) "The Spread of Security Communities: Communities of Practice, Self-Restraint, and NATO's Post-Cold War Transformation", *European Journal of International Relations* 14(2): 195–230.

(2010) "Europe as a Civilizational Community of Practice", in: Peter J. Katzenstein (ed.), *Civilizations in World Politics: Plural and Pluralistic Perspectives*, London and New York: Routledge, 67–90.

Adler, Emanuel and Michael Barnett (eds.) (1998) *Security Communities*, Cambridge: Cambridge University Press.

Adler, Emanuel and Patricia Greve (2008) "When Security Community Meets Balance of Power: Overlapping Regional Mechanisms of Security Governance", *Review of International Studies* 35(S1): 59–84.

Adler, Paul S. and Seok-Woo Known (2002) "Social Capital: Prospects for a New Concept", *Academy of Management Review* 27(1): 17–40.

Adler, Emanuel and Vincent Pouliot (eds.) (2011) *International Practices*, Cambridge: Cambridge University Press.

Albert, Mathias and Yosef Lapid (1997) "On Dialectic and IR Theory: Hazards of a Proposed Marriage", *Millennium* 26(2): 403–415.

Aldrich, Daniel P. (2012) *Building Resilience: Social Capital in Post-Disaster Recovery*, Chicago: University of Chicago Press.

Alfred, Michael F. and Bruce Bueno de Mesquita (1979) "Choosing Sides in Wars", *International Studies Quarterly* 23(1): 87–112.

Alker, Hayward R. (1996) *Rediscoveries and Reformulations: Humanistic Methodologies for International Studies*, Cambridge: Cambridge University Press.

Alker, Hayward R. and Thomas J. Biersteker (1984) "The Dialectics of World Order: Notes for a Future Archaeologist of International Savoir Faire", *International Studies Quarterly* 28(2): 121–142.

Allison, Graham T. (1977) *Essence of Decision: Explaining the Cuban Missile Crisis*, Boston: Little Brown.

Ames, Roger T. and David L. Hall (2001) *Focusing on the Familiar: A Translation and Philosophical Interpretation of Zhongyong*, Honolulu: University of Hawaii Press.

(2003) *Daodejing – "Making This Life Significant": A Philosophical Translation*, New York: Ballantine Books.

Ames, Roger T. and Henry Rosemont Jr. (1998) *The Analects of Confucius: A Philosophical Translation*, New York: Ballantine Books.

Ashley, Richard K. (1986) "The Poverty of Neorealism", in: Robert O. Keohane (ed.), *Neorealism and its Critics*, New York: Columbia University Press, 255–300.

Austin, J. L. (2002) *How to Do Things with Words*, Beijing and Cambridge: Foreign Language and Research Press and Oxford University Press.

Avant, Deborah D., Martha Finnemore, and Susan Sell (2010) "Who Governs the Globe?", in: Deborah Avant, Martha Finnemore, and Susan Sell (eds.), *Who Governs the Globe?* Cambridge: Cambridge University Press, 14–17.

Avineri, Shlomo (1972) *Hegel's Theory on the Modern State*, Cambridge: Cambridge University Press.

Axelrod, Robert (1984) *The Evolution of Cooperation*, New York: Basic Books.

Axelrod, Robert and Robert O. Keohane (1985) "Achieving Cooperation under Anarchy: Strategies and Institutions", *World Politics* 38(1): 226–254. Also in: David Baldwin (ed.) (1993) *Neorealism and Neoliberalism: The Contemporary Debate*, New York: Columbia University Press, 85–115.

Axelrod, Robert, David E. Axelrod, and Kenneth J. Pienta (2006) "Evolution of Cooperation among Tumor Cells", *Proceedings of the National Academy of Sciences of the United States of America* 103(36): 13474–13479.

Baldwin, David A. (1971) "Money and Power", *Journal of Politics* 33(3): 578–614.

(1978) "Power and Social Exchange", *The American Political Science Review* 72(4): 1229–1242.

Baldwin, David A. (ed.) (1993) *Neorealism and Neoliberalism: The Contemporary Debate*, New York: Columbia University Press.

Barkin, J. Samuel (2003) "Realist Constructivism", *International Studies Review* 5(3): 325–342.

Barnett, Michael and Raymond Duvall (2005) "Power in International Relations", *International Organization* 59(1): 39–75.

Barnett, Michael and Martha Finnemore (2004) *Rules for the World: International Organizations in World Politics*, Ithaca: Cornell University Press.

Berenskoetter, Felix (2007) "Friends, There Are No friends? An Intimate Reframing of the International", *Millennium* 35(3): 647–676.

Berger, Peter L. and Thomas Luckmann (1966) *The Social Construction of Reality: A Treatise in the Sociology of Knowledge*, New York: Doubleday.

Bian, Yanjie (2011) "Daoyan: Guanxi Shehuixue Jiqi Xueke Diwei (Introduction: Relational Sociology and its Status in the Discipline)", in: Bian Yanjie (ed.), *Guanxi Shehuixue: Lilun yu Yanjiu (Relational Sociology: Theories and Studies)*, Beijing: Social Sciences Academic Press, 1–14.

Blaney, David and Naeem Inayatullah (1998) "International Political Economy as a Cultural of Competition", in: Dominique Jacquin-Berdal, Andrew Oros, and Marco Verweij (eds.), *Culture in World Politics*, Houndmills and London: Macmillan, 61–88.

Blaney, David L. and Arlene B. Tickner (2013) "Introduction: Claiming the International Beyond IR", in: Arlene B. Tickner and David L. Blaney (eds.), *Claiming the International*, London and New York: Routledge, 1–24.

Bleiker, Roland (1998) "Neorealist Claims in Light of Ancient Chinese Philosophy: the Cultural Dimension of International Theory", in: Dominique Jacquin-Berdal, Andrew Oros, and Marco Verweij (eds.), *Culture in World Politics*, Houndmills and London: Macmillan, 89–115.

Bollier, David (2001) "The Cornucopia of the Commons", *YES! Magazine*, June 30.

Boulding, Kenneth (1990) *Three Faces of Power*, Newbury Park: SAGE Publications.

Bourdieu, Pierre (1977) *Outline of a Theory of Practice*, Cambridge: Cambridge University Press.

(1990) *The Logic of Practice*, Stanford: Stanford University Press.

(2012) "Structure, Habitus, Practices", in: Craig Calbourn, Joseph Gerteis, James Moody, Steven Pfaff, and Indermohan Virk (eds.), *Contemporary Sociological Theory*, UK: Wiley-Blackwell, 345–358.

Brincat, Shannon (2009) "Negativity and Open-Endedness in the Dialectics of World Politics", *Alternatives* 34(4): 455–493.

(2011) "Towards a Social-Relational Dialectic for World Politics", *European Journal of International Relations* 17(4): 680–709.

Brincat, Shannon and L. H. M. Ling (2014) "Dialectics for IR: Hegel and the Dao", *Globalizations* 11(5): 661–687.

Bull, Hedley (1969) "International Theory: The Case for a Classical Approach", in: Klaus Knorr and James N. Rosenau (eds.), *Contending Approaches to International Politics*, Princeton: Princeton University Press, 20–38.

(1977) *The Anarchical Society: A Study of Order in World Politics*, New York: Columbia University Press.

Bull, Hedley and Adam Waston (eds.) (1984) *The Expansion of International Society*, Oxford: Oxford University Press.

Burchill, Scott (1996) "Introduction", in: Scott Burchill and Andrew Linklater with Richard Devetak, Matthew Paterson, and Jacqui True (eds.), *Theories of International Relations*, New York: St. Martin's, 1–27.

Burt, Ronald S. (1992) *Structural Holes: The Social Structures of Competition*, Cambridge, MA: Harvard University Press.

Buzan, Barry (1993) "From International System to International Society: Structural Realism and Regime Theory Meet the English School", *International Organization* 47(3): 327–352.

(2001) "The English School: An Underexploited Resource in IR", *Review of International Studies* 27(3): 471–488.

(2004) *From International Society to World Society?: English School Theory and the Social Structure of Globalization*, Cambridge: Cambridge University Press.

(2010) "Culture and International Society", *International Relations* 86(1): 1–25.

Buzan, Barry and Richard Little (2000) *International Systems in World History: Rethinking the Study of International Relations*, Oxford: Oxford University Press.

Buzan, Barry, Charles Jones, and Richard Little (1993) *The Logic of Anarchy: Neorealism to Structural Realism*, New York: Columbia University Press.

Buzan, Barry, Ole Wæver, and Jaap de Wilde (1998) *Security: A New Framework for Analysis*, Boulder: Lynne Reinner.

Byers, Michael (1999) *Custom, Power, and the Power of Rules: International Relations and Customary International Law*, Cambridge: Cambridge University Press.

Callahan, William (2002) "Nationalizing International Theory: The Emergence of the English School and IR Theory with Chinese Characteristics", Paper Presented at *IR Theory in the 21st Century: British and Chinese Perspectives*, Beijing: Renmin University of China.

(2004) "The Next Big Idea: Great Harmony and Chinese IR Theory", *International Review* 36(Autumn): 33–43.

Caporaso, James A. (1978) "Dependence and Dependency in the Global System: A Structural and Behavioral Analysis", *International Organization* 32(1): 13–43.

Cardoso, Fernando Henrique and Enzo Faletto (1979) *Dependency and Development in Latin America*, Berkeley: University of California Press.

Carr, Edward Hallet (1964) *Twenty Years Crisis, 1919–1939: An Introduction to the Study of International Relations*, New York: Harper and Row.

Checkel, Jeffrey (1998) "The Constructivist Turn in International Relations Theory", *World Politics* 50(2): 324–348.

——— (2005) "International Institutions and Socialization in Europe: Introduction and Framework", *International Organization* 59(4): 801–826.

——— (2007) "Social Mechanisms and Regional Cooperation: Are Europe and the EU Really All that Different?", in: Amitav Acharya and Alastair Iain Johnston (eds.), *Crafting Cooperation: Regional International Institutions in Comparative Perspectives*, Cambridge: Cambridge University Press, 221–243.

Cheng, Chung-ying (1991) *Lun Zhong Xi Zhexue Jingshen (On the Spirits of Chinese and Western Philosophies)*, Shanghai: Oriental Press.

——— (2005) *Cong Zhongxi Hushi zhong Tingli: Zhongguo Zhexue yu Zhongguo Wenhua de Xindingwei (Rising from the Mutual Interpretation of Chinese and Western Cultures: Creative Renewal of Chinese Philosophy)*, Beijing: Renmin University Press.

——— (2006) "Toward Constructing a Dialectics of Harmonization: Harmony and Conflict in Chinese Philosophy", *Journal of Chinese Philosophy* 33(S1): 25–59.

Coleman, James S. (1988) "Social Capital in the Creation of Human Capital", *American Journal of Sociology* 94(Supplement): S95–S120.

Collins Cobuild English Dictionary (1995), London: HarperCollins Publishers.

Compact Edition of the Oxford English Dictionary (1971), Oxford: Oxford University Press.

Confucius (1998) *The Analects*, trans. Arthur Waley, Beijing: Foreign Languages and Research Press.

Confucius et al. (2014) *Chinese Classics: Confucian Analects, The Great Learning, and The Doctrine of the Mean*, trans. James Legge, Shanghai: Shanghai Sanlian Press.

Cook, K. S. and J. M. Whitmeyer (1992) "Two Approaches to Social Structure: Exchange Theory and Network Analysis," *Annual Review of Sociology* 18: 109–127.

Copeland, Dale (2000) "The Constructivist Challenge to Structural Realism", *International Security* 25(2): 187–212.

Coulter, Jeff (1982) "Remarks on the Conceptualization of Social Structure", *Philosophy of the Social Sciences* 12(March): 33–46.

Cox, Robert W. (1986) "Social Forces, States, and World Orders: Beyond International Relations Theory", in: Robert O. Keohane, *Neorealism and its Critics*, New York: Columbia University Press, 204–254.

——— (2002) "Universality in International Studies: A Historicist Approach", in: Michael Brecher and Frank Harvey (eds.), *Critical Perspectives in International Studies: Millennial Reflections on International Studies*, Ann Arbor: University of Michigan Press, 209–216.

Crawford, Neta C. (2002) *Argument and Change in World Politics: Ethics, Decolonization, and Humanitarian Intervention*, Cambridge: Cambridge University Press.

Crawford, Robert M. A. (2001) "International Relations as an Academic Discipline: If It's Good for America, Is It Good for the World?", in: Robert M. A. Crawford and Darryl S. L. Jarvis (eds.), *International Relations Theory: Still an American Social Science?* Albany: State University of New York Press, 1–26.

Crawford, Robert M. A., and Darryl S. L. Jarvis (eds.) (2001) *International Relations Theory: Still an American Social Science?* Albany: State University of New York Press.

Dahl, Robert (1957) "The Concept of Power", *Behavioral Science* 2(3): 201–215.

Dahrendorf, Ralf (1958) "Out of Utopia: Toward a Reorientation of Sociological Analysis", *American Journal of Sociology* 64(2):115–127.

Deutsch, Karl W. (1963) *The Nerves of Government: Models of Political Communication and Control*, New York: The Free Press.

Di, Bairui (William Theodore de Barry) (2011) "Women Weishenme Yaodu *Lunyu* (Why do We Need to Read *the Analects*)?" *Kaifang Shidai (Open Times)* 3: 61–68.

Donnelly, Jack (2000) *Realism and International Relations*, Cambridge: Cambridge University Press.

Doty, Roxanne Lynn (2000) "Desires All Way Down", *Reviews of International Studies* 26(1): 137–139.

Dougherty, James E. and Robert L. Pfaltzgraff, Jr. (2001) *Contending Theories of International Relations: A Comprehensive Survey*, 5th edn., New York: Addison Wesley Longman.

Doyle, Michael W. (1997) *Ways of War and Peace*, New York: Norton.

Dunne, Tim (1998) *Inventing International Society: A History of the English School*, New York: St. Martin's Press.

Duvall, Raymond D. and Arjun Chowdhury (2011) "Practices of Theory", in: Emanuel Adler and Vincent Pouliot (eds.), *International Practices*, Cambridge: Cambridge University Press, 335–354.

Dyer, Jeffery H. (1996) "Does Governance Matter: Keiretsu Alliances and Asset Specificity as Sources of Japanese Comparative Advantages", *Organization Science* 7(6): 649–666.

Dyer, Jeffery H. and Harbir Singh (1998) "The Relational View: Cooperative Strategy and Sources of Interorganizational Competitive Advantage" *The Academy of Management Review* 23(4): 660–679.

East Asia Vision Group (2001) "Towards an East Asian Community: Region of Peace, Prosperity and Progress", www.mofa.go.jp/region/asia-paci/report2001 .pdf, accessed October 26, 2017.

East Asia Vision Group II (2012) "Report of the East Asia Vision Group II". www .mofa.go.kr/mofat/htm/issue/2012a.pdf, accessed November 6, 2017.

Editors (2002) "Editorial Note", *Millennium* 31 (3): iii–iv.

Elias, Norbert (1939/2012) *On the Process of Civilization: Sociogenetic and Psychogenetic Investigations*, Dublin: University College Dublin Press.

Emirbayer, Mustafa (1997) "Manifesto for a Relational Sociology", *American Journal of Sociology* 103(2): 281–317.

Esperne, Eric G. P. (2010) "Contractual and Relational Governance Practices", Paper for the 95th ISM Annual International Supply Management

Conference, April 2010, www.instituteforsupplymanagement.org/files/Pubs/ Proceedings/2010ProcGC-Esperne.pdf, accessed October 26, 2017.

Fei, Xiaotong (2012) *From the Soil: The Foundation of Chinese Society*, Beijing: Foreign Language Teaching and Research Press.

Feng, Tianyu, He Xiaoming, and Zhou Jiming (2005) *Zhonghua Wenhuashi (A History of Chinese Culture)*, Shanghai: Shanghai People's Publishing House.

Feng Youlan (Fung, Yu-lan) (1962) *Zhongguo Zhexue Shi (A History of Chinese Philosophy)*, Beijing: Zhonghua Shuju.

(1991) "Why China Has No Science – An Interpretation of the History and Consequences of Chinese Philosophy", in: Feng Youlan (Fung Yu-lan), *Selected Philosophical Writings of Fung Yu-lan*, Beijing: Foreign Language Press, 571–595.

(2004) *Feng Youlan Zishu (Autobiography)*, Beijing: Renmin University Press.

Finnemore, Martha (1996) *National Interests in International Society*, Ithaca: Cornell University Press.

(2001) "Exporting the English School", *Review of International Studies* 27(3): 509–513.

Finnemore, Martha and Kathryn Sikkink (1998) "International Norm Dynamics and Political Change", *International Organization* 52(4): 887–917.

Foucault, Michel (1972) *The Archaeology of Knowledge*, London: Tavistock.

(1991) *Discipline and Punish: The Birth of a Prison*, London: Penguin.

Frank, André Gunder (1967) *Capitalism and Underdevelopment in Latin America*, New York: Monthly Review Press.

Frank, André Gunder and Barry K. Gills (eds.) (1993) *The World System: Five Hundred Years of Five Thousand Years*, London and New York: Routledge.

Friedberg, Aaron L. (1993/1994) "Ripe for Rivalry: Prospects for Peace in a Multipolar Asia", *International Security* 18(3): 5–33.

Gao, Cheng (2010) "Quyu Hezuo Moshi Xingcheng de Lishi Genyuan he Zhengzhi Luoji: yi Ouzhou he Meizhou wei Fenxi Yangben (Historical Origins and Political Logics in the Formation of the Patterns of Regional Cooperation: Case Studies on Europe and North America)", *Shijie jingji yu Zhengzhi (World Economics and Politics)* 10: 33–57.

Geertz, Clifford (1973) *The Interpretation of Cultures*, New York: Basic Books.

Gernet, Jacques (1985) *China and the Christian Impact: A Conflict of Cultures*, trans. Janet Lioyd, Cambridge: Cambridge University Press.

Ge, Zhaoguang (2001) *Zhongguo Sixiangshi (A History of Chinese Thinking)*, Shanghai: Fudan University Press.

Gheciu, Alexander (2005) "Security Institutions as Agents of Socialization? NATO and the 'New Europe'", *International Organization* 59(4): 973–1012.

Gill, Stephen (ed.) (1993) *Gramsci, Historical Materialism and International Relations*, Cambridge: Cambridge University Press.

Gilpin, Robert (1981) *War and Change in World Politics*, Cambridge: Cambridge University Press.

Gold, Thomas, Doug Guthrie, and David Wank (2002) "An Introduction to the Study of Guanxi", in: Thomas Gold, Doug Guthrie, and David Wank (eds.),

Social Connections in China: Institutions, Culture, and the Changing Nature of Guanxi, Cambridge: Cambridge University Press, 3–20.

Goldstein, Joshua S. (2001) *War and Gender: How Gender Shapes the War System and Vice Versa*, Cambridge: Cambridge University Press

Goldstein, Judith and Robert O. Keohane (eds.) (1993) *Ideas and Foreign Policy: Beliefs, Institutions, and Political Change*, Ithaca and London: Cornell University Press.

Grieco, Joseph M. (1988) "Anarchy and the Limits on Cooperation: A Realist Critique of the Newest Liberal Institutionalism", *International Organization* 42(3): 485–507. Also in: David Baldwin (ed.) (1993) *Neorealism and Neoliberalism: The Contemporary Debate*, New York: Columbia University Press, 250–266.

Griffiths, Martin and Terry O"Callaghan (2001) "The End of International Relations?", in: Robert M. A. Crawford and Darryl S. L. Jarvis (eds.), *International Relations Theory: Still an American Social Science?* New York: State University of New York Press, 187–202.

(2006) *International Relations: The Key Concepts*, London and New York: Routledge.

Groom, A. J. R. and Peter Mandaville (2001) "Hegemony and Autonomy in International Relations: The Continental Experience", in: Robert M. A. Crawford and Darryl S. L. Jarvis (eds.), *International Relations Theory: Still an American Social Science?* New York: State University of New York Press, 151–165.

Gu, Hongming (Ku Hung-Ming) (2006) "Chinese Scholarship: Part II", in Gu Hongming (Ku Hung-Ming) ed., *Spirit of Chinese People* (English-Chinese bilingual edition), Xi"an: Shaanxi Normal University Press, 212–223.

Gulick, Edward Vose (1967) *Europe's Classical Balance of Power: A Case History of the Theory and Practice of One of the Great Concepts of European Statecraft*, New York: Norton.

Guzzini, Stefano (2013) *Power, Realism and Constructivism*, London: Routledge.

Haas, Mark L. (2007) "The United States and the End of the Cold War: Reactions to Shifts in Soviet Power, Policies, or Domestic Politics?", *International Organization* 61(1): 145–179.

Habermas, Jürgen (1984) *Theory of Communicative Action Vol. I: Reason and the Rationalization of Society*, trans. Thomas McCarthy, Boston: Beacon Press.

Hafner-Burton, Miles Kahler, and Alexander H. Montgomery (2009) "Network Analysis for International Relations," *International Organization* 63(3): 559–592.

Hall, David L. and Roger T. Ames (1987) *Thinking through Confucius*, New York: State University of New York Press.

(1995) *Anticipating China: Thinking through the Narratives of Chinese and Western Culture*, Albany, New York: State University of New York Press.

(1998) *Thinking from the Han: Self, Truth, and Transcendence in Chinese and Western Culture*, New York: State University of New York Press.

Hamilton, W. D. (1964) "The Genetical Evolution of Social Behavior", *Journal of Theoretical Biology* 7(1): 1–16.

Harrison, Lawrence E. and Samuel P. Huntington (eds.) (2000) *Culture Matters: How Values Shape Human Progress*, New York: Basic Books.

Haugaard, Mark (2012) "Rethinking the Four Dimensions of Power: Domination and Empowerment", *Journal of Political Power* 5(1): 33–54.

He, Zhaowu, Bu Jinzi, Tang Yuyuan, and Sun Kaitai (1991) *An Intellectual History of China*, Beijing: Foreign Languages Press.

He, Zhipeng and Sun Lu (2015) "Zhongguo de Guojifa Guannian: Jiyu Guoji Guanxi Shi de Fenxi (Chinese Views of International Law: An Analysis Based on History of International Relations)", *Guoji Guanxi yu Guojifa Xuekan (Journal of International Relations and International Law)*, 5: 42–94.

Hegel, G.W.F. (1991) *The Philosophy of History*, trans. J. Sibee, Buffalo: Prometheus Books.

Heine, Christian and Benno Teschke (1996) "Sleeping Beauty and the Dialectical Awakening: On the Potential of Dialectic for International Relations", *Millennium* 25(2): 399–423.

Herz, John (1950) "Idealist Internationalism and the Security Dilemma", *World Politics* 2: 157–180.

Ho, D. Y. F. (1991) "Relational Orientation and Methodological Individualism", *Bulletin of the Hong Kong Psychological Society* 26/27: 81–95.

(1995) "Selfhood and Identity in Confucianism, Taoism, Buddhism, and Hinduism: Contrasts with the West", *Journal for the Theory of Social Behavior* 25(2): 115–139.

(2000) "Dialectical Thinking: Neither Eastern nor Western", *American Psychology*, 55(9): 1064–5.

Hobson, John A. (1965) *Imperialism: A Study*, Ann Arbor: University of Michigan Press.

Hopf, Ted (1998) "The Promise of Constructivism in International Relations Theory", *International Security* 23(1): 171–200.

(2010) "The Logic of Habit in International Relations", *European Journal of International Relations* 16(4): 539–561.

Hu, Shi (1919/1991) *Hu Shi Xueshu Wenji: Zhongguo Zhexueshi (Collective Works of Hu Shi: A History of Chinese Philosophy)*, Beijing: Zhonghua Press.

Huang, Chiung-chiu and Chih-yu Shih (2014) *Harmonious Intervention: China's Quest for Relational Security*, Surrey, England: Ashgate.

Hui, Victoria Tin-bor (2005), *War and State Formation in Ancient China and Early Modern Europe*, Cambridge: Cambridge University Press.

Huntington, Samuel (1993) "The Clash of Civilizations?", *Foreign Affairs* 72(3): 22–49.

(1996) *The Clash of Civilizations and the Remaking of World Order*, New York: Simon and Schuster.

Hurrell, Andrew (2001) "Keeping History, Law and Political Philosophy Firmly within the English School", *Review of International Studies* 27(3): 489–494.

Hwang, Kwang-kuo (1987) "Face and Favor: The Chinese Power Game", *American Journal of Sociology* 92(4): 944–974.

(2006) *Rujia Guanxizhuyi: Wenhua Fansi yu Dianfan Chongjian (Confucian Relationalism: Cultural Reflection and Theoretical Construction)*, Beijing: Peking University Press.

Hwang, Kwang-kuo, Hu Xianjin et al. (2004) *Mianzi: Zhongguoren de Quanli Youxi (Face: Power Game of Chinese People)*, Beijing: Renmin University Press.

Ikenberry, John (2001) *After Victory: Institutions, Strategic Restraint, and the Rebuilding of Order after Major Wars*, Princeton: Princeton University Press.

(2008) "The Rise of China and the Future of the West: Can the Liberal System Survive?", *Foreign Affairs* 87(1): 23–37.

(2009a) "Liberalism in a Realist World: International Relations as an American Scholarly Tradition", *International Studies* 46(1&2): 203–219.

(2009b) "Liberal Internationalism 3.0: America and the Dilemmas of Liberal World Order," *Perspectives on Politics* 7(1): 71–87.

Ikenberry, John and Ann-Marie Slaughter (2006), *Forging the World of Liberty under Law, US Strategic Security in the 21st Century – Final Report of the Princeton Project on National Security*, www.princeton.edu/~ppns/report/FinalReport.pdf, accessed October 26, 2017.

Jackson, Patrick Thaddeus (2008) "Foregrounding Ontology: Dualism, Monism, and IR Theory", *Review of International Studies* 34(1): 129–153.

Jackson, Patrick Thaddeus and Daniel H. Nexon (1999) "Relations before States: Substance, Process and the Study of World Politics", *European Journal of International Relations* 5(3): 291–332.

Jervis, Robert (1976) *Perception and Misperception in International Politics*, Princeton: Princeton University Press.

Johnston, Alastair Iain (1995), *Cultural Realism: Strategic Culture and Grand Strategy in Chinese History*, Princeton: Princeton University Press.

Jones, Bruce, Carlos Pascual, and Stephen John Stedman (2009) *Power and Responsibility: Building International Order in an Era of Transnational Threats*, Washington: The Brooking Institution Press.

Jones, Candace, William S. Hesterly, and Stephen P. Borgatti (1997) "A General Theory of Network Governance: Exchange Conditions and Social Mechanisms", *The Academy of Management Review* 22(4): 911–945.

Kagan, Jerome (2009) *The Three Cultures: Natural Sciences, Social Sciences, and the Humanities in the 21st Century*, Cambridge: Cambridge University Press.

Kang, David (2007) *China Rising: Peace, Power, and Order in East Asia*, New York: Columbia University Press.

Kant, Immanuel (1997) *Critique of Pure Reason*, translated and edited by Paul Guyer and Allen W. Wood, Cambridge: Cambridge University Press.

Kaplan, Morton (1969) "The New Great Debate: Traditionalism vs Science in International Relations", in: Klaus Knorr and James N. Rosenau (eds.), *Contending Approaches to International Relations*, Princeton: Princeton University Press, 39–61.

Katzenstein, Peter J. (ed.) (1996) *The Culture of National Security: Norms and Identity*, New York: Columbia University Press.

(2005) *A World of Regions: Asia and Europe in the American Imperium*, Ithaca and London, Cornell University Press.

(2010a) "A World of Plural and Pluralistic Civilizations: Multiple Actors, Traditions, and Practices", in: Peter J. Katzenstein (ed.), *Civilizations in World Politics: Plural and Pluralistic Perspectives*, London and New York: Routledge, 1–40.

(2010b) "A World of Plural and Pluralistic Civilizations", *World Economics and Politics* 11: 45–53.

(2012a) (ed.) *Sinicization and the Rise of China: Civilizational Processes beyond East and West*, London and New York: Routledge.

(2012b) (ed.) *Anglo-America and Its Discontents: Civilizational Identities beyond West and East*, London and New York: Routledge.

Katzenstein, Peter J., Robert O. Keohane, and Stephen D. Krasner (eds.) (1999) *Exploration and Contestation in the Study of World Politics*, Cambridge, MA: The MIT Press.

Keck, Margaret M. and Kathryn Sikkink (1998) *Activists beyond Borders: Advocacy Networks in International Politics*, Ithaca: Cornell University Press.

Keene, Edward (2007) "A Case Study of the Construction of International Hierarchy: British Treaty-making Against the Slave Trade in the Early Nineteenth Century", *International Organization* 61(2): 311–339.

Keeny, Spurgeon M. and Wolfgang K. H. Panofsky (1981) "MAD versus NUTS: Can Doctrine or Weaponry Remedy the Mutual Hostage Relationship of the Superpowers", *Foreign Affairs* 60(2): 287–304.

Kegley, Charles (ed.) (1995) *Controversies in International Relations Theory: Realism and Neoliberal Challenges*, New York: St. Martin's.

Kennan, George (1947) "The Sources of the Soviet Conduct", *Foreign Affairs*, 25(4): 566–82.

Kennedy, Paul (1987) *The Rise and Fall of Great Powers: Economic Change and Military Conflict from 1500–2000*, New York: Random House.

Keohane, Robert O. (1984) *After Hegemony: Cooperation and Discord in World Political Economy*, Princeton: Princeton University Press.

(1989a) (ed.) *International Institutions and State Power: Essay in International Relations Theory*, Boulder: Westview Press.

(1989b) "Neoliberal Institutionalism: A Perspective on World Politics", in: Robert O. Keohane (ed.), *International Institutions and State Power: Essay in International Relations Theory*, Boulder: Westview Press, 1–20.

(1989c) "Theory of World Politics: Structural Realism and Beyond", in: Robert O. Keohane (ed.), *International Institutions and State Power: Essay in International Relations Theory*, Boulder: Westview Press, 35–73.

(1989d) "The Demand for International Regimes", in Robert O. Keohane, *International Institutions and State Power: Essays in International Relations Theory*, Boulder: Westview Press, 101–131.

(1989e) "International Institutions: Two Approaches", in: Robert O. Keohane (ed.), *International Institutions and State Power: Essay in International Relations Theory*, Boulder: Westview Press, 158–179.

(1993) "Institutional Theory and the Realist Challenge after the Cold War", in: David Baldwin (ed.), *Neorealism and Neoliberalism: The Contemporary Debate*, New York: Columbia University Press, 269–300.

(2000) "Ideas Part-way Down", *Reviews of International Studies* 26(1): 125–130.

(2012) "Twenty Years of Institutional Liberalism", *International Relations* 26 (2): 125–138.

Keohane, Robert O. and Joseph S. Nye (2000) "Introduction", in: Joseph Nye and John Donahue (eds.), *Governance in a Globalizing World*, Washington: The Brookings Institution Press, 1–44.

(2001) *Power and Interdependence*, 3rd edn., New York: Longman.

Kindleberger, Charles (1973) *The World in Depression, 1929–1939*, Berkeley: The University of California Press.

King, Ambrose Y. (1985) "The Individual and Group in Confucianism: A Relational Perspective", in: Donald J. Munro (ed.) *Individualism and Holism: Studies in Confucian and Taoist Values*, Ann Arbor: Center for Chinese Studies, the University of Michigan, 57–68.

King, Gary, Robert Keohane, and Sidney Verba (1994) *Designing Social Inquiry: Scientific Inference in Qualitative Research*, Princeton: Princeton University Press.

Kipnis, Andrew (2002) "Practices of *Guanxi* Production and Practices of *Ganqing* Avoidance", in: Thomas Gold, Doug Guthrie, and David Wank (eds.), *Social Connections in China: Institutions, Culture, and the Changing Nature of Guanxi*, Cambridge: Cambridge University Press, 21–34.

Kissinger, Henry (1973) *A World Restored: Metternich, Castlereagh and the Problems of Peace, 1812–1822*, Boston: Houghton Mifflin.

(2011) *On China*, New York: The Penguin Press.

Klotz, Audie (1995) "Norm Reconstituting Interests: Global Racial Equality and U.S. Sanction against South Africa", *International Organization* 49(3): 451–478.

Klotz, Audie and Cecelia Lynch (2007) *Strategies for Research in Constructivist International Relations*. Armonk: M.E. Sharpe.

Kornprobst, Markus (2007) "Argumentation and Compromise: Ireland's Selection of the Territorial Status Quo Norm", *International Organization* 61(1): 69–98.

Krasner, Stephen (ed.) (1983) *International Regimes*, Ithaca: Cornell University Press.

(1991) "Global Communications and National Power: Life on the Pareto Frontier", *World Politics* 43 (3): 336–366. Also in: David Baldwin (ed.) (1993), *Neorealism and Neoliberalism: The Contemporary Debate*, New York: Columbia University Press, 234–249.

Kratochwil, Friedrich (1989) *Rules, Norms, and Decisions: On the Conditions of Practical and Legal Reasoning in International Relations and Domestic Affairs*, Cambridge: Cambridge University Press.

Kratochwil, Friedrich and Edward D. Mansfield (eds.) (2006) *International Organization and Global Governance: A Reader*, 2nd edn. (English reprinted edition), Beijing: Pearson Education Asia Limited and Beijing University Press.

Kugler, Jacek and Marina Arbetman (1989) "Choosing among Measures of Power: A Review of the Empirical Record", in: Richard J. Stoll and Michael D. Ward (eds.), *Power in World Politics*, Boulder and London: Lynne Reinner, 49–68.

Kuhn, Thomas (1962) *The Structure of Scientific Revolutions*, Chicago: The University of Chicago Press.

Kurth, James (2010) "The United States as a Civilizational Leader", in Peter Katzenstein (ed.), *Civilization in World Politics: Plural and Pluralistic Perspectives*, London and New York: Routledge, 41–66.

Lakatos, Imre (1978) *The Methodology of Scientific Research Programmes: Philosophical Papers I*, London: Cambridge University Press.

Lapid, Yosef (1997) "Culture's Ship: Returns and Departures in International Relations Theory", in: Yosef Lapid and Friedrich Kratochwil (eds.), *The Return of Culture and Identity in IR Theory*, Boulder and London: Lynne Rienner Publishers, 3–20.

Lebow, Richard Ned (2008) "Identity and International Relations", *International Relations* 22(4): 473–492.

Lebra, T. S. (1976) *Japanese Patterns of Behavior*, Honolulu: The University of Hawaii Press.

Legro, Jeffrey (1997) "Which Norms Matter? Revisiting the 'Failure' of Internationalism", *International Organization* 51(1): 31–63.

Lenin, V. I. (1939) *Imperialism: The Highest Stage of Capitalism*, New York: International Publishers.

Li, John Shuhe (2003) "Relation-based Versus Rule-based Governance: An Explanation of the East Asian Miracle and Asian Crisis", *Review of International Economics* 11(4): 651–673.

Li, Minghui (2005), *Rujia Shiye xia de Zhengzhi Sixiang (Political Thought within the Confucian Framework)*, Beijing: Peking University Press.

Li, Zehou (2004) *Lunyu Jindu (Reading the Analects Today)*, Beijing: Sanlian Press.

(2011) *Zhexue Gangyao (An Outline of Philosophy)*, Beijing: Peking University Press.

Liang, Shuming (1933/1992) "Zhongguo Minzu Zijiu Yundong zhi Zuihou Juewu (The Last Consciousness of China's National Self-salvation Movement)", in: *Minguo Congshu (A Series of Writings during the Period of the Republic of China)*, Shanghai: Shanghai Shudian.

(1949/2012), *Zhongguo Wenhua Yaoyi (The Essential Features of Chinese Culture)*, Shanghai: Shanghai Century Press.

Lin, Nan (1999) "Social Networks and Status Attainment", *Annual Review of Sociology* 25: 467–487.

(2001) "*Guanxi*: A Conceptual Analysis", in: Alvin Y. So, Nan Lin, and Dudley Poston (eds.), *The Chinese Triangle of Mainland, Taiwan, and Hong Kong: Comparative Institutional Analysis*, Westport: Greenwood, 153–167

Ling, L. H. M. (2013) "Worlds beyond Westphalia: Daoist Dialectics and the 'China threat'", *Review of International Studies* 39(3): 549–568.

Linklater, Andrew and Hidemi Suganami (2006) *The English School of International Relations: A Contemporary Reassessment*, Cambridge: Cambridge University Press.

Liu, Qing (2015) "Xunqiu Gongjian de Pubianxing: Cong Tianxia Lixiang dao Xin Shijie Zhuyi (In Search for a Jointly Built Universality: From the *Tianxia* Ideal to New Worldism)", in: Xu Jilin and Liu Qing (eds.), *New Worldism*, Shanghai: Shanghai People's Publishing House, 54–63.

Lou, Yulie (2016) "Guoyi: Chuantong Wenhua de Shijianzhe (Chinese Medicine: A Practice of Traditional Chinese Culture", in: Lou Yulie, *Zhongguo Wenhua de Genben Jingshen (The Essence of the Chinese Culture)*, Beijing: Zhonghua Shuju, 116–132.

Lowe, Victor (1966) *Understanding Whitehead*, Baltimore: The Johns Hopkins Press.

Luo, Hua (2006) "Lun Renmin Tiaojie Zhidu de Xianzhuang, Bianhua jiqi Jiazhi Neihan (The Condition, Change and Inherent Value of People's Mediation)", *Lilun yu Gaige (Theory and Reform)* 6: 121–123.

Luo, Jiade and Wang Jing (2011) "Quanzi Lilun: Yi Shehui Wangluo de Shijiao Fenxi Zhongguoren de Zuzhi Xingwei (Circle Theory: An Analysis of Chinese Organizational Behavior from the Perspective of Social Networking", in: Bian Yanjie (ed.), *Guanxi Shehuixue: Lilun yu Yanjiu (Relational Sociology: Theories and Studies)*, Beijing: Social Sciences Academic Press, 205–223.

Ma, Jianzhong (1898) *Mashi Wentong (Ma's Grammar)*, Shanghai: Commerce Press.

Maliniak, Daniel, Susan Peterson, Ryan Powers, and Michael J. Tierney (2014) *TRIP 2014 Faculty Survey*. Williamsburg: Institute for the Theory and Practice of International Relations, https://trip.wm.edu/reports/2014/rp_2014/, accessed November 6, 2017.

Mansbach, Richard W. and John A. Vasquez (1981) *In Search of Theory – A New Paradigm for Global Politics*, New York: Columbia University Press.

March, James G. and Johan P. Olsen (1998) "The Institutional Dynamics of International Political Orders", *International Organization* 52(4): 943–969.

Mastanduno, Michael (1991) "Do Relative Gains Matter?: America's Response to Japanese Industrial Policy", *International Security*, 16 (1): 73–113. Also in: David Baldwin (ed.) (1993) *Neorealism and Neoliberalism: The Contemporary Debate*, New York: Columbia University Press, 250–266.

Mencius (2014) *Chinese Classics: The Works of Mencius*, trans. James Legge, Shanghai: Shanghai Sanlian Press.

Milner, Helen (1993) "The Assumption of Anarchy in International Relations Theory", in: David A. Baldwin (ed.), *Neorealism and Neoliberalism: The Contemporary Debate*, New York: Columbia University Press, 143–169.

(1997) *Interest, Institutions, and Information: Domestic Politics and International Relations*, Princeton: Princeton University Press.

Morgan, Patrick (2011) "The Practice of Deterrence", in: Emanuel Adler and Vincent Pouliot (eds.), *International Practices*, Cambridge: Cambridge University Press, 139–173.

Morgenthau, Hans J. (1961) *Politics among Nations: The Struggle for Power and Peace*, 3rd edn., New York: Alfred A. Knopf.

Mou, Zongsan (1985), *Yuan shan lun (On Realization of Virtue)*, Taibei: Taiwan Xuesheng Shuju.

Munro, Donald (ed.) (1985) *Individualism and Holism: Studies in Confucian and Taoist Values*, Ann Arbor: Center for Chinese Studies, The University of Michigan.

Neufeld, Mark A. (1995) *The Restructuring of International Relations Theory*, Cambridge: Cambridge University Press.

Ni, Peimin (2010) "Zhongyi de Kexuexing yu Liangzhong Kexue Gainian (Scientific-ness of Traditional Chinese Medicine and Two Understandings of Science)", *Zhexue Fenxi (Philosophical Analysis)* 1(1): 139–146.

Nicholson, Michael (1996) "The Continued Significance of Positivism?", in: Steve Smith, Ken Booth, and Marysia Zalewski (eds.), *International Theory: Positivism and Beyond*, Cambridge: Cambridge University Press, 128–145.

Nisbett, Richard E. (2003) *The Geography of Thought: How Asians and Westerners Think Differently . . . and Why*, New York: Free Press.

Nisbett, Richard, Kaiping Peng, Incheol Choi, and Ara Norenzayan (2001) "Culture and System of Thought: Holistic Versus Analytical Cognition", *Psychological Review* 108(2): 291–310.

North, Douglass C. (1990) *Institutions, Institutional Change and Economic Performance*, Cambridge: Cambridge University Press.

(2005) *Understanding the Process of Economic Change*, Princeton and Oxford: Princeton University Press.

Nossal, Kim Richard (2001) "Tales that Textbooks Tell: Ethnocentricity and Diversity in American Introductions to International Relations", in: Robert M. A. Crawford and Darryl S. L. Jarvis (eds.), *International Relations – Still an American Social Science: Toward Diversity in International Thought*, Albany: State University of New York, 167–186.

Nowak, Martin (2006) "Five Rules for the Evolution of Cooperation", *Science* 314 (5805): 1560–1563.

(2012) "Evolving cooperation", *Journal of Theoretical Biology*, 299: 1–8.

Nowak, Martin, with Roger Highfield (2011) *Super Cooperators: Evolution, Altruism and Human Behaviour or Why We Need Each Other to Succeed*, Edinburgh: Canongate.

Nye, Joseph S. (1993) *Understanding International Conflict: An Introduction to Theory and History*, New York: HarperCollins College Publishers.

(2002) *The Paradox of American Power: Why the World's Only Superpower Can't Go It Alone*, New York: Oxford University Press.

(2004) *Soft Power: The Means to Success in World Politics*, New York: Public Affairs.

(2015) "The Future of U.S.-China Relations", *China-US Focus Digest* 6: 16–18.

Olson, Mancur (1965) *The Logic of Collective Action: Public Goods and the Theory of Groups*, Cambridge, MA: Harvard University Press.

Onuf, Nicholas Greenwood (1989) *World of Our Making: Rules and Rule in Social Theory and International Relations*, London and New York: Routledge.

(1998) "Constructivism: A User's Mannual", in: Vendulka Kubálková, Nicholas Onuf, and Paul Kowert (eds.), *International Relations in a Constructed World*, Armonk and London: M.E. Sharpe, 58–78.

Organski, A. F. K. and Jacek Kugler (1980), *The War Ledger*, Chicago: The University of Chicago Press.

Ou, Jiecheng (2005), *Dang Zhongyi Yushang Xiyi: Lishi yu Xingsi (When Chinese Medicine Meets Western Medicine: History and Ideas)*, Beijing: Sanlian Press.

Oye, Kenneth A. (ed.) (1986) *Cooperation under Anarchy*, Princeton: Princeton University Press.

Paltiel, Jeremy (2010) "Mencius and the World Order Theories", *The Chinese Journal of International Politics* 3(1): 37–54.

Pang, Pu (1980) "Zhongyong Pingyi (An Analysis of *Zhongyong*)", *Zhongguo Shehui Kexue (Social Sciences in China)* (1): 75–100.

(1986) "Daojia Bianzhengfa Lungang (An Outline of the Daoist Dialectics) Part I", *Xueshu Yuekan (Academic Monthly)* (12): 4–10.

(1987) "Daojia Bianzhengfa Lungang (An Outline of the Daoist Dialectics) Part II", *Xueshu Yuekan (Academic Monthly)* (1): 29–33.

Peng, Kaiping and Richard Nisbett (1999) "Culture, Dialectics, and Reasoning about Contradiction", *American Psychology* 54(9): 741–754.

Polanyi, Michael (1998) *Personal Knowledge: Towards a Post-critical Philosophy*, London and New York: Routledge.

Popper, Karl (1959) *The Logic of Scientific Discovery*, London: Hutchinson.

Poppo, Laura and Todd Zenger (2002) "Do Formal Contracts and Relational Governance Function as Substitutes or Complements?", *Strategic Management Journal* 23(8): 707–725.

Porter, Tony (2001) "Can there be National Perspectives on International Theory", in: Robert M. A. Crawford and Darryl S. L. Jarvis (eds.), *International Relations Theory: Still an American Social Science?*, Albany: State University of New York Press, 131–147.

Portes, Alejandro (1998) "Social Capital: Its Origins and Applications in Modern Sociology", *Annual Review of Sociology* 24: 1–24.

Pouliot, Vincent (2008) "The Logic of Practicality: A Theory of Practice of Security Communities", *International Organization* 62(2): 257–288.

(2016) *International Pecking Orders: The Politics and Practice of Multilateral Diplomacy*, Cambridge: Cambridge University Press.

Powell, Robert (1991) "Absolute and Relative Gains in International Relations Theory", *American Political Science Review* 85(4): 1303–1320. Also in: David Baldwin (ed.) (1993) *Neorealism and Neoliberalism: The Contemporary Debate*, New York: Columbia University Press, 209–233.

Prakash, Aseem and Mathew Potoski (2010) "The International Organization for Standardization as a Global Governor: A Club Theory Perspective", in: Deborah D. Avant, Martha Finnemore, and Susan K. Sell, *Who Governs the Globe?*, Cambridge: Cambridge University Press, 72–101.

Pye, Lucian (1968) *The Spirit of Chinese Politics: A Psychocultural Study of the Authority Crisis in Political Development*, Cambridge, MA: The MIT Press.

Qian, Mu (Ch"ien Mu) (1994) *Zhongguo Wenhuashi Daolun (An Introduction to the Cultural History of China)*, Beijing: The Commercial Press.

(2005) *Xiandai Zhongguo Xueshu Lunheng (On Modern Chinese Academic Development)*, Guilin: Guangxi Normal University Press.

Qin, Yaqing (2004) "Guoji Guanxi Yanjiu zhong Kexue yu Renwen de Qihe (Combination of Science and Humanities in the Study of International Relations)", *Zhonguo Shehui Kexue (Social Sciences in China)* (1): 78–82.

(2009a) "Guanxi Benwei yu Guocheng Jiangou: Jiang Zhongguo Linian Zhiru Guoji Guanxi Lilun(Relationality and Processual Construction: Bringing Chinese Ideas into International Relations Theory)", *Zhongguo shehui Kexue (Social Sciences in China)* xxx(4): 5–20.

(2009b) "Diqu Goujia yu Dongya Hezuo: Duoyuan Duochong de Diqu Zhili Tixi (Regional Architecture and East Asian Cooperation: A Multiple and Plural Framework for Regional Governance)", in: Qin Yaqing (ed.) *Dongya Diqu Hezuo: 2009 (East Asian Cooperation: 2009)*, Beijing: Jingji Kexue Chubanshe, 1–14.

(2010) "International Society as a Process: Institutions, Identities, and China's Peaceful Rise", *The Chinese Journal of International Politics* 3(2): 129–153.

(2011) "Possibility and Inevitability of a Chinese School of International Relations Theory", in: William A. Callahan and Elena Barabantseva (eds.), *China Orders the World: Normative Soft Power and Foreign Policy*, Baltimore: The Johns Hopkins University Press, 37–53.

(2013) "Guojia Xingdong de Luoji: Guoji Guanxi Lilun de Zhishi Zhuanxiang jiqi Yiyi (Logics of State Action: The Knowledge Turn and its Implications)", *Zhongguo Shehui Kexue (Social Sciences in China)*, 6: 182–198.

(2014) "Continuity through Change: Background Knowledge and China's International Strategy", *The Chinese Journal of International Politics* 7(3): 285–314.

(2016a) "A Relational Theory of World Politics", *International Studies Review* 18(1): 33–47.

(2016b) "Zhongguo Canyu Guoji Tixi: Jiyu Shijian de Shijiao (China's Engagement with the International System: A Perspective of Practice)", in: Qin Yaqing (ed.) *Shijian yu Biange: Zhongguo Canyu Guoji Tixi Jincheng Yanjiu (Practice and Coevolution: China's Engagement with the International System)*, Beijing: World Knowledge Press, 1–18.

Qin, Yaqing and Wei Ling (2008) "Structure, Process, and the Socialization of Power: East Asian Community Building and the Rise of China", in: Robert Ross and Zhu Feng (eds.), *China's Ascent: Power, Security, and the Future of International Relations*, Ithaca and London: Cornell University Press, 115–140.

Reiter, Dan and Allan C. Stam (2002) *Democracies at War*, Princeton: Princeton University Press.

Ringma, Erik (2012) "Performing International Systems: Two East-Asian Alternatives to the Westphalian Order," *International Organization* 66(1):1–25.

Risse, Thomas (2000) "Let's Argue!: Communicative Action in World Politics", *International Organization* 54(1): 1–39.

Rittberger, Volker (1993) *Regime Theory and International Relations*, Oxford: Clarendon.

Roberson, B. A. (1998) *International Society and the Development of International Relations Theory*, London and New York: Continuum.

Rosenau, James (1982) *The Scientific Study of Foreign Policy*, London: Frances Printer.

(2003) *Distant Proximities: Dynamics beyond Globalization*, Princeton: Princeton University Press.

Rosenau, James and Ernst-Otto Czempiel (eds.) (1992) *Governance without Government: Order and Change in World Politics*, Cambridge: Cambridge University Press.

Rostow, W. W. (1966) *The Stage of Economic Growth: A Non-Communist Manifesto*, Cambridge: Cambridge University Press.

Ruggie, John Gerard (ed.) (1993) *Multilateralism Matters: The Theory and Praxis of an Institutional Form*, New York: Columbia University Press.

(1999) "What Makes the World Hang Together? Neo-Utilitarianism and the Social Constructive Challenge", in: Peter J. Katzenstein, Robert O. Keohane, and Stephen D. Krasner (eds.), *Exploration and Contestation in the Study of World Politics*, Cambridge, MA: The MIT Press, 215–245.

Russett, Bruce (1993) *Grasping the Democratic Peace: Principles for a Post-Cold War World*, Princeton: Princeton University Press.

Russett, Bruce and John Oneal (2001) *Triangulating Peace: Democracy, Interdependence, and International Organizations*, New York: Norton.

Russett, Bruce, Harvey Starr, and David Kinsella (2006) *World Politics: The Menu for Choice*, 8th edn., Belmont: Wadsworth/Thomson Learning.

Saussure, Ferdinand de (1959) *Course in General Linguistics*, New York: McGraw-Hill.

Schatzki, Theodore R. (2001) "Introduction: Practice Theory", in: Theodore R. Schatzki, Karin Knorr Cetina, and Eike Von Savigny, (eds.), *The Practice Turn in Contemporary Theory*, London and New York: Routledge, 1–14.

Schelling, Thomas (1980) *The Strategy of Conflict*, Cambridge, MA: Harvard University Press.

Schwartz, Benjamin (1964) "Some Polarities in Chinese Thought", in: Arthur Wright, ed., *Confucianism and Chinese Civilization*, New York: Atheneum Press, 3–15.

Searle, John R. (1995) *The Construction of Social Reality*, New York: The Free Press.

Shang, Huipeng (2015) "Lun Gudai Nanya Guoji Tixi: 'Dafa Tixi' de Tedian ji Yuanli (The International System in Ancient South Asia: The Logic of the Dharma System)", *Guoji Zhengzhi Yanjiu (The Journal of International Studies)* 141(5): 9–27.

Shannon, Thomas Richard (1989) *An Introduction to the World-System Perspective*, Boulder: Westview.

Shih, Chi-yu and Chiung-chiu Huang (2015) "China's Quest for Grand Strategy: Power, National Interest, or Relational Security", *The Chinese Journal of International Politics* 8(1): 1–26.

Shweder, Richard A. (2000) "Moral Maps, 'First World' Conceits, and the New Evangelist", in: Lawrence E. Harrison and Samuel P. Huntington (eds.), *Culture Matters: How Values Shape Human Progress*, New York: Basic Books, 159–176.

Shweder, Richard A. and Robert A. LeVine (eds.) (1984), *Cultural Theory: Essays on Mind, Self, and Emotion*, Cambridge: Cambridge University Press.

Sil, Rudra and Peter Katzenstein (2010) *Beyond Paradigms: An Analytical Eclecticism in the Study of World Politics*, London and New York: Palgrave Macmillan.

Simon, Herbert A. (1955) "A Behavioral Model of Rational Choice", *The Quarterly Journal of Economics* 69(1): 99–118.

(1985) "Human Nature in Politics: The Dialogue of Psychology with Political Science", *American Political Science Review* 79 (2): 293–304.

Simon, Burton, Jeffery A. Fletcher, and Michael Doebeli (2012) "Hamilton's Rule in Multi-level Selection Models", *Journal of Theoretical Biology* 299: 55–63.

Singer, J. David (1961) "The Level-of-Analysis Problems in International Relations", in: Klaus Knorr and Sidney Verba (eds.), *The International Studies: Theoretical Essays*, Princeton: Princeton University Press, 77–92.

Slaughter, Anna-Marie (2009) "America's Edge: Power in the Networked Century", *Foreign Affairs* 88(1): 94–113

Slaughter, Anna-Marie, Bruce W. Jentleson, Ivo H. Daalder, etc. (2008) *Strategic Leadership: Framework for a 21st Century National Security Strategy*, http://fsi .stanford.edu/sites/default/files/StrategicLeadership.pdf, accessed October 26, 2017.

Smith, Steve (2000) "Wendt's world", *Reviews of International Studies*, 26(1): 151–63.

Smith, Steve, Ken Booth, and Marysia Zalewski (eds.) (1996) *International Theory: Positivism and Beyond*, Cambridge: Cambridge University Press.

Song, Zhiming (1998) "Zhongguo Gudai Bianzhengfa de Leixing yu Hexin (Types and Core Ideas of the Dialectics in Ancient China)", *Journal of Renmin University* 12(5): 39–44.

Stein, Arthur (1982) "Coordination and Collaboration: Regimes in an Anarchic World", *International Organization* 36(2): 299–324. Also in: David Baldwin (ed.) (1993) *Neorealism and Neoliberalism: The Contemporary Debate*, New York: Columbia University Press, 29–59.

Sterling-Folker, Jennifer (2002) "Realism and the Constructivist Challenge: Rejecting, Reconstructing, or Rereading", *International Studies Review* 4(1): 73–97.

Stern, Geoffrey (1995) *The Structure of International Society*, London and Washington: Pinter.

Sun, Zhongyuan (2014) *Zhongguo Luojixue Shijiang (Ten Lectures on Chinese Logic)*, Beijing: Renmin University Press.

Sun Tzu (Sun Zi) (2015) *The Art of War*, trans. Roger T. Ames, London: Frances Lincoln.

Sylvester, Christine (1994) *Feminist Theory and International Relations Theory in a Postmodern Era*, Cambridge: Cambridge University Press.

Szabó, György and Attila Szolnoki (2012) "Selfishness, Fraternity, and Other-regarding Preference in Spatial Evolutionary Games", *Journal of Theoretical Biology* 299: 81–87.

Tao, Shuya (1999) "Lun Renmin Xietiao Zhidu (On People's Mediation System)", *Xiandai Faxue (Modern Law Science)* 20(3): 66–68.

Thornton, John (2008) "Long Time Coming", *Foreign Affairs* 87 (1): 2–22.

Tian, Chenshan (2005) *Chinese Dialectics: From Yijing to Marxism*, Lanham: Lexington.

Tickner, J. Ann (2011) "Dealing with Difference: Problems and Possibilities for Dialogue in International Relations", *Millennium* 39 (3): 607–618.

Tickner, Arlene B. and David L. Blaney (eds.) (2012) *Thinking International Relations Differently*, London and New York: Routledge.

(2013) *Claiming the International*, London: Routledge.

Tickner, Arlene B. and Ole Wæver (eds.) (2009) *International Relations Scholarship around the World*, London and New York: Routledge.

Tilly, Charles (1996) "International Communities, Secure or Otherwise", Center for the Social Sciences at Columbia University Pre-Print Series.

Tu, Wei-Ming (1985) "Selfhood and Otherness: The Father-Son Relationship in Confucian Thought", in: Tu Wei-Ming, *Confucian Thought: Selfhood as Creative Transformation*, Albany, NY: State University of New York Press, 113–130.

(2008) *An Insight of Chung-yung* (the Chinese and English bilingual edition), Beijing: People's Press.

Tylor, Edward B. (1871), *Primitive Culture: Researches into the Development of Mythology, Philosophy, Religion, Art, and Custom*, London: John Murray.

Uzzi, Brian (1997) "Social Structure and Competition in Interfirm Networks: The Paradox of Embeddedness", *Administrative Science Quarterly* 42(1): 35–67.

Veelen, Matthijs van, Julián García, Maurice W. Sabelis, and Martijn Egas (2012) "Group Selection and Inclusive Fitness are not Equivalent; The Price Equation vs. Models and Statistics", *Journal of Theoretical Biology* 299: 64–80.

Vincent, R. J. (1986) *Foreign Policy and Human Rights in International Relations: Issues and Responses*, Cambridge: Cambridge University Press.

Wæver, Ole (1996) "The Rise and Fall of the Inter-paradigm Debate", in: Steve Smith, Ken Booth, and Marysia Zalewski (eds.), *International Theory: Positivism and Beyond*, Cambridge: Cambridge University Press, 149–185.

Wallerstein, Immanuel (1974) *The Modern World-System I*, New York: Academic Press.

Waltz, Kenneth (1959) *Man, the State, and War*, New York: Columbia University Press.

(1979) *Theory of International Politics*, Readings: Addison-Wesley.

(1995) "Realist Thought and Neo-realist Theory", in: Charles Kegley (ed.), *Controversies in International Relations Theory: Realism and Neoliberal Challenges*, New York: St. Martin's, 67–82.

Wang, Yangming (2014) *Chuanxi Lu (Wang Yangming's Teachings)*, Beijing: Beijing Shidai Huawen Shuju.

Ward, Mchael D., Katherine Stovel, and Audrey Sacks (2011) "Network Analysis and Political Science", *Annual Review of Political Science* 14: 245–264.

Watson, Adam (1992) *The Evolution of International Society: A Comparative Historical Analysis*, London and New York: Routledge.

Weber, Max (1949) *The Methodology of the Social Sciences*, trans. and edited by Edward A. Shils and Henry A. Finch, Glencoe: Free Press.

Weber, Max (1999) "Die 'Objektivität' Sozialwissenschaftlicher und Sozialpolitischer Erkenntnis", in: Elizabeth Flitner (ed.), *Gesammelte Aufsätze zur Wissenschaftslehre*, Potsdam: Internet-Ausgabe.

Webster's Third New International Dictionary of the English Language (1986), Springfield: Merriam-Webster Inc.

Wei, Ling (2010) *Guifan, Wangluohua yu Diquzhuyi: Dier Guidao Jincheng Yanjiu (Norms, Networking, and Regionalism: A Study of Track Two Processes)*, Shanghai: Shanghai People's Publishing House.

Weldes, Jutta (1996) "Constructing National Interests", *European Journal of International Relations* 2(3): 273–318.

Wellman, Barry, Wenhong Chen, and Dong Weizhen (2002) "Networking Guanxi," in: Thomas Gold, Doug Guthrie, and David Wank (eds.), *Social Connections in China: Institutions, Culture, and the Changing Nature of Guanxi*, Cambridge: Cambridge University Press, 221–241.

Wemheuer-Vogelaar, Wiebke, Nicholas J. Bell, Mariana Navarrete Morales, and Michael J. Tierney, (2016) "The IR of the Beholder: Examining Global IR Using the 2014 TRIP Survey", *International Studies Review* 18: 16–32.

Wendt, Alexander (1987) "The Agent-Structure Problem in International Relations Theory", *International Organization* 41(3): 335–370.

(1992) "Anarchy is What States Make of It: The Social Construction of Power Politics", *International Organization* 46(2): 391–425.

(1994) "Collective Identity Formation and the International State", *American Political Science Review* 88(2): 384–396.

(1999) *Social Theory of International Politics*, Cambridge: Cambridge University Press.

(2001) "Driving with the Rearview Mirror: On the Rational Science of Institutional Design", *International Organization* 55(4): 1019–1049.

Whitehead, Alfred North (2010) *Process and Reality*, corrected edn., edited by David Ray Griffin and Donald W. Sherburne, 2nd edn., New York: Free Press.

Womack, Brantly (2006) *China and Vietnam: The Politics of Asymmetry*, Cambridge: Cambridge University Press.

(2016) *Asymmetry and International Relationships*, Cambridge: Cambridge University Press.

Wu, Jingrong and Cheng Zhenqiu (eds.) (2000) *New-Age Chinese-English Dictionary*, Beijing: Commerce Press.

Xie, Y. (2017) "It's Whom You Know That Counts", *Science* 355(6329): 1022–1023.

Xu, Jin (2009) "Mengzi de Guojiajian Zhengzhi Sixiang ji Qishi (The International Thought of Mencius and its Implications)", *Shijie Jingji yu Zhengzhi (World Economics and Politics)* 1: 6–16.

Xu, Shen (2006) *Shuowen Jiezi (Xu Shen's Etymological Dictionary)*, Beijing: Social Sciences Academic Press.

Xu, Zhuoyun (Hsu, Cho-yun) (2006) *Zhongguo Wenhua yu Shijie Wenhua (Chinese Culture and Cultures of the World)*, Guilin: Guangxi Normal University Press.

Xunzi (1999) *Xunzi (I)*, trans. John Knoblock, Changsha: Hunan People's Publishing House.

Yan, Xuetong (2011) *Ancient Chinese Thought, Modern Chinese Power*, trans. Edmund Ryden, Princeton and Oxford: Princeton University Press.

Yang, Kuo-shu (1993) *Zhongguoren de Shehui Quxiang – Shehui Hudong de Guandian (Social Orientation of the Chinese: A Social Interaction Perspective)* Taipei: Guiguan Press.

Zaheer, Akbar, Bill McEvily, and Vincenzo Perrone (1998) "Does Trust Matter? Exploring the Effects of Interorganizational and Interpersonal Trust on Performance", *Organization Science* 9(2): 141–159.

Zalewski, Marysia (1996) "'All These Theories yet the Bodies Keeping Piling Up': Theory, Theorists, Theorizing", in: Steve Smith, Ken Booth, and Marysia Zalewski (eds.), *International Theory: Positivism and Beyond*, Cambridge: Cambridge University Press, 346–351.

Zehfuss, Maja (2002) *Constructivism in International Relations: The Politics of Reality*, Cambridge: Cambridge University Press.

Zhai, Xuewei (2005) *Renqing, Mianzi, and Quanli de Zai Shengchan (Renqing, Face, and Reproduction of Power)*, Beijing: Peking University Press.

——— (2011) *Zhongguoren de Guanxi Yuanli: Shikong Zhixu, Shenghuo Yunian Jiqi Liubian (The Principle of Chinese Guanxi: Time-space Order, Life Desire, and their Changes)*, Beijing, Peking University Press.

Zhang, Shuguang (2009) *Jiechu Waijiao: Nikesong Zhengfu yu Jiedong Zhongmei Guanxin (Diplomacy of Engagement: Nixon Administration and Relaxation in Sino-US Relations)*, Beijing: World Knowledge Press.

Zhao, Tingyang (2009) "Gongzai Cunzai Lun: Renji yu Xinji (Ontology of Coexistence: Relations and Hearts)", *Zhexue Yanjiu (Philosophical Researches)* 8: 22–30.

——— (2010) "Hezuo de Tiaojian (Conditions for Cooperation)", in: Zhao Tingyang, *Meigeren de Zhengzhi (Politics of Everybody)*, Beijing: Social Sciences Academic Press, 18–49.

——— (2016) *Tianxia de Dangdaixing: Shijie Zhixu de Shijian yu Xiangxiang (A Possible World of All-under-heaven System: The World Order in the Past and for the Future)*, Beijing: China Citic Press.

Zhou, Kevin Zheng, Laura Poppo, and Zhilin Yang (2008) "Relational Ties or Customized Contracts? An Examination of Alternative Governance Choices in China", *Journal of International Business Studies* 39(3): 526–534.

Zhu, Zhirong (2005) *Zhongguo Shenmei Lilun (A Theory of Chinese Aesthetics)*, Beijing: Peking University Press.

Zhuangzi (2012) *Zhuangzi (Chuang-Tze): A New Selected Translation with an Exposition of the Philosophy of Kuo Hsiang*, trans. Feng Youlan, Beijing: Foreign Language Teaching and Research Press.

Index